Studies in Eighteenth-Century Culture

Volume 44

Studies in Eighteenth-Century Culture

Volume 44

Studies in Eighteenth-Century Culture

Volume 44

Published by The Johns Hopkins University Press for the
American Society for Eighteenth-Century Studies

The Johns Hopkins University Press
Baltimore and London
2015

Printed in the United States of America on acid-free paper.
9 8 7 6 5 4 3 2 1

The Johns Hopkins University Press
2715 North Charles Street
Baltimore, Maryland 21218-4363
www.press.jhu.edu

ISBN 978-1-4214-1862-9
1-4214-1862-9
ISSN 0360-2370

Articles appearing in this annual series are abstracted and indexed in *Historical Abstracts* and *America: History and Life*.

Contents

Editor's Note

In 2013, the annual meeting of the American Society for Eighteenth-Century Studies took place in Cleveland, Ohio for the first time since the organization's inaugural convention met there in 1970. That first ASECS meeting was followed up, one year later, with the publication of the first volume of *Studies in Eighteenth-Century Culture*, which included exceptional papers drawn from among those delivered at that gathering. For 44 years and 44 volumes, the annual publication of *SECC* has accompanied and celebrated the scholarly life of ASECS by providing a space in which to acknowledge and share the excellent and wide-ranging work exchanged at the most recent meetings of its sponsoring organization.

Over the four intervening decades, the journal has, of course, undergone changes as both the field of eighteenth-century studies and the ASECS organization itself have developed and grown. *SECC* has long since, for example, moved to a double-blind peer review process for submissions, keeping pace with the increasing number and quality of scholarly journals dedicated to eighteenth-century studies. At the same time, however, *SECC* has remained committed to considering for publication only articles that have been developed and revised from conference papers originally presented at the national or regional ASECS conferences, or those sponsored by its affiliate societies. Perhaps the journal's most consistent commitment has been to representing the extraordinary interdisciplinary vibrancy that has sustained and continues to animate the organization. Year after year, the journal's pages bring into proximity and dialogue the diversity of fields (such as art history, history, literature, musicology, dance, theater, women's and gender studies, religious studies, and political science) as well as the transnational range of languages and cultures (including French, English, German, Italian, and Spanish studies) that converge at ASECS meetings. At the same time, the journal offers a rich record of the ways in which eighteenth-century studies has grown over the years to incorporate and intersect with emergent fields such as race and empire studies, disability studies, and material culture studies.

Volume 44 opens with the 2013 Presidential Address delivered at the Cleveland meeting by Julie Candler Hayes. Hayes examines the overlooked genre of moralist writings to find subtle treatments by French women of the unequal power relations that characterized marriage. These reflections also changed over the course of the century, as earlier writers such as Lambert and Puisieux often reflected on how female unhappiness almost unavoidably led to female infidelity in marriage, while later writers such as Verzure and d'Arconville tied their critiques of marriage and their celebration of the single life to an emergent political language of liberty and independence.

The following three articles turn to the figure of the body and the growing field of disability studies in the context of eighteenth-century visual culture, philosophical writing, and medical discourse. Teresa Michals examines the changing visual representation of amputation from its comical exposure in caricature to its concealment in the genre of the formal portrait. Her close examination of portraits of Lord Nelson, however, reveal how these images of Nelson broke with this tradition by making amputation visible—a shift that revised or challenged conventional models of masculine and military heroism that relied on images of bodily integrity and gentlemanly status. Paul Kelleher illustrates how ideas of disability deeply inform the understanding of sympathy and morality developed in Adam Smith's *Theory of Moral Sentiments*. In a subtle and careful reading, Kelleher shows how disability (or what Smith refers to as deformity) is, in fact, the precondition for fellow feeling and moral subjectivity—a reading that makes Smith newly relevant for issues central to contemporary disability studies. Lucas Hardy considers the significance of the body in pain in the context of colonial New England and its 1721 smallpox epidemic. Focusing on the figure of Cotton Mather and his medical handbook, *The Angel of Bethesda*, Hardy argues that for Mather the bodily pain associated with inoculation and disease is a precondition not only for physical health but for spiritual conversion. Mather developed a theory of pain that challenged Lockean ideas by emphasizing the necessity of confronting rather than avoiding pain, as a spur to clear the body both of disease and sin.

The following two pieces engage with debates about slavery and literary history in transatlantic, global, and multigeneric contexts. Andrew Pisano takes us from Puritan New England to evangelical South Carolina to offer a truly significant revision to dominant literary histories and understandings of African American print culture. While conventional narratives begin that history with Gronniosaw in 1760, Pisano makes a compelling case that African American participation in a transatlantic Awakening print culture ought to begin instead with the slaves on the South Carolina plantation of Jonathan Bryan, and their contributions to the 1742 letter attributed first to George Whitefield and later to Anne Dutton. Turning to the representation of slavery in Restoration literature, Adam Beach argues that Dryden's *Don Sebastian* offers a unique representation of the sexual threats faced by male as well as female slaves. By bringing together a formal analysis of the split-plot structure of Dryden's tragicomedy with attention to its context of Mediterranean slavery, Beach also interweaves two critical schools on Dryden that have long remained separated.

Questions of literary genre and form are at the center of the next four contributions, beginning with Rachael Scarborough King's examination of epistolarity and the central role of letters in early periodical culture. King locates in John Dunton's use of the question-and-answer format in *The Athenium Mercury* a model of authorship and ownership that communally and cyclically interweaves readers with writers. As Dunton enters into plagiarism debates with Daniel Defoe about the latter's use of reader letters in periodicals, King shows that a split—between readers and authors, and between writing and printing—begins to emerge, and to herald modern hierarchies between the production and consumption of print. Selective reprinting in the periodical press played a significant role, Kelly Battles argues, in the public reception and perceptions of Anna Leititia Barbauld, who also fashioned her own authorial identity in ways that have made it difficult for scholars to recognize the continuities between her early and later work. Her late political poem *Eighteen Hundred and Eleven*, which sharply criticized Britain and its future, therefore maintains her sustained commitment to universal rights.

Samara Anne Cahill locates in the two final novels of Jane Barker's "Galesia trilogy" a "textilic nationalism" that identifies Barker's fictional form of the patchwork with the materiality of global textile production and exchange. Barker's quilted texts argue for the absorption of foreigners and exiles into a hybrid and cosmopolitan England aligned with the Stuarts, and opposed to more recent importations of Dutch financial and political influences. Yann Robert identifies the development of a new form of theatrical production by the late eighteenth-century French playwright Louis-Sébastien Mercier. Mercier's advocacy for a silent form of pantomime emphasized indeterminacy and incompletion so as to cede a radical creative agency to the audience. Mercier thereby challenged traditional notions of authorship and of aesthetics, while at the same time individualizing theater's effects in ways that rejected Jacobin commitments to theatrical production and performance as a source of ideological uniformity.

Heidi Kraus makes a groundbreaking contribution to studies of the French landscape tradition by overturning the claims of earlier scholars to convincingly attribute the painting, *View From the Luxembourg*, to Jacques-Louis David. Kraus also reassesses David's contribution to the genre of landscape painting by considering his Roman sketches and the influence on his work by the landscape painter Valenciennes. The volume concludes with Jonathan Blake Fine's fascinating examination of the role of heretical writing in the Prussian public sphere and subsequent Counter-Enlightenment. Publications by Gotthold Ephraim Lessing, Karl Friedrich Bahrdt, and Christian Ernst Wünsch—whom Fine refers to as "the new heathens"—circulated challenges to religion in forms that appealed to lay readers with increasing access to print. These publications prompted not only the strong reaction by Johann Christoph Woellner but the Counter-Enlightenment's collapse of radical and mainstream Enlightenment ideas.

This collection of exceptional scholarship could not have been assembled without the indispensable help of those involved with producing this volume. I would like to thank especially my excellent co-editor, Eve Tavor Bannet, for her support and assistance; Sarah Scheutze, for her careful copyediting work; Ashley Barros, for her enthusiastic and reliable help as student assistant for the volume; the Dean's Office of the College of Arts and Sciences at Santa Clara University, for resources to support my editorial work; Dan Sallaberry, for his timely help with the list of readers; Vickie Cutting, for indispensable support from the ASECS office; and the editorial board and the many external readers who generously contributed their time and intelligence to this project.

Michelle Burnham
Santa Clara University
2014

Editorial Readers for Volume Forty-four

NATHAN ABRAMS / Film Studies / Bangor University, Wales
JULIA ABRAMSON / Modern Languages, Literatures, & Linguistics / University of Oklahoma
LAURA AURICCHIO / Humanities / The New School
EVE TAVOR BANNET / English / University of Oklahoma
WILLIAM BARCHAM / History of Art / Fashion Institute of Technology
JOSEPH BARTOLOMEO / English / University of Massachusetts at Amherst
TUSKA BENES / History / College of William & Mary
DAVID BREWER / English / Ohio State University
KRISTINA BROSS / English / Purdue University
TONI BOWERS / English / University of Pennsylvania
JEFFREY BURSON / History / Georgia Southern University
ANDREW BUSH / Hispanic Studies / Vassar College
VINCENT CARRETTA / English / University of Maryland
ANNE CHANDLER / English / Southern Illinois University
RANDALL CLACK / English / Wesley College
EMMA CLERY / English / University of Southampton
MATT COHEN / English / University of Texas at Austin
MICHÈLE COHEN / Humanities / Richmond University
SARAH COHEN / Art History / SUNY at Albany
JEFFREY COLLINS / Art & Culture / Bard Graduate Center
KEVIN COPE / English / Louisiana State University
DREW EDWARD DAVIES / Musicology / Northwestern University
JOELLEN DELUCIA / English Language & Literature / Central Michigan University
HELEN DEUTSCH / English / University of California, Los Angeles
JESSE EDWARDS / English / Manchester Metropolitan University
SARAH ELLENZWEIG / English / Rice University
MATT ERLIN / Germanic Languages & Literatures / Washington University in St. Louis
RICHARD FROHOCK / English / Oklahoma State University
NOELLE GALLAGHER / English / University of Manchester
SOPHIE GEE / English / Princeton University
ERIK GOLDNER / History / California State University, Northridge
THOMAS HALLOCK / English / University of South Florida
BREAN HAMMOND / English / University of Nottingham
JULIE CANDLER HAYES / Languages, Literature, & Cultures / University of Massachusetts, Amherst
ROB HUME / English / Pennsylvania State University
CHRIS IANNINI / English / Rutgers University
CATHERINE INGRASSIA / English / Virginia Commonwealth University
GREG JACKSON / English / Rutgers University
CHRISTOPHER JOHNS / History of Art / Vanderbilt University

Philosophical about Marriage: Women Writers and the Moralist Tradition ASECS Presidential Address, 2013

JULIE CANDLER HAYES

When we think of early modern women's intellectual and cultural production, we are probably more likely to think of genres other than moralist writing—letters and novels, translation, even history and science. Women left their mark in all of these domains. Moralist writing, however, possessed an innate cultural capital derived from the authority of Montaigne, a modern classic, and classical antecedents in Cicero and Seneca, yet it eluded the increasingly pejorative connotations, especially for women, of "erudition"—however erudite the moralist's allusions might be—by assuming a worldly, detached form of spectatorship. Thus, even as other genres, notably the novel, were assuming the moralist role of social commentary and analysis of the human heart, the novel explicitly blurred the lines between subject and object, between the spectator and his or her world, lines that moralist discourse sought to maintain. By writing in this older mode, women writers engaged with a distinguished tradition and claimed for themselves the right to observe and to analyze. Thus, the choice of genre is in itself a statement on women's participation in intellectual life and their relationship to the production of knowledge.

William Reddy and Jerrold Seigel have commented on the fraught nature of interpersonal relationships, "laced with intrigue and a wounding struggle for preeminence," as Seigel puts it, as a distinctive feature of élite

French social life under the ancien régime.[1] Classical moralist writing has indeed been one of our chief means for imaginatively recreating this world through the eyes of François de La Rochefoucauld and Jean de La Bruyère. Eric Méchoulan has argued that moralist writing comes into its own in the wake of the sixteenth-century Wars of Religion, the retreat of the Church as guarantor of state morality, and the new location of personal morality within the individual.[2] The moralist practices the courtier's "art of prudence" both as a form of self-regulation and, through deeper understanding of their motives, as a means to control or surpass others.

In the longer project of which this is a part, I look at the ways in which women take on some of the great topoi of traditional moralist writing: friendship, the passions, old age, knowledge of oneself and of the world. One topic, however, runs through their works far more prominently than in those of their male interlocutors and predecessors: marriage.

Classical moralist thought, whether ancient or modern, has remarkably little to say on the subject of marriage. Montaigne describes a good marriage as "representing" the conditions of friendship—as analogous to friendship, in other words, but not quite the same. He tells us that one marries not for oneself, but rather for one's posterity, one's family. Under ideal conditions, marriage can be a source of profound happiness, but it is not to be confused with love. "These things are distantly related [*ont quelque cousinage*], but they are very different."[3] The leading moralists of the following century are less nuanced on the subject, and indeed not particularly interested in it. As usual, in his one maxim on marriage, La Rochefoucauld sums up the thinking of an era with devastating concision: "Il y a de bons mariages, mais il n'y en a point de délicieux."[4] La Bruyère scatters reflections on marriage in various chapters of *Les Caractères*, where it is invariably linked to questions of wealth, social advancement, and hypocrisy. Among eighteenth century moralists, Luc de Clapiers, marquis de Vauvenargues, and Chamfort both take a jaundiced view of marriage, seeing it simply as a "commerce" of material interests, and hardly conducive to personal (masculine) happiness. Take Chamfort, for example: "Le mariage et le célibat ont tous deux des inconvénients: il faut préférer celui dont les inconvénients ne sont pas sans remède."[5] Much of the 17th and 18th century iconography of marriage further suggests ways in which the topic lent itself to comic, misogynistic, or sentimental representations.

Not surprisingly, marriage is a subject on which the female moralists differ sharply from their male interlocutors. I distinguish female moralist writing from the huge volume of texts related to the "querelle des femmes" or even to much salon-related cultural production. I would argue that many of these texts take a dim view of marriage without actually examining it in any depth. Marriage equals "slavery" in the eyes of many elite women, but their critique remains abstract; their interest lies in analyzing the inner recesses of the human heart, the infinite variety of forms of emotional attachment and disaffection. For instance, marriage is largely absent from Madeleine de Scudéry's world, hovering on the horizon, urged by male suitors, but indefinitely deferred by the heroine.

The remarkable treatise by the late 17th-century feminist philosopher Gabrielle Suchon, *Du célibat volontaire, ou la vie sans engagement* (1700), has an analytic structure which places it squarely within the realm of philosophy and theology. As her title suggests, Suchon proposes a critique not of marriage per se, but of the inexorable rule by which women are forced to choose between marriage and the convent. Suchon argues in favor of a "third way," a single life devoted to study and meditation, lived in the world rather than in the convent. As we shall see, her choice remains a compelling one for women throughout the century to come.

Marriage is a difficult topic. The ideology of passionate love and heroic friendship left no place for it. Madame de Lafayette claimed that her heroine's husband was unique among men in being able to sustain passion after marriage—but only because the object of his love was never truly present. By failing to reciprocate her husband's desire, the princesse de Clèves insured its continuation. Lafayette's analytical eye is directed not at marriage, but at passion: what nourishes it, and what kills it. Marriage is a social and legal structure, not an emotion or feeling, yet as Montaigne observes, the two have *quelque cousinage*. Although as a social practice it is visibly manifest in political and religious institutions, it is nevertheless akin to what Raymond Williams calls a "structure of feeling" because as a practice it carries with it a host of assumptions, "social experiences," and unarticulated or pre-articulated thoughts, thoughts "at the very edge of semantic availability" as Williams puts it.[6] Needless to say, it is also a practice that channels feeling, often dramatically, and becomes the locus for heightened social anxieties—anxieties in evidence not long ago in debates over gay marriage and the so-called "Defense of Marriage Act." As Tony Tanner argues in his classic study of the centrality of the topoi of marriage and adultery in the rise of the novel, "marriage is the all-subsuming, all-organizing, all-containing contract" for bourgeois society— adultery, "the possible breakdown of all the mediations on which society depends."[7]

Over the course of the eighteenth century, thinking about marriage would evolve. Many commentators have pointed to the rise of companionate marriage as one significant shift. In France, the revolutionary government's move to legalize divorce in 1792 was another.[8] The moralists that I look at in this essay point less to either of these changes than to the tensions, internal contradictions, and inconsistencies within both the traditional understanding of marriage and the emergent companionate ideal. Far from offering an idealized view of marriage, even in its companionate form, women moralists emphasize its unequal power relationships and the improbability of conjugal happiness. The demystification of marriage norms may be quite unconscious, as it appears to be in the marquise de Lambert, or quite overt, as in the présidente d'Arconville; yet not one of these figures contests the institution itself or postulates grounds on which a different understanding of marriage might arise.

Undoubtedly the best known figure that I will discuss here is Anne-Thérèse de Marguenat de Courcelles, marquise de Lambert. Her early 18th-century salon would come to represent the refinement, taste, and intelligence of the bygone *siècle classique*, a refuge from the vulgarities of Regency society. She wrote both moralist essays and conduct books. For most of her life, she preferred to circulate her manuscripts privately among her circle of friends, who appreciated both the purity of her prose and the judiciousness of her thought. She was deeply distressed when her essay on friendship was published without her permission.

A symptom of the uncertain relationship between moralist writing and the topic of marriage is the blurring of the (never completely water-tight) boundary between moralist writing and conduct literature. Hence we find Lambert's reflections on marriage as much or more in her didactic *Avis d'une mère à sa fille* as in her more distinctly moralist text, the *Réflexions nouvelles sur les femmes*. In the *Réflexions*, the discussion centers on the social and affective lives of adult women—hence married women, although their marriage is never mentioned as such. Lambert observes that most or many of these women will be "tempted by love"—again, the unstated understanding is that she is speaking of adulterous love. Conjugal love is simply not a topic. Women who let themselves be touched by love "pass from folly to folly" to the detriment of their reputation and, more damagingly, to their sense of personal integrity. The unconscious assumptions are also present in the *Avis d'une mère à sa fille.* Here the text is ostensibly addressed to a young unmarried woman. Again, amidst the complex texture of stated and unstated advice is the unavoidable observation that many married women are unfaithful to their husbands. While it is imaginable that the discussion of how to flee the "attack" of love might possibly apply to an unmarried girl, clearly Lambert's discussion of how best to comport oneself in society after having committed "une faute" does not. "Les femmes qui ont eu le malheur de se dérober à leur devoir, de blesser la bienséance, doivent ce respect à l'usage et à l'honnêteté violée, de paroître avec un air humilié; c'est une espèce de réparation que le Public demande; il se souvient de vos fautes dès que vous les oubliez."[9]

A similar understanding, and far more explicit, informs *Conseils à une amie*, another text that blurs the line between conduct literature and moralist writing. Madeleine d'Arsant de Puisieux (1720–1798) was a writer of moralist works and novels. She gained a certain notoriety from a liaison with Diderot in the late 1740s. Her early prefaces echo her pleasure at being taken seriously as a writer by "Monsieur D***," but she later expresses her annoyance that others were attributing her work to him. *Conseils à une amie* is undoubtedly her best-known work among scholars today, but she would enjoy a long, prolific literary career and in her final years would receive a pension from the revolutionary government.

While ostensibly written as "advice," much of the discussion in *Conseils* is concerned with the analysis of a wide range of social questions and human relationships, especially as they affect women. It is in the course of a discussion of power dynamics and dependency that Puisieux observes that women are better off if they do not owe their fortunes to their husbands—a situation she describes as "humiliating"[10]—and she has this to say about the proper behavior between married couples:

> Une femme doit avoir de la complaisance, de la douceur, de l'indulgence pour son mari; mais elle s'avilit au-dessous d'une domestique, si elle lui est trop soumise. La soumission marque de la subordination; & entre des gens mariés, tout est égal. Un mari n'a pas moins de devoirs à remplir qu'une femme. … Je ne sçais si mon coeur me trompe; mais il me dit qu'ils n'étoient pas destinés à nous imposer la loi; & l'expérience m'apprend qu'ils l'auroient peut-être reçue, si les femmes d'autrefois avoient eu autant de fermeté & de la résolution qu'il y en a dans la plupart de celles d'à-présent: mais le joug est donné; il faut s'y soumettre.[11]

The grim acknowledgement of the final line clashes discordantly with the egalitarian feminism of the first part.

Ultimately, in Puisieux's view, while a woman should make every effort to remain virtuous, it remains the case that "one mustn't count on one's strength": many women will ultimately cede to their hearts and take a lover. There are mitigating circumstances: most young women are sent into marriage without having the chance to get to know their future spouses, and husbands are frequently unfaithful themselves. Puisieux's worldly narrator even assures her young friend that ultimately the wandering husband's "passions" will cool and that he'll again seek refuge in his family and appreciate the friendship of his wife ("*sa meilleure amie*").[12] This less-than-rosy prospect of lukewarm domestic bliss aside, however, the fact remains that women may well seek their happiness elsewhere. Should such be the case, Puisieux advises, then one must choose well: "It is not the attachment which dishonors us, but rather the object."

Conseils à une amie has a titillating reputation as a sort of misconduct book, a lesson in worldliness, and in that respect it's hard to imagine an approach farther from that of Lambert, whose writings were seen by her contemporaries as exemplifying virtue. Puisieux's breezy manner is at antipodes from Lambert's measured pronouncements, yet the two concur that adultery is a fundamental fact of married life.

My next example comes from a fascinating anonymous work that deserves to be better known, the *Réflexions hazardées d'une femme ignorante* of 1766. Nothing is known for certain of the author of the *Réflexions*. She was first identified as "Madame de Verzure" in a literary compendium from 1778.[13] That attribution was picked up by nineteenth-century bibliographers, with the additional bit of information that she was the wife of a Genoese banker. However, a reviewer in the *Correspondance littéraire* of December 1765 attributes the work to Madame Bontemps, "la douce amie" of the marquis de Mirabeau, to whom the work was dedicated. Mme Bontemps, or Marie-Jeanne de Châtillon, had published an anonymous translation of James Thomson's *The Seasons*, making her a plausible candidate. Following scholarly custom, however, I shall refer to the author of the *Réflexions hazardées* as Verzure.

Madame de Verzure's essay, "Sur le célibat et le mariage," offers a disenchanted outlook. Like Mme d'Arconville, as we shall see, Verzure holds a generally pessimistic view of humanity as enslaved by passion, driven by *amour-propre* and venal interests. Her chapter on marriage sums up the numerous ways in which the institution has been perverted by the social and economic interests of noble and elite non-noble families. Although the married state favors males, it is hardly conducive to happiness for either partner.

> Les filles sont des victimes qu'on éleve avec soin, pour les immoler à l'orgueil de ceux qui leur ont donné le jour…
>
> Le sort du sexe en général, & sa destination est d'être privé de sa liberté. On ne sçauroit donc trop accoutumer de bonne heure les filles à la dépendance: elles doivent l'envisager comme une chose de droit, contre laquelle il seroit inutile de se révolter.
>
> Heureuses encore, quand on leur laisse le choix du genre d'esclavage.[14]

In its purest form, moralist writing is less concerned with finding a remedy to a situation than with analyzing and articulating the situation. Thus

Verzure offers no advice, but instead focuses on the existential situation of the married woman. For her, there is only one form of freedom for men or women, freedom from the passions, "détachement de nous-mêmes."[15]

I will be discussing the work of Marie-Geneviève-Charlotte Darlus, présidente Thiroux d'Arconville, to a greater extent than the others here, for she is a truly exceptional figure. She was the daughter of a wealthy farmer general and wife of a magistrate and member of the Parlement de Paris. Having received only a minimal education in her childhood, she embarked on a project of self-education in her twenties, following the births of her sons. She published novels, moralist works, histories, scientific and literary translations, and carried out original research in chemistry. She insisted on anonymous publication, but when some of her works were attributed to Diderot in the 1770s, she brought out a seven-volume set of her published works to date in order to indicate their common authorship. In her final years, her eyesight failing, she dictated hundreds of essays on a wide range of topics, including her autobiography. Those manuscripts, long thought to be lost, have recently been acquired by the Morisset Library at the University of Ottawa.

Like Verzure, d'Arconville sees the loss of liberty as a central truth of marriage, even companionate marriage. Reflections on the married state arise throughout her writing career, and while her thinking is generally consistent, it is also nuanced and complex, suggesting an ongoing effort to reconcile singularity and belonging, autonomy and dependence. The key texts that I'll discuss are an early essay in her *Pensées et réflexions morales* (1760), a chapter in *De l'amitié* (1761), and several of her late essays from the years 1801–1805.

The topic of marriage recurs in several of the essays in *Pensées et réflexions*. In "Sur les femmes," d'Arconville offers a series of portraits of adulterous women: Lucinde, who takes lovers out of sheer boredom; Pauline and Zenobie, who delude themselves into believing that they love both their husbands and their lovers; and Dorothée, whose fall into a series of superficial affairs is the fault of her unpleasant, jealous husband. While she condemns infidelity and promiscuity, d'Arconville sees mitigating circumstances in the cases of women who are lucid about their desires (unlike Pauline and Zénobie) or who experience a profound passion (something that Dorothée's constricted life precludes).[16] The asymmetry of marriage reveals itself in a paradox:

> Il y a plus de maris qui aiment leur femmes, que de femmes qui aiment leurs maris; & je crois avoir trouvé la raison dans l'amour que tous les hommes ont en général pour la liberté. Les femmes dépendent de leurs maris, & les maris ne dépendent point de leurs femmes.[17]

Echoes of the companionate ideal can be heard, as when a woman is said to lose more in the death of a husband for whom she feels “esteem and trust” than in the loss of the most passionate lover. Even so, d’Arconville points out, a woman who loses a good husband “at least acquires her liberty.”[18]

Marriage fares no better in the chapter in *De l’amitié* on friendship between husbands and wives. Marriage ought to be the source of greatest felicity to which mortals might aspire, according to d’Arconville, but all too often self-interest and passions conspire to wreck marriages.[19] In effect, the discussion of friendship vanishes in a series of paralipses in which the speaker repeatedly refuses to name or describe what is happening: the failure of the marriage, the inevitability of adultery. “Let us forget these misfortunes that perversity has rendered all too common….”[20]

Marriage enters the discussion only indirectly in d’Arconville’s second moral treatise, *Des Passions*, as one of the sites where lives are shipwrecked by twin passions of desire and ambition. It is only in the moralist essays left among her late manuscripts that she turns again to the topic with attentiveness, complexity, and depth. While many of the essays take up related issues of personal freedom, fidelity, and love, I shall examine three in which the question of marriage is central, then turn briefly to pertinent passages in her autobiographical writing.

One of the earliest pieces in the late manuscripts, “Sur le mariage” offers a vision of the institution of marriage even bleaker than Mme de Verzure’s.[21] Beginning with the historical observation that marriage was hardly “respectable” prior to being elevated by Christianity to a sacrament, she goes on to critique it as irretrievably damaged by social norms and familial ambitions. Young people are never consulted on the choice of a partner, she observes, and girls in particular have no basis for judgment because of their sheltered upbringing, particularly if they have received a convent education. While the young bride, touched by her husband’s attention and thrilled by her new clothes and jewels, may be inclined to fall in love, such feelings are not made to last. A husband’s self-interest consists not in seeking his wife’s love, which is unpredictable and dangerous, but rather in deserving her esteem, which lays the groundwork for mutual affection and respect. A wife’s self-interest lies in obeying her husband, since his “absolute empire” over her grants him the power to “la rendre malheureuse impunément.”[22]

Describing marriage as “a yoke” imposed by religion, d’Arconville notes that it furthermore requires a constancy not found in nature.[23] Given the severity of the moral code manifest throughout her writings, it comes as something of a surprise that d’Arconville, like Lambert, appears to acquiesce to the quasi inevitability of marital infidelity, though she imputes the blame for the majority of unfaithful wives to their unsatisfactory husbands.[24] She concludes with a scathing image:

> Il résulte de ces réflexions que l'état de mariage remplit rarement d'une part l'idée que se fait une jeune personne de la félicité dont elle espère jouir dès qu'elle sera mariée, et qu'on l'aura décorée du collier sur lequel on devrait inscrire comme sur celui d'un chien, *j'appartiens à Mr. un tel.*[25]

Happy—or at least "bearable" (*supportables*)—marriages exist, but they require much patience, flexibility, a clear mind, and iron-clad virtue ("une vertu à toute épreuve").[26]

Freedom, *la liberté*, remains the highest good, to which all creation aspires—except for humanity, whose desire for voluntary servitude seemingly knows no bounds.[27] Despite her largely negative assessment of human relationships, her writings abound with heartfelt evocations of moments of intimacy and mutual understanding.[28] Such deep connections are possible through friendship, but, as we have seen, friendship rarely makes it into marriage at all, and never, apparently, with any intensity.

The essay "Sur l'intérieur des ménages" ("On the Interior of Households") begins with an evocation of how difficult in general it is to be happy, then considers the chances for happiness in different social classes. Although manual labor drives away inappropriate thoughts that might lead one astray, conjugal happiness is infrequent among *le peuple*, where the men too often squander their substance on drink and are brutal to their wives and children. Prospects for happiness in wealthy families are no better: arranged marriages leave no place for individual desires, and young wives are often either humiliated by their husbands' bad example or corrupted by it.[29] Only those of "the middling sort" have a solid chance at true conjugal happiness, although the principles of even the bourgeoisie, formerly "the seat of virtue," have foundered in the wake of the Revolution. Nevertheless, d'Arconville sees in this group, free on the one hand from the stress of poverty and on the other from the ambitions and frivolous desires that accompany great wealth, the best chance for happy households where, "reciprocal trust uniting hearts, they have nothing to hide from one another."[30] Love is not necessary and indeed could only disturb the state of plenitude.

In a later volume, d'Arconville will echo this thought in her essay "Du célibat" ("On Celibacy"), adding an autobiographical reference. Happy marriages do exist, she tells us:

> J'en ai connu plusieurs, et particulierement dans ma famille [;] il est certain qu'alors ce lien si redoutable…est un paradis anticipé; en effet, tout ce qui met souvent le trouble dans cette union, contribue à sa félicité: les communs intérets, l'empressement que deux époux trouvent à satisfaire leurs désirs mutuels et à

> y contribuer réciproquement, la naissance de leurs enfants, les progrès de leurs éducations…rendent leurs jours délicieux; il n'y a point de vuide dans leur vie….[31]

The essay as a whole, however, is an extended plea in favor of the single life. Feelings of love can obviate the loss of freedom in marriage, but they cannot last when sexual pleasure is no longer *une faveur* bestowed willingly, but rather *un devoir*, a duty. In short, she tells us, marriage is not a natural state: "J'en reviens à mon *refrain*, que la liberté est le premier des biens, et que c'est la *prostituer* pour ainsi dire, que de l'abandonner au hazard en se mariant."[32] Personal observations of happy marriages notwithstanding, d'Arconville's first allegiance is to the ideal of the unattached life.[33]

The personal observations at the beginning and end of "Du célibat" might appear somewhat at odds with one another. Should we make something of the fact that the "several" happy marriages that she has observed do not appear to include her own, at least not explicitly? The references to her marriage in her autobiographical writings are rare and extremely brief. Her marriage "at fourteen years, four and a half months" puts an abrupt end to the account of her childhood, "Histoire de mon enfance."[34] The story of her intellectual development, "Histoire de ma littérature," contains a passing reference to her marriage at fourteen as the occasion of a temporary pause in her writing. That essay goes on to detail her self-education in literature, translation, and science, as well as the progress of her writing and publishing career, but says nothing of her personal and family life.

Louis-Lazare Thiroux d'Arconville, président at the Parlement de Paris, was eight years her senior, hence a young man at the time of their marriage. Their three sons were born within fairly quick succession, and it is likely that d'Arconville's turn to self-education coincided with the birth of her third son at age twenty. She refers with deep affection to her sister, her brother-in-law Angran d'Alleray, and her husband's brother Thiroux d'Epersenne. One of her autobiographical essays, "Mes Voyages," includes an amusing anecdote from the early months of their marriage of a misadventure at a friend's country house: when she walked into a swamp and was unable to extricate herself, her husband came to help her and found himself similarly trapped; both had to be rescued by their host. The husband surfaces occasionally in other essays, but his death in May 1789 is mentioned only as the occasion for her decision to leave Paris and retire to her beloved estate in Meudon.

Such references tell us little, but should warn against a simplistic biographical reading of her discussions on marriage. Reticence, *pudeur*, would seem to be one of the primary traits of this woman who avoided *le grand monde* for a select group of friends and mentors, who always published anonymously or elected not to publish at all, and for whom public revelations of either the joys or chagrins of married life must have seemed unthinkable. We may assume that Thiroux d'Arconville offered no obstacles to his wife's determined quest for knowledge, but whether he actively supported her efforts and took pride in them, we cannot know. He is absent from her accounts of her philosophical, literary, scientific, and historical projects; not he but her brother-in-law d'Alleray offers advice on setting up her study at Meudon. She appears to have had great autonomy in arranging her life and determining the use of her time.

Such a life would not appear, at least, to inspire the devastating image discussed earlier of the young bride "decorated" with a dog collar, "I belong to Mr. So-and-So" ("*j'appartiens à M^r. un tel*"). On the other hand, it's clear that wealth, autonomy, and the ability to select her friends and pursue her interests did not in any way constitute "liberty." Writing at the end of her long life, she speaks of her "penchant" for the single state and describes even a good marriage as antithetical to personal liberty. Some women writers and intellectuals came to writing in the wake of unhappy marriages—for example, Lambert, Graffigny, and Riccoboni—or after widowhood left them free to write or hold salons. For Emilie Du Châtelet, born in a higher social class and in the generation of d'Arconville's parents, marriage seems to have been a simple fact of life, but hardly one that limited her in any way; like d'Arconville, she complains of the late start of her "real" education, her self education, but this seems to be the only limitation against which she struggles. Marriage is not viewed as a constraint for the aristocrat, but for d'Arconville, marriage is an existential and moral reality. Hence even marriage with a high degree of autonomy constitutes a form of voluntary (or involuntary) servitude, and had she been offered the choice, she would not have chosen it.

* * *

Not surprisingly, given all that was at stake, marriage is a considerably weightier subject for women moralists than for their male counterparts. They offer no witty jabs at convention, no clever wordplay. As we've seen, there is a distinction, but also some overlapping, between the advice of conduct writing and the analysis of more thoroughly moralist texts. All underscore the asymmetrical power relations of marriage and young women's—and young men's—lack of choice. The terms of the argument have not greatly changed since the seventeenth-century *querelle des femmes* and the critique of marriage levied by Madeleine de Scudéry and her contemporaries, but the evolving social and political context lends a different meaning to the terms by setting them in a different horizon of expectations. It is one thing to compare marriage to slavery at the height of the absolute monarchy; it is another to make the same comparison a century later, in a world where concepts of natural rights and natural law held increasing currency, where companionate, freely chosen marriage was the ideal, even if arranged marriages were still largely the norm.

Over the course of d'Arconville's lifetime, the confluence of the new affectivity and new social and political ideas produced what Dror Wahrman calls a "sea change" in the constitution of personal identity on both sides of the English Channel.[35] The scope of this talk does not allow a thorough examination of all the issues that converge here, but it has allowed us to chart a double movement: first, women writers' turn to marriage as a legitimate object of moralist inquiry, rather than as a subject of satire; second, a shift in the attitudes of these women writers over the course of the eighteenth century. All recognize the centrality of the institution to the shape of women's lives—how could they not?—but whereas Lambert and Puisieux unblinkingly acknowledge the likelihood of infidelity by both partners, but do not see infidelity in itself as an indication of a broken marriage, or marriage as a poor choice, Verzure and especially d'Arconville discuss presumably "intact" marriages in much bleaker terms. In other words, the earlier writers appear to expect less of marriage by way of sexual or emotional fulfillment, but view it with equanimity. Verzure and d'Arconville, on the other hand, assume companionate marriage as the basic model, but find it unsatisfying and confining.

In the studies of Old Regime affectivity that I alluded to earlier, marriage is one form of what William Reddy calls "emotional refuge" from the pressures of social hierarchies and intense self-regulation. Other forms include the entire range of practices linked to the period's new emphasis on affectivity: spiritual self-examination, salon conversation, letter writing, biography and autobiography, and, of course, the reading of novels.[36] As we have seen, however, marriage offers little or no refuge for the women of this study.
There is a tension in the works discussed here between the moralist tradition's emphasis on cold observation and mastery of self and others, and our writers' desire to explore lived experience and personal vulnerability. It is the novel that will ultimately take on the cultural analysis performed by moralist writing; not the moralists' sometime will to power, but their quest to understand human motives and interactions. The entwinement of novel and moralist analysis emerges with the rise of extended prose fiction over the course of the seventeenth century; even the novel's earliest theoreticians

propose that fiction may indeed be the bearer of truth.[37] The discourse of self-regulation remains important for the women moralists, particularly Verzure and d'Arconville, for whom it stems from the Stoic tradition of the mastery of the passions—and neo-Augustinian distrust of *amour-propre*—rather than from models of court behavior. Stoic self-discipline, however, ultimately repeats and converges with the ancien régime's worldly disciplines of self-control, which may explain part of the reason why the ideal of freedom, even when internalized and separated from social institutions such as marriage, remains elusive. D'Arconville's sense of self may be bound up in the world of the ancien régime, but her expectations for marriage are subtly colored by a profound sense that this world was not enough.

NOTES

1. Jerrold Seigel, *The Idea of the Self* (Cambridge, UK: Cambridge University Press, 2005), 37; see also William Reddy, *The Navigation of Feeling: A Framework for the History of Emotions* (Cambridge, UK: Cambridge University Press, 2001), 324–26.

2. Eric Méchoulan, "La Prudence de l'homme de cour: De Gracián à Amelot de la Houssaye," in *Le Moraliste, la politique et l'histoire*, ed. Jean-Charles Darmon (Paris: Desjonquères, 2007), 96.

3. Michel de Montaigne, "Sur quelques vers de Virgile," *Essais*, ed. Maurice Rat, 2 vols. (Paris: Garnier, 1962), 2:274.

4. "There are good marriages, but none are delicious." François, duc de la Rochefoucauld, *Maximes (1678)*, n.113, in *Moralistes du XVIIe siècle*, ed. Jean Lafond (Paris: Robert Laffont, 1992), 144.

5. Chamfort, *Maximes et pensées* (Paris: Union générale d'éditions, 1963), 103. "Marriage and celibacy each have their drawbacks: I prefer the one whose drawbacks are not irreversible."

6. Raymond Williams, *Marxism and Literature* (Oxford, UK: Oxford Univ. Press, 1977), 133–4.

7. Tony Tanner, *Adultery and the Novel: Contract and Transgression* (Baltimore: Johns Hopkins Univ. Press, 1979), 15, 17.

8. See among many recent studies on changes in family life under the ancien régime and revolution: Suzanne Desan, *The Family on Trial in Revolutionary France* (Berkeley: Univ. of California Press, 2004); Jennifer Ngaire Heuer, *The Family, Nation, and Gender in Revolutionary France, 1789–1830* (Ithaca: Cornell Univ. Press, 2005). For a useful overview of the historiography of the family, see Suzanne Desan and Jeffrey Merrick, Introduction, *Family, Gender, and Law in Early Modern France*, ed. S. Desan and J. Merrick (University Park, PA: Pennsylvania State Univ. Press, 2009), xi–xxvi. Margaret R. Hunt provides a thoughtful cross-cultural survey

of the parameters defining women's lives in *Women in Eighteenth-Century Europe* (Harlow, UK: Pearson, 2010).

9. Anne-Thérèse de Marguenat de Courcelles, marquise de Lambert, *Avis d'une mère à sa fille*, in *Oeuvres complètes* (Paris: Léopold Collin, 1808), 89. "Women who have had the misfortune to fail in their duty and injure propriety owe this sign of respect to convention and violated morality: to humble themselves when they appear in society. The Public requires these reparations; it remembers your failings the instant that you forget them."

10. Madeleine d'Arsant de Puisieux, *Conseils à une amie* (n.p.: [1749].), 129–30. "Il est bien humiliant de devoir tout à un homme." [It is humiliating to owe everything to a man.]

11. Puisieux, *Conseils*, 131–32. "A woman should have kindness, gentleness, and indulgence for her husband; but she degrades herself below a servant's place if she is too submissive. Submission is a mark of subordination, but in a married couple everything is equal. A husband has no fewer obligations to fulfill than a wife. … I know not if my heart deceives me, but it tells me that [men] were not destined to rule over us; and experience teaches me that the reverse might have occurred if the women of yesteryear had as much strength and resolution as the women of the present day. But the yoke is given, and we must submit."

12. Puisieux, *Conseils*, 146.

13. Jacques Hébrail and Joseph de la Porte, eds., *Supplément à La France littéraire* (Paris: Chez la Veuve Duchesne, 1778), 185.

14. Mme de Verzure, "Sur le célibat et le mariage," in *Réflexions hazardées d'une femme ignorante*, 2 vols. (Amsterdam: Chez Vincent, 1766), 1:146, 147–48. "Girls are victims who are raised with care in order that they be sacrificed to the pride of those who gave them life—I refer to people of consequence in the world. The fate of the female sex and its destiny is to be deprived of liberty. One cannot therefore begin too early to accustom young girls to dependency; they must see it as a matter of course against which it is useless to rebel. Fortunate are those who are allowed to choose the nature of their enslavement."

15. Verzure, "La Liberté" in *Réflexions hazardées*, 1:178.

16. Marie-Geneviève-Charlotte Thiroux d'Arconville, "Sur les femmes," in *Pensées et réflexions morales*, *Mélanges de littérature, de morale et de physique*, 7 vols. (Amsterdam: Au dépens de la Compagnie, 1775), 1:379–83.

17. D'Arconville, "Sur le mariage," *Mélanges*, 1:385. "There are more husbands who love their wives, than wives who love their husbands. I believe that I have discovered the reason in humanity's love of liberty. Women depend on their husbands, but husbands are independent of their wives."

18. D'Arconville, "Sur le mariage," *Mélanges*, 1:387.

19. D'Arconville, *De l'amitié*, *Mélanges*, 2:73.

20. D'Arconville, *De l'amitié*, *Mélanges*, 2:74.

21. D'Arconville's late manuscripts are bound in twelve volumes under the title *Pensées, réflexions et anecdotes* (hereafter *PRA*). For a description of the manuscripts, see Emilie Joly et Patrice Bret, "Corpus des oeuvres de Madame d'Arconville," in *Madame d'Arconville: Une femme de lettres et de sciences au siècle des Lumières*,

ed. Patrice Bret et Brigitte Van Tiggelen (Paris: Hermann, 2011), 151–58.

22. D'Arconville, "make her unhappy with impunity," *PRA*, 1:50.

23. D'Arconville, *PRA*, 1:46–47. In her essay "Sur la constance et de l'inconstance" in the same manuscript volume as "Sur le mariage," D'Arconville elaborates on this notion, arguing that inasmuch as both depend on desires and drives that are not under our control, fidelity is not a virtue, nor infidelity a vice. *PRA* 1:54–65. See also "Sur l'inconstance en amour," *PRA*, 4:346–57.

24. D'Arconville, *PRA*, 1:43, 48. D'Arconville returns to this point in "Sur l'intérieur des ménages," *PRA* 6:38.

25. D'Arconville, *PRA*, 1:52. "I conclude from these reflections that the conjugal state rarely fulfills a young girl's expectations of the felicity that she hopes to enjoy once she is married, and once she is bedecked with a collar inscribed like a dog's, "*I belong to Mr. So-and-So.*"

26. D'Arconville, *PRA*, 1:52.

27. D'Arconville, "Sur la liberté," *PRA*, 1:349–59.

28. D'Arconville, "Sur le tête a tête," *PRA*, 3:256.

29. Here d'Arconville returns to the image, present in many of her evocations of marriage among the wealthy, of the young woman whose head has been so turned by the prospect of new clothes and jewels that she doesn't realize immediately the burden she has taken on. *PRA*, 6:30.

30. D'Arconville, *PRA*, 6:25.

31. D'Arconville, *PRA*, 11:145–46. "I have known several, particularly in my family. In such cases, it is certain that this redoubtable bond… is paradise on earth. All that could potentially trouble the union instead contributes to its happiness: common interests, the eagerness of the couple to satisfy their mutual desire and to reciprocate, the births of children and the progress of their education… All this renders their days delicious; their lives are never empty."

32. D'Arconville, *PRA*, 11:137–38. "I come back to my *refrain* that liberty is the greatest of goods, and that we *prostitute* it, so to speak, by abandoning it to chance through marriage."

33. Verzure had also begun her essay on the single life with an admission of partiality: "Etant attachée à mon idée sur le mariage & le célibat, je crains de ne pas appercevoir bien clairement ce qui peut la combattre; je veux cependant tâcher de mettre de côté toute prévention." *Réflexions hazardées*, 1:136.

34. D'Arconville, *PRA*, 3:488–89.

35. Dror Wahrman, *The Making of the Modern Self: Identity and Culture in Eighteenth-Century England* (New Haven: Yale Univ. Press, 2004), xiii, 312–21. See similar comments on the political thrust of the new affectivity in Reddy, 154; and Seigel, 83.

36. Reddy, 149–54, Louis Dupré, *The Enlightenment and the Foundations of Modern Culture* (New Haven: Yale Univ. Press, 2004), 45–67.

37. See Camille Esmein-Sarrazin, "Fiction et morale au XVIIe siècle: La Recherche d'un bon usage du roman," in *Pensée morale et genres littéraires*, eds. Jean-Charles Darmon and Philippe Desan (Paris: Presses Universitaires de France, 2009), 105–21; and in the same volume, Barbara Carnevali, "L'Observatoire des

moeurs: Les Coutumes et les caractères entre littérature et morale," 159–78. Joan DeJean argues for the central role of the novel in promoting the new affectivity and new sense of identity; see *Ancients Against Moderns* (Chicago: Univ. of Chicago Press, 1997), 78–123.

Invisible Amputation and Heroic Masculinity

TERESA MICHALS

In portraits and prints of the Napoleonic era, heroes cannot be amputees and amputees cannot be heroes—except for Admiral Lord Horatio Nelson. Nelson's iconography confronts the observer with a full-frontal view of the bodily mutilation of a military hero. Although amputation was widely represented in the eighteenth century, Nelson's portraits are unusual in incorporating it into images of heroic masculinity and national identity. Why did heroic portraits generally render amputation invisible, and what are we to make of the departure from this practice seen in Nelson's portraits? More broadly, how does physical disability relate to portraiture's claim that in delineating how people look, the painter's eye and hand can make visible what they truly are? Answering these questions requires us to consider how disability or "defect" relates to key conventions of eighteenth-century portraiture. As Marcia Pointon remarks, portraiture "makes graspable the elusive body" by bringing together "the conscious and the unconscious, the historical and the actual, the real and the imagined.[1] When the elusive body that the portraitist seeks to capture is disabled, then the representational choices made call attention to certain larger ways of thinking that give meaning to a likeness. The portraits examined here reveal the complexity of the visual codes through which bodies signify as particular kinds of people—as national heroes in the late eighteenth and early nineteenth centuries.

Lord St. Vincent's complaint that "that foolish little fellow has sat to every painter in London" is an exaggeration, but Nelson did get his portrait painted often. Despite frequently being unwell or at sea and dying at the age of forty-seven, he is the subject of more formal portraits than any military hero except the Duke of Wellington.[2] Nelson was also a popular subject for caricatures, in addition to commemorative consumer goods such as mugs and decanters, fans, and fabrics.[3] And the body that all of these images sought to represent was conspicuously disabled: shattered by musket ball as he led a raid at Santa Cruz de Tenerife on July 25, 1797, Nelson's right arm was amputated immediately below the shoulder.

As a highly visible amputee, Nelson was part of a trend. After long being suspect as a presumptuous act that, among other things, disfigured the image of God, elective limb amputation had become fairly widely accepted by the end of the 17th century, largely due to the rise of gunpowder and the particular kinds of damage that gunpowder inflicts on human tissue and bones.[4] Moreover, in Nelson's own time, medical advances in amputation combined with the wars of 1793–1815 greatly increased the number of disabled veterans in England, who often appeared as stock figures occasioning laughter or pity in popular print and literary and visual arts.[5] However, Nelson's social class and professional status were less typical among military amputees: he was not a disabled and discharged soldier or sailor, but rather a disabled officer on active duty. He lost his right arm early in his career and lost the sight in one eye even earlier. He fought and won his three great battles, the Nile (1798), Copenhagen (1801), and Trafalgar (1805), as a disabled active-duty officer—as a one-armed, half-blind Admiral who was working at the very peak of his administrative genius, technical expertise, and charismatic leadership.

"Disabled active-duty officer" is a less familiar category than "disabled veteran."[6] Nelson was wounded more often than any other senior officer of his day, but he was not alone in returning to duty after amputation.[7] Rear Admiral Sir Thomas Pasley, a friend of Nelson's, provides a useful comparison. At the age of sixty, Pasley lost his left leg below the knee in the Battle of the First of June, 1794.[8] Although Pasley did not command at sea again, he continued to serve and to be promoted, first as Commander-in-Chief (the Nore) then Commander-in-Chief (Plymouth). He retired in 1801 as a full admiral. We should note that among sailors rather than officers the familiar rank "Able-Bodied Seaman" referred to skills rather than to a physical norm. An able-bodied seaman was a sailor with at least two years of experience at sea and the specialized skills that went with such experience. The rank did not contrast with "disabled" but with "Ordinary Seaman" or "Landsman," sailors who had served less time at sea.

In September 1797, the Admiralty's Lord Spencer describes Nelson's physical condition optimistically: "I am very happy to have it in my power to inform you that he seems likely to recover entirely from the effect of his Wound, & to be able to serve."[9] At first there may be something surprising about this official statement that a one-armed man who was also permanently blind in one eye was expected to be "entirely recovered" and so fit to return to active military duty—fit to go to war. But that surprise is a reminder of the difference between the continuing power of an ideal of heroic military masculinity and the requirements of actual military service. Nelson's military success did not depend on his own physical strength or wholeness but his ability to command men and ships. Upon first seeing him after Teneriffe, King George remarked "You have lost your right arm." Nelson purportedly answered, "But not my right hand," and presented to the king Captain Berry, his second in command.[10] Such anecdotes suggest that Nelson was adept at incorporating disability into his version of military heroism, here pointing out the difference between an ideal of physical wholeness and the actual requirements of his position. Similarly, in his famous refusal to obey the signal to withdraw at the Battle of Copenhagen, he told his flag captain "You know, Foley, I only have one eye — I have the right to be blind sometimes." Holding the telescope to his blind eye, he said "I really do not see the signal!"

Social class informs the visual codes that helped to frame public perceptions of Nelson's career as a disabled active duty officer, and his body itself. As we have suggested, the most common image of the military amputee during the Napoleonic era was the disabled, discharged, and impoverished soldier or sailor. These men were most often represented as helpless, an image of physical vulnerability compounded by economic dependence. Encounters with such veterans figured in Nelson's progress through cheering crowds. Here, for example, is the *Gentleman's Magazine's* account of such a moment during Nelson's visit to Salisbury in December, 1800:

> Another man presented himself, who at the Helder Point has met with a similar fate with his Lordship off Tenerife in the loss of an arm. Every circumstance of greatness or distinction vanished for the moment from the brave Admiral's mind...his sympathy was awakened...a proof of which his fellow sufferer soon experienced in a generous token of the hero's feeling.[11]

As historian Timothy Jenks has described, such stories reflect the teller's "desire to view Nelson's body as a conduit to plebeian patriotism." Banishing "every circumstance of greatness or distinction," if only momentarily, the juxtaposition of these two disabled bodies could be seen to represent the "enduring loyalty of disabled veterans, and a class-transcendent sense of national community."[12] The structure of such charitable encounters, however, foregrounds class even as it transcends it: one disabled man generously hands over coins, the other gratefully pockets them. Even as he acknowledges their common loss, Nelson affirms his social difference.

In *Cruelty and Laughter*, Simon Dickie summarizes the eighteenth century's "deep-seated comic associations about amputees," particularly the amputee military veterans who posed a "justifiable claim on one's charity." Although missing arms also elicit this kind of laughter, missing legs seem to come to mind first as a natural source of hilarity. A wooden leg marks the far edge of sensibility. Often, it is simply over the line:

> From Adam Smith to Goldsmith, James Beattie, and countless lesser authors, the man with a wooden leg becomes almost a master trope for testing the possibilities and limitations of sympathy. These men had been wounded in the service of their country, but there were just too many of them – and, anyway, who could possibly look at someone with a wooden leg and not burst out laughing?[13]

This common eighteenth-century assumption that amputation is naturally risible has a number of sources. Perhaps most relevant for portraiture is the sense that purely mental or emotional pain is of a higher order than suffering caused by visible damage to the body. For example, in *The Theory of Moral Sentiments*, Adam Smith sees amputation as a very "real calamity," but one that lacks the dignity of solely emotional pain: "The loss of a leg may generally be regarded as a more real calamity than the loss of a mistress. It would be a ridiculous tragedy, however, of which the catastrophe was to turn upon a loss of that kind."[14] Here a disabled body is incompatible with the high seriousness that establishes suffering as the proper subject of tragic drama. Similar assumptions about dignity, humor, and amputation may reduce the likelihood of such a body appearing in a heroic portrait.

Even more relevant to the visual arts than the discourse of sensibility is the idea of "defect," another context for Smith's assumption that the natural response to the sight of amputation is laughter and scorn. As the word itself suggests, a 21st-century understanding of "disability" purports to focus on how bodies function in relation to their social and physical environment—what disabled people can or cannot do in a given set of circumstances. In contrast, as critics such as Lennard Davis and David Turner argue, the eighteenth-century idea of "defect" is largely framed in terms of aesthetic ideals, as "the opposite of beauty." Scholars such as Helen Deustch, Felicity

Nussbaum, and Roger Lund have shown that the energetic derision of ideas of ugliness or "defect" is entwined with familiar eighteenth-century aesthetic theories that see beauty as a sign of God's design: a "defect" is a falling away from a divinely-ordained order, an order that beauty makes visible.[15] The claim that the sight of amputation will naturally elicit derision reflects this larger habit of thinking about the human body in terms of ideal form. As a way of making abstract qualities visible, ideal form relates to the portraitist's professional responsibility to show an inner truth about a sitter's character rather than merely to duplicate accurately his or her external appearance. This ability to give concrete form to abstractions is important to the professional status of the portraitist. As Jonathan Richardson insists in his *Essay on the Theory of Painting* (1725), "'Tis not enough to make a Tame, insipid Resemblance of the Features, so that everybody shall know who the Picture was intended for." Catching a mere likeness "is often done by the lowest of Face-Painters, but then 'tis ever with the Air of a Fool, and an Unbred Person."[16] In contrast, the true artist will reveal what the sitter is, not merely what he looks like, proving that the artist himself is an insightful and cultured gentleman rather than an under-bred "face-painter."

Outside of the realm of the visual arts, people seem to have seen Nelson after the loss of his arm in terms of both "defect" and "disability." "I find it looks shocking to be without one arm," writes a friend on seeing him for the first time after Tenerife, summing up the impact of amputation as a deviation from a visual ideal. Nelson himself was concerned about how he would be seen, especially by his superiors. However, he seems to have thought more in terms of preconceptions about what a one-armed senior officer could or could not do rather than external signs of divine order, worrying that "A left-handed admiral will never again be considered as useful."[17] As we have seen, the Admiralty's verdict that Nelson was "entirely recovered" suggests that that they ultimately relied less on an idea of "defect" in his case than on something like a framework of disability, assessing his usefulness in the context of their particular needs.

Within the visual arts, "defect" has greater weight. This is evident when we compare representations of Nelson to those of other military amputees and to the generic figure of the disabled veteran in two genres: caricature and the formal portrait. Generally appearing in the press without any direct involvement by the person represented, caricatures offer an external commentary on their subject in the context of various political issues of the day. In contrast, a formal portrait generally requires the subject's active participation in sitting for the painter, if not in commissioning and paying him or her. Unlike formal portraits, caricatures often call attention to the physical difference of amputees. Both caricatures and portraits provide a valuable context for representations of Nelson. Although created after Nelson's time, George Cruikshank's sentimental caricature, *The Battle of the Nile* (1825), still draws on some of the "deep-seated comic associations" that Jenks describes, presenting drunken and disabled seamen as an occasion for laughter, pity, and—implicitly—alms-giving. This caricature represents pensioners at Greenwich Hospital celebrating the anniversary of the Battle of the Nile. Founded in 1694, Greenwich Hospital's charter directed it to provide "reliefe and support of seamen serving on board the shipps or vessells belonging to the Navy Royall who by reason of Age, Wounds or other disabilities shall be uncapable of further service at sea and being unable to maintain themselves."[18] Whatever moral or emotional connotations military disability may carry today, Margarette Lincoln claims that this image "is without a trace of respect" for the service of the veterans whom it depicts celebrating the anniversary of the Battle of the Nile: "Their mutilated condition – most are missing arms, eyes or legs – is used to make the scene more humourous, since the gestures that accompany their dramatic reconstruction of the battle seem incongruous and extravagant given their obvious incapacity to wield arms."[19] (Fig. 1) As a representation not of an individual but rather a group of disabled military men who are dependent on a charitable foundation, the caricature may invoke the sense mentioned above that "there are just too many of them." In addition, it suggests an aspect of humor that William Gilpin notes in his influential *Essay upon Prints containing remarks on Picturesque Beauty*...(1768, 1802). Gilpin claims that the distinguishing marks of any profession become ridiculous when we see them multiplied among a group of members of that profession, praising, for example, Hogarth's "collections of natural curiosities": "The Oxford-heads, the physician's-arms, are expressly of this humourous kind. They are truly comic; though ill-natur'd effusions of mirth..."[20] Finally, Cruikshank's caricature invites the viewer to see the wooden leg of the pensioner on the extreme left as one of a group of wooden legs belonging to a chair, a dehumanizing detail.

More unusually, Thomas Rowlandson's c. 1800 caricature, "The Tough Old Commodore," presents a specific individual, Nelson's friend Admiral Sir Thomas Pasley, rather than anonymous types of the invalided sailor. (Fig. 2) Instead of an object of charity, Pasley is an officer on active duty, and a gentleman. His bulging gut and the lumpy skin of his face and neck invite laughter, but his facial expression is indeed tough, especially in comparison with the blandly pretty young couple behind him and the oblivious tooth-picker in the foreground. The image's rhyming caption ("The bullets and gout have knocked his hulk about") is humorous, not heroic, but the title, like the image itself, seems to leave open a greater possibility

Figure 1. George Gruikshank, *The Battle of the Nile*.
National Martime Museum.

Figure 2. Thomas Rowlandson, *The Tough Old Commodore*.
National Maritime Museum

of a respectful response than does the image of the Greenwich pensioners. Unlike Cruikshank, Rowlandson makes no visual analogies between Pasley's prosthesis and an object unconnected to his body.

As one might expect given the number and military significance of his victories, Nelson was more widely represented than any other naval officer of his time. The wartime appetite for public images of the victor of England's greatest battles posed a number of interesting choices for the artist: should he render such a man's physical difference visible or invisible? If visible, how could it be incorporated into an image of heroism rather than comedy or pathos? Caricatures usually present Nelson both as visibly disabled and as the active champion of his country. For example, "Extirpation of the Plagues of Egypt;—Destruction of Revolutionary Crocodiles; —or, ye British Hero Cleansing ye Mouth of ye Nile," James Gillray's caricature celebrating Nelson's decisive victory over the French fleet at the Battle of the Nile, offers a giant, stern-faced British Hero, striding through the waves and bludgeoning revolutionary crocodiles to death with his left hand, which holds a club labeled "British Oak." Gillray includes the wound that Nelson's forehead received in the battle but takes some license in representing amputation. He gives Nelson back nearly all of his right arm and adds a hook, tethered to which are the crocodiles that represent captured French ships; the one belching flame behind Nelson's left shoulder is L'Orient. Having perished in a spectacular explosion, L'Orient's destruction dominates most visual representations of this battle. (Fig. 3)

More unusually, in "The Hero of the Nile," Gillray attacks the personal rewards that this battle brought Nelson rather than celebrating his triumph. The humor of this image does not focus on amputation, however, but rather on the visible signs of wealth and honor. An oversized version of one of these signs towers over Nelson's head, the diamond chelengk that he was given by the grateful Sultan of Turkey. Nelson's "most spectacular decoration," this "plume of triumph" consisted of thirteen sprays of diamonds representing the French ships at the Battle of the Nile, with a "large central diamond… mounted on a clockwork motor so that it rotated and sparkled as it caught the light."[21] The chelengk was a fine target for those wishing to ridicule what they saw as Nelson's excessive display of his many military decorations, which he made a point of wearing, apparently out of a combination of personal pride and deliberate self-promotion.[22] About 140 x 105 x 25 mm in size, twirling and sparkling in Nelson's hat, the chelengk is said to have made an "unusual" impression. In Gillray's hands, it grows to nearly the size of the hat itself. In the shield at the bottom of the print, Gillray replaces Nelson's arms with moneybags and a scroll inscribed £2000 per Ann., the pension Nelson was awarded for this victory. (Fig. 4) Unlike Gillray's celebratory

Figure 3. James Gillray, *Extirpation of the Plaques of Egypt;—Destruction of Revolutionary Crocodiles;—or, ye British Hero Cleansing ye Mouth of ye Nile.* National Martime Museum

Figure 4. James Gillray, *The Hero of the Nile*. National Martime Museum.

caricatures, "The Hero of the Nile" does not include the actual scarring on Nelson's forehead nor the imaginary hook that Gillray often gave him with which to manipulate representations of French ships. Here, the empty opening at the end of Nelson's right sleeve is visible, and its drooping folds seem of a piece with the oversized chelengk, the baggy uniform, and the robe of honor that hangs too loosely on his sloping shoulders and small frame.

Turning from caricatures to formal portraits of naval officers dating from the long wars of 1793–1815, we find a genre unified by a broad political purpose: the production of heroes. As Margarette Lincoln notes, "Portraiture was the major genre of this period and did much to create popular naval heroes."[23] Eighteenth-century painter Joshua Reynolds explains the necessity of making a hero look like a hero: "a painter of history shews the man by shewing his action…He cannot make his hero talk like a great man; he must make him look like one."[24] As Jonathan Richardson also asserts, the portrait artist's responsibility is to make visible and compelling not a literal likeness but rather an inner truth: in this case, military heroism. A successful portraitist produced an image of ideal masculinity that could represent to a wide audience the strength of the nation as a whole. More generally, Richard Brilliant argues that portraits of significant public figures such as "statesmen, intellectuals, creative artists, war heroes, and approved champions" use visual cues to demand respect from their viewers, figures that "usually bear the gravamen of their 'exemplary' public roles; they offer up images of serious men and women, worthy of respect, persons who should be taken equally seriously by the viewing audience."[25] "Gravamen" is an interesting word to use to describe the outwards sign of a public role. Perhaps chosen because of its closeness to "gravitas," "gravamen" is a legal term related to *gravis* or "heavy."[26] In late Latin it means a physical inconvenience; later, it means the strongest part of an accusation. In any case, one likely gravamen for a war hero to bear in a portrait might seem to be a mark of battle, such as a missing arm or leg.

Historically, however, heroic portraits seem to follow a different convention: they make such physical losses disappear. Amputation becomes invisible. Unlike caricatures, portraits of distinguished amputee naval officers tend to conceal the fact of amputation, either angling the figure away from the viewer to hide a missing arm or truncating it to hide a missing leg. For example, Arline Meyer describes Sir Peter Lely's portrait of Sir Frescheville Holles as an example of "the discreet three-quarters view": Holles brandishes a naked sword at the viewer in one hand, standing so as to conceal the fact that his other arm was lost in battle.[27] (Fig. 5) Similarly, unlike Rowlandson's caricature, Lemuel Francis Abbott's half-length formal portrait of Rear Admiral Pasley does not represent his prosthesis. In both of these portraits, amputation has become invisible. Why is this the case?

Figure 5. Sir Peter Lely, *Fresheville Holles*. National Maritime Museum.

In part, naval portraiture's convention of invisible amputation seems to reflect the larger habit, discussed above, of imagining the body in terms of ideal form, a way of thinking that conceptualizes physical difference in general as "defect" rather than "disability." Perhaps the more committed a visual tradition is to such an ideal of the body, then the less free it will be to represent amputation without evoking derision. More particularly, representing amputation conflicted with the goal of producing a certain image of ideal masculinity. Unlike the actual bodies of military men, this ideal image was invulnerable to injury. As Jenks explains, "The male body…was centrally located in contemporary patriotic discourse. Threats to it were, both metaphorically and literally, threats to the stability and permanence of the wider body politic."[28] To this way of thinking, not only was the nation literally defended by the physical strength and wholeness of its military men, but the physical strength and wholeness of these men also metaphorically represented the strength and wholeness of the nation. If the military hero's life and character were understood as the expression of such an ideal, then representing amputation would obscure rather than reveal the truth about him.

The commitment to ideal form in general portraiture and to a particular ideal of heroic masculinity in military portraiture provides a plausible explanation for the general invisibility of amputation in the formal portraits of eighteenth-century naval heroes. In Nelson's case, these factors figure explicitly in the controversy over the proper way to make his body express the truth of his life after it ended at the Battle of Trafalgar. Strong opinions were expressed about how to represent the moment of Nelson's death. Like an amputated body, a dead or dying body differs from the ideal figure most commonly used to suggest the invulnerability of military masculinity and national identity. Representing Nelson's last moments at Trafalgar meant confronting all of these issues: "The dilemma over truth versus epic imagination pervades all the 'death tableaux' pictures of the Georgian era, none more so than the many pictures of the death of Nelson," as Peter Harrington notes.[29] A deluxe set of prints sold after Trafalgar tried to satisfy the demands of both versimilitude and the heroic ideal by representing Nelson in one print "in the full vigor of manhood, with both his arms; [in] the other after he had lost one arm."[30] Even images of Nelson that were not death tableaux, such as monumental statues, struggled with the problem of incorporating amputation into a visual code that relied on the physical strength and wholeness of the male body to stand for the strength and wholeness of the nation. When the Trafalgar Square memorial was planned, for example, serious consideration was given to the idea that it should represent Nelson "in his perfect figure," his entire body unmarked by battle.[31] Like many allegorical representations, Benjamin West's 1807 painting "The Immortality of Lord Nelson" avoids the question by placing a cherub immediately below Nelson's bare chest and right shoulder, as Sir Peter Lely avoids it by angling Freschville Holles away from the viewer. (Fig. 6) In the case of portraits of Nelson painted during his lifetime, however, something surprising occurs. They consistently confront the viewer with the loss of his arm. Lemuel Francis Abbott's 1797 portrait is probably the most influential of them all, much copied by painters and engravers.[32] It was commissioned by William Locker, Nelson's mentor and the Lieutenant Governor of Greenwich Hospital, as part of his plan to create a "National Gallery of Marine Paintings, to commemorate the eminent services of the Royal Navy of England" in the Painted Hall at Greenwich Hospital. Locker's hopes were not fully realized until 1824 (seventy-two years before the founding of England's National Portrait Gallery), when the Naval Gallery became England's first "national historical" art museum, dedicated to fostering patriotism and the Hospital's charitable purpose. Nevertheless, Locker's intention was clear.[33] This 1797 portrait of Nelson is, then, a very good example of the impulse to enlist portraiture in the creation of naval heroes that Lincoln describes. Its relatively direct representation of amputation becomes even more remarkable in this context. (Fig. 7) It offers a full-frontal view, with the right shoulder and amputated arm of the

Figure 6. Benjamin West, *The Immorality of Lord Nelson*. National Maritime Museum.

Figure 7. Lemuel Francis Abbott . *Horatio Nelson* (1797). National Maritime Museum.

figure angled slightly towards the viewer rather than away. This portrait also shows the viewer that the right sleeve of Nelson's jacket has been cut open to accommodate the dressing of his still unhealed wound, and is held together by black ribbons. Abbott's portrait exploits a possibility that is not offered by an allegorical representation such as West's. Neither Abbot nor West, in fact, show the viewer Nelson's "fin," as he called the stump of his right arm, but in place of this missing arm Abbot foregrounds signs of Nelson's military status: the empty sleeve of a Royal Navy rear-admiral's uniform coat is neatly secured across his chest, the cuff angling up towards the gold star of the Order of the Bath.

With the exception of death tableaux and allegories, formal portraits of Nelson consistently foreground this empty right sleeve. Why do these heroic representations depart from convention to acknowledge the fact of amputation in this way? One factor may be the cultural use of Nelson's body to cross boundaries of social class, forming a "conduit to plebian patriotism."[34] The visibility of amputation in Nelson's heroic portraits may attempt to transmute the grotesque into the heroic, as did popular written accounts of his battles and injuries. As Jenks explains, in such accounts, Nelson "came to heroically personify the progressive mutilation that was grotesquely addressed in the annals of tarism."[35] Elite officers were more commonly praised for their mental fortitude under fire rather than for physical combat. For example, in what David McNeil calls "the brain-splattering motif," admiring anecdotes typically describe the officer coolly issuing orders while other men's bodies are blown up around—and onto—his own.[36] If such an officer's elite body did receive any injury, then indirect and deferential language was most often used to indicate it. In contrast, grotesque language was commonly used explicitly to describe the wounded body and the superhuman—or sub-human—endurance of the common sailor or "Jack Tar." Fanciful, patriotic, and gory, the annals of tarism describe common sailors performing feats such as "smiling, and with a steady clear voice," singing "the whole of *Rule Britannia*" while having an arm amputated. In a more extreme form, when a tar is cut in two at Trafalgar, fragments of his body continue to defy the French with plebian patriotism: "strange to tell, his legs were left standing upon the deck, with all the firmness and determination of life!"[37] Although he benefited from well-placed family connections, Nelson was the son of a relatively obscure Norfolk clergyman. Because of the perceived liminality of his social position, together with the number and severity of his wounds in battle, he seems to have attracted some of the physically explicit or even grotesque language more commonly used to describe the body of the common sailor.[38]

Marianne Czisnik suggests another factor that also helps to explain the unusual visibility of amputation in Nelson's formal portraits, one that, like tarism, relates to the use of his body to promote plebian loyalty. During his lifetime, relatively cheap commemorative goods such as pottery and glass paintings commodified a simple, easily reproduced and easily recognized image of Nelson as the one-armed admiral. By the time monumental statues such as the Trafalgar Square memorial began to appear, Czisnik asserts, this "image ... seems to have been too settled to allow for a right arm to be added."[39] That is, no statue representing Nelson "in his perfect figure" would actually look like Nelson to a wide popular audience. Given the political function of heroic military portraits, the image popularized by commemorative goods may have shaped these portraits in the same way that it shaped Nelson's later monumental statues.

One very specific convention is also evident in Nelson's portraits, one that is not connected to the uses of Nelson's image to foster plebian loyalty to the nation but linked to the formal portrait's ability to announce its sitter's elite status. As Meyer points out, the way Nelson wore his empty right sleeve in person and in his portraits conforms to a portrait type that "appeared with relentless frequency in England in the eighteenth century... the familiar image of a gentleman poised with one hand inside his partially unbuttoned waistcoat." The "hand-in" pose was a genteel staple, one of the most popular of the standard poses that portraitists employed.[40] Rear Admiral Sir Thomas Pasley assumes it in the caricature by Rowlandson that we have seen above, as does Nelson in Cruikshank's satirical caricature of the rich Hero of the Nile. In formal portraits, the hand-in pose alluded to traditions of self-presentation derived from classical oratory. It conventionally represented "manly boldness tempered with modesty," often implying a contrast between the solid reticence of the English national character and the unstable volubility of gesticulating Frenchmen. Ironically, as Meyer notes, today the pose is best known as that of a Frenchman's, Napoleon in David's famous 1812 portrait.[41] A less celebrated example is the portrait of Jane Austen's brother, Admiral Charles Austen. Robert Home's 1805 portrait of the Duke of Wellington as a young major general in India also uses this pose. In this case the hand is completely hidden. As the hand-in-waistcoat pose primarily signified gentlemanly status rather than martial valor, portraits of gentlemen with no connection to any branch of the military also favored it. (Fig. 8) and (Fig. 9)

Abbott's much-copied 1797 portrait of Nelson showcases all the gentlemanly qualities of dignity and restraint that are associated with the hand-in waistcoat pose. Consider this 1799 version of the portrait, updated to include Nelson's later decorations, including the chelengk in his hat. Although by 1799 Nelson no longer had the right sleeve of his uniform

Figure 8. *Admiral Charles Austen.* Jane Austen Memorial Trust.

Figure 9. Robert Home. *Arthur Wellesley.* National Portrait Gallery.

jackets altered, Abbott does not remove the black ribbon ties from the image. (Fig. 10) Compare this image, the dominant way of representing Nelson, with a much less popular variant, attributed to Guy Head (c. 1800): a portrait of Nelson after he was wounded in the head at the Battle of the Nile. The contrast between Guy Head's portrait and the dominant image of Nelson shows how the ideal of invulnerable heroic masculinity could be more effectively created or pre-empted by a range of visual codes rather than the fact of amputation itself. (Fig. 11)

This portrait represents a climactic moment in the battle: the injury to Nelson's head was being dressed when he heard that L'Orient was on fire and ran up on deck without his coat. Unpopular as it was with the public, Nelson is believed to have owned this portrait himself.[42] Sometimes criticized as "effeminate" and never widely reproduced, it departs in a number of ways from the heroic masculine ideal seen in his more popular portraits. Nelson was almost always painted in uniform—suggesting, like the hand-in waistcoat pose itself, authority and self-control. Although in this portrait Nelson still wears one military decoration (his St. Vincent medal), without his coat he appears to be out of uniform with a concomitant loss of authority. Here, the soft flesh of his throat is exposed rather than being encased in the usual stiff collar and stock. The parted lips, upturned gaze, and soft facial contours of this figure differ from the composed expression more generally seen. The fresh blood on the bandage and shirt also suggest the immediacy of crisis rather than the settled composure of a formal portrait. This image's overall air of intimacy has given rise to speculation that it was intended less for a general public eager for patriotic images of invulnerable masculinity than for one particular viewer, Emma Hamilton, whom Nelson was eager to supply with an image of himself looking vulnerable.

Whether or not it played a role in that personal story, for a general viewer, this portrait calls attention to hands and arms. Instead of being covered by a uniform sleeve following the familiar and gentlemanly hand-in waistcoat pose, here Nelson's amputated right arm simply ends, revealing the most dramatic spectacle of the battle: the explosion of L'Orient. Although the blood sprayed over his right shoulder comes from his recent head wound, it is difficult not to visually associate this blood with the violence of amputation. And nearly as conspicuous as his missing hand is his remaining hand, for Nelson's left hand is central to this image, resting prominently over his heart. Echoing the conventions of a love portrait in the midst of a scene of battle, as the National Portrait Gallery notes, this "curious gesture" is striking.

Like the hand-in waistcoat pose and Head's portrait, a strangely whimsical, mock-satirical essay on Nelson in the *St. James Chronicle* calls attention to hands: this piece is supposedly written in the voice of (as well as

Figure 10. Lemuel Francis Abbott. *Horatio Nelson* (1799). National Maritime Museum.

Figure 11. Guy Head, *Horatio Nelson*. National Maritime Museum.

signed by) "Admiral Nelson's LEFT HAND." It takes a comic tone towards Nelson's amputation that recalls the light-hearted accounts of Jack Tar's mutilated plebian body, but discusses a convention strongly associated with England's social elite: primogeniture. Even more directly than the hand-in waistcoat pose, this piece uses hands to represent social class. It attacks the privileged social status of right hands and asserts the left hand's right to an equal education in the gentlemanly arts of writing, drawing, and fencing:

> Whereas, your humble petitioner has had the misfortune to lose his brother in his Majesty's service. . . . This is to certify, in behalf of himself and the whole race, that they have been from time immemorial, greatly abridged of their just rights and privileges... you must acknowledge, that at present, We, the Left hands, have been kept in a state of comparative ignorance and barbarism. This arises solely from our want of education: for while the favoured Right hand is attended by the very best masters, in writing, drawing, fencing, &c. &c. the poor Left hand is neglected and forgotten, and hangs aukwardly dangling at the side ...[43]

The Left Hand's complaints go on at length and include the convention of lover's hands: "How often has your Petitioner itched to take a Lady by the hand, but yet never was permitted, though the Right was engaged in all the offices of gallantry." Although the premise of this piece is the kind of explicit, flippant treatment of mutilation that characterizes the annals of tarism, its focus is social inequality between the older and younger sons of propertied families—the kind of limited social inequality that shaped Nelson's own experience and career path. Like the caricatures and formal portraits we have considered here, in the juxtapositions of tone and subject that are strange to us today, it recalls the much wider gap between common sailors and officers, plebian and elite bodies, pathetic objects of charity and a nation's heroes.

Finally, we should note that even aside from scars, blindness, and amputation, Nelson's short, slight, and frequently fever-ridden body differed markedly from the heroic masculine ideal whose power Jenks describes: "Nelson is one of the most insignificant figures I ever saw...a more miserable collection of bones and wizened frame cannot be imagined," noted one observer.[44] As a child, Benjamin Robert Haydon was surprised to see that the mighty defender of Britain was a "little diminutive man with a green shade over his eye." Later, Haydon's inscription on a portrait of Nelson shows how the incongruity between his physical weakness and his military might could be rephrased as a compelling paradox: "NELSON a little body with a Mighty Heart."[45]

The portraits we have considered here try to incorporate Nelson's "little body" as well as his empty right sleeve into an ideal of heroic masculinity, and they were generally well-received. However, in 1807, a *Times* review of Samuel Drummond's death tableaux, "The Death of Nelson," suggests the enduring association of masculinity, military might, physical strength, and physical wholeness. (Fig. 12) The reviewer praises the painting by praising the impressive manliness of the large, brawny, and un-mutilated figures who surround their dying, drooping Admiral: "each of them is a true soldier or sailor…none are maimed or halt, but the wounded or the dying, all else are men and heroes!"[46] Here, a Christ-like Nelson is bathed in the white light appropriate to the savior of Britain, and the loss of his right arm is strategically concealed by the white-shirted sailor who helps to carry him below deck, performing the same function as the cherub in Benjamin West's allegory. According to *The Times*, this Nelson is, nevertheless, not quite a man and not quite a hero. The very familiarity of the earlier heroic images of Nelson that we have considered here, their very success in drawing together eighteenth-century visual codes, may obscure for us the extent to which they depart from convention in incorporating disability into the representation of heroic military masculinity. The casualness with which this reviewer excludes the maimed and halt from the ranks of men and heroes reminds us that is a remarkable achievement.

Figure 12. Samuel Drummond. "The Death of Nelson." National Maritime Museum.

NOTES

For invaluable help with this article, the author would like to thank the Disability Studies Caucus of the American Society for Eighteenth-Century Studies, the insightful readers at *SECC*, and Dr. Angela Ka-Yan Ho, Assistant Professor of Art History at George Mason University.

1. Marcia R. Pointon, *Hanging the Head: Portraiture and Social Formation in Eighteenth-Century England* (New Haven: Yale Univ. Press, 1993), 6, 9.

2. Colin White, *The Nelson Companion* (Annapolis, MD: Naval Institute Press, 1995), 33.

3. For a fine collection of such goods available for on-line viewing, see the National Maritime Museum http://www.rmg.co.uk/national-maritime-museum.

4. See John Kirkup, *A History of Limb Amputation* (London: Springer, 2007).

5. See Timothy Jenks, *Naval Engagements: Patriotism, Cultural Politics, and the Royal Navy, 1793–1815* (Oxford; New York: Oxford Univ. Press, 2006); Margarette Lincoln, *Representing the Royal Navy: British Sea Power, 1750–1815* (Burlington, VT: Ashgate, 2002).

6. As a point of reference, in the contemporary United States military, returning to active duty after the loss of a limb is an unusual but possible path for a military career. In the 1980s, only a little more than 2 percent of U.S. amputee soldiers returned to duty, and that number includes partial-foot, partial-hand and below-knee amputation. More recently, greater numbers of "injured service members from Afghanistan and Iraq with higher levels of amputations, including transfemoral (above-knee)…continue to serve successfully." "Military in Step: The Process of Returning to Duty or Not After Limb Loss," *A Publication of the Amputee Coalition of America in Partnership with the U.S. Army Amputee Patient Care Program.* 86 https://www.amputee-coalition.org/military-instep/returning-to-duty.html

7. Jenks, *Naval Engagements*, 218.

8. In April 1801, Nelson dined with "another one-armed admiral," Vice-Admiral Alexander Greame. John Sugden, *Nelson: The Sword of Albion*, (New York: Henry Hold and Co., 2013), 495; R. J. B. Knight, *The Pursuit of Victory: The Life and Achievement of Horatio Nelson* (New York: Basic books, 2005), 261.

9. Richard John Boileau, *The Nelson Portraits: An Iconography of Horatio, Viscount Nelson, Vice Admiral of the White* (London: Royal Naval Museum Publications, 1998), 22; Knight, *The Pursuit of Victory*, 256.

10. Knight, *The Pursuit of Victory*, 257.

11. *Gentleman's Magazine*, 89, (1801) 207, quoted in Jenks, *Naval Engagements*, 216 .

12. Jenks, *Naval Engagements*, 215, 217.

13. Simon Dickie, *Cruelty and Laughter: Forgotten Comic Literature and the Unsentimental Eighteenth Century* (Chicago: Univ. of Chicago Press, 2011), 93.

14. Adam Smith, *The Theory of Moral Sentiments* (New York: Penguin, 2010), Part I, "Of the Propriety of Action," Section I, "Of the Sense of Propriety," I II 9.

15. Helen Deutsch and Felicity Nussbaum, eds., *Defects: Engendering the Modern*

Body, (Ann Arbor: Univ. of Michigan Press, 2000); Roger D. Lund, "Laughing at Cripples: Ridicule, Deformity and the Argument from Design," *Eighteenth-Century Studies* 39, no. 1 (2005): 91–114; Lennard J. Davis, *The Disability Studies Reader*, 4th ed. (New York, NY: Routledge, 2013).

16. Jonathan Richardson, *An Essay on the Theory of Painting.* (London: A.C. and A. Bettesworth, 1725), 22, quoted in Pointon, *Hanging the Head.*

17. Knight, *The Pursuit of Victory*, 253, 252.

18. *Greenwich Hospital: Supporting the Royal Navy Since 1694.* 2013. http://www.grenhosp.org.uk/

19. Lincoln, *Representing the Royal Navy*, 197.

20. William Gilpin, *An Essay upon Prints: Containing Remarks upon the Principles of Picturesque Beauty, the Different Kinds of Prints, and the Characters of the Most Noted Masters; Illustrated by Criticisms upon Particular Pieces: to which are Added, Some Cautions that May be Useful in Collecting Prints* (London: G. Scott, for J. Robson, 1768), 170.

21. See The National Maritime Museum, Orders and Decorations.

22. See Knight, *The Pursuit of Victory,* 347; Sugden, *Nelson,* 2.

23. Lincoln, *Representing the Royal Navy*, 33.

24. Joshua Reynolds, *Seven Discourses Delivered in the Royal Academy by the President*, (London: T. Cadell, 1778) 110, quoted in Marianne Czisnik, *Horatio Nelson: A Controversial Hero* (London: Hodder Arnold, 2005), 99.

25. Richard Brilliant, *Portraiture* (Cambridge, Mass: Harvard Univ. Press, 1991), 10.

26. *Oxford English Dictionary*, 2nd ed., s.v. "gravamen."

27. Arline Meyer, "Re-Dressing Classical Statuary: The Eighteenth-Century 'Hand-in-Waistcoat' Portrait," *The Art Bulletin* 77, no. 1 (March 1995): 63.

28. Jenks, *Naval Engagements*, 204.

29. Peter Harrington, *British Artists and War: The Face of Battle in Paintings and Prints, 1700–1914* (London : Greenhill Books ; Pennsylvania : Stackpole Books in association with Brown Univ. Library, Rhode Island, 1993), 87.

30. Jenks, *Naval Engagements*, 197.

31. Czisnik, *Horatio Nelson* 113. For an interesting discussion of the continuing controversy over the representation of disability in public monuments, now in the context of femininity rather than masculinity but still under the very shadow of Nelson's Column in Trafalgar Square, see Ann Millett, "Zola Award Honorable Mention: Sculpting Body Ideals: Alison Lapper Pregnant and the Public Display of Disability," *Disability Studies Quarterly* 28, no. 3 (July 31, 2008).

32. Walker and National Maritime Museum (Great Britain), *The Nelson Portraits*, 33.

33. Grenwich Hospital, http://www.grenhosp.org.uk.

34. Jenks, *Naval Engagements*, 194.

35. Jenks, *Naval Engagements*, 213.

36. David McNeil, *The Grotesque Depiction of War and the Military in Eighteenth-Century Fiction* (Univ. of Delaware: 2005), 20, quoted in Jenks, *Naval Engagements*, 207.

37. Jenks, *Naval Engagements*, 200, 208.

38. Jenks, *Naval Engagements*, 213.
39. Czisnik, *Horatio Nelson*, 103,116.
40. Meyer, "Re-Dressing Classical Statuary," 45, 49.
41. Jenks, *Naval Engagements*, 53.
42. The National Maritime Museum , Description BHC2903. collections.rmg.co.uk/collections/objects/14376.html
43. *The St. James Chronicle.* 14–16 September, 1797. No page numbers.
44. Knight, *The Pursuit of Victory*, 48.
45. *The Nelson Companion*, 51.
46. Quoted in *The Times*, No. 7031, April 1807: 3C. Nicholas Tracy, *Britannia's Palette: the Arts of Naval Victory* (Montreal [Que.]: McGill-Queen's Univ. Press, 2007) 178.

The Man Within the Breast: Sympathy and Deformity in Adam Smith's *The Theory of Moral Sentiments*

PAUL KELLEHER

> He is a bold surgeon, they say, whose hand does not tremble when he performs an operation upon his own person; and he is often equally bold who does not hesitate to pull off the mysterious veil of self-delusion, which covers from his view the deformities of his own conduct.
>
> —Adam Smith, *The Theory of Moral Sentiments*

In this essay, I explore a mode of experience that is an abiding concern in both eighteenth-century British moral philosophy and contemporary disability studies: the intersubjective bonds of sympathy. There is no question that considerable differences—historical, cultural, and discursive—separate the forms of thought that characterize moral philosophy and disability studies. Nevertheless, when read by one another's lights, significant cross-historical relays emerge between the moral-philosophical speculations of the eighteenth century and the relatively recent critiques of ableist ideology. Moreover, while disability studies generally has tended to focus on nineteenth-, twentieth-, and twenty-first-century contexts, groundbreaking work by scholars such as Lennard J. Davis, Felicity Nussbaum, Helen Deutsch, and David M. Turner, among others, has revealed the eighteenth century to be an important chapter—perhaps even a decisive turning point—in the history of disability.[1] Scholarship on eighteenth-century disability has interrogated how a society ostensibly devoted to "enlightenment" represented, taxonomized, judged, excluded, and (too often) brutalized disabled individuals and populations. More recently, there has been an effort to recover and to theorize the lived, subjective experience of the disabled in the eighteenth century—and more broadly still, to understand what Deutsch refers to as "the history of the link between disability and subjectivity" as such.[2] It will be my contention that eighteenth-century moral philosophy's sustained inquiry into the process of sympathy—how it works, why it often fails, and who does and does not deserve the balm of fellow-feeling—played a vital, but little examined, role in fashioning both disabled and non-disabled forms of subjectivity.

Although my analyses largely focus on the eighteenth century, I draw inspiration from contemporary critiques of sympathy's impact on the lives of the disabled. For instance, Joseph P. Shapiro's trenchant history of the disability rights movement, *No Pity*, makes clear that the lived experience of disability is intertwined—often painfully and oppressively—with the experience of being pitied. Shapiro stresses that when the disabled claim forms of socio-political agency and power, or undertake acts of culture-building predicated on positively inflected notions of disabled identity, the first order of business is calling into question the historically overdetermined relationship between disability and pity (and pity's seemingly less patronizing counterparts, such as sympathy, compassion, and empathy). In addition to intervening in the arenas of legislation and policy-making, politicizing disability requires us to challenge the cultural politics of the "poster child," the spectacularized image-parade of Tiny Tims and "supercrips" who are offered up respectively as objects of pity and sources of "inspiration"—but who embody the non-disabled population's fear of atypical mental and bodily states.[3] Lennard J. Davis reinforces this point, and broadens its theoretical import, in his editor's introduction to the ground-breaking volume, *The Disability Studies Reader* (1997). Most "normals," Davis suggests, assume they can intuitively understand what disability entails, and he ventriloquizes their attitude thus: "What could be simpler to understand? One simply has to imagine the loss of the limb, the absent sense, and one is half-way there. Just the addition of a liberal dose of sympathy and pity along with a generous acceptance of ramps and voice-synthesized computers allows the average person to speak with knowledge on the subject."[4] However, in Davis's reckoning, if sympathy seemingly affords the "normal" individual spontaneous and immediate access to the life experience of the disabled, this promise of intersubjective connection across the divide of difference is an illusion at best and a disguised form of discrimination at worst. "Pity and empathy do not lend themselves to philosophy, philology, or theoretical considerations in general"; indeed, as Davis stresses, those working in disability studies explicitly work against pity and empathy, in order to "articulat[e] and theoriz[e] a political, social, and ideological critique."[5]

I take seriously Shapiro's and Davis's assessments of the distorting—indeed oppressive—effects that sympathy has on the ways that disabled minds and bodies, lives and experiences, are conceptualized and represented.[6]

There is no question that appeals to sympathy have been used to reaffirm the ideological distinction between the so-called "normal" and the disabled. However, while these contemporary critiques of the ideological pretensions of sympathy are vitally necessary, I explore other aspects of the historical relationship between sympathy and disability, ones that nuance and complicate our sense that sympathy, across the centuries, merely has aided and abetted an oppressive dispensation in which "normal" subjects pity—and thereby objectify and marginalize—disabled minds and bodies. I qualify Davis's position by arguing that sympathy does in fact have the potential to provoke general philosophical and theoretical considerations; by reconsidering eighteenth-century theorizations of sympathy from the vantage point of contemporary disability studies, I argue that a critical engagement with sympathy affords new strategies for mounting the kinds of "political, social, and ideological critique" that Davis and other disability scholars advocate.

To this end, I focus on what is without question the eighteenth century's most influential philosophical treatment of sympathy: Adam Smith's *The Theory of Moral Sentiments* (1759). More specifically, I demonstrate that Smith's exploration of the workings of sympathy is thoroughly enmeshed, both conceptually and rhetorically, in an ambivalent relationship with figures of disability. On the one hand, when he turns his attention to disabilities that affect the mind or the body, disability seems to provide just another empirical example through which Smith will articulate the ways that an individual forms a conception of the thoughts and passions of other individuals. References to the mad, to "idiots," or to men who have lost a leg sit alongside discussions of aggrieved lovers, generous benefactors, and fictional heroes, suggesting, it would seem, that figures of disability bear no special explanatory power within Smith's account of the formation of the sympathetic subject.[7] On the other hand, these discrete appearances of the disabled within *The Theory of Moral Sentiments* are only one—and perhaps the most superficial—way that disability informs Smith's philosophical enterprise.

While he may be merely reproducing the commonplace attitudes of his contemporaries when he renders scenes in which spectators sympathize with the disabled body or the disordered mind, elsewhere the rhetoric of disability provides the language through which Smith articulates the internal workings of sympathy and the instantiation of moral subjectivity. It is true that the term "disability" does not explicitly appear in *The Theory of Moral Sentiments*, but as David M. Turner has shown, a writer in Smith's historical moment certainly would have been familiar with the terms "disability," "disabled," and "able-bodied."[8] In the absence of a direct reference to "disability," what we do find in the twists and turns of Smith's philosophical exposition is the language of "defect," "excess," and "deformity," a cluster of terms that function as figurative or conceptual counterparts to the more materially inflected notions of "disabled" and "able-bodied." I pay particularly close attention to the ideological work that deformity performs in *The Theory of Moral Sentiments*, and further, I show how Smith's philosophical system renders the notion of self-interested "partiality" a form of moral disability. In Smith's hands, the rhetoric of disability underwrites the logic of sympathy, and by extension, his understanding of moral subjectivity and affective interiority (what he calls the "man within the breast" [130]) is constitutively entwined with the ostensible "otherness" of the disabled. Thus, within the pages of *The Theory of Moral Sentiments*, when sympathetic spectators engage in affectively charged encounters with disabled minds and bodies, these "normals" (to recall Davis's term) are not simply pitying the disabled "other"; rather, they are on the verge of recognizing what Smith calls the "precariousness of human life," the shared human condition of being unavoidably exposed to the vicissitudes—that is, the calamities, disorders, and deformations—of embodied life (136).

Face to Face

Before going further, I want to touch on some of Smith's key arguments and formulations regarding how sympathy operates. Early on, he broadens more familiar understandings of "sympathy." Whereas pity and compassion typically "signify our fellow-feeling with the sorrow of others," Smith uses "sympathy" to "denote our fellow-feeling with any passion whatever" (10). In other words, while the idea of sympathizing with another's grief or distress is common enough, and is perhaps even today what most readily comes to mind when we speak of sympathy, Smith is equally interested in thinking about how we come to sympathize with passions that do not arise from hardship or pain, such as the passion of joy. In addition to expanding what it means and how it functions, from the beginning Smith conceptualizes sympathy as a form of moral judgment. The alignment of sympathy and judgment brings us to the "impartial spectator," the theoretical centerpiece of *The Theory of Moral Sentiments*. The "impartial spectator" signifies an internalized figure of judgment, the "great inmate of the breast," whose calculus of the proper and the improper determines how we perceive and assess the feelings and the conduct of others (134). Our capacity to feel sympathy for another is, according to Smith, entirely bound up with our capacity to judge, to approve and disapprove of, the causes and the effects of his or her passions.[9] As he phrases it, "To approve of the passions of another…as suitable to their objects, is the same thing as to observe that we entirely sympathize with them; and not to approve of them as such, is the same thing as to observe that we do not entirely sympathize with them" (16).

Before Smith equates sympathy and judgment, in the opening pages of *The Theory of Moral Sentiments* he briefly entertains the possibility of unchecked sympathetic connection: "Upon some occasions sympathy may seem to arise merely from the view of a certain emotion in another person. The passions, upon some occasions, may seem to be transfused from one man to another, instantaneously, and antecedent to any knowledge of what excited them in the person principally concerned. Grief and joy, for example, strongly expressed in the look and gestures of any one, at once affect the spectator with some degree of a like painful or agreeable emotion. A smiling face is, to every body that sees it, a cheerful object; as a sorrowful countenance, on the other hand, is a melancholy one" (11). However, as the careful qualifications in this passage begin to suggest, while *The Theory of Moral Sentiments* offers the eighteenth century's most elaborate meditation on sympathy, Smith's moral punchline ultimately is *we sympathize, but only imperfectly, and it's a good thing, too*. From the perspective of the spectator, the incompleteness of sympathy makes judgment both possible and essential. As the moral spectator, I sympathize only to the extent that I approve or disapprove of the other's feelings or conduct; my approval or disapproval is guided by how I imagine the impartial spectator would approve or disapprove of the scene before me. When I find myself in the position of the one whose feelings or conduct are being viewed and judged, my previous experiences as a spectator (and my own internalization of the impartial spectator) already have taught me that sympathy is incomplete. Consequently, my desire for the spectator's sympathy is checked, and in order to secure some modicum of sympathy, I call upon my powers of self-discipline; these for Smith are the lessons learned in the Stoic school of self-command. By lowering the pitch of my passions, I achieve the moral self-composure that will be judged as a "proper" reaction to life's vicissitudes. In this way, I become a proper object of sympathy; the spectator's sympathetic approval, and my own self-approval, conform as closely as possible to the expectations and the dictates of the abstract impartial spectator that thoroughly inform this moral drama.

Smith often describes the intersubjective connection formed between spectator and spectatee (so to speak) as a face-to-face encounter, a scene of seeing and being seen, but as he makes clear, the formation of the impartial spectator within the human subject is only possible within the broader context of civil society. Without the presence of others, who en masse constitute a social realm of passion, action, and thought beyond the self, the impartial spectator would remain unrealized and, in some sense, so too would the human subject itself. Unlike Rousseau, Smith does not seriously explore the possibility that a human could exist apart from society. "[M]an," he asserts, "can subsist only in society" (85).[10] At the same time, though, he finds it philosophically useful to imagine at some length what, most likely, could never be: "Were it possible that a human creature could grow up to manhood in some solitary place, without any communication with his own species, he could no more think of his own character, of the propriety or demerit of his own sentiments and conduct, of the beauty or deformity of his own mind, than of the beauty or deformity of his own face" (110). By entertaining for a moment the fiction of a human creature developing alone, apart from others, Smith has no intention of entering into a debate regarding a pre-social state of nature. His purpose, rather, is to reaffirm the naturalness and the propriety of the aesthetic criteria—the beautiful and the deformed—that structure his philosophical account of how self and other enter into and sustain a system of moral relationality.[11] Smith doesn't believe that a human creature can reach "manhood" alone, either physically or morally. And when he speaks of "manhood" in *The Theory of Moral Sentiments*, he most often has in mind a Stoic version of masculinity, one that privileges self-command and self-sacrifice, one that strives to achieve a reasoned and restrained relationship to external events and misfortunes in order to cultivate and preserve a "tranquillity" of mind that best predisposes one to feel and act virtuously (151).[12] The Stoic concern with regulating how external phenomena impact our internal state—and how our internal state, when properly developed, assumes a kind of mastery over external phenomena—informs Smith's introduction of aesthetic criteria into his moral philosophy. Simply put, the relation of outside to inside, and inside to outside, is important to both Stoic and aesthetic discourse. Smith's conflation of these two discourses accounts for a great deal of the rhetorical power of his text; at the same time, this discursive conflation, as we will see, introduces a set of problems, both ideological and moral, that trouble some of Smith's central premises and thereby make his text available for counterreadings and reappropriations from the perspective of contemporary disability studies.

In the fictional state of nature that Smith briefly invokes and quickly discards, a solitary human creature has no occasion to contemplate the beauty or deformity of his own face or his own mind. "All these are objects which he cannot easily see, which naturally he does not look at, and with regard to which he is provided with no mirror which can present them to his view" (110). The deformed face and the deformed mind, Smith seems to suggest, do exist in a pre-social state (albeit a conjectural one), but in the absence of other human creatures, their existence has no empirical or moral consequences. Differently put, whatever material form they may take, this materiality is virtually nonexistent, there and not there at the same time—but importantly, deformity always is waiting in reserve. Once the scene becomes populated with other people, once the human creature is brought into society, "he is immediately provided with the mirror which he wanted [that is, lacked] before" (110). Of what does this figurative mirror consist? Echoing a similar image in David Hume's *Treatise of Human Nature* (1739–40), Smith asserts that this mirror is "placed in the countenance and behaviour of those he lives with, which always mark when they enter into, and when they disapprove of his sentiments" (110).[13] Society and judgment simultaneously spring into being as the faces and bodies of others embody a visceral moral calculus. Smith exploits the connotations of this figurative mirror, in which the once-solitary human creature "first views the propriety and impropriety of his own passions, the beauty and deformity of his own mind" (110). By apprehending himself in others and seeing there a reflection of his own beauty and deformity, the human creature becomes a social being. He becomes acutely aware that others judge his appearance, his sentiments, and his conduct; in return, he will learn to exercise the same form of judgment in his perceptions and assessments of others.

Judging those with whom he shares the realm of civil society, though, is predicated on a certain intensification and deepening of what we now would call "interiority." By reading the approval or disapproval of others in their faces and bodies, the socialized human creature not only comes under the sway of moral judgment. He also is subjected, and subjects himself, to a new economy of the passions. Moral judgment and the inner life of the passions develop alongside—and indeed, depend on—one another. The fictional "man who from birth was a stranger to society" possesses a limited range of passionate attachment and intellectual deliberation (110). The "external bodies which either pleased or hurt him" engross him thoroughly and exhaust his concern with the external world (110). Even the most insistent passions would lose some of their power because, despite their strength, they would be fleeting. The things "most immediately present to him," the sources of his pleasures and pains, "could scarce ever be the objects of his thoughts" (110). In society, though, the passions are not only more intensely engaged. Importantly, they are themselves multiplied and diversified. "Bring him into society," Smith observes, "and all his own passions will immediately become the causes of new passions" (111). Desire breeds new desires, joy and sorrow give rise to new joys and sorrows. This profusion of new passions is set into motion by "[o]ur first ideas of personal beauty and deformity," which are "drawn from the shape and appearance of others"; this process is then accelerated and compounded when we "become sensible … that others exercise the same criticism upon us" (111).

Beauty and Deformity

According to Smith's own terms, it would not be an overstatement to suggest that the experience of becoming cognizant of our own beauty and deformity (and the beauty and deformity of others) is the condition of possibility for morality itself. Accordingly, we would be right to say that Smithean civil society is underwritten, from first to last, by an ideological dispensation that divides the beautiful from the deformed. Smith inherits the binary of "beauty" and "deformity" from the moral philosophy of his teacher, Francis Hutcheson, who in turn derives it from the work of Anthony Ashley Cooper, the third earl of Shaftesbury.[14] Looking forward, the aesthetic ideology that informs eighteenth-century moral philosophy lays the groundwork for, and is recapitulated in, the ideology of the normal and the abnormal, which begins in the nineteenth century and continues unabated into the contemporary moment.[15] The notions of normality and abnormality have been recruited to identify, classify, and pathologize atypical bodies and minds, frequently, of course, to disastrous ends. As we already have seen, Smith freely applies the criteria of beauty and deformity to describe the external (appearance and conduct) and the internal (thoughts and passions) characteristics of the human creature. He moves easily and without comment from discussions of pleasing and displeasing bodies to pleasing and displeasing actions. An almost comic scene is offered in which "we," newly sensitized to the aesthetic effects of personal appearance, rush to an actual mirror after having regarded ourselves in the figurative mirror of society. "We become anxious to know how far our appearance deserves either their blame or approbation," and so we "examine our persons limb by limb, and by placing ourselves before a looking-glass, or by some such expedient, endeavour, as much as possible, to view ourselves at the distance and with the eyes of other people" (111–12). Those lucky few who discover that they are "tolerably handsome" are afforded in the future a kind of psychological buffer, whereby they will be better able to withstand the "most disadvantageous judgments of others" (112). Unfortunately, those who discover that they are the "natural objects of distaste," must ready themselves for a lifetime of criticism and anxiety, given that every sign of another's disapprobation will trigger in them a mortification "beyond all measure" (112).[16]

Smith follows these scenes of bodies examined and judged with a discussion of how these social processes carry over into judgments regarding our character and our conduct. As before, "we" find ourselves before a mirror, and begin to "examine our own passions and conduct" (112). "We suppose ourselves," Smith writes, "the spectators of our own behaviour, and endeavour to imagine what effect it would, in this light, produce upon us" (112). But unlike the moment of self-examination in which we scrutinized our bodies, there is no mirror that can reflect back to us the image of our behavior other than the mirror found in other people. "This is the only looking-glass by which we can, in some measure, with the eyes of other people, scrutinize the propriety of our own conduct" (112). Also as before, some will like what they see and others will not. Those who are "tolerably satisfied" when they behold their moral character through the eyes of others will grow "indifferent" to applause, and perhaps even despise the "censure of the world" should they be "misunderstood or misrepresented," because comfort will be found in the knowledge that they are "the natural and proper object of approbation" (112). And those who have reason to doubt how their moral characters appear will grow "more anxious" for approbation, and will feel every instance of "censure" with a "double severity" (112).

Over a period of time that Smith does not specify, the repeated act of routing our self-perception and self-understanding through the minds and bodies of others consolidates the power of the impartial spectator. The virtual eyes of the impartial spectator, we come to feel, are always upon us, and this experience of becoming habituated to the scrutiny of moral spectatorship transforms the shape of our thoughts and passions. Indeed, we are not only internally transformed but also internally divided. The circuit established between self and society, in which seeing and being seen constitute our apprehension of the proper and the improper, fashions a split social subject. As Smith phrases it, "[w]hen I endeavour to examine my own conduct, when I endeavour to pass sentence upon it, and either approve or condemn it, it is evident that, in all such cases, I divide myself, as it were, into two persons; and that I, the examiner and judge, represent a different character from that other I, the person whose conduct is examined into and judged of" (113). The first "I" is the impartial spectator, a "particular point of view" that also represents a general and abstract point of view. The second "I" is the "person whom I properly call myself" (113). In this somber scene of judgment, Smith does not suggest that any sort of communication occurs between these two selves. The one sees and judges, the other remains silent and accepts whatever judgment is handed down. Smith underscores the absolute divide that must remain in place when he refutes, in advance, the idea that these two selves might collapse again into one undivided person.

This would be as impossible, he claims, as discovering that cause and effect were one and the same (113).

The strict opposition Smith wishes to maintain between these two selves, I would argue, draws inspiration from what he claims is the absolute and immediately recognizable difference between beauty and deformity. If morality depends on our ability to divide ourselves in two, this resonates with Smith's penchant for drawing on the discourse of aesthetics to articulate the workings of morality. In other words, the internal scene of judgment in which one "I" confronts another "I" should be read as precisely that: a *scene*, one which bears all the marks of aesthetic construction.[17] The aesthetic ideology that informs *The Theory of Moral Sentiments* privileges the classical idea of beauty as that which is synonymous with symmetry, order, and harmony.[18] Throughout his text, Smith applies this vision of beauty to matters large and small. His frequent appeals to Nature stress the beneficial orderliness of what he will designate as "natural" and thus attempt to render inarguable. "The rules which [Nature] follows are fit for her," he writes, "those which [man] follows for him: but both are calculated to promote the same great end, the order of the world, and the perfection and happiness of human nature" (168). When Smith turns his attention to more local matters—for instance, in his discussion of how we assess the passions of others (and ourselves) as being either "proportionate" or "disproportionate" to their causes—he implicitly aestheticizes both the language and the process of moral judgment. And so, when he invites his reader to imagine that each human subject who has properly internalized the impartial spectator does so through a process of self-division, we can read this self-division as a recapitulation within the human subject of the providential order manifested in Nature more generally. By erecting and preserving within ourselves a scene of orderly opposition, in which "I" faces "I," we participate in the "order of the world." At the same time, I would suggest, by staging this scene of self-judgment, we also internalize and reaffirm the binary of the beautiful and the deformed. Aligned with the principles of beauty, the impartial spectator examines the accused, looking closely and carefully for traces of deformity. Were this moral drama played out in a real courtroom, one might reasonably consider the possibility that the accused will be found not guilty. But when we recall Smith's earlier observation that "no human conduct ever did, or ever can come up to" the "idea of complete propriety and perfection," we realize that this scene of judgment will necessarily find something to condemn, and thus repeat once again the moral and aesthetic deprecation of deformed minds and bodies (26).

Imagining Morality

As I suggested above, the opposition between beauty and deformity is fundamental to the philosophical enterprise of *The Theory of Moral Sentiments*, and so it comes as no surprise that Smith consciously works to diminish the possibility that this opposition will be called into question. He is particularly vigilant, as we will see, when he discovers that he himself has introduced a troublesome and potentially destabilizing element into his text. After the passage in which the eyes of other people are figured as the "looking-glass" in which we "scrutinize" our own behavior, Smith notes the following: "Unfortunately, this moral looking-glass is not always a very good one. Common looking-glasses, it is said, are extremely deceitful, and by the glare which they throw over the face, conceal from the partial eyes of the person many deformities which are obvious to every body besides. But there is not in the world such a smoother of wrinkles as is every man's imagination, with regard to the blemishes of his own character" (112). This short passage appears only in the first edition of *The Theory of Moral Sentiments*; all subsequent editions eliminate these lines and move immediately to the discussion of self-division and self-judgment. Why, we might ask, would Smith remove this passage? To my mind, it reads as both a witty and realistic aside about the vagaries of moral life. And throughout the text, Smith amply demonstrates a sardonic familiarity with the foibles and lapses that plague even the best-intentioned moral subjects.

Smith rethinks the wisdom of this observation, I argue, because it explicitly threatens to undermine the status of the imagination in his text, and more particularly, the role that the imagination plays in bringing us into relation with others and thus into the sphere of morality. On the opening page of *The Theory of Moral Sentiments*, Smith both acknowledges and partially refutes the conventional wisdom that humans are inherently selfish. Yes, he concedes, humankind may be naturally inclined to gratify self-interested desires. But at the same time, they are animated by other principles, such as the active desire to see, to be aware of, and thereby to become "interested" in the fortunes of others (9). Even when faced with the spectacle of another's distress, we derive a "pleasure" merely from "seeing it" (9). As an example of this sort of pleasure, he refers to "pity or compassion, the emotion which we feel for the misery of others, when we either see it, or are made to conceive it in a very lively manner" (9). The phrase "or are made to conceive it" signals the work of the imagination. "As we have no immediate experience of what other men feel," he notes, "we can form no idea of the manner in which they are affected, but by conceiving what we ourselves should feel in the like situation" (9). It goes without saying that Smith invokes the act of seeing everywhere; but without the imagination, without this capacity to project beyond the confines of our experience and "conceive" ourselves as another, sight would never give rise to the intersubjective realm of morality.

In order to make his vision of the imagination rhetorically powerful and to set firmly in place the moral dynamic of imaginatively trading places with another, Smith conjures up a famously lurid scene of torture:

> Though our brother is upon the rack, as long as we ourselves are at our ease, our senses will never inform us of what he suffers. They never did, and never can, carry us beyond our own person, and it is by the imagination only that we can form any conception of what are his sensations. Neither can that faculty help us to this any other way, than by representing to us what would be our own, if we were in his case. It is the impressions of our senses only, not those of his, which our imaginations copy. By the imagination we place ourselves in his situation, we conceive ourselves enduring all the same torments, we enter as it were into his body, and become in some measure the same person with him. … His agonies, when they are thus brought home to ourselves, when we have thus adopted and made them our own, begin at last to affect us, and we then tremble and shudder at the thought of what he feels. (9)

One of the ironies of this scene, which certainly provides one of the most memorable openings of any philosophical work, is that Smith will progressively temper the immediacy and intensity of feeling we have before us here. As we move forward in *The Theory of Moral Sentiments*, much importance will be given to the fact that we cannot, in fact, feel another's pain as sharply as he does. This, as I have discussed earlier, teaches us to moderate the expression of our pain, thus enabling a sympathetic onlooker to share our passion, albeit in a lower register and to a lesser degree. Nevertheless, this remains a sensory connection between the self and the other, and as Smith explains, when we attempt to conceive within ourselves what the impassioned situation of another feels like, the imagination "copies" the impressions of our own senses and "excites some degree of the same emotion" (9). Smith needs the imagination to operate with a considerable amount of fidelity as it performs its work of copying, for only through the imagination is it possible to "become in some measure the same person" as the suffering person we contemplate.

A great deal depends on the imagination serving the cause of moral order.[19] Were the imagination chronically or constitutionally prone to making inaccurate or infelicitous sensory reproductions, the moral subject would be imprisoned within the boundaries of the self and the entire system of intersubjective relationality would either dissipate or, perhaps worse, become a tangled web of improper—not to say, deformed—correspondences. Thus, when Smith remarks in the excised passage how the imagination is an extraordinary "smoother of wrinkles" and a deft concealer of the "blemishes" of our character, he introduces precisely this possibility. Just as the glare of a "common looking-glass" helps to disguise the "deformities" our "partial" eyes wish to ignore, he momentarily figures the imagination as a force through which we enact another kind of trading of places, an improper exchange of beauty and deformity. This is the reason, I argue, that Smith, when it came time for a second edition of his treatise, eliminated this unflattering depiction of the imagination. Correct moral perception depends on the imagination being a reasonably reliable relay between my senses and those of another; it also depends on the imagination being a faculty that does *not* habitually undo the distinction between the beautiful and the deformed. With this textual revision, Smith prevents the imagination as such from becoming allied with partiality and deformity. He does, however, leave in place his condemnation of a cast of characters—the "woman who paints," the "foolish liar," and the "important coxcomb"—whose self-deluding "vanity arises from so gross an illusion of the imagination, that it is difficult to conceive how any rational creature should be imposed upon by it" (115). The moral power of the imagination, somewhat paradoxically, is thus shored up by Smith's admission that it is "difficult" for the philosopher "to conceive"—that is, to imagine—how and why the imagination can be so grossly abused.

A Stronger Love

The rhetoric of deformity, as we have seen, is indissociable from Smith's philosophical account of how the individual enters into and assumes the moral duties entailed by civil society. Having fashioned the contours of his moral subject, Smith continues to deploy the trope of deformity as he refines and specifies the ways that sympathy sustains the relationship between self and other. For instance, in a chapter entitled "Of the Influence and Authority of Conscience," Smith considers how individuals are able to make "any proper comparison" between their own interests and the interests of others (135). Only by consulting the impartial spectator, Smith tells us, can we see our self-interest in its "proper shape and dimensions" (134). At first, our desires and concerns appear urgent and imposing. But this perception is analogous to the optical tricks a person experiences when viewing a landscape. Just as "to the eye of the body," the greatness and smallness of objects is determined by the distance between the object and the viewer, so to "the natural eye of the mind," the interest closest to hand—that is, our own self-interest—appears great and the interests furthest from us—that is, the interests of others—appear small (134, 135). As Smith argues, both of these organs—"the eye of the body" and "the natural eye of the mind"—are inherently imperfect and flawed and their respective "defects" are corrected in similar fashion (135). The person beholding a landscape and the person calculating his own self-interest are both taught by "habit and experience" to imaginatively assume the position and adopt the eyes of a "third person" (135). Only by aligning ourselves with the perspective of this third person, this impartial spectator who embodies an ideal form of moral perception, can we properly judge and correct our seemingly congenital tendency to see and judge improperly. Smith understands habit and experience as, in a sense, prosthetic devices that correct the perceptual defects that are inherent in the human creature. Be it the eye of the body or the eye of the mind, the formation within ourselves of the impartial spectator promises to replace our "improper" forms of seeing with a form of moral spectatorship that "correct[s] the otherwise natural inequality of our sentiments" (136).

From here, Smith immediately turns to one of the most striking, indeed shocking, philosophical thought exercises in *The Theory of Moral Sentiments*. He asks us to entertain in our mind's eye the following catastrophe: "Let us suppose that the great empire of China, with all its myriads of inhabitants, was suddenly swallowed up by an earthquake, and let us consider how a man of humanity in Europe, who had no sort of connexion with that part of the world, would be affected upon receiving intelligence of this dreadful calamity" (136). How does this man of humanity react?[20] As Smith tells us, "He would, I imagine, first of all, express very strongly his sorrow for the misfortune of that unhappy people, he would make many melancholy reflections upon the precariousness of human life, and the vanity of all the labours of man, which could thus be annihilated in a moment" (136). However, these sorrowful feelings and somber meditations quickly enough come to an end. "And when all this fine philosophy was over," he regretfully observes, "when all these humane sentiments had been once fairly expressed, he would pursue his business or his pleasure … with the same ease and tranquillity, as if no such accident had happened" (136). And then Smith really raises the moral stakes: "The most frivolous disaster which could befal [*sic*] himself would occasion a more real disturbance. If he was to lose his little finger to-morrow, he would not sleep to-night; but, provided he never saw them, he will snore with the most profound security over the ruin of a hundred millions of his brethren, and the destruction of that immense multitude seems plainly an object less interesting to him, than this paltry misfortune of his own" (136–37).

The philosophical question that follows is disconcerting, but given Smith's assumption that the uncorrected human creature tends to indulge in morally defective judgments, the question is also inevitable: would this so-called man of humanity, who has been tossing and turning over the prospect of losing a finger, sacrifice the lives of millions of Chinese men, women, and children in order to avoid being bodily mutilated? The answer of course is a resounding *no*—or in any case, it should be a resounding *no*—for "human nature startles with horror" at such a thought. And why, Smith asks, "When our passive feelings are almost always so sordid and so selfish, how comes it that our active principles should often be so generous and so noble?" (137). Here again the impartial spectator—variously glossed as "reason, principle, conscience, the inhabitant of the breast, the man within, the great judge and arbiter of our conduct"—intervenes to save us from our imperfect and defective selves (137).

> It is he who, whenever we are about to act so as to affect the happiness of others, calls to us, with a voice capable of astonishing the most presumptuous of our passions, that we are but one of the multitude, in no respect better than any other in it; and that when we prefer ourselves so shamefully and so blindly to others, we become the proper objects of resentment, abhorrence, and execration. It is from him only that we learn the real littleness of ourselves, and of whatever relates to ourselves, and the natural misrepresentations of self-love can be corrected only by the eye of this impartial spectator. It is he who shows us the propriety of generosity and the deformity of injustice; the propriety of resigning the greatest interests of our own, for the yet greater interests of others, and the deformity of doing the smallest injury to another, in order to obtain the greatest benefit to ourselves. (137)

Smith here recapitulates the moral drama of a self divided into accuser and accused. The "man within," the impartial spectator, sternly hails the self that presumptuously—albeit "naturally"—follows the dictates of self-love. It is important to note that Smith explicitly draws on the trope of blindness in this passage. Shame covers those who "blindly" prefer their own interest to the interests of others; the self is morally disabled by the blindness that encourages the undisciplined individual to embrace the partial and the deformed. Only the eyes of the impartial spectator can correct the disabling effects of self-love. And yet, having chastened us for our predisposition toward moral defect and deformity, Smith takes away a bit of his argument's sting by opening before us a path to a higher kind of love: "It is not the love of our neighbour, it is not the love of mankind, which upon many occasions prompts us to the practice of those divine virtues. It is a stronger love, a more powerful affection, which generally takes place upon such occasions; the love of what is honourable and noble, of the grandeur, and dignity, and superiority of our own characters" (137). However, without saying so explicitly, I would argue that Smith has outlined a moral-philosophical rationale for how our self-love can be both transcended and preserved. That is, we are being invited to indulge not our undisciplined, uncorrected, deformed, and deforming self-love, but rather a love of the "superiority of our own characters," which is made possible by the moral intervention of the impartial spectator.

In short, then, treating others properly means loving ourselves properly. And loving ourselves properly is a moral accomplishment grounded in habit and experience—specifically, the habit and experience of overcoming our deformities and adopting the ideal, undeformed perspective of the impartial spectator.[21] But as we ascend the heights of moral grandeur, we must remember that impartiality can only be fashioned through partiality, and propriety can only be fashioned through deformity. In other words, disability is the condition of possibility for Smithean sympathy and morality. And, finally, we also must remember that Smith's appropriation of the language of disability, although it is often pitched at the level of the abstract and the figurative, takes for granted the existence and experience of those disabled minds and bodies for whom a morally transcendent self-love is often an exceedingly challenging proposition.

NOTES

I would like to thank Michelle Burnham, the editor of *Studies in Eighteenth-Century Culture*, and *SECC*'s two anonymous readers for their invaluable feedback.

1. See Lennard J. Davis, *Enforcing Normalcy: Disability, Deafness, and the Body* (New York: Verso, 1995); Lennard J. Davis, *Bending over Backwards: Essays on Disability and the Body* (New York: NYU Press, 2002); Helen Deutsch, *Resemblance and Disgrace: Alexander Pope and the Deformation of Culture* (Cambridge: Harvard Univ. Press, 1996); Felicity Nussbaum, "Feminotopias: The Pleasures of 'Deformity' in Mid-Eighteenth-Century England," in *The Body and Physical Difference: Discourses of Disability*, ed. David T. Mitchell and Sharon L. Snyder (Ann Arbor: Univ. of Michigan Press, 1997), 161–73; Helen Deutsch and

Felicity Nussbaum, eds., *"Defects": Engendering the Modern Body* (Ann Arbor: Univ. of Michigan Press, 2000); and David M. Turner, *Disability in Eighteenth-Century England: Imagining Physical Impairment* (New York and London: Routledge, 2012).

2. Helen Deutsch, "The Body's Moments: Visible Disability, the Essay, and the Limits of Sympathy," *Prose Studies* 27.1–2 (April-August 2005): 14. Chris Mounsey, for instance, calls for more detailed explorations of the "immediacy of individual lived experience"; further, he stresses that we need to attend to how individuals with the "same" disability are, in fact, both "same" and "different"—not least because disabilities exhibit synchronic and diachronic variation. See Chris Mounsey, "Introduction: Variability: Beyond Sameness and Difference," in *The Idea of Disability in the Eighteenth Century*, ed. Mounsey (Lewisburg: Bucknell Univ. Press, 2014), 18.

3. Joseph P. Shapiro, *No Pity: People with Disabilities Forging a New Civil Rights Movement* (New York: Three Rivers Press, 1994), 30, 38.

4. Lennard J. Davis, "Introduction," *The Disability Studies Reader*, ed. Davis (New York: Routledge, 1997), 2.

5. Davis, "Introduction," 2–3.

6. Elsewhere, Davis observes that "by narrativizing an impairment, one tends to sentimentalize it, and link it to the bourgeois sensibility of individualism and the drama of the individual story." Davis, *Enforcing Normalcy*, 11. David T. Mitchell and Sharon L. Snyder elaborate on Davis's position as follows: "The personal narrative expands the boundaries of our understanding of disability on an individual level, but its attendant social and political contexts tend to be overshadowed by the emotions of pity and/or sympathy evoked by the reader's identification with the narrator's personal plight. Consequently, first person narratives cannot singularly provide the interpretive paradigms needed to revise cultural understandings of disability." David T. Mitchell and Sharon L. Snyder, "Introduction: Disability Studies and the Double Bind of Representation," in *The Body and Physical Difference: Discourses of Disability*, ed. Mitchell and Snyder (Ann Arbor: Univ. of Michigan Press, 1997), 11. From the perspective of disability studies, Smith's *The Theory of Moral Sentiments* represents an important chapter in the history of disability, affect, and self-narration. More specifically, *The Theory of Moral Sentiments* philosophically narrates the ideological instantiation of the "first person" moral subject, and along the way, reveals how sympathy—the capacity to think and feel intersubjectively—is indissociable from the social and political contexts that give rise to the "first person."

7. Adam Smith, *The Theory of Moral Sentiments*, ed. D.D. Raphael and A.L. Macfie (Indianapolis: Liberty Fund, 1984), 12, 260–61, 148. All further references will be to this edition and cited parenthetically in the text.

8. See Turner's first chapter, "Defining Disability and Deformity," in *Disability in Eighteenth-Century England*, 16–34.

9. See Hina Nazar, *Enlightened Sentiments: Judgment and Autonomy in the Age of Sensibility* (New York: Fordham Univ. Press, 2012), for a consideration of how Enlightenment notions of judgment are grounded in (rather than merely repudiate or transcend) the aesthetics and ethics of sentimentalism. Her

discussion of *The Theory of Moral Sentiments* (e.g., 24–25, 52–56) highlights the determinative role Smith accords to affective experience and social relations in the formation of moral duty. James Chandler offers a brilliant reading of Smithean sympathy in relation to sentimentalism's revolutionizing of literary form, communication, and perception in *An Archaeology of Sympathy: The Sentimental Mode in Literature and Cinema* (Chicago: Univ. of Chicago Press, 2013). For other discussions that situate Smith's theory of sympathy within Enlightenment debates regarding reason and sentiment, see Charles L. Griswold Jr., *Adam Smith and the Virtues of Enlightenment* (Cambridge: Cambridge Univ. Press, 1999); Pierre Force, *Self-Interest Before Adam Smith: A Genealogy of Economic Science* (Cambridge: Cambridge Univ. Press, 2003); and Michael L. Frazer, *The Enlightenment of Sympathy: Justice and the Moral Sentiments in the Eighteenth Century and Today* (Oxford: Oxford Univ. Press), 89–111.

10. Throughout this essay, I typically will use male or masculine pronouns and references, in order to remain consistent with Smith's linguistic habits. It goes without saying that Smith's philosophical thought is tendentiously grounded in a gender ideology that opposes, in conventional and often facile ways, male and female forms of thought, feeling, and action.

11. Disability studies scholars have begun to interrogate the ways that aesthetic ideology historically aids and abets the pathologization of the so-called abnormal or anomalous. See, for instance, Ato Quayson, *Aesthetic Nervousness: Disability and the Crisis of Representation* (New York: Columbia Univ. Press, 2007), and Tobin Siebers, *Disability Aesthetics* (Ann Arbor: Univ. of Michigan Press, 2010).

12. For considerations of masculinity and Stoicism in Smith, see Stewart Justman, *The Autonomous Male of Adam Smith* (Norman: Univ. of Oklahoma Press, 1993), 24–81; and Julie Ellison, *Cato's Tears and the Making of Anglo-American Emotion* (Chicago: Univ. of Chicago Press, 1999), 10–12, 69–73. Additionally, Wendy Motooka offers a suggestive reading of masculinity in *The Theory of Moral Sentiments* in *The Age of Reasons: Quixotism, Sentimentalism and Political Economy in Eighteenth-Century Britain* (London: Routledge, 1998), 205–20.

13. As Hume writes, "the minds of men are mirrors to one another, not only because they reflect one another's emotions, but also because those rays of passions, sentiments and opinions may be often reverberated, and may decay away by insensible degrees. Thus the pleasure, which a rich man receives from his possessions, being thrown upon the beholder, causes a pleasure and esteem; which sentiments again, being perceiv'd and sympathiz'd with, encrease the pleasure of the possessor; and being once more reflected, become a new foundation for pleasure and esteem in the beholder." David Hume, *A Treatise of Human Nature*, ed. David Fate Norton and Mary J. Norton (Oxford: Oxford Univ. Press, 2000), 236. Hume conceives of sympathy as a fairly immediate form of emotional communication, even contagion, whereas Smith stresses that sympathy typically involves a spectator's assessment of an emotional "situation," in which emotional immediacy is subordinated to and tempered by considerations of propriety and impropriety, merit and demerit. Sympathy, Smith observes, "does not arise so much from the view of the passion,

as from that of the situation which excites it" (12). Nevertheless, when he imagines the human creature first encountering others of his kind, Smith seems to imply that physical deformity is immediately sensed and identified, whereas moral deformity only becomes possible within a social system of comparative perceptions and assessments.

14. References, both explicit and implicit, to "deformity" are everywhere to be found in Shaftesbury's *Characteristics of Men, Manners, Opinions, Times* and Hutcheson's *An Inquiry into the Original of Our Ideas of Beauty and Virtue*. For Shaftesbury, see *Characteristics of Men, Manners, Opinions, Times*, ed. Lawrence E. Klein (Cambridge: Cambridge Univ. Press, 1999), 93, 172–73, and 415. For Hutcheson, see *An Inquiry into the Original of Our Ideas of Beauty and Virtue*, ed. Wolfgang Leidhold (Indianapolis: Liberty Fund, 2004), 25, 61, 92, 124, 139, and 168. Elsewhere, I have considered how the notion of deformity is central to Shaftesbury's moral philosophy. See Paul Kelleher, "Defections from Nature: The Rhetoric of Deformity in Shaftesbury's *Characteristics*," in *The Idea of Disability in the Eighteenth Century*, ed. Mounsey, 71–90.

15. For an incisive account of the rise of "normality" in the nineteenth century and its relationship to conceptions of disability, see Davis, *Enforcing Normalcy,* in which Davis draws on Michel Foucault's critique of the norm. See especially, Foucault, *The History of Sexuality, Vol. 1: An Introduction* (New York: Vintage, 1990) and Foucault, *Abnormal: Lectures at the Collège de France, 1974–1975* (New York: Picador, 2003).

16. Smith's description of the individual's disorienting encounter with his own deformity, which, in some sense, functions as the primal scene of moral subjectivity, resonates with Lennard J. Davis's definition of "physical disability" as "a disruption in the sensory field of the observer." Disability, for Davis, "is located in the observer, not the observed, and is therefore more about the viewer than about the person using a cane or a wheelchair." Davis, "Dr. Johnson, Amelia, and the Discourse of Disability in the Eighteenth Century," in *"Defects,"* ed. Deutsch and Nussbaum, 56.

17. In *The Figure of Theater: Shaftesbury, Defoe, Adam Smith, and George Eliot* (New York: Columbia Univ. Press, 1986), 167–92, David Marshall offers a subtle discussion of how Smith's conception of sympathy relies extensively on the tropes of theatricality.

18. See Terry Eagleton, *The Ideology of the Aesthetic* (Oxford, UK: Blackwell, 1990).

19. Drawing on Michel Foucault's well-known discussion of panopticism in *Discipline and Punish*, John Bender argues that the moral order envisioned by Smith is at the same time a social order that enacts discipline and control through sympathetic spectatorship. See Bender, *Imagining the Penitentiary: Fiction and the Architecture of Mind in Eighteenth-Century England* (Chicago: Univ. of Chicago Press, 1987), 218–28.

20. For a rigorous consideration of Smith and the challenges of enacting sympathy in a global context, see Fonna Forman-Barzilai, *Adam Smith and the Circles of Sympathy: Cosmopolitanism and Moral Theory* (Cambridge: Cambridge Univ. Press, 2011).

21. In the larger project from which this article is drawn, I offer a comparative reading of Smith's *The Theory of Moral Sentiments* and Rosemarie Garland-Thomson's *Staring: How We Look* (New York: Oxford Univ. Press, 2009). Both Smith and Garland-Thomson investigate the ways that the human subject visually encounters and ideologically processes the spectacle of mental and bodily difference. For Smith, our "untaught and undisciplined feelings" are corrected through the agency of the impartial spectator (148). In contrast, Garland-Thomson argues that the experience of staring can trigger an ethical transformation, through which we can unlearn our normative habits of seeing and become "undisciplined spectator[s]" (21).

"The Practice of Conveying and Suffering the Small-pox": Inoculation as a Means of Spiritual Conversion in Cotton Mather's *Angel of Bethesda*

LUCAS HARDY

> You may see (said they) what hee is by his Diseases!
> —Cotton Mather, *The Diary*, 1692

Smallpox arrived for the sixth time in the city of Boston in late April of 1721.[1] Reacting to the outbreak in his diary, Cotton Mather—the eminent Puritan theologian and first proponent of inoculation in America—wrote, "The grievous Calamity of the *Small-pox* has now entered the Town. The practice of conveying and suffering the *Small-pox* by *Inoculation*, has never been used in *America*…But how many lives might be saved by it, if it were practiced? I will procure a Consult of our Physicians, and lay the matter before them."[2] If his first remark about smallpox was an apparently scientific one, Mather's second comment, which came just two days later, looked entirely ministerial. He noted, again in his diary, "The Entrance of the Small-pox into the Town must awaken in me several Tempers and Actions of Piety relating to myself, besides a Variety of Duty to the People."[3] Throughout the nearly yearlong epidemic, Mather oscillated between his interest in medicine and his deeply-entrenched sense of Protestant ethics to determine the proper course of action in assisting the community with the outbreak.

Since the middle of the twentieth century, medical historians have paid special attention to the scientific impact of Mather's work on inoculation. Otho T. Beall, Jr. and Richard H. Shryock, for instance, in *Cotton Mather: First Significant Figure in American Medicine* (1954), were the first to show in a book-length study the importance of Mather's role in the smallpox epidemic. They asserted that "the history of immunology, with all its ultimate values in overcoming infectious diseases, began...in the Boston of 1721."[4] Three decades later, Arthur M. Silverstein, in *A History of Immunology* (1989), argued that Mather "not only advanced a theory of acquired immunity in natural smallpox infection but also explained...why variolation [or inoculation] is effective in inducing lasting immunity."[5] More recently, Ed Cohen, in *A Body Worth Defending: Immunity, Biopolitics, and the Apotheosis of the Modern Body* (2009) has suggested that "the first person to adapt the notion of 'self-defense' to a medical context, thereby foreshadowing what we now call immunity, is the most iconic and bombastic of American Protestants, Cotton Mather."[6] While these studies have positioned Mather as a progressive scientist on the verge of discovering concepts that would become theories of contagion and acquired immunity well over a century after the 1721 outbreak, their tendency to follow the scientific legacy of inoculation has overlooked the fact that Mather viewed the procedure chiefly as a method for obtaining resistance to the pathogenic force of innate sin. In this regard, inoculation served as the very "action of piety" and "duty to the people" he mentioned in his diary.[7]

This essay proves that Mather viewed inoculation not just as a medical procedure but, more accurately, as a new scientific means for inducing spiritual conversion. For the Puritans, the ultimate purpose of conversion was to produce the assurance that God had bestowed saving grace upon the repentant. Early in the twentieth century, Perry Miller explained that this process began within each person by some contact with a conversionary "means." "Conversion," Miller writes, "is an event in nature, and as in other natural events, the process of regeneration is initiated by an external object from which the senses derive a phantasm, exactly as in any other act of apprehension."[8] The experience Miller describes began with the convert capturing a sensation, but it quickly became an intellectual operation wherein she sought to interpret the spiritual meaning of both the stimulus and the sensation. Inoculation, then, promoted such a conversion in two specific ways. First, it kindled a weak form of smallpox in the patient and produced symptoms that could be read for signs of healing in both the body and the soul. Second, and of most importance to Cotton Mather, was the idea that it induced a prescribed amount of physical pain for the patient to contemplate as she completed her conversion. In pain, Mather identified a naturally-occurring force that, through its association with Christ's suffering, contained a trace of the divine. Thus, pain could give meaning to human pathology by connecting the body with Christian salvation.

While medical historians have focused primarily on the science of inoculation, literary scholars have proposed ways of understanding its theological implications in the Puritan population of early New England. Perhaps the most compelling idea to emerge from studying the intersection between the science of inoculation and the theology of conversion is Gregory S. Jackson's concept of "inoculation theology" from *The Word and its Witness: The Spiritualization of American Realism* (2009).[9] Jackson argues that with inoculation theology, ministers—particularly those in the middle of the eighteenth century and into the nineteenth—taught their congregants to "interpret their own lived experiences through spiritual templates."[10] He suggests that by turning sensory events, especially alarming ones, into antidotes that would prevent future lapses into sin, preachers could metaphorically immunize the regenerate against spiritual corruption.[11] Jackson contends that like medical inoculation, this theology of inoculation operated on the premise that humans could "alter the moral world," a notion that the inoculations of 1721 had instilled in later clergymen (like the formidable Jonathan Edwards) by providing them with a "model for how to shape volition."[12] Jackson's emphasis on the role that spiritual immunity plays in Puritan experience thus reveals that the idea of eradicating sin—or, at the very least, preventing it from spreading across communities—was a common component of early New England's theological experimentation.

Jackson's study positions Mather as a figure who negotiated an earlier theology that privileged religious discourse over personal experience and a later one that blended sensation with doctrine. Mather's pivotal status in revising Puritan theology was likely owing to his lifelong interest in the benefits that science offered to religion. Indeed, while a student at Harvard, he had been steeped in natural philosophy and had even trained briefly for a career in medicine before a childhood speech impediment subsided and he became better suited for the demands of the pulpit.[13] As Ed Cohen rightly points out, then, Mather recognizes in *The Angel of Bethesda*, the medical handbook he completed in 1724, that smallpox contagion occurred, at least in part, by a failure of bodily defenses, as external "animalcula" (or microscopic animals) and "miasms" entered the mouth and nose during respiration. But Mather says very little about this hypothesis in *The Angel*. He contends only that "the *Small-Pox* may be more of an *Animalculated Business*, than we have been generally aware of" and remarks that "the venomous *Miasms* (Lett *That* Word serve at the present) of the *Small Pox*, entering the Body, in the Way *Inspiration*, are...taken into the *Blood* of the *Lungs*."[14] He surmises that these miasms are more potent in natural instances of smallpox than in cases that occur by way of inoculation. While he appears incidentally attuned to something like a germ theory of contagion, he never attempts to explain how miasms and animalcula produced smallpox once inside the body.[15] Neither does he connect this theory to the idea of immunity. In fact, he downplays his remarks both by showing uncertainty about using the word "miasm" and by finally referring to his comments as "jargon" (110).

Given his mixed academic background, it should not surprise us that Mather's theology contradicts the biological means by which smallpox immunity worked. Indeed, he remains brief about acquired resistance to the disease in *The Angel*, explaining very simply that "*No Man undergoes it Twice*" (97). Though this claim was verifiable, in the remainder of the paragraph, he suggests that immunity owes more to piety than to biology, writing, "*O Man* ... This observation will be verified in thy *Moral Experience*; and that the *Grosser Sins*, which thou hast once Repented of, thou wilt *Never again* fall into them" (97). Mather begins on scientific grounds by employing the word "observation" to prove the empirical means by which he knows that people usually did not contract the pox twice, but he quickly moves into speculative terrain by arguing that immunity resulted from the patient's repentance for particular sins through moral behavior. While the relationship between disease and immorality is not immediately clear in this passage, Mather's extensive commentary on the subject throughout the *Angel of Bethesda* reveals specific connections between sin and pathology and discloses how resistance to smallpox was, for him, a firmly theological problem.

The Imposition of Inoculation

Mather had first learned about inoculation from his slave Onesimus, who underwent a variation of the procedure in Africa. "Something of the smallpox" was transplanted into Onesimus, in order to "forever preserve him from it," Mather explained in a letter to London scientist John Woodward.[16] Not long after conversing with Onesimus, he read two descriptions of inoculation in the *Philosophical Transactions of The Royal Society*. One account had been related in 1714 by John Woodward himself on the behalf of Emanuel Timoni, an Italian physician practicing in Turkey, where inoculations had been performed for at least forty years.[17] The other account was composed in 1716 by Giacomo Pylarini, who reported on the procedure's successful use in both Turkey and Greece. Inspired by the apparently providential convergence of several inoculation stories, Mather became convinced that the procedure should be employed in Boston during the next inevitable outbreak. The opportunity finally presented itself in 1721.

With several other ministers and the physician Zabdiel Boylston, Mather set out in the earliest days of the epidemic to familiarize the population with the procedure and to begin inoculating patients. The cohort quickly met with stiff opposition, however, from other ministers, physicians, and concerned citizens. Two of the more vigorous critiques came from Boston schoolmaster Samuel Grainger and William Douglass, the only doctor residing in Boston who held the degree of M.D.[18] In pamphlets and letters published in newspapers during the epidemic, these anti-inoculators focused on the perceived unlawfulness of ministers and physicians deliberately inflicting injury upon otherwise healthy and law-abiding citizens. In particular, the epistemology of sin enabled the debate. If Mather saw inoculation as a means to fight sin and, consequently, disease in Boston, his opponents viewed it as a sinful practice in and of itself, as a technological affront to God's sovereignty.

Samuel Grainger argued that citizens should "reject [inoculation] as scandalous to the Gospel of JESUS CHRIST and Dangerous to Society." In a tract titled *The Imposition of Inoculation as a Duty Religiously Considered* (1721), published in the *New-England Courant* newspaper, he criticized the evidence inoculators had been using to validate the procedure. He remarked, "Had those gentlemen [Mather and Boylston any other Authority than an *ipse dixit*, to support and prove what they had taken a profane liberty to affirm; they had put the matter beyond dispute."[19] Grainger took exception with the fact Mather had relied only on three distant accounts of inoculation and not on firsthand observation of its success while promoting the procedure. His concern led him to pose two basic questions about the theological legality of inoculation. First, he asked whether it was lawful to seek "preservation FROM [God's] desolating judgment," and especially from a so-called "Pestilential Distemper" like smallpox.[20] Second, provided that it was permissible to preserve oneself from God's wrath, he questioned whether inoculation would count as a legal means to prevent the disease. With respect to his first question, he determined that only certain defenses proposed in the Bible were acceptable attempts to end such a punishment—specifically, any form of "repentance" or "reformation" that "removes the *Cause* which brings the Judgment."[21] His determination that only acts of devotion were appropriate reactions to an event like smallpox rendered his second question essentially moot, since inoculation would appear to fall well outside of the doctrinal parameters of reformation and repentance.

The nature of Grainger's anxiety spoke to the fact that the inoculation debate had emerged out of a crisis of religious ethics, from a tension rooted in the "scruples of earnest and devout people," as historian John B. Blake has remarked.[22] There was no clear precedent for inoculation in New England, and determining where and how it fit within Puritan life was entirely open to interpretation. But for physician William Douglass, as for Grainger, it was clearly antithetical to the ordinary practices of New England medicine and religious orthodoxy alike. In a December 20, 1721 letter to one Alexander

Stewart, M.D., F.R.S in London, titled *Inoculation of the Smallpox as Practiced in Boston*, Douglass drew attention to the incongruous use of prayer as a supplement to inoculation:

> In the beginning of the Small Pox, they pray *God may put a stop to its spreading*, and at the same time do all they can to *propagate it by Inoculation*, which is equally as infectious as in the natural Way....In one part of prayer *to thank God for the Discovery*, and a little after to pray conditionally *that if it be not of God he may put a stop to it*; with many other such Expressions in their Prayers, which in my humble Opinion, seem to be a *mocking of God*, and an *Abuse on their Hearers*, whereof the greatest Part are against procuring of Self-Illness. What shall a Man do in such Cases? Go to worship where he cannot join in Prayer with the Minister?[23]

For Douglass, the perpetuation of inoculation worked in blatant contradiction to prayers appealing for God's help in ending the outbreak. Moreover, he contended that pro-inoculation pastors were forsaking their parishioners by participating in such a controversial and potentially dangerous public health project. For Douglass, more than for someone like Grainger, the debate was about the importance of maintaining professional boundaries. Indeed, his claim that ministers were disrupting the spiritual lives of their flocks can be read as a tongue-in-cheek reaction to Mather's very public intrusion into Douglass's field of medicine. In another letter to Alexander Stewart on February 15, 1722, titled *The Abuses and Scandals of Some Late Pamphlets in Favour of Inoculation of the Small Pox*, Douglass continued his criticism of the inoculators—and "DR. C.M.," specifically—by arguing that they lacked the necessary medical qualifications to manage an epidemic and, especially, to administer a procedure as radical as inoculation: "To be more or less *Book learned*," he contended, "is not a sufficient qualification for a *Physician*."[24] Douglass resented the absence of a physician holding the degree of M.D. on the inoculators' side and concluded, therefore, that inoculation was a "headstrong irregular procedure."[25]

If, as John B. Blake argues, the debate was ultimately about the relationship between inoculation and devotion, what failed to register for both Grainger and Douglass was that Mather's epidemiology was structured on a unique understanding of pathology, one derived from the connected presence of sin and disease in the body. Mather's view of his own involvement in the epidemic and in medicine more broadly was tied to his complicated understanding of the relationship between the human body and Christian theology. More than his contemporaries in either the medical profession or the clergy, he understood the body to be at the center of divine experience, as the material through which God communicated with his subjects. In *The Angel of Bethesda*, which he completed three years after the 1721 smallpox epidemic, Mather attempted to make a final statement on the theological origins of health and sickness. In this text, he clarified his position on the nature of disease by arguing that smallpox—and, indeed, all illness—began as corruption in the mind that spread to the body and the soul.

Sin and Disease in *The Angel of Bethesda*

Mather opens *The Angel of Bethesda* by mapping out the Adamic origin of disease, in order to prove that the human body's natural state of being was pathological.[26] The underlying spiritual crisis forming the root of his inquiry in *The Angel* is that the mind had been corrupt since the moment of original sin. He remarks explicitly in the first chapter, "Some Remarks on the Grand Cause of Sickness," that sin began with a problem of thinking, with Adam and Eve consciously choosing knowledge in the Garden of Eden: "Had our First Parents eaten of the *Tree of Life*, doubtless a confirm'd state of *Perfect Health*, both in Themselves and their Offspring had been the *Fruit* of it. But our *First Parents* criminally applied themselves to the forbidden *Tree of Knowledge*. This proved a *Tree of Death* … and *Sicknesses* are among the *Punishments* of that nefandous Crime" (6). In this claim, sickness corresponds with the attainment of knowledge through the transgression of the sentient body: a human being ate the apple and gained new comprehension of the world specifically through the senses. For Mather, the mind had been polluted by terrestrial thoughts since the Fall, and it continued to produce corruption in the body. Writing often from the point of view of the patient he was instructing in *The Angel*, Mather indicts the poisoned mind repeatedly. Several chapters into the book, he proclaims, "How Empty has my Head been of such Thoughts, as a Reasonable and Religious Mind ought continually to have been replenish'd with!" (58). The absence of moral thoughts, he contends, left the mind in a sinful disposition, one open to bad brainwaves that eventually promoted physical sickness in the patient. He reinforces this idea by remarking that "as long as … *Passions of the Mind* continue, the Diseases may indeed change their *Forms*, but they rarely quitt the Patient" (35). Until the mind gained control over its thoughts, the body would remain in an unhealthy state.

Mather makes clear that this sinful mind injured the patient specifically by altering a tripartite formulation of spirit, body, and soul that he terms "the scriptural anatomy of man" in the fifth chapter of *The Angel of Bethesda*.

Referencing Matthew 26:4, he explains that "mind" and "spirit" were synonymous in this anatomical constellation. "When our SAVIOR so excused His drowsy Disciples, *The Spirit is willing, but the Flesh is Weak*," Mather writes, "Doubtless, By *the Spirit*, he means what His Apostle afterwards called *The Mind*" (28). This mind-as-spirit designation was crucial because Mather went on to write that a clear connection existed not only between the health of the mind and the health of the body, but also between the health of the mind and the soul: "the *Health* of the *Soul*...lies in *Obeying* and not *Opposing* the empire of the *Mind*" (29). By indicating that the wellbeing of both the body and the soul was dependent upon the mind's good health, he reveals that the cornerstone of his medical advice is to promote a way in which the congenitally poisoned mind might be transformed into a healthy state. Thus, Mather proposes a flexible, largely indeterminate physiological configuration that remained outside of other philosophies of mind and body circulating early in the eighteenth century—the materialism of Hobbes and mechanistic dualism of Descartes, for instance.[27]

This lack of any clear distinction between the material and immaterial parts of the scriptural anatomy meant that the body and soul remained open to conventional physical remedies and spiritual methods of healing. In this chapter, then, he implies that the patient's recovery from both physical and spiritual sickness was best begun by his conscious attempt to undergo a transformation of mind—in short, to experience conversion. Mather's notion that the mind was the source of this spiritual corruption was not a new concept in reformed theology. Indeed, since the advent of Puritanism in late sixteenth-century England, the renewal of the mind had been prescribed in the form of spiritual conversion, in order to transport adherents from an unregenerate state to a sanctified condition. Edmund Morgan, perhaps more succinctly than any other scholar of Puritanism, summarizes the conversion experience: "The [conversion] pattern is so plain as to give the experience the appearance of a stereotype." He continues, "First comes a ... false awakening to God's commands and a pride in keeping them pretty well, but also much backsliding. Disappointments and disasters lead to other fitful harkenings of the word. Sooner or later ... conviction enables the individual to see his hopeless...condition and to know that his own righteousness cannot save him, that Christ is his only hope. Thereafter comes the infusion of saving grace."[28] While these phases were essentially standardized parts of the Puritan conversion process, there was much flexibility in how the repentant interpreted each step toward grace.[29]

The assurance of grace—the conviction that one was finally saved—remained one of the most challenging problems in Puritan life. It presented a two-pronged dilemma. First, the repentant had to contend with the idea that grace took root in the metaphorical space of the heart, or what Norman Pettit refers to as "the biblical metonym for the inner man."[30] Second, converts were required to use their own interpretive skills to examine this "heart" for some indication that it had received grace. Thus, they alternated between doubt and conviction that they were in a sanctified state. Eighty-four years before Mather finished *The Angel*, the minister Thomas Hooker, in his *Soul's Humiliation* (1640), envisioned such a heart in a specifically pathological context by writing about "choleric distemper" as a symbolic condition of the heart in want of transformation. He writes, "See how thy heart behaves it self, in regard of the strict commands of God. … If thou find thy heart swelling and bubbling against the truth, and thy heart begins to be angry with the Word … then know this, that certainly so much of this as there is in thy heart, so much thy soul wants of Humiliation."[31] Hooker remains on metaphorical terrain in explaining that the volatility of heart represented the soul's need for a humbling sort of alteration through self-reflection. He continues, "But some may say, Can the saints of God be thus transported with this vile distemper? Yes, this choleric distemper of heart, sometimes creeps in upon a soul. Look therefore into your own hearts."[32] In this argument, the "swelling" and "bubbling" heart remains the primary representation of the subject's interiority, while choleric distemper serves only as a trope (and not as an actual disease) reflecting his or her unregeneracy.[33] As Hooker extends the metaphor by allowing this distemper to migrate from the metonymic heart to the soul, his teaching remains dependent upon exhortatory language and the convert's imagination of his own sinful corruption.

The heart was often the epicenter of such violent transformation in the Puritan. Cotton Mather's maternal grandfather, John Cotton, used his treatise *The Covenant of Grace* (1655) to instruct his flock that "the Spirit of God becometh unto the Soul, not only as a Spirit of burning to consume all that is like stubble, but doth also melt the iron-stone of the heart and soften it into flesh, that the word may take deep impression in it."[34] In Cotton's conversion rhetoric, as in Hooker's, the vehicle of the metaphor changes shape, as the heart is softened from metal into flesh, but less clear is how its tenor—the conscience or mind—is affected by his changed heart. While it was the *sine qua non* of Puritan life, the process of transformation from a depraved to a so-called "saintly" condition had, by the time Mather wrote *The Angel of Bethesda*, been dependent upon tropes of the heart for over 100 years. It seemed to Mather that these polyvalent rhetorical figures could no longer ensure religious uniformity across a Boston population that appeared increasingly corrupt, sinful, and diseased.

Early in 1721, just prior to the smallpox outbreak, Mather had noticed that members of his church were excessively lazy. He wrote in his diary on February 27, "I observe a great Number of People in the Flock, whose Employments are so circumstanced, that while their Hands are employ'd, their Minds are very much at leisure, and others, in whose Business both Hands and Minds are so."[35] For Mather, if Bostonians' minds were at "leisure," then the city was host to an epidemic of disfigured scriptural anatomies—a crisis that yielded a pervasive sort of sinful corruption and, in his medical reasoning, smallpox itself. Later that spring, he recorded in his diary that a group of congregants were intent on defecting from the North Church, where he had served as pastor since 1685.[36] They had begun work on a new meeting house, and he feared that the building would draw the flock away until there was little, if any, kinship left among his parishioners.[37] Mass regeneration could perhaps stem this problem of widespread declension, but as it had stood until 1721—and as Hooker and John Cotton reveal—there was an inherent amount of ambiguity in the conversion process, and there was no guarantee that it could be carried out uniformly enough to save the city. Sarah Rivett makes an important point about the insecurities accompanying regeneration, contending that "Puritans understood conversion as an uncertain process whose truth could be understood only allegorically as a movement between the desolation of the world and the inner strength of the soul."[38] If negotiating this figural terrain between the inner and outer world wasn't complicated enough, the repentant Puritan would find little hope in relying on her inherently corrupt soul for assurance. A more visible method of conversion that recognized sense perception as the key component, rather than the personal interpretation of the metonymic heart, could potentially solve this problem of inward doubt and stabilize Mather's heterodox flock.

Conversion Pathology

Louise A. Breen was the first historian to recognize that smallpox inoculation and conversion were related forces during the 1721 outbreak. In "Cotton Mather, the 'Angelical Ministry,' and Inoculation," Breen suggests that for Mather inoculation was a clear attempt to promote widespread regeneration.[39] She argues that in the wake of the Glorious Revolution, Mather understood that "mass regeneracy would guarantee New England's emergence as the world's sole bastion of true religion."[40] While he had proposed many medically-oriented "emblems" for conversion, he was finally "able to unveil inoculation as his most refined illustrative example of the morphology of conversion. The analogy…he believed would save the eternal lives of his fellow colonists," Breen writes.[41] Thus, she makes the crucial observation that inoculation operated through the same social framework as spiritual conversion. Like regeneration, inoculation was a singular event in one's life, but the experience stood to protect the entire community from corruption. The comparison worked according to the following logic: "Mather taught that the sinner could 'prepare' himself for conversion by relinquishing all to God; in smallpox, the patient could prepare himself for immunity to future epidemics only by taking a deadly virus into his system. Sinner and patient willingly abased themselves."[42] Here the inoculation procedure was parallel to conversion. For both events required risky and, indeed, painful steps in which the subject accepted a certain amount of corruption in order to negotiate a move away from sin. The analogy was carried even further by the common experience of doubt—the convert's doubt that he was saved, and the patient's doubt that she would live.

For Breen, as for Gregory S. Jackson, inoculation remains a trope or model for regeneration, a point Breen makes clear by remarking, "This is not to say inoculation was thought to be a spiritual experience in itself."[43] Though inoculation was certainly not viewed by observers like Samuel Grainger or William Douglass as a spiritual endeavor (quite the opposite), in *The Angel of Bethesda*, Mather reveals in specific steps how the procedure fit into a plan for conversion. Indeed, Breen's compelling analysis of the relationship between inoculation and conversion itself points to this unexplored, yet palpable, link between inoculation and religious experience. For Mather, inoculation enabled the immaterial experience of conversion by materially creating the sensation of pain in the body. In *The Angel of Bethesda*, he addresses explicitly the apparent connections between conversion and inoculation by showing how the depraved scriptural anatomy stood to be transformed by the procedure. Unlike the repentant in Hooker's and Cotton's conversion theologies, Mather's patient in *The Angel* does not engage with the semiotics of a metaphorical organ but instead enlists in a more quantifiable renewal where conversion theology was synthesized with the symptomatology of inoculated smallpox.

The inoculated patient in *The Angel of Bethesda* suffers a mild—yet highly programmed—bout of disease. Mather rather enthusiastically prescribes the appropriate behavior for the patient once he contracted the pox. In his chapter on smallpox in *The Angel*, titled "Variolae Trimphatae," he best shows how the regeneration of the pathological mind might be executed through the physiology of the body. Here, he most explicitly addresses the idea of Puritan conversion by introducing the language of "turning," or the conceptual model by which converts transitioned from corruption to sainthood. Sarah Rivett has effectively explained that the Puritan sermon, the conventional technology for inspiring conversion, "urges the repentant to 'turn' to Christ, establishing a rhetorical frame that acts as an invitation to…empirical searching for gracious affection."[44] In "Variolae Trimphatae," Mather focuses on this mechanism of the turn by claiming that those facing smallpox were "Certainly Stupid and out of Measure, and more Foolish, than the *Wild Asses Colts*, if they do not Immediately Turn and Live unto God, and gett into such a *State of Safety for Eternity*, that they may be *Ready* for whatever *Event* this *Distemper* may have upon them" (94). If Mather insists upon a turn, his rhetoric in *The Angel*, unlike in a sermon, relies on the visible presence of an actual disease to urge the turn to Christ.

Faced with the symptoms of smallpox—particularly, with what he calls "the nasty *Pustules* which now fill thy *Skin*," which "are but Little Emblems of the *Errors* which thy *Life* has been filled Withal"—he suggests that the patient obtain proof that conversion was necessary (96). The errors being made visible were, of course, those "passions of the mind" that emanated from the immoral head and bubbled onto the surfaces of the body. By joining the corporeality of smallpox with the language of regeneration, Mather amplifies both the nature of the "stimulus" that Perry Miller identifies and the "empirical searching" that Rivett describes as key moments in the conversion process. Mather uses conversionary language in "Variolae Trimphatae" not just in chastening his patient, but also in implicating the mind's role in the recovery from smallpox. Once again referencing the visibility of the disease, he writes, "Be Restless, until *the Things that accompany Salvation*, and the *Evident Tokens* of it, be plainly to be found upon thee: Until thou art able to say, *My Mind by a New and strong Biass given from Heaven unto it, is come to make the Serving and Pleasing of the Glorious God, the Chief End of my Life*" (94). Here, he reinforces that the mind needed renewal in the presence of smallpox. Moreover, the phrase "evident tokens" underscores the physicality that defined this sort of conversion. Expanding on his claim, he implies that the transformation of the patient's mind could be validated as she registered the visibly changing symptoms of smallpox. If the patient's life prior to the onset of the disease could be viewed as the phase of initial backsliding Edmund Morgan discusses, this restless waiting became the stage in the conversion process where the repentant abided in a state of hopelessness while acknowledging the necessity in relinquishing himself to God.

Thinking in Pain

In the conversion theology developed in *The Angel of Bethesda*, the patient's relinquishment of himself is marked less by indefinite waiting and more by the deliberate performance of intellectual work meant to please God. When he introduces inoculation for the first time in *The Angel*, in an appendix to the "Variolae Trimphatae" chapter, Mather reveals that inoculation promoted conversion not only by forcing into view "tokens" of corruption, but also by providing the patient with a critical dose of pain to contemplate, in order to stop his mind from thinking poorly. While Mather's interest in "conveying and suffering the small-pox" implies an element of pain, by "suffer," he likely means to "undergo" or "endure" the procedure. Pain became an explicit component of this conversion process only once smallpox presented itself in the patient. He includes a paragraph in "Variolae Trimphatae" outlining the symptoms of inoculation and reveals exactly how pain surfaced. He writes, "About the *Seventh Day*, the Patient feels the *Usual Symptoms* of the *Small-Pox* coming on him; and he is now managed as in an ordinary *Putrid Fever*. If he can't *hold up*, he goes to Bed. If his *Head* ake too much, we putt a Common *Poultis* to his *Feet*. If he be very Qualmish in the *Stomach*, we give him a gentle *Vomit*....If the Fever be too high, in some Constitutions, we bleed a Little" (114). As Mather makes obvious here, inoculation was a viable conversion tool only because it reduced the likelihood of death in the sufferer, not because it spared him from the disease. As the patient experinced these symptoms, he was assigned a very specific task in order to execute his conversion: think in pain.

As the most important sensation for the sick mind and body to endure, pain is at the core of Mather's argument in *The Angel*. In two key chapters, he reveals that the best way to improve thinking and transform the mind was by provoking pious ideas with pain. In a chapter titled "Stimulator," which is devoted to describing the general attributes of pain, he contends that pain should be a "spur" that "hastens [the patient] into those dispositions of PIETY" (55). Moreover, he makes clear that the arrival of pain within the body must compel the patient to "get good" by his pain, to embark on a hermeneutic project whereby he reads his natural pain, and not his "heart," for divine meaning (62). Pain thus focused thinking during sickness in order to change the "sinful" and "empty" head. While inoculation was only one medical circumstance in which pain played a key part for Mather, its role was certainly central in this conversion scenario. In describing the symptoms of inoculation, Mather observes that one specific form of pain—headache—would very likely occur in an inoculated patient. Though it is one in a list of many possible infirmities, headache was a critical symptom for the patient to experience when read in light of Mather's pain theory in *The Angel*. In particular, chapter ten of the handbook explains the spiritual consequences of headache.

In this chapter, titled "Cephalica," Mather exclaims: "Think; 'What a *Forge of Sins* against the Glorious God, has been this Poor, Vile, Sinful *Head* of mine! ... How *Empty* has my *Head* been of such *Thoughts*, as a Reasonable and a Religious Mind ought continually have been replenish'd with!" (58). Mather's use of the imperative, demanding that the patient "think," indicates the didactic nature of his medical advice. He is, as he implies, teaching his patient a new, experimental way of converting. He also suggests in this pedagogy that the steps he outlines must be followed carefully, since the acceptance of smallpox into the body was a dangerous endeavor. Most importantly, however, the command to "think" reinforces that in this conversion theology, the patient must act responsibly and morally by participating in the Word and by gaining a new capacity for religious imagination. It was with this pain, then, that the patient moved specifically toward a state of grace. Mather further suggests to his reader, "Lett not the *Pains* of thy *Head*, chase or keep away those *Thoughts* out of thy *Head*, which ought now more than ever, to have a Lodging there" (58). In this prescription, as he twists science into theology, it becomes the head's physiological function to monitor the body's spiritual health. Thus, he reinforces that pain should be contemplated and not quickly dismissed, implying that it was a force that helped, rather than hurt, the patient.

For Mather, pain was so critical to this medical conversion because it was the natural phenomenon Christ suffered for mankind's redemption. He writes, "He suffered grievous *Pain* to purchase for me a Deliverance from the eternal Miseries in the Punishment of the Wicked, and the Benefit of my having these my Temporal Miseries made profitable to me" (55). As Mather details it, Christ's experience left every subsequent moment of pain with a divine connotation. If pain was part of Adam and Eve's consequence for transgressing in the Garden, Christ counteracted the destructive power of pain when he felt it, effectively purchasing pain back and giving it salvific meaning. Functioning as a gift to the patient—one meant to produce a healthier state of mind and soul through the sensations of the body—pain, in a sense, became a sign of grace. About the way in which headache might be seen as a part of salvation, then, Mather urges the patient in pain to "Think; 'What *Pains* did my dear SAVIOR suffer in His *Head*, when he felt the *Crown of Thorns* Violently Struck into it! What my Savior Suffered in His *Head*, has purchased for me, the Pardon of the *Sins*, which has Exposed my *Head* unto all its *Pains*" (58). While he identifies a commodity exchange of pain in which Christ has "purchased" man's salvation by paying with pain, what most resonates in this passage is the reference to the crown of thorns. This image portrays Christ not simply as feeling pain consistent with being stuck by thorns but, more invasively, as being stunned by pain within his head, and not just on it, while he secured redemption for humankind. In the case of the inoculated patient, just such an internal shock could be safely produced through the symptom of headache.

The Spectacle of Pain

Like his theory of the "scriptural anatomy" that existed in an oblique relationship to materialist and dualist conceptions of body and mind, Mather's theory of pain was unusual, too. In fact, his conception of pain resulted precisely from the idea that the body's sensations were endowed with spiritual significance. His approach to pain functioned outside of the empirical understanding of pain that John Locke had elucidated in the seventeenth century. Though he does not cite Locke directly in his discussion of pain in *The Angel*, Mather would have been familiar with Locke's classification of pain as a simple idea in the *Essay Concerning Human Understanding* (1689).[45] In "Stimulator," Mather both builds upon Locke's empiricism and exploits gaps in his logic. In the *Essay*, for instance, Locke describes pain as a pure moment of "sensation" or "reflection" that "molests" the afflicted person.[46] For him, pain entered the mind passively, and it could be neither described nor defined when it occurred. By contrast, Mather saw pain along the lines of one of Locke's complex ideas, as a composite of multiple perceptions existing in specific contexts that, Locke says, could be "considered each by itself, as one entire thing, and signified by one name."[47] Parsing the terminological distinctions between Locke and Mather shows the very different ways in which each understood the relationship between theology and the force of pain. Locke indicates, "The wisdom and goodness of our maker, who designing the preservation of our being, has annexed pain to the application of many things to our bodies, to warn us of the harm that they will do; and as advices to withdraw from them."[48] According to his impression of pain, the sufferer should alter his state of being as quickly as possible in order to end pain. The action of withdrawing from the stimulus was itself a tribute to God, a fitting recognition for Locke of God's wisdom in creating the human being with a self-defense mechanism.

Mather, too, saw pain as a warning sign, but the sufferer's withdrawal from the pain stimulus was a secondary concern to his interpretation of pain's spiritual stakes, since pain was an important condition of conversion. In "Stimulator," Mather reminds the reader to "Lett all thy *Pains* be so many *Spurs*, to quicken thy Pace in the Race of Christianity: And Lett them hasten thee into those Dispositions of PIETY, which will be rich Compensations for all that thou mayest Suffer from them (55)." The thoughts produced under pain—indeed, the thoughts generated by the headache and other afflictions associated with inoculation—became the very impulses through which the scriptural anatomy healed itself and by which God recognized the patient's religious sacrifice. Locke observes that in tending towards pleasure and away from pain, humans tended toward God, "'with whom there is fullness of joy, and at whose right hand are pleasures for evermore,'" he says quoting Psalm 16.[49] While for Locke pain was oppositional to God, for Mather, pain was a natural force that originated with God and was mediated through Christ. During the 1721 epidemic, Samuel Grainger had been adamant in *The Imposition* that inoculation was a practice intended to "overrule" the "pestilential sickness" God had sent to punish Boston. What Mather failed to make clear to Grainger and other critics at the time was that inoculation wasn't an attempt to overrule or preempt smallpox; rather, it was meant to treat the source of the disease by removing sin and transforming the depraved mind through pain. In this regard, Mather saw inoculation along the very same lines that Grainger viewed reformation or repentance, for both strategies were meant to "remove the cause" of the sickness, as Grainger phrased it.

As a phenomenon that could effectively unify the body and soul in the act of thinking piously, then, pain joined the scriptural anatomy together and made the patient into "a grateful Spectacle" to "The Glorious God," Mather contends in "Stimulator" (55). This moment wherein the patient became a spectacle can be read as the final conversionary outcome of inoculation, as the moment when grace was bestowed. While the patient engaged in thinking during pain and generated ideas of God, he was healed, as proven by his ability to focus finally on "reasonable" and "religious" ideas. Connected by the variolous matter, the visible symptoms, and especially the shared pain of inoculation, citizens of Boston were asked to direct their thoughts toward spiritual ends through a physiological process. In Mather's view, if inoculation provided acquired immunity to smallpox, it occurred by pain in the patient's body enacting pious thoughts in the mind that would prevent him from falling to "grosser sins" in the future.

NOTES

1. Ola Elizabeth Winslow, *A Destroying Angel: The Conquest of Smallpox in Colonial Boston* (Boston: Houghton Mifflin, 1974), 27.

2. Cotton Mather, *The Diary of Cotton Mather*, 2 vols. (New York: Frederick Ungar Publishing, 1954), 2:620–621.

3. Mather, *Diary*, 2:621.

4. Otho T. Beall and Richard H. Shryock, *Cotton Mather: First Significant Figure in American Medicine* (Baltimore: Johns Hopkins Univ. Press, 1954), 126.

5. Arthur M. Silverstein, *A History of Immunology* (New York: Academic Press, 1989), 13.

6. Ed Cohen, *A Body Worth Defending: Immunity, Biopolitics, and the Apotheosis of the Modern Body* (Durham, NC: Duke Univ. Press, 2009), 62.

7. Beall and Shryock, in *Significant Figure*, 93–95, contend that Mather's inoculation plan was influenced partly by his religious mission to "do good," but they and others have stopped short of proving how deeply rooted in theology the human body and its diseases were for Mather. See also Maxine Van De Wetering, "A Reconsideration of the Inoculation Controversy," *The New England Quarterly* 58 (1985): 46–67. Van De Wetering suggests that Mather's interest in inoculation was motivated by a turn later in his life to a more compassionate style of ministry.

8. Perry Miller, *The New England Mind: The Seventeenth Century* (Cambridge: Harvard Univ. Press, 1939), 288–289.

9. Beall and Shryock, Silverstein, Cohen, and Jackson represent only a portion of a much larger body of scholarship on inoculation in early America. Indeed, many scholars have considered the medical, rhetorical, and political stakes of Mather's involvement with inoculation. See, for example, John B. Blake, "The Inoculation Controversy in Boston: 1721–1722," *New England Quarterly* 25 (1952): 489–506; Mitchell Robert Breitwieser, "Cotton Mather's Pharmacy," *Early American Literature* 16 (1981): 42–49; Jeffery Jeske, "Cotton Mather: Physico-Theologican," *Journal of the History of Ideas* 47 (1986): 583–594; Carla Mulford, "'Pox and Hellfire': Boston's Smallpox Controversy, the New Science, and Early Modern Liberalism," *Periodical Literature in Eighteenth-Century America*, eds. Mark L. Kamrath and Sharon M. Harris (Knoxville: Univ. of Tennessee Press, 2005); Kelly Wisecup, "African Medical Knowledge, the Plain Style, and Satire in the 1721 Boston Inoculation Controversy," *Early American Literature* 46 (2011): 25–50; Robert Tindol, "Getting the Pox off all their Houses: Cotton Mather and the Rhetoric of Science," *Early American Literature* 64 (2011): 1–23; Cristobal Silva, *Miraculous Plagues: An Epidemiology of Early New England Narrative* (New York: Oxford Univ. Press, 2011).

10. Gregory S. Jackson, *The Word and its Witness: The Spiritualization of American Realism* (Chicago: The Univ. of Chicago Press, 2009), 189.

11. Jackson, *Word and its Witness*, 16.

12. Jackson, *Word and its Witness*, 53.

13. Winton U. Solberg, Introduction to *The Christian Philosopher* by Cotton Mather, ed. Winton U. Solberg (Chicago: Univ. of Illinois Press, 2000), xxvi–xxvii.

14. Cotton Mather, *The Angel of Bethesda*, ed. Gordon W. Jones (Barre, MA: American Antiquarian Society and Barre Publishers, 1972), 94, 110. References will hereafter be provided parenthetically within the text.

15. For a view on Mather's understanding of animalcula, see Beall and Shryock, *Significant Figure*, 87–92, 113.

16. Kenneth Silverman, *Selected Letters of Cotton Mather* (Baton Rouge: Louisiana State Univ. Press, 1971), 214.

17. Emanuel Timoni and John Woodward, "An Account, or History of the Procuring of the Small Pox by Incision, or Inoculation; As It Has for Some Time Been Practiced at Constantinople," *Philosophical Transactions of the Royal Society* B 29 (1714–1716): 72–82.

18. Patricia Cline Cohen, *A Calculating People: The Spread of Numeracy in Early America* (Chicago: The Univ. of Chicago Press, 1982), 98; Beall and Shryock, *Significant Figure*, 102.

19. Grainger, *Imposition*, 3.

20. Grainger, *Imposition*, 4.

21. Grainger, *Imposition*, 4–5.

22. Blake, "The Inoculation Controversy," 498.

23. William Douglass, *Inoculation of the Smallpox as Practiced, Consider'd in a Letter to A—S—M.D. & F.R.S. In London* (Boston: James Franklin, 1722), 19.

24. William Douglass, *The Abuses and Scandals of Some Late Pamphlets in Favour of Inoculation of the Small Pox* modestly obviated, and inoculation further consider'd in a letter to A—S—M.D. & F.R.S. in London (Boston, James Franklin, 1722), 8.

25. Douglass, *Abuses and Scandals*, 11.

26. Mather's idea that disease was the inherent condition of the human body marked a reversal of seventeenth-century Puritan thought. According to Cristobal Silva, in *Miraculous Plagues*, 102–104, first-generation New England colonists like William Bradford and John Winthrop considered good health to be the norm and saw in it signs of providence and justification for their mission in the New World. When sickness arrived, it was an omen that God was displeased with the community. Mather viewed sickness as a providential experience, but he saw it more as a self-produced phenomenon than a punishment handed down directly by God. Patricia A. Watson, in *The Angelical Conjunction: The Preacher-Physicians of Colonial New England* (Knoxville, TN: The Univ. of Tennessee Press, 1991), underscores the close connection between sin and sickness in Puritan thought, explaining that "Puritan theologians used illness and suffering as concrete indicators of the power of sin to corrupt not only the soul but the body itself" (13). While Watson details an impressive history of the sociological and biblical relationship between sin and disease in early New England, she stops short of explaining how sin was transformed into disease within the body and how medical procedures like inoculation could stop or prevent sin from affecting the body. In outlining how the immaterial problem of sin impacted Mather's patient through the materiality of disease, I aim, at least partially, to fill this gap.

27. For Thomas Hobbes's materialist conception of anatomy, see Part One, "Of Man," in *Leviathan* (New York: Penguin, 1985). For René Descartes' philosophy of mind-body dualism, see especially the Sixth Meditation in *Meditations on First Philosophy with Selections from the Objections and Replies*, trans. John Cottingham and Bernard Williams (New York: Cambridge Univ. Press, 1996), 50–62.

28. Edmund Morgan, *Visible Saints: The History of a Puritan Idea* (Ithaca: Cornell Univ. Press, 1963), 91.

29. For more on variations in Puritan conversion morphology, see Janice Knight, *Orthodoxies in Massachusetts: Rereading American Puritanism* (Cambridge: Harvard Univ. Press, 1994); see also Patricia Caldwell, *The Puritan Conversion Narrative: The Beginnings of American Expression* (New York: Cambridge Univ. Press, 1983).

30. Norman Pettit, *The Heart Prepared: Grace and Conversion in Puritan Spiritual Life* (New Haven: Yale Univ. Press, 1966), 1.

31. Thomas Hooker, *The Soul's Humiliation* (London, 1640), 191–192.

32. Hooker, *Soul's Humiliation*, 192.

33. Since the fifth century BCE, choleric distemper was believed to be caused by an imbalance in the four elemental "humors" that maintained health in the body. Roy Porter, *The Greatest Benefit to Mankind: A Medical History of Humanity* (New York: Norton, 1998), 9.

34. John Cotton, *The Covenant of Grace: Discovering The Great Work of a Sinners Reconciliation to God* (London: Francis Eglesfield and John Allen, 1655), 27.

35. Mather, *Diary*, 2:603–604.

36. Solberg, Introduction to *The Christian Philosopher*, xxviii.

37. Mather, *Diary*, 2:615–616.

38. Sarah Rivett, *The Science of the Soul in Colonial New England* (Chapel Hill: Univ. of North Carolina Press, 2011), 338.

39. Louise A. Breen, "Cotton Mather, the 'Angelical Ministry,' and Inoculation," *The Journal of the History of Ideas* 46 (1991): 356.

40. Breen, "Angelical Ministry," 336.

41. Breen, "Angelical Ministry," 338.

42. Breen, "Angelical Ministry," 356.

43. Breen, "Angelical Ministry," 356.

44. Rivett, *Science of the Soul*, 99.

45. While Mather does not mention John Locke explicitly in "Stimulator," he does reference him in a chapter on diseases common to infants in *The Angel of Bethesda*.

46. John Locke, *An Essay Concerning Human Understanding*, ed. Roger Woolhouse (New York: Penguin, 1997), 129.

47. Locke, *Essay*, 160.

48. Locke, *Essay*, 130.

49. Locke, *Essay*, 131.

Reforming the Literary Black Atlantic: Worshipful Resistance in the Transatlantic World

ANDREW M. PISANO

Early Black Atlantic literature emerged in large part due to the transatlantic evangelical revivals commonly known as the First Great Awakening. The list of early black writers whose works directly reflect the Awakening's influence is extensive and spans nearly thirty years, from 1760 to1789.[1] James Albert Ukawsaw Gronniosaw's *A Narrative of the Most Remarkable Particulars in the Life of James Albert Ukawsaw Gronniosaw, An African Prince* (1772), represents the black authorship not as a region- or nation-bound curiosity, but rather as a testament to the universal power of Christian conversion. Gronniosaw's *Narrative* is the first black-authored text to be sponsored by (and dedicated to) Selena Hastings, the Countess of Huntingdon. The *Narrative* also marks the first time the renowned British evangelicals, who would later establish themselves as the Huntingdon Connexion with Hastings as the grand patron, actively sponsored a writer of African descent.[2] The move from the spiritual and material support of black people to the transatlantic introduction of black authorship is essential for the emergence of Anglophonic black authorship.

While scholars consider Gronniosaw's *Narrative* to be the first Anglophonic text narrated by a person of African-descent and sold throughout the British Atlantic world, I read the religious participation in 1740 of Jonathan Bryan's slaves as a foundational moment in Black Atlantic literary history. These slaves' public engagement in the evangelicalism of the First Great Awakening captured the attention of the South Carolina public, forging a discursive space in a transatlantic print culture consumed with ideas of spiritual and social renewal. We must address some southern slaves as influencers and active participants in the formation of a print culture that encourages an even earlier emergence of Anglophonic black authorship than scholars have recognized. Drawing from the theoretical framework posited by Lara Langer Cohen and Jordan Alexander Stein in their edited collection of essays, *Early African American Print Culture*, I conclude that South Carolina planter elite Jonathan Bryan's slaves participated in the modification of mid-eighteenth-century transatlantic evangelical print discourse.[3]

This reconsideration challenges extant understandings of the origins of the literary Black Atlantic. Critics rightfully identify the First Great Awakening as generating the potential for the emergence of Black Atlantic writers.[4] But we should also consider that the writings of Briton Hammon, Jupiter Hammon, and especially Ukawsaw James Gronniosaw were only possible because people of African descent, most notably South Carolina planter Jonathan Bryan's slaves, influenced the emergence of a literary Black Atlantic. These slaves' participation in the evangelical community captured the attention of George Whitefield during his second American tour. In turn, Whitefield reported his excitement and wonder at these slaves' enthusiasm back to his colleague and friend, in England, Anne Dutton. In 1743, Dutton took the opportunity at both the behest of Whitefield and the print debate regarding the Christianization of slavery circulating throughout the colonies, to publish a letter to Bryan's slaves, praising their piety and subservience. Like Whitefield's *To the Inhabitants of Maryland, Virginia, North and South-Carolina* (1740), Dutton's *A Letter to the Negroes Lately Converted to Christ in America* maintained the position that slavery is compatible with Christianity. However, unlike Whitefield's *Letter*, Dutton positioned slaves as readers and participants in the transatlantic epistolary print community, a shift bondspeople inspired by teaching one another how to read, engaging with the evangelicalism of the Great Awakening, and affecting the composition of Dutton's *Letter*.

Dutton's *Letter* opens a textual, rhetorical space for black readers and black participants, thus intervening in white-dominated, transatlantic evangelical print discourse. Current scholarship in early African American print culture reconsiders the dimensions of the discursive origins of the literary Black Atlantic. Cohen and Jordan Stein's *Early African American Print Culture* challenges the relationship between "'print,' a technology that fixes impressions, and 'print culture,' a world in which print both integrates with other practices and assumes a life of its own." For Cohen and Stein, such rigid distinctions do not hold up when studying early African American writing because of its historically vexed association with white editors, publishers, and sellers. Therefore, the critical thrust of the collected essays seeks an "expansive understanding of print," examining "the ways that print affects (and sometimes effects) personhood, circulates to unintended readers, is subject to reiteration and reappropriation, solicits publics that may not recognize themselves as such, and allows equally for representation and misrepresentation."[5] Although Dutton's *Letter* itself is not written by the slaves, its composition closely aligns with later amanuensis-composed narratives, such as Gronniosaw's. Dutton's *Letter*, too, is a "historically vexed" text, composed for slaves so they may know that their religious fervor has not gone unnoticed. Whitefield and Dutton's praises are self-congratulatory: they wish to acknowledge what they perceive as evidence of successful religious colonization, nothing more.[6]

Therefore, we must consider the slaves' marginalized actions subordinated by Dutton's praises of religious enthusiasm and calls for continued obedience to their master. Cohen and Stein contest the more traditional argument that African American literature, especially in its earliest form, is designated by black authorship.[7] They argue that one of the critical contentions channeled throughout the collected essays is the positing of "an alternative paradigm to the study of 'black authorship' that has for so long been the only significant paradigm by which to estimate African American print culture, and African American literature more generally." Cohen and Stein are careful to point out, however, that they and their fellow contributors, by reconsidering accepted qualifiers of traditional authorship, "d[o] not and should not displace" "attention to racialization or its historically lived experience." [8] Rather, they urge the recognition of early black "narrative protagonists," "performers," "booksellers," "editors," and "signifiers" as "participants in a rapidly emergent media culture whose impact on everyday life scholars are only beginning to understand." [9] If we are to engage in Cohen and Stein's critical schema, this list should also include the slave recipients of Dutton's *Letter*, because they are the performers and signifiers in the text: their public demonstrations of faith co-authored a literary presence in the transatlantic world.

Scholars of the First Great Awakening have argued for the correlation between the revivals and an expansion of colonial print. The circulation of (anti) revivalist news, letters, journals and diaries, autobiographies and sermons, fashioned a culture of eager readers and listeners on both sides of the Atlantic. More specifically, however, the evangelicalism-inspired dialogue circulating in print throughout the British American colonies contributed to the formation of a spiritual sovereignty, to an imagined community of believers, regardless of which side of the debate they stood.[10] Yet, critical discussion of this developmental moment in early American culture continues to maintain the position that this print culture is entirely bound to white participation. As the scholarly record stands, black participation in print culture, religious and otherwise, does not occur until 1760; this period also marks the beginning of Black Atlantic literature.[11] Writers such as Briton Hammon and Jupiter Hammon, Ukawsaw James Gronniosaw and Phillis Wheatley emerge, in part, out of the post-Awakening stir to meet evangelicals' demands for public demonstrations of black conversion.

There are, in fact, two reasons to consider Bryan's slaves as the significant agents who mediate colonial American print culture. The first is the slaves' adaption of New Light Christianity and acquisition of literacy. As reports such as Whitefield's shows, Bryan's slaves adapted and practiced their faith freely on Bryan's plantation. They were preached to each other and taught one another how to read scripture. Their resolve to participate in the religious fervor active in much of South Carolina ultimately garnered the attention of Whitefield who, in turn, promoted their actions to Dutton, asking her also to address them in her public writings. The publication and transatlantic circulation of Dutton's *Letter* broadened the Anglo-centric parameters of the British Atlantic evangelical community. Thus, no longer can we ascribe a white-participant parameter around colonial American print culture.

Second, following Cohen and Stein, I urge an assessment of Dutton's *Letter* as being co-authored by Bryan's slaves. Their dynamic and unique participation in the larger faith community broke through the Anglo-centric sphere of public evangelicalism. By their own actions of empowerment, these slaves created their own public personas. They, in short, subverted their public and political marginality as non-entities expelled from engaging in public dialogue by choosing to form their own culture of education and faith. It seems only fitting, then, to reevaluate Black Atlantic literary production, and to establish Bryan's slaves as participants in the literary Black Atlantic.

"An Inconsiderable Evil," Comparatively Speaking: Religion, Slavery, and the Formation of South Carolina Evangelical Print Culture

The polarization occurring between New England and Mid Atlantic New and Old Lights during Whitefield's first American preaching tour overlapped with other troubles brewing in South Carolina. In 1739, the Low Country witnessed or read about a slave uprising in South Carolina, known as the Stono Rebellion. While not directly related to the preaching of New Light evangelicals, the slaves' violent revolt had proved to many southern planters that slaves were prepared to revolt. Whitefield's landing in South Carolina for what would be his second American visit but first American preaching tour, could not have been fraught with more tension. Shortly after his arrival, Whitefield took note of the deplorable conditions under which slaves suffered. Unable to stay silent on the issue, Whitefield published in 1740, *A Letter to the Inhabitants of Maryland, Virginia, North and South Carolina*. In the *Letter*, Whitefield chastised southern slave owners for their negligence of slaves' physical and spiritual well-being. At one point, Whitefield observes:

> How you will receive it I know now; whether you will accept it in Love, or be offended with me…I am uncertain. Whatever be the Event, I must inform you in the Meekness and Gentleness of *Christ*, that I think God has a Quarrel with you for your Abuse and Cruelty to the poor Negroes …Your Dogs are caressed and fondled at your Tables: But your Slaves, who are frequently styled Dogs or Beasts, have not an equal Privilege. They are scarce permitted to pick up the Crumbs which fall from their Masters' Tables.[12]

Whitefield's comments clearly admonished slave owners for their dehumanization of slaves, and put pressure on the absence of moral integrity in the institution of slavery. Whitefield was not, however, an abolitionist; rather, at this stage in his life, he had strong opinions about the harsh treatment of slaves in the colonial South.[13]

Whitefield alludes to what many readers believed was a rationale for slaves to rise up against their masters. "[C]onsidering what Usage they commonly meet with," ponders Whitefield, "I have wondered, that we have not more Instances of Self-Murder among the Negroes, or that they have not more frequently rose up in Arms against their Owners." [14] Nevermind that Whitefield goes on to acknowledge with scriptural authority, slaves' "relative Duties" as "the Yoke of Bondage" in "all lawful Things, to their Masters."[15] Southern planters saw Whitefield's remarks as offensive and dangerous, especially given the close temporal proximity to the Stono Rebellion.

The Stono Rebellion was the most violent slave revolt South Carolina had seen until that point. The uprising demonstrated, to the horror of whites, that slaves were not insentient beings devoid of personal and cultural histories. Just as there were pockets of first generation slaves who came from various tribes and regions, speaking disparate languages, there were other groups who shared similar-enough origins where language, customs, and even experiences in military service overlapped. Many slaves, in fact, shared common histories and experiences—especially the rebellious group of Angolanese slaves near Stono Creek, South Carolina. Historian Jack Shuler observes that by 1729, when South Carolina officially became a royal colony and the importation of slaves from Africa and stop-overs in the Caribbean was rapidly increasing, plantation violence, disease, heat, and constant humidity clearly took a toll on the slaves. By 1738, "relations between Spain and Britain were dissolving rapidly, especially since Spain had published a royal edict in 1738 promising freedom to any slave who could escape to Florida." [16] As a result, some slaves attempted to flee and, with some success, reached northern Florida. In 1739, an organized effort was made by slaves to hack and shoot their way to Spanish Florida. On Sunday, September 9, 1739, "about twenty Kongolese slaves led by a man named Jemmy or Cato," found their way to Stono Bridge, "about fifteen miles outside of Charles Town next to a road that followed the coastline southward." [17] These twenty men raided plantations and other homesteads, killing dozens of white men, women, and children. They also attempted to recruit other slaves along the way with varying success. The revolt was quickly put down by better-armed Carolina militia men. What lingered in the minds of many Carolinians, though, was a clear example of the slaves' "propensity for multiple layers of communication and organization."[18]

There are two competing theories regarding the causes and motivations for the Stono Rebellion. John K. Thornton contends that one motivational force behind the Stono Rebellion was the slaves' urge to practice their Catholicism, a liberty certainly encouraged by the Spanish. Thornton observes that "South Carolina slaves were in all likelihood not drawn from the Portuguese colony of Angola (as the account implies) but from the kingdom of Kongo (in modern Angola), which was a Christian country and had a fairly extensive system of schools and churches in addition to a high degree of literacy (at least for the upper class) in Portuguese." Furthermore, writes Thornton, "the Kongolese were proud of their Christian and Catholic heritage, which they believed made them a distinctive people; thus, Kongolese slaves would have seen the Spanish offers in terms of freedom of religion (or rather, freedom of Catholic religion) as additionally attractive beyond promises of freedom in general." [19] Thornton's interpretation of the Stono resistance, however, assumes that the primary motivations fueling the slaves' resistance was a regional and ethnic commonality. In short, their shared origin of Angolan (Portuguese) Catholic folkways and, as Thornton observes, the possibility of time served in Angolan military service were primary forces in their violent, seemingly militaristic revolt.

Perry L. Kyles disagrees with Thornton's analysis, however. Kyles argues that rather than ascribing regional and cultural origins as an organizing force of resistance, a critical impulse that is "somewhat static" in its reliance on ethno-cultural origins as a primary motivator, "the harsh conditions on Carolina plantations generated acts of resistance among oppressed men, women, and children who formed meaningful relationships, irrespective of their places of birth." [20] Here, Kyles' counterargument recalls Paul Gilroy's widely influential concept of the "politics of transfiguration." Gilroy writes: "[The politics of transfiguration] emphasizes the emergence of qualitatively new desires, social relations, and modes of association within the racial community of interpretation and resistance and between that group and its erstwhile oppressors...This is not a counter-discourse but a counterculture that definitely reconstructs its own critical, intellectual, and moral genealogy." [21] Kyles' reevaluation of the scholarship on the Stono Rebellion thus concludes that the slaves' revolt was a diasporic response to the racialized, oppressive hierarchy of white South Carolina plantation culture rather than an enactment of ethno-cultural origins.[22]

Kyles' thesis is important to my discussion for two reasons. First, his argument encourages scholarly attention to the formation of a diasporic community conjoined by the shared horrors of the Middle Passage, Caribbean seasoning, and the harsh treatment and policing of African peoples' bodies and minds in colonial South Carolina.[23] Second, it underscores the vitality and assertiveness of a South Carolina slave culture that was responding and adapting to political and cultural changes in a world that actively excluded them. We know slaves reacted to the evangelicalism of Whitefield and his fellow itinerant preachers, because the print war between Alexander Garden, Bishop of London Commissary and Minster and Whitefield came to a brief truce over the mistreatment of slaves and their seemingly squandered potential as converts and ministers of the gospel. In other words, the responses of the enslaved to the awakenings in the Low Country influenced public dialogue between Whitefield and Garden.

Responding to Whitefield's criticism of slave owners in his *Letter to the Inhabitants*, Garden admitted that planters had indeed strayed from the Christian principle of open conversion. Agreeing with Whitefield, Garden concluded that planters "[took] little or no proper Care...of the Souls of their Slaves." [24] Sylvia Frey and Betty Wood contend that Garden's reaction "was because of the lack of 'one certain uniform Method of Teaching' bondpeople." Instead, Garden had a plan to open a school in Charlestown with the intention of training black peoples to eventually become self-sufficient in their teaching of reading, writing, and study of scripture. Frey and Wood assert that "Garden hoped that his institution would appeal to the planters as a way of nullifying the impact of the evangelical Protestantism already beginning to infiltrate the slave quarters of the Low Country." [25] But he also sincerely wished to nurture what he saw as a burgeoning demographic of converts. Garden wanted to see slaves' physical conditions improve and, if possible, steer them away from the fervor of New Light evangelicalism towards what he considered to be a more level-headed religious self-reliance.

During the early 1740s, the *South-Carolina Gazette* was awash with both regional and intercolonial talk of awakenings and was, at one point, a leader of awakening news in the colonies. Discussing the awakenings' presence in the *South-Carolina Gazette* during the early 1740s, Lisa Smith notes that "[n]o other region of the colonies experienced such lengthy paper wars with so many contributors." [26] Furthermore, "[t]he *Gazette* holds the distinction of printing the fourth-highest number of revival related items in the colonies during the years 1739–1748 with 149 items, behind only the *Boston Evening-Post*, *Boston Gazette*, and *Pennsylvania Gazette*." "In fact," writes Smith, "during 1740 and 1741, the *Gazette* printed more items on the revival than did any other newspaper in the colonies except the *New England Weekly Journal*." [27] The sheer volume of public discourse on the topic of evangelicalism— from the debates between Whitefield and Garden to the many anonymous and pseudonymous editorials— clearly indicates readers' demand for the latest news on the topic.

As one would expect in a slave-based society, the *South-Carolina Gazette's* structure and content was geared towards white merchants and plantation and business owners. Hennig Cohen observes that a "fairly typical subscriber, Dr. Richard Bohum Baker, paid [editor] Peter Timothy" for "subscriptions covering a period of two years and three months." [28] Indeed, for editor Peter Timothy, "[s]ubscriptions and advertising were the *Gazette's* two main sources of income," as were the inclusion of "unsolicited essays and poems, particularly writing of a satiric or controversial nature." [29] Advertisements and the inclusion of dialogues such as the exchange between Whitefield and Garden kept the *Gazette* running, but it also further emphasized the readership and content of the newspaper. Timothy's *Gazette* was by and for white readers as was, by the very nature of colonial print culture, other colonial printings on the New Light/Old Light debate. People of color were not part of the formation of an intercolonial or even regional imagined community, yet they may still have accessed these popular printed debates.

Slaves, free blacks, and Native Americans were exposed to the religious debates of the awakenings through public spaces such as taverns and, of course, through interactions with itinerant preachers. During the colonial period, taverns were occupied by a variety of people: blacks, whites, and Native Americans. Even after the Slave Law of 1740, a consequence of the Stono Rebellion which prohibited black peoples from publicly congregating or securing rooms or other lodgings in South Carolina, they still managed to drink and socialize in public. Philip D. Morgan observes that in 1744, "[a]n advertisement for a runaway slave mentioned a sighting at a tavern," and in another account, "a mistress who objected to her hired slave's failure to turn over his wages explained that the money was lost 'either by Gaming or spend[ing] among the lettle Punch-Houses.'" [30] Historian Donald R. Wright further widens the geographical scope of tavern patronage, writing that "[a] black/Indian/lower-class-white tavern culture existed in cities of any size" during the colonial period.[31] Indeed, David Conroy writes: "In 1751 [a] Boston town meeting discussed the 'great disorders and disturbances which have been frequently made' by black and Indian servants collecting into 'companies at night' for drinking and gaming." Conroy continues, writing that "[p]oor drinksellers, legal and illegal, undermined these [legal and communal] efforts by their readiness to sell to blacks, Indians, and white servants." [32] More went on in taverns than drinking and gaming, however.

Taverns were a site where public opinion was formed. In *Taverns and Drinking in Early America*, Sharon V. Salinger contends that "[t]averns could be depended upon to have the local newspaper, and at times it was read aloud." It was, in fact, common for readers to "voic[e] their individual and collective opinions on topics ranging from local gossip to imperial politics." [33] We must, therefore, consider the very real possibility that printed evangelical debates, sermons, journals, and advertisements were openly discussed in taverns. Allan Gallay agrees, writing: "[The First Great Awakening] brought a storm of interest to religion in colonial society and became the premier issue discussed in taverns, newspapers, and pamphlets." [34] Unfortunately, the response of people of color to printings, public readings, and discussions on the awakenings is unknown. There is a strong likelihood, however, that people of color, literate and illiterate alike, plugged into the intercolonial awakening discourse via tavern culture.[35] There was also the matter of slaves' direct contact with itinerant preachers such as Whitefield and his followers. At this meeting point, the most substantial evidence exists of slaves' adaption of and influence on transatlantic Awakening print culture.

"The Most Beautiful Order of Housekeeping": Andrew Bryan and the Print Legacy of the Bryan Plantation Slaves

Andrew Bryan's connection to the First Great Awakening and the importance of print stands alone in scholarly conversations on the formation of the early African American Church. Bryan was a former slave of wealthy South Carolina planter Jonathan Bryan who recognized the power of print in his ministry. However, his only real presence in scholarship is as one of the first leaders of the early African American Church. Scholars of black colonial revivalism, such as Eugene D. Genovese, Mechal Sobel, Alan Gallay, and others, say nothing of slaves' or former slaves' influence on religious public thought aside from being the subject of larger debates over slavery, and functioning as entities that bear the brunt of shifting Christian missionary politics. In his chapter on black preachers, Genovese notes that "blacks preached with some ease during the eighteenth century," but Genovese almost immediately digresses into anecdotes from the antebellum period, leaving the topic of slaves' interaction with the awakenings unexplored.[36] Sobel, on the other hand, offers ample discussion on slaves' participation in the Virginia awakenings of the 1750s. Keeping in line with this general argument, Sobel contends that "blacks and whites shared spiritual experiences, and the effect was deep and lasting in both communities."[37] But outside of a Virginia religio-communal analysis, Sobel's only discussion of a black-affiliated print contribution is John Marrant's *Narrative,* published in 1785, decades after the revivals of the 1740s and 50s.[38]

Gallay, too, in *The Formation of the Planter Elite*, gives a detailed overview of the awakenings, looking mostly at South Carolina. His discussion of South Carolina's evangelical print culture is insightful for any scholar researching the topic. However, he does not mention slaves' impact on print during this period, aside from being passive subjects in debates on slavery.[39] Therefore, we must begin by studying Andrew Bryan and his origins as a means of broadening the history of black participation in American print culture.

Bryan's story is notable to historians and sociologists interested in tracing the origins of African American religious communities, but his life (and, of course, the founding of the First Black Baptist Church) illustrates the very real praxis that stemmed from some African slaves' adaption of ideals promoted during the First Great Awakening. Bryan's recognition of the power of print is evident in his letter to Rev. Dr. Rippon. On December 23, 1800, Bryan wrote a letter to Rippon, thanking him for his material support. Of particular interest to Bryan were the books sent by Rippon, for Bryan saw print as a necessary component to a healthy religious community. Bryan writes:

> All the books mentioned in your truly condescending and affectionate letter, came safe, and were distributed according to your humane directions. You can scarcely conceive, much less than I describe, the gratitude excited by so seasonably and precious a supply of the means of knowledge and grace, accompanied with benevolent proposals of further assistance.[40]

Bryan's letter was composed during his time as pastor at the Second African

Baptist Church of Savannah, Georgia. In addition to Bryan, Henry Francis, former slave of Colonel Leroy Hammond, also shared in the pastoral duties at that church. Like Bryan, Francis' talents for religious oration attracted the attention of both blacks and whites. Francis was, in fact, granted manumission after some wealthy white attendees purchased his freedom. Andrew Bryan, on the other hand, purchased his freedom following the death of Jonathan Bryan.[41]

Andrew Bryan's remarkable ascension from slave to one of the first sanctioned black Baptist clergy is emblematic of some African Americans' adaption of the religious ideals preached during the First Great Awakening. Born to slaves in 1737 on Jonathan Bryan's plantation at Goose Creek, South Carolina, Andrew Bryan "converted under the preaching of [another slave preacher] George Liele." [42] Milton C. Sernett writes that, "Liele, baptized around 1774, preached in the area of Silver Bluff, South Carolina," and "founded a black congregation in 1777 at Yama Craw, outside Savannah." During Liele's absences, which oftentimes found him in Jamaica, Bryan "reorganized" the work begun by Liele in Savannah, "and established the First African Church" there in 1788.[43] Liele's religious conversions were largely unchallenged by whites because "he would not receive any slaves who had not the permission of their owners." "This not only increased the membership of the church," observes Davis, "but it made friends for their cause among the masters and overseers."[44]

Liele's time in Savannah was also under radically different conditions. As Davis points out, not only was Liele's cooperation with white slave owners beneficial but he also preached while the British remained in control of the colony. Once Bryan took over in 1788, the aftermath of the American Revolution saw British soldiers stealing away slaves to join their ranks, thus encouraging others to escape. As a result, many white slave owners restricted their slaves' movements and demanded Bryan cease preaching, as it enticed slaves to travel outside the physical boundaries of the plantation. Bryan refused and was "twice imprisoned," whipped, and "cut and bled abundantly." [45] Bryan's perseverance paid off, however, and he was eventually granted another location for worship by Jonathan Bryan. Andrew Bryan continued preaching well beyond the Revolution, eventually returning to Savannah, later dying in 1812. His recognition of the power of print, as noted in his letter to Rippon, draws from a unique set of circumstances, events that altered lives and communities in Scotland and, especially, the American colonies.

Unfortunately, what exists of Andrew Bryan's writings come from his later years, and even these texts give little information about growing up on the Bryan plantation. Most of what we have are the now well-known accounts of Jonathan and Hugh Bryans' participation in the revivals, some of which have already been discussed in this essay. Thus far, I have noted some examples of the dynamic, dialogic print culture affiliated with the First Great Awakening. This shifting print culture, however, needs to include the participation and interaction of Jonathan Bryan's slaves. Slaves, too, engaged with and influenced printed public discourse.

In 1742, the slaves on Jonathan Bryan's plantation joined the transatlantic evangelical print culture, moving from rhetorically crafted passive subjects discussed in print to readers and participants in the composition of one of the earliest black Atlantic texts. Stephen J. Stein argues that Whitefield is the author of a 1742 anonymous epistle entitled *A Letter to the Negroes Lately Converted to Christ in America. And Particularly to Those Lately Called out of Darkness, into God's Marvelous Light, at Mr. Jonathan Bryan's in South Carolina.* Stein bases his argument on the Whitefieldian structure and rhetoric of the letter, and on the well-known association between Whitefield and Bryan.[46] In a follow-up article, however, Stein recants his thesis: "Anne Dutton, not George Whitefield, wrote the anonymous letter."[47] Stein remarks that this conclusion is based on an "oblique reference to Dutton [which] appears in *The Christian History*, an early American periodical supportive of the Great Awakening."[48] The reference in question comes from editor Thomas Prince, Jr., who included writings in *History* by Scottish evangelical James Robe. I cite Robe's notice in full:

> I received a Letter about two weeks ago, directed to them [that is, the youth of his congregation], from an *English* Gentlewoman, who is Author of the *Letter to the Negroes converted in America.* It is so good, and may be so encouraging, and useful to all such *young Ones*, who set themselves to seek the LORD, That I give it a Place here.[49]

In mentioning Dutton's *Letter* in context of Dutton's other community-minded writings, Robe indicates that Dutton's London-published *Letter* was making its rounds throughout evangelical communities in England and Scotland. Its circulation also underscores the influence it and other writings by Dutton had on the enthusiastic desire to communicate across the Atlantic, furthering an emphasis on Christian community-building. Prince's inclusion of Robe's account in his *History* emphasizes the transatlantic presence of the Great Awakening.[50] But it also presented readers with the importance of a particular subject matter: slavery and the slave as reader and participant in the transatlantic evangelical community.

Dutton's *Letter* was inspired by both her close friendship and correspondence with Whitefield and what she deemed to be the remarkable piety and education of Bryan's slaves. Stein observes that Dutton's "role [in evangelical matters] increased substantially as Whitefield's circle of acquaintances and influence widened." "At his urging," writes Stein, "she assumed a part of the burden of corresponding with the widely-scattered segments of the evangelical community, including those in America." Moreover, in "July 1741 the evangelist again asked Dutton to correspond with his 'dear little orphans' in Georgia. 'I would have you also write to Mr. J___B___, a converted planter,' and to others in the area."[51] Stein writes that in "late 1741 on Bryan's plantation twelve black slaves were converted." Stein continues, noting that "[n]ews of that 'fresh awakening' among his friends in America caused Whitefield to write in February 1742, 'I am informed, that twelve negroes, belonging to a planter lately converted at the Orphan house, are savingly brought home to Jesus Christ.'" "The same news," writes Stein, "provided the occasion for Dutton's *Letter to the Negroes* ... [Dutton] wrote with confidence to the blacks because she was a correspondent of their master and fully accustomed to writing such pastoral letters."[52] Dutton's composition of the *Letter* was also contingent on the influence Bryan's slaves had on their local religious culture. They, in fact, willed their participatory actions into being, thus establishing their presence in Dutton's text.

The influence of the slaves' actions and their influence on Dutton's subsequent publication apparently made its way into South Carolina print culture. In *Virginia Genealogies*, Horace Edwin Hayden contends that Dutton's *Letter* was "republished by Jonathan Bryan in South Carolina," due to the "great attention" that "was awakened in behalf of the religious instruction among the negroes."[53] Unfortunately, evidence of where or when Bryan republished Dutton's *Letter* remains unknown. Nonetheless, the transatlantic, circuitous journey of Dutton's *Letter* establishes the text as evidence of black agency in transatlantic print culture.

The circulation of Dutton's *Letter* throughout the evangelical transatlantic community signals a turn in how scholars should discuss colonial South Carolina print culture and the origins of early Black Atlantic authorship. The suggestion that Bryan republished Dutton's *Letter* is striking because it directly and publicly includes slaves as readers and participants in the dynamic print culture of the colonies, most notably in South Carolina. Furthermore, Prince's inclusion of Robe's notice in his widely read *History* and Jonathan Bryan's apparent republishing of the *Letter* in South Carolina signals an evolution in black peoples' ecclesiastical association. The inclusion of Dutton's *Letter* in South Carolina evangelical print culture transforms slaves from the passive, unidentifiable entities in SPG accounts, Jonathan

Edwards's conversion narratives, and publishings by Whitefield and Hugh Bryan into active readers and participants in the authorship of Dutton's widely read *Letter*. With Dutton's *Letter*, its transatlantic print life, and its apparent inclusion in South Carolina print discourse, slaves were recognized as participants in an imagined community of the like-minded faithful. Thus, Dutton's *Letter* is an example of Black Atlantic print culture and an important associative to the emergence of formal black authorship in 1760.

Following Whitefield's and then Hugh Bryan's ill-received letters deploring slavery and clergy irresponsibility, South Carolina evangelicals thought it time to ease their printed criticism of slavery practices and instead focus on private education. Alexander Garden, critic of Whitefield's and Hugh Bryan's attack on clergy, established the Charleston Negro School in 1742. Garden, an affiliate of the SPG, "had faith in the Negroes' ability to succeed, and remained steadfast in his efforts to provide South Carolina Negroes with enlightenment." "Garden firmly believed," continues Shawn Comminey, that "slaves could be trained to teach other slaves, in hopes of creating a perpetual cycle of plantation education among Negroes in South Carolina."[54] At the same time, Jonathan Bryan adopted such a plan. In 1743, the same year Dutton composed and printed her *Letter* in London, Johann Martin Boltzius, fellow evangelical and friend of the Bryans, visited Jonathan Bryan's plantation. While there, Boltzius made careful observations of Bryan's slave community. He notes, "[at Bryan's plantation, I] found the most beautiful order in the house-keeping [by which he 'meant the entire economy of a household, especially the agriculture'] and among the Negroes, of whom several were honestly converted to God." Boltzius continues, stating "[a]lthough the people in the land say that his [Bryan's] Negroes do nothing but pray and sing and thereby neglect their work, this calumny is clearly contradicted… He and his Negroes are experiencing the truth of the words of Christ."[55] Boltzius's allusion to Jonathan Bryan and his slaves' affiliation with scriptural analysis, "experiencing the truth of the words of Christ," is emblematic of Bryan's larger agenda: to teach slaves to be literate so they can read scripture and—fulfilling Garden's pedagogical plan—be self-reliant, independent perpetuators of Christian education.

Like Jonathan Bryan's slaves, Hugh's slaves were also adapting their evangelical instruction, practicing amongst themselves in private. Two years earlier, in 1741, travelers near Hugh Bryan's plantation reported hearing "a Moorish slave woman, singing a spiritual near the water's edge." "She evidently," Leigh Eric Schmidt observes, "had been a part of those 'great Bodies of Negroes' who assembled for 'Religious Worship."[56] Schmidt concludes that the Bryans' "evangelicalism could readily be appropriated by slaves and transformed into their own Christianity."[57] Indeed, Dutton's

Letter, inspired by Whitefield's enthusiastic observations, acknowledged this diasporic community of African slaves as true participants in the southern awakenings. Their unique affiliation with a benevolent master provided them the opportunity to organize their own faith community. This ultimately gave them the ability to practice their faith-based literacy and make an indelible impression on the transatlantic evangelical print network. If we are to rely on Hayden's notice of Bryan's republishing of Dutton's *Letter* in South Carolina, such an impression also found its way into the South Carolina readership, which should encourage scholars to rethink the ways we discuss colonial (and early) American print culture studies.

The First Great Awakening had myriad effects on colonial American and early American culture. Former slave Andrew Bryan's leadership of the First Black Baptist Church, which remains a formidable religious institution some two hundred years after his death, speaks to the enormous influence the southern awakenings had on planters and slaves. Most importantly, however, the slaves adapted an evangelical theology that initially sought to convert bodies rather than rethink a collective identity. As Tim D. Hall argues, "the periodical [and newspaper] played an important role in the emergence of a provincial public sphere of print discourse." "In the hands of Thomas Prince Jr. [and others]," writes Hall, "the periodical also became a powerful tool for the construction of what Benedict Anderson has termed an 'imagined community,' not of nation, but of a transatlantic company of people transformed by empire-wide revival."[58] The First Great Awakening's influence on the coalescing of national identity—an early threading together of the very body politic that declared American national sovereignty in 1776—began with the dynamic print culture of the 1740s.[59] We now need to acknowledge the participation of slaves in this print sphere, thus including these bondpeople in the formation of early American sovereignty.

Although slaves' participation in early evangelical print culture is indirect and filtered by a white writer, it nonetheless forms the crucial prehistory to individual black authorship. Like James Albert Ukawsaw Gronniosaw, southern slaves too embraced the spiritual egalitarianism of Calvinist Protestantism as a means of lessening the strain of social marginalization and, in doing so, sought out and adapted the Christian virtues of reciprocal love and personal responsibility to Christ—notions that, for many, complemented existing African beliefs. Bryan's slaves' proactive adaption of evangelical beliefs for fostering their own unique plantation communities ultimately drew the attention of Whitefield, and they, thus, entered into the transatlantic religious print culture as pioneers of the early literary Black Atlantic.

NOTES

1. Slaves Jupiter Hammon and Briton Hammon, whose writings were both published in New England in 1760, are the earliest texts composed by black authors. Jupiter Hammon's published broadside poem, *An Evening Thought. Salvation, by Christ, with Penitential Cries: Composed by Jupiter Hammon, a Negro Belonging to Mr. Lloyd,* is not only his first publication but, as the title suggests, one of his most notable didactic writings. Briton Hammon's *A Narrative of the Most Uncommon Sufferings and Surprizing Deliverance of Briton Hammon, a Negro Man* is also meant to be morally instructive, but is more associative of an adventure tale and captivity narrative. James Albert Ukawsaw Gronniosaw's *A Narrative of the Most Remarkable Particulars in the Life of...an African Prince, as Related by Himself,* an as-told-to account of his capture in Africa and subsequent passage to British America and finally Britain, is widely considered to be the first slave narrative. Published in 1772, the *Narrative* shares many similarities with the writings of Briton Hammon and Jupiter Hammon: Gronniosaw is explicit in his restoration of Christianity and is anecdotal in his recounting of his experience at sea and contact with various Anglos prior to landing in Britain. However, Gronniosaw's *Narrative* shares the distinct honor of being the first transatlantic publication by a former slave, and as such, the first widely read account of an African detailing his Christian conversion.

2. Adam Potkay and Sandra Burr, *Black Atlantic Writers of the 18th Century: Living the New Exodus in England and the Americas* (New York: St. Martin's Press, 1995), 25–26. Regarding Gronniosaw's route to publication, Adam Potkay and Sandra Burr conclude that the narrative was related by Gronniosaw to Hannah Moore, a "religious author and social reformist in England" who suggested Gronniosaw's story might sell and earn him and his family some desperately needed income. In turn, Moore passed the *Narrative* off to Walter Shirley, evangelical, publisher, and cousin to Selena Hastings. With the backing of Hastings, Shirley composed the authenticating preface to the *Narrative* and then passed the manuscript off to printer Samuel Hazard in 1772 for publication.

3. Laura Langer Cohen and Jordan Alexander Stein ed., *Early African American Print Culture* (Philadelphia: University of Pennsylvania Press, 2012).

4. Vincent Carretta, "Back to Future: Eighteenth Century Transatlantic Black Authors," *A Companion to African American Literature*. ed. Gene Andrew Jarrett (Oxford: Wiley-Blackwell, 2011), 13 and Eve Tanor Bannet, *Transatlantic Stories and the History of Reading, 1720–1810* (Cambridge: Cambridge University Press, 2011), 157.

5. Cohen and Stein, *Early African American Print Culture*, 7.

6. In fact, by 1751, Whitefield was a strong advocate for slavery. He saw slavery as necessary in order to supplement the labor needed to maintain the Bethesda Orphanage. See Frank Lambert, *'Pedlar in Divinity': George Whitefield and the Transatlantic Revivals* (Princeton: Princeton University Press, 1994), 204–05.

7. Cohen and Stein clarify their use of "early" African American literature as follows: "'Early,' in the present usage, refers to African American print culture before the Harlem Renaissance. This aesthetic movement—along with an attendant constellation of developments in American culture, critical practices, and the literary

marketplace—established an undeniable place for African American writing in the United States. But it did so in part by crystallizing a set of concepts, including 'author,' 'literature,' and even 'African American.' These categories subsequently helped carve out claims for African American literature in the canon (including those made by post-1960s critics); but, conversely, their fixity seems to have hampered scholars' abilities to understand the terrain of African American print during a period before these definitions gained purchase" (4–5).

8. Cohen and Stein, *Early African American Print Culture*, 14.

9. Cohen and Stein, *Early African American Print Culture*, 14–15.

10. I borrow the term "imagined community" from Benedict Anderson. See Anderson, *Imagined Communities: Reflections on the Origin and Spread of Nationalism*. Revised Edition (London: Verso, 2006), 33–34.

11. The term "Black Atlantic" comes from Paul Gilroy's widely influential *The Black Atlantic: Modernity and Double Consciousness* (Cambridge: Harvard University Press, 1993), ix.

12. Whitefield, "To the Inhabitants…" from *Three Letters from the Reverend Mr. G. Whitefield* (Philadelphia, 1740), 13–15, quoted in Thomas S. Kidd, *The Great Awakening: A Brief History with Documents* (Boston: Bedford St. Martin's, 2008), 112–15.

13. Whitefield's stance on slavery changed dramatically by 1749. In 1749, Whitefield successfully argued for the adoption of slave labor in Georgia. Georgia formally legalized slavery in 1751. That same year, Whitefield purchased several slaves to work at his Bethesda Orphanage and encouraged his patron, Selena Hastings, to make additional investments in slave labor. Hastings agreed, purchasing around two hundred slaves to labor on the grounds of Bethesda. See Lambert, *'Pedlar'* 200–20.

14. Whitefield, "To the Inhabitants," 113.

15. Whitefield, "To the Inhabitants," 114.

16. Jack Shuler, *Calling Out Liberty: The Stono Slave Rebellion and the Universal Struggle for Human Rights* (Jackson: The University Press of Mississippi, 2009), 69.

17. Schuler, *Calling Out*, 70.

18. Schuler, *Calling Out*, 73.

19. John K. Thornton, "African Dimensions of the Stono Rebellion," *The American Historical Review* 96.4 (1991): 1101–1113.

20. Perry L. Lyles, "Resistance and Collaboration: Political Strategies within the Afro-Carolinian Slave Community, 1700–1750," *The Journal of African American History* 93.4 (2008), 506, 503.

21. Gilroy, *Black Atlantic*, 37–38.

22. Kyles' argument also considers accounts of slave resistance prior to the Stono Rebellion where, according to some records, there was no evidence of an ethno-cultural origin as a force of organization. In addition, Kyles also includes an array of runaway slave ads—both prior to and following the Stono Rebellion—that suggests there is more evidence of ethno-cultural heterogeneity taking part in acts of resistance than Afro-cultural similarities.

23. For more on Slave Seasoning in the Caribbean, see Anthony B. Pinn's *Terror and Triumph: The Nature of Black Religion* (Minneapolis, MN: Fortress Press, 2003).

24. Garden, *Mr. Commissary Garden's Six Letters. With Mr. Whitefield's Answer to the First Letter* (Boston: T. Fleet, 1740), 51–54.

25. Sylvia R. Frey and Betty Wood, *Come Shouting To Zion: African American Protestantism in the American South and British Caribbean to 1830* (Chapel Hill: The University of North Carolina Press, 1998), 72.

26. Lisa Smith, *The Great Awakening in Colonial American Newspapers: A Shifting Story* (Lanham, MD: Lexington Books, 2012), 80.

27. Smith, *Newspapers*, 76–77.

28. Hennig Cohen, *The South Carolina Gazette, 1732–1775* (Columbia: The University of South Carolina Press, 1953), 8.

29. Cohen, *Gazette*, 7, 10.

30. Morgan, "Black Life in Eighteenth-Century Charleston," *Articles on American Slavery: Colonial Southern Slavery*. ed. Paul Finkelman (New York: Garland Publishing, 1989), 207.

31. Wright, *African Americans in the Colonial Era: From African Origins through the American Revolution* (Second Ed. Wheeling, IL: Harlan Davidson, 2000), 143.

32. Conroy, *In Public Houses: Drink and the Revolution of Authority in Colonial Massachusetts* (Chapel Hill: The University of North Carolina Press, 1995), 125–126.

33. Sharon V. Salinger, *Taverns and Drinking in Early America* (Baltimore: The Johns Hopkins University Press, 2004), 56, 244.

34. Alan Gallay, *The Formation of the Planter Elite: Jonathan Bryan and the Southern Colonial Frontier* (Athens: The University of Georgia Press, 2007), 31.

35. Locating evidence of people of colors' participation in tavern culture is that much more important for the field of early American print culture or public sphere studies because, as David Conroy attests, "informal tavern gatherings came closest to incarnating representative versions of [a democratic] public, because rank was often slighted or submerged in such gatherings or absent altogether." On this discussion, Conroy concludes: "Thus the expansion of the printed political discourse and the emergence of a critical reading public paradoxically rendered the oral culture of taverns even more important" (177). Up until this point, people of color in the American colonies are mostly if not entirely absent from the critical discussions emerging out of Jürgen Habermas's widely influential *The Structural Transformation of the Public Sphere: An Inquiry into a Category of Bourgeois Society*. 1962. (Boston: MIT Press, 1991) and Michael Warner's more recent study of the American colonies, *The Letters of the Republic: Publication and the Public Sphere in Eighteenth-Century America* (Boston: Harvard University Press, 1990). To include people of color in Warner's study (and more recent works taking up Warner's ideas) would further subvert any argument that early American print culture and, in turn, the formation of a public sphere was entirely bound to white hegemony.

36. Eugene D. Genovese, *Roll, Jordan, Roll: The World the Slaves Made* (New

York: Vintage Books, 1974), 257.

37. Mechal Sobel, *The World They Made Together: Black and White Values in Eighteenth-Century Virginia* (Princeton: Princeton University Press, 1989), 180.

38. Sobel, *Jordan*, 183.

39. For discussion of the Great Awakening in colonial South Carolina, see Gallay's second chapter, 30–54.

40. Bryan, "A Letter From the Negro Baptist Church in Savannah, Addressed to the Reverend Doctor Rippon," *African American Religious History: A Documentary Witness*, ed. Milton C. Sernett, (Durham: Duke University Press, 2000), 49–50.

41. John W. Davis, "George Liele and Andrew Bryan, Pioneer Negro Baptist Preachers," *The Journal of Negro History* 3.2 (1918), 126–27.

42. Davis, "Preachers," 123–24.

43. Sernett, *African American Religious History*, 43.

44. Davis notes that "So careful was Liele to get the confidence of the masters and overseers that he ordered a bell for his church just a mile and half out of Spanish Town in Jamaica, not particularly to give warning to the slaves but to the owners of slaves that they might know the time when their slaves should return to the plantations." In addition, church readings were "shown to members of the legislature, the magistrates and justice to secure their approval that they might give their slaves permission to become members of the congregation" (123).

45. Davis, "Preachers," 124.

46. Stephen J. Stein, "George Whitefield on Slavery: Some New Evidence," *Church History* 42.2 (1973), 243–56.

47. Stein, "A Note on Anne Dutton, Eighteenth Century Evangelical," *Church History* 44.4 (1974), 486.

48. Stein, "A Note on Anne Dutton," 485; Prince's *Christian History* was in print for only two years, from 1743–45. For an excellent analysis and history of Prince's *Christian History*, see Tim D. Hall's "Imagining a Transatlantic Awakening: *The Christian History* and the Hermeneutics of Revival," *Periodical Literature in Eighteenth-Century America*, ed. Mark L. Kamrath and Sharon M. Harris (Knoxville: The University of Tennessee Press, 2005), 29–46.

49. Stein, "A Note on Anne Dutton," 485.

50. Hall, "Imagining a Transatlantic Awakening," 33.

51. Stein, "A Note on Anne Dutton," 489.

52. Stein, "A Note on Anne Dutton," 489–90.

53. Hayden, *Virginia Genealogies: A Genealogy of the Glassell Family of Scotland and Virginia* (Wilkes-Barre, 1891), 208.

54. Shawn Comminey, "The Society for the Propagation of the Gospel in Foreign Parts and Black Education in South Carolina, 1702–1764," *The Journal of Negro History* 84.4 (1999), 363.

55. Gallay, *Planter Elite*, 47.

56. Schmidt, "'The Grand Prophet,' Hugh Bryan: Early Evangelicalism's Challenge to the Establishment and Slavery in the Colonial South," *The South Carolina Historical Magazine* 87.4 (1986), 248.

57. Schmidt, "'The Grand Prophet,'" 248.

58. Hall, "Imagining a Transatlantic Awakening," 31.

59. Nancy Ruttenburg, *Democratic Personality: Popular Voice and the Trial of American Authorship* (Stanford: Stanford University Press, 1998), 85–86.

Literary Form and the Representation of Slavery in Dryden's *Don Sebastian*

ADAM R. BEACH

In the past ten years, two distinct schools of criticism on *Don Sebastian* (1690) have emerged. The first focuses on Dryden's use of tragicomedy and on the play as a complex political response to the Glorious Revolution, while the second situates the play in a Mediterranean context dominated by a history of Christian-Islamic conflict and, to a much lesser extent, slavery. Curiously, these two schools have had little overlap. The second school rarely attends to the issues of literary form raised by the first, while the first school has hardly anything to say about Dryden's views on Islam, slavery, or the Mediterranean world, which are the main topics that dominate the second. In fact, neither school treats Dryden as an important figure in the history of literary representations of slavery; this is a larger problem in Restoration studies more generally, which has lavished attention on both Aphra Behn's *Oroonoko* (1688) and its dramatic adaptation by Thomas Southerne (1695) but has generally neglected Dryden's important contribution to a royalist Restoration discourse on slavery.[1]

This essay brings Dryden front and center to our discussions of slavery in Restoration literature by drawing together some of the emphases and insights of these two schools of criticism. By attending to issues of literary form and the tragicomic split-plot structure of the play, I argue that *Don Sebastian* is unique among Restoration dramatic treatments of slavery in that

Dryden assigns different sets of slaves to both the high and low plots. As a result, Dryden is able to put into conversation his sense of the very different options that defeated peoples have when confronting the existential threats of enslavement, particularly in the way that slavery threatens to annihilate the slave's previous identity, especially in terms of their sexuality and status. While Behn and Southerne focus only on the sexual threats faced by female slaves, Dryden makes a unique and striking contribution to the period's literary discourse on slavery by exploring and drawing parallels between the sexual threats faced by both male and female slaves once they become, to use Orlando Patterson's term, "socially dead."[2] In so doing, Dryden invokes an English discourse about sodomy in North African slavery to underscore the point that all slaves are always potential victims of sexual violence.

Even though I turn to issues of tragicomedy and the depiction of slavery in the play, this does not mean that I will ignore Dryden's response to the Glorious Revolution, an emphasis that has been a hallmark of the first school of *Don Sebastian* criticism. Rather, my approach opens up another way to understand Dryden's play as his public response to the Revolution. Both politically defeated and increasingly persecuted for his Catholicism, Dryden uses the split-plot structure of *Sebastian* to put into dialectical tension two strategic modes available to defeated people. The first is the heroic resistance of the upper plot, which is associated with Sebastian and Almeyda's brazen and noble refusal to be cowed by their conditions of slavery. This form of resistance is familiar from the story of *Oroonoko*, in both Behn's and Southerne's versions, and it typically leads to torture, tragedy, and death. Sebastian and Almeyda are unwilling to accommodate the desires of their slave master and, thus, are willing to risk all forms of pain and punishment to maintain their personal integrity, their status as sovereigns, and their right, tragically as it turns out, to keep control of their sexuality. The second form of resistance involves Antonio's passive obedience and his playful attempts to use his charm and sexuality to entertain and pleasure his potential and actual masters. Having no regard for personal integrity, Antonio will do or say anything in order to survive and improve his slave condition. In striking contrast to Sebastian and Almeyda's strategies of resistance, Antonio's less assertive response to slavery ironically leads to wealth, love, and escape.

By putting these modes of resistance into dialectical play in the tragicomic structure, Dryden offers his audience a remarkable literary exploration of the plight of slaves. Additionally, he provides an outlet to think through his own options, and that of other deposed pro-Stuart Royalists, in the face of his own newly defeated and metaphorically enslaved position in English society. At the end of the essay, I will argue that Dryden self-deprecatingly associates his own role as a playwright with Antonio's lower-plot attempts to entertain and pleasure his way of out slavery. Given the gross existential threats faced by Antonio, including rape by both male and female slave owners, Dryden's comedy here has a dark edge, as does his own self-portrayal in the prologue as a type of reduced Antonio figure, posturing before his audience in order to gain the mercy of his new political masters.

Before further expanding on my argument, I would like to review the recent schools of criticism that I mention above, for the divergence between them speaks to a methodological impasse within Dryden studies, and Restoration studies more generally. The first school is best represented by Richard Kroll, whose work illuminates the theoretical, ethical, and political principles that animate Dryden's drama. Kroll focuses specifically on Dryden's split-plot tragicomedies and argues that they are purposely artificial in their construction. For Kroll, they reveal Dryden's investment in a specifically English, anti-absolutist, Fletcherian mode and its "suspended, contingent, and dialectical ethic." The split-plot structure that Dryden uses, much like the dialogic structure in *Of Dramatic Poesy*, "floats several technically incommensurable theses at once" that are meant to be kept suspended in unresolvable tension.[3] In his reading of *Don Sebastian*, Kroll argues that the play is not a piece of Jacobite propaganda. Rather, it represents a complex, equivocating response to the events of 1688 and to the crises of conscience and political ambiguity that it brought about for many people. In this way, Kroll participates in and fruitfully extends a long-standing conversation about the play's relationship to political issues in England and the tumultuous events of 1688.[4]

Kroll's book represents a wholesale rethinking of Restoration literary culture and an argument that Dryden's Fletcherian mode should be seen as its center; it is exemplary in its attention to the intellectual and political contexts that structured Dryden's complex literary productions. Kroll's work strikes a similar note to that of Elliott Visconsi, in that both argue that Dryden thought of drama as a medium that ideally should force its audience into situations wherein they have to deliberate about, without necessarily resolving, difficult ethical and political questions.[5] However, Kroll's work entirely brackets another emerging conversation about *Don Sebastian*, one that seeks to understand Dryden's relationship to a Mediterranean world and history structured by slave institutions in which many Englishmen and other Europeans had been caught up as well as to the history of Christian-Islamic struggle in the region. Kroll's work suggests that those interested in literary form and the intellectual contexts of Restoration literature see their work as incompatible with larger questions about imperialism and slavery in the early modern world. In fact, Kroll completely ignores Bridget Orr's previous reassessment of Restoration drama that demonstrates that playwrights frequently used their plays to engage in serious discussions about global affairs and imperial concerns. Writing some six years before Kroll, Orr notes that scholars of Restoration drama lag behind their counterparts in other fields in addressing concerns of imperialism and further argues: "Critics have traditionally read through the exoticism of the Restoration heroic drama, to locate a political meaning allegorized."[6] If Kroll's reading of *Don Sebastian* is any evidence, then it appears that this critical tendency to allegorically locate the meaning of every Restoration imperial play in immediate English political contexts—to the exclusion of any other kind of reading—continues unabated.[7]

In her own brief reading of *Don Sebastian*, Orr argues that Dryden "rings the death-knell not just on Stuart monarchy *per se*, but the heroic conception of Christian empire, certainly as it related to the English."[8] Further, she examines the vehement anti-Islamic ideology of the play and the way that Dryden attends to the actual enslavement of Europeans in the Mediterranean as a way to puncture the Whig ideology that decried the Stuarts' supposed desire to "enslave" Englishmen in an absolutist state.[9] Orr's productive work has been followed recently by that of Nabil Matar, who further investigates Dryden's vitriolic attacks on Islam and the Islamic world, as well as by that of Geraldo U. de Sousa, who attempts to further contextualize the play in terms of the history of Portugal and Christian-Islamic conflict in the Mediterranean.[10] What is striking about this group of scholars, however, is their general lack of interest in exploring questions of literary form. None of these critics raises the question of the relationship between the play's split-plots or Dryden's larger purposes in using the tragicomic form to engage with this particular content.

My essay bridges these two schools by arguing that we can better understand Dryden's approach to the enslavement of Europeans in a complex Mediterranean world when we attend to his use of the tragicomic literary form. In his fascinating preface to the published edition of the play, Dryden himself highlights its tragicomic structure in a way that opens up the text to our explorations of his depiction of slavery. In his preface, Dryden instructs his readers on how to best appreciate *Sebastian*'s split-plot structure and the manner in which the two plots form an organic unit. Speaking of the general desire of English audiences to have their tragic dramas "*lightned with underparts of mirth*," Dryden goes on to brag about the particular success of his split-plot:

> It had been easier for me to have given my Audience a better course of Comedy, I mean a more diverting, than that of *Antonio*

> and *Morayma.* But I dare appeal even to my Enemies, if I or any man cou'd have invented one, which had been more of a piece, and more depending, on the serious part of the design: for what cou'd be more uniform, than to draw from out of the members of a Captive Court, the Subject of a Comical entertainment?[11]

Dryden goes on to highlight the structural importance of Antonio, reminding his readers how Antonio appears with Don Sebastian and Almeyda as a captive in the first scene, then splits into his own lower plot when separated from them, and rejoins the high plot in Act 4 when he helps to save Almeyda from the rabble.

I am interested here in Dryden's notion that the lower plot might not have been as "diverting" as possible, and I believe he means this term in several senses. The lower plot is not as diverting in a comic entertainment sense because it does not depart nearly enough from the serious concerns and topics of the upper plot. The two plots are "of a piece" because they both explore potential responses to the existential horrors imposed by slave institutions. As the play demonstrates, Dryden understands that all slaves are potential victims of horrific acts of sexual violence and that slave masters have the capability of annihilating the bodies and identities of their human chattel. Dryden is also interested in the fact that, as Orlando Patterson puts it, a slave "always had *some* choice" in the face of this overwhelming power and violence of the master.[12] Patterson wants to draw attention to the fact that, even though rendered socially dead within the master's society, the slave has some agency in deciding how to proceed within the matrix of power, punishment, and reward created by the master. Dryden, too, is interested in these slave strategies, and he contrasts bombastic resistance in the tragic high plot with a sly, self-deprecating, and sometimes comedic form of resistance in the lower plot. For this reason, Dryden's play provides a striking comparison to Southerne's *Oroonoko*, which examines slavery in the upper plot but turns to the comedic enterprises of the Welldon sisters in the rather "diverting" lower plot, which only has loose thematic associations with the upper plot.

Dryden's play is much more "of a piece" in that its narrative structure resembles a stream that is only briefly split or is, in another sense of the term, "diverted" into two channels and then quickly rejoined. This splitting happens in the opening scene in which the captured Portuguese soldiers are forced to draw lots with the understanding that Muley-Moluch will sacrifice those who pick the black tiles to the Prophet Muhammad. As Matar has pointed out, this moment represents a prime example of Dryden's egregious anti-Islamic polemic.[13] Dryden also uses this lottery to mark out the very different ways that Sebastian and Antonio will respond to their new circumstances. Alvarez and Sebastian approach the urn in a masculine, undisturbed way that marks them as superior to their fellow Portuguese slaves, who cower and quake at the thought of death. Initially, Antonio emulates his fallen king, but he quickly shows signs of fear and cowardice during the process—thus, Dryden uses the scene to begin "diverting" Antonio into a lower plot register. For example, Antonio comically refuses to look at his tile because he is afraid to know his fate, a move which quickly draws Dorax's disdain: "There's th' Amorous airy spark, *Antonio*;/ The wittiest Womans toy in *Portugal*./ Lord what a loss of Treats and Serenades!/ The whole She Nation will b' in mourning for him" (I.i.293–96). After Antonio holds up his black tile for all to see, Dorax again insults him for his response: "He looks uneasie at his future Journey:/ And wishes his Boots off again; for fear/ Of a bad Road, and a worse Inn at night./ Go to bed fool, and take secure repose/ For thou shalt wake no more" (I.i.305–39). Antonio's response is pointedly contrasted to that of Alvarez, who smiles upon his black tile, and especially to that of Sebastian, who heroically reveals himself and rants in the face of Muley-Moluch after drawing his dark lot.

Sebastian welcomes the opportunity to die as the lone sacrifice, as this will show his heroic spirit and his dedication to his fallen soldiers. While his body has been captured, Sebastian remains unbowed and indomitable, declaring to a stunned and shaken Muley-Moluch that "Souls know no Conquerors" (I.i.369). Later in the scene, Almeyda also bombastically proclaims herself to Muley-Moluch and continues to claim her importance, her resolute spirit, and her freedom: "Hear me; I will be heard:/ I am no Slave; the noblest blood of *Affrick*/ Runs in my Veins; a purer stream than thine;/ For, though deriv'd from the same Source, thy Current/ Is puddl'd, and defil'd with Tyranny" (I.i.428–32). This opening signals that the upper plot will focus on Sebastian and Almeyda's noble and principled response to slavery, one predicated on vainglorious defiance and on the preservation of one's integrity, identity, and agency even if it means torture or death. Here, slavery provides a test of the character of the noble slave, and serves as a crucible in which to examine whether Sebastian and Almeyda's principles and greatness of soul can survive their radical change of fortune.

After Muley-Moluch retires, subdued by the heroic ranting of Sebastian and Almeyda, Benducar shunts them off the stage, styling them "Royal Captives" (I.i.476) while, at the same time, ordering the slave market to be opened in order to dispose of the "inferior Captives" (I.i.478), Antonio included. It is at this precise moment that the two plots "divert," yet what is remarkable is how centrally they both deal with issues of slavery and sexuality, especially the ways that slaves lose control over their bodies and decisions about their sexuality as a result of their debased condition.

The upper plot takes a somewhat traditional heroic drama approach to this subject, as Almeyda becomes involved in multiple triangulated struggles between Sebastian and a host of other men, including Muley-Moluch, the Mufti, and Benducar.

Because of her enslaved condition, Almeyda is under constant threat of rape, a fact that is highlighted from the beginning scene when Dorax speculates on her fate and tells Benducar: "I hope she dy'd in her own Female calling,/ Choak'd up with Man, and gorg'd with Circumcision" (I.i.132–33). Here, Dorax articulates a noxious vision of sexual violation in which he hopes that Almeyda is killed during a gang-rape, presumably his idea of what should happen to enemy women who are defeated and caught on the wrong side of a political struggle. As the play continues, multiple men attempt to gain control over Almeyda's body, from the Mufti, whose lascivious intentions are clear to all when he tries to save Almeyda from death early on (I.i.260–61; I.i.420–24), to Muley-Moluch himself, who becomes smitten with Almeyda and immediately starts to meditate on raping her once she scornfully rejects his advances. Muley-Moluch threatens her over and over with rape and murder, as the following demonstrates: "Well then, I love,—/ And 'tis below my greatness to disown it:/ Love thee implacably, yet hate thee too;/ Wou'd hunt thee bare-foot, in the mid-day Sun,/ Through the parch'd Desarts, and the scorching Sands,/ T' enjoy thy Love, and once enjoy'd, to kill thee" (II.i.442–47). Here, Muley-Moluch's language echoes that of Dorax, as both fantasize about Almeyda being raped and then murdered in a single violent episode.

After Muley-Moluch leaves Sebastian and Almeyda and gives her one more chance to willingly accept his sexual advances, the couple engage in an extended heroic dialogue in which they debate the proper response to their predicament. Much like Oroonoko in both Behn's novella and especially in Southerne's play, Sebastian is forced to contemplate the fact that he is powerless to prevent the violation of Almeyda's body by her slave master: "And is't not strange, that Heav'n shou'd bless my Arms/ In common Causes, and desert the best?/ Now in your greatest, last extremity,/ When I wou'd ayd you most, and most desire it,/ I bring but Sighs, the succors of a Slave" (II.i.511–15). Here, Dryden highlights the stunning powerlessness that confronts the slave in matters of marriage and sexuality and the near impossibility of even a ranting masculine hero like Sebastian to contest successfully the power of his master. In the face of this powerlessness, Almeyda, much like Imoinda in both Behn and Southerne, urges suicide as a possible heroic strategy in order to avoid ravishment and to maintain control over her own body: "Expos'd to this inhuman Tyrant's lust;/ My Virtue is a guard beyond my strength,/ And Death, my last defence, within my call" (II.i.519–21). In the end, the two forge a new, heroic path towards reclaiming their bodies, their integrity, and their social status by deciding to marry secretly in the face of Muley-Moluch's rage and, in the case of Sebastian in Act III, to go calmly to his death. Facing a typical love and honor struggle, Almeyda eventually does capitulate somewhat to Muley-Moluch, briefly sacrificing her honor to beg at his feet for Sebastian's life, but the third act ends with the implacable emperor sending Sebastian off to death and Almeyda to face her impending rape at his hands. Much like slave masters everywhere, Moluch claims the power to define the status of his slaves: he refers to Sebastian as a piece of dehumanized property, ordering Dorax to "Take hence that, once a King; that sullen pride/ That swells to dumbness; lay him in the Dungeon" (III.i.300–301). If earlier in the scene, Sebastian ranted that he would "shew thee/ How a Man shou'd, and how a King dare dye" (III.i.214–15), here Moluch has the last word and the final act of definition in reducing Sebastian from a "King" into a "that," an abject object not even worthy of a name.

Scholars have not remarked on the way that Dryden expertly deploys the conventions of the love and honor struggles of the heroic drama in order to examine the struggles of slaves, nor have they acknowledged that Southerne's *Oroonoko* owes just as much to these powerful scenes in *Don Sebastian* as it does to the similar material in Behn's text. Scholars have not followed the manner in which the lower plot echoes these issues surrounding the sexuality and identity of slaves, but Dryden is just as interested in the ways that male slaves are subject to the same forces of sexual degradation as women. As the scene turns from the high to the low plot, Dryden creates a slave market that becomes a theater within a theater where male slaves are forced, as Dryden's stage direction indicates, to "*do Tricks*" in an attempt to entertain prospective buyers as well as show off their physical abilities (96). Here is a site in which the masters and the associated onlookers are in complete control—the slaves become puppets in the world of the market, a place where their full reduction from people to socially dead tools is enacted. While the upper plot trucks in the somewhat romantic world of "royal slavery," the lower plot strikes a grittier, more menacing tone. In this setting, verbal resistance to the slave master, however forceful, has no possibility of overcoming or even delaying the master's desires. Rather, the marketplace as well as the violence enacted within it swiftly leaves the slave a stark choice: obedience or torture, rape, and death.

From the very first moment Antonio is brought to the slave market, his identity as a Portuguese nobleman is erased even as his body is subject to the constant threat of violation, violence, and rape. To begin with, Antonio mistakenly responds to Mustapha in a way that would have been more appropriate to his previous free identity rather than to his new position as a slave:

> *Anton.* Dog, what wou'dst thou have?
> *Must.* Learn better manners, or I shall serve you a Dog-trick; come, down upon all four immediately; I'll make you know your Rider.
> *Ant.* Thou wilt not make a Horse of me?
> *Must.* Horse or Ass, that's as thy Mother made thee:—But take earnest in the first place for thy Sawcyness. [*Lashes him with his Whip.*] Be advis'd Friend, and buckle to thy Geers: Behold my Ensign of Royalty display'd over thee. (I.i.507–15).

In this exchange, Mustapha responds with a sexual threat, an assertion of Antonio's reduction to an animalistic abject status, and a violent reminder that, given this new status, he is a nobody who can be preyed upon, violated, and beaten with impunity. Not only can a shifty "Captain of the Rabble" like Mustapha assert sovereignty over Antonio, but so can any other number of men who come to the market to purchase slaves. Faced with such overwhelming force and violence, Antonio quickly decides on a remarkably different strategy to deal with his enslavement than that of Sebastian and Almeyda. Lying down on the ground in order to provide full mastery to Mustapha, Antonio placates him by saying, "Hold, my dear Thrum-cap: I obey thee cheerfully, I see the Doctrine of Non-Resistance is never practis'd thoroughly but when a Man can't help himself" (I.i.520–22).[14] From this point forward, Antonio responds to his slavery by attempting to appease and entertain his masters, whatever the consequences for his own honor, identity, and sexuality.

Even this gesture does not necessarily protect Antonio from the possibility of horrible violation. If Dorax uses language of gang-rape and murder to fantasize about Almeyda's fate earlier in the scene, Dryden echoes this imagery when the scene shifts to an episode where, according to the stage directions, both Mustapha and a "2d. merchant" force Antonio to do his "*Postures*" (98), a term with decidedly sexual connotations in the Restoration, by bridling him and having him move around on his hands and knees while also physically "*feeling about him*" (99) and stroking him.[15] Like Almeyda, who is sexually threatened throughout the play by multiple men, Antonio is also the victim of any number of sexual predators here, as Dryden plays darkly with discourses of domination and animality. There is something ambiguous and unnerving about this scene, and while some have found in it a farcical engagement with issues of slavery, Orr is more convincing when she states that it simultaneously contains a "comic turn," "erotic overtones," and a “frightening edge” as men haggle over Antonio’s body and want to see him stripped naked for their inspection.[16]

In this scene, Dryden engages with a powerful English discourse about sodomitical rape in North African slavery. Scholars have staked out varied explanations for the frequency with which English writers claimed that sodomy was widely practiced and that male slaves were frequently raped in the Islamic Mediterranean. Nabil Matar argues, for example, that this was part of a larger anti-Islamic invective and that English writers used this charge to denigrate Muslims and prepare the discursive ground for imperial ventures in later years.[17] Linda Colley takes a very different tack when she denies that English authors turned to charges of sodomy solely to attack and denigrate Muslims. Instead, she argues, sodomy “was rather a metaphor, a particularly acute expression of the fear and insecurity that Britons and other Western Europeans continued to feel in the face of Islamic power and, as they saw it, aggression.”[18] Both Matar’s and Colley’s arguments help to explain Dryden’s use of the trope, as it both feeds the general anti-Islamic tenor of the play and helps him to further explore the vulnerabilities of defeated and enslaved peoples held by powerful and aggressive enemies. It seems likely that Dryden was particularly interested in the rape of male slaves at this time because of his own “fear and insecurity” in post-Revolution England. Perhaps Dryden suggests that, after the Revolution, pro-Stuart Catholic men are in a similar position to that of Antonio—they are about to be metaphorically, if not literally, raped by those aggressive and domineering men who emerged on the winning political side.[19]

Regardless of what inspired him, we should acknowledge that Dryden’s play is unique in the ways he explores rape as a form of violence legitimated within slave cultures and directed not only at female but also at male bodies. Both enslaved men and women are subject to gross violations of their bodies by those in power, and Dryden’s play represents a fascinating literary engagement with these realities. Returning to Antonio in the slave market, Dryden represents the market as an institutional space in which many different kinds of men, both masters and potential masters, can enact any sexual fantasy upon the body of the slave.[20] Entering into a homosocial and homoerotic relationship with each other and the slave, these men participate in a group violation of Antonio’s body while other men, both on the stage and in the audience, watch and are entertained. Dryden’s play provides a “frightening edge” indeed as it investigates the way the violation of the slave’s body becomes a theater of cruelty in which anything is possible and people can engage in both active and spectatorial roles.

As the scene unfolds, however, Antonio’s turn to “non-resistance” does not mean complete inaction—rather, he uses his wit, charm, and ability to entertain in an attempt to escape the most horrible effects of slavery. Initially, he does this by telling Mustapha that he will "obey thee cheerfully," suggesting that a likely staging of the horse scene involved Antonio playfully taking up the role of a horse in order to whinny suggestively, rear up, and show off his body to the erotically interested men as he trots around on all fours. Indeed, something of the kind is suggested by Dryden's direction that indicates he "does all his Postures" while tethered to the end of a bridle. If Antonio does play along in a somewhat seductive turn as a horse, this would be in keeping with Dorax's initial assessment of his character: "There's th' Amorous airy spark, *Antonio*;/ The wittiest Womans toy in *Portugal*" (I.i.293–94). Here, Dorax suggests that Antonio has already been accustomed to being the plaything of others, one who uses wit and deference to take a subordinate role in his sexual affairs with women. In this way, Antonio is a foppish character both before and after his enslavement—his gender position provides a striking and pointed contrast to that of Almeyda, who has a masculine edge in her ranting and who, at one point, imagines herself as Sebastian's "Brother" (V.i.605). If Dorax condemns Antonio for not taking up a domineering masculine role with women, this does not mean that the play ratifies his assessment. Both in this opening scene and in the later episodes with Johayma and Morayma, Antonio is able to use his sexual charm and ability to cater to the desires of others in order to better his own situation. And, since Antonio ultimately wins out at the end, the play suggests that men who are used to accommodating female desires and willing to play the subordinate role may, in fact, be better positioned than other types of men to maneuver after experiencing defeat and slavery.

Consider, for example, how Antonio makes a joke after being bridled and stroked by Mustapha by personally taking up the extended metaphor of horse-trading that Mustapha and the merchant have been using to discuss his sale: "For Heaven's sake Owner spare me; you know I am but new broken" (I.i.541–42). His acquiescence to the degrading conceit of his immediate masters as well as his announcement that he considers himself a "broken" and compliant slave seems to have some effect. The men quit galloping Antonio around the stage and, instead, start to haggle over the price for his body. By entertaining those who have power over him and by playing along with their idiom of power and sex, Antonio can partially mitigate his situation and forestall further physical violence, even as he is unable to change radically the facts of his enslavement and his position as a socially dead member of his new society. Rather than following Almeyda and Sebastian in railing against the system of enslavement in which he finds himself, he works within the system to find the most advantageous situation possible. Antonio, in effect, plays the role of the slave to perfection. Thus, if there is comedy in the scene, it does indeed have a dark edge as it explores the self-debasement and the performances that slaves enact in their attempt to escape the most spectacular forms of bodily violation and torture to which they are subject. This is the type of comedy that disturbs even as it may make the audience laugh at Antonio's scrambling antics—in the end, a man employing comedic strategies in order to avoid torture and rape is not exactly funny.

Dryden's depiction of the overwhelming violence and vulnerability faced by slaves also greatly tempers the comedic turn that occurs when Antonio becomes embroiled in a plot development that echoes traditional English cuckold comedies. No doubt, Antonio's adventures with Johayma, Morayma, and the Mufti contain brisk sexual language full of double entendres and traditional comedic scenes involving disguises, mistaken identity, night antics, and the scrambling of lovers almost caught in the act. However, I differ from those, like Derek Hughes, who argue that the shift in scene to the Mufti's garden and the shift in comedic register to the cuckold comedy represent a substantial departure from the violent world of the play's upper plot or even of the slave market scene.[21] Rather, I argue that the noxious atmosphere of sexual violence and degradation found earlier in the play also pervades the Mufti's garden, and this puts the cuckold comedy into a much darker and more disturbing mode than the normal Restoration fare.

Consider, for example, the second scene of Act II, where Antonio, now fully transformed into the garb of a slave, meets Johayma for the first time. Johayma's opening lines contain a joke about the possible pleasures offered by the uncircumcised penises of Christian slaves as well as a veiled threat of castration that sets the tone for their relationship, one in which she eventually offers Antonio the choice of sexually pleasuring her or death:

> *Mufti*. Why honey-bird, I bought him a purpose for thee; didst not thou say thou long'dst for a Christian slave?
> *Joh*. Ah, but the sight of that loathsom creature has almost cur'd me; And how can I tell that he's a Christian? and he were well search'd he may prove a *Jew* for ought I know. And besides I have always long'd for an Eunuch; for they say that's a Civil Creature, and almost as harmless as your self, Husband. Speak fellow, are not you such a kind of peaceable thing? (II.ii.8–15)

Just as Sebastian is reduced to the status of a "that" by Muley-Moluch, Antonio is here figured as a sexually objectified and "peaceable thing" whose body is controlled by others. In response, Antonio quickly picks up on Johayma's double entendres and works within the terms of her discourse. He shows that he has fully absorbed the lesson he learned in the marketplace when he seductively displays his body for the gaze of this new master by "*making legs*" (123), and he further offers to submit sexually and serve her in every way possible: "I can carry your Umbrella, and fan your Ladyship, and cool you when you are too hot: in fine, no Service either by day or by night shall come amiss to me; and besides am of so quick an apprehension, that you need but wink upon me at any time, to make me understand my duty" (II.ii.29–33). Just like the men in the marketplace, Johayma takes to "*Turning him about*" (124) in order to subject his body to her lascivious gaze, even as the Mufti seconds Johayma's menacing reference to eunuchs earlier in the scene by openly threatening to use his knife to circumcise or castrate Antonio for his "sawciness" (II.ii.63). Antonio's penis and his sexual identity are subjected to the gaze, discipline, and desire of both his male and female masters, and Dryden's focus on these issues here seriously complicates the "comedy" of this part of the lower plot and creates, once again, a very dark comedic effect.

After Antonio is left by himself, he returns to the issue of the extent to which a slave is able to resist the desires of his master: "How far a Christian shou'd resist, I partly know; but how far a lewd young Christian can resist is another question. She's tolerable, and I am a poor Stranger, far from better Friends, and in a bodily necessity" (II.ii.67–70). Here, Dryden eschews any fantasies about the life of a male sex slave—rather, Antonio realizes that he is being forced to comply of "necessity" and that by so doing he might make Johayma into a more beneficent master. Here, Antonio posits sexual enslavement to a "tolerable" woman as a strategic choice for a slave. Instead of emulating the Biblical Joseph, who rejected Potiphar's wife and ended up in jail, Antonio will choose the path of non-resistance and compliance. The fact that this type of slavery may give this "lewd young Christian" some sexual pleasure is only a secondary consideration that leads him to this choice.[22]

Of course, this sexual enslavement to Johayma becomes completely repugnant to Antonio once he meets Morayma and sees an opportunity for freedom; his resistance to Johayma's sexual advances in the garden sends him, like Joseph, briefly down the path of possible torture and death. In the face of Johayma's subsequent deployment of violence, he quickly retreats into a more compliant mode, desperately telling her that, "I shall refuse no drudgery" (III.ii.153–54) and later complaining that, "Fear of Death has gone farther with me in two Minutes, than my Conscience wou'd have gone in two Months. I find my self in a very dejected condition, all over me" (III.ii.195–97). Unable here to assert control of his body or his sexuality, Antonio is, once again, forced to confront the abject condition of the slave. When Morayma upbraids him later in the scene for his fawning compliance to Johayma by claiming that he did not behave like a "Cavalier of honour,"

Antonio replies, "Not very heroic; but self preservation is a point above Honour and Religion too" (III.ii.232–34). This position forms in tension with the upper-plot heroic rhetoric of Sebastian, who at all times prefers to die than to acquiesce to Muley-Moluch's will, even as it also draws a parallel between Antonio and the heroic Almeyda, who is not as steadfast in following the heroic code as Sebastian. For, in the previous scene, she sacrifices the "greatness" of her "Soul" by kneeling to Muley-Moluch to save Sebastian's life (III.i.240–42). This moment is brief and ineffectual, and Almeyda eventually returns to rant against Muley-Moluch and to resist her master despite his threats of death and rape. Nevertheless, this subtle dialectical engagement between the two plots shows Dryden's complex thinking about the issue of resistance to slavery. In the end, heroic resistance and abject non-resistance are not mutually exclusive, as Almeyda's episode of kneeling suggests. Dryden also hints that, ultimately, it does not matter which strategy the slave takes, for all slaves face potential and actual violence every minute of their lives, no matter how heroic or pleasing they are. This idea is emphasized when Morayma tells Antonio the likely outcome of Johayma's sexual use of him: "for when she has worn you out, she will certainly dispatch you to another world, for fear of telling tales; as she has already serv'd three Slaves, your Predecessors, of happy memory, in her favours" (III.ii.253–56). In this, Johayma echoes Muley-Moluch from the high plot in that both threaten to rape and then murder their slaves. Just as male and female slaves are subjected to the same kinds of violent rape, both male and female masters have access to similar regimes of violence in which they can satiate their urges to dominate, violate, and dispose of their human chattel.

In the end, Dryden's anti-Islamic fantasy that a Muslim woman would convert to Christianity, steal from her father, and run off with a slave to Europe forestalls Antonio's dark fate at the hands of Johayma. For all of his promises of sexual drudgery and fawning, Antonio does later take heroic action by assaulting the Mufti, escaping, and then convincing Mustapha to work to overthrow the Emperor. Just as Almeyda briefly acts in a non-resistant manner that is inconsistent with her character, Antonio is briefly heroic in a way that is inconsistent with his. This forms part of a larger pattern of echo and reversal found in the play's structure. In the end, Dryden shows a flexibility about the issue of slave resistance—placed in the position of being socially dead, the slave can choose to comply or resist or, at times, both. The play does not ultimately endorse either strategy, but rather chooses to put them in dialectical tension, to force the audience to confront the ethical and practical choices faced by those who have been defeated and enslaved. In this way, *Don Sebastian* presents what is likely the most intellectually, emotionally, and formally complex exploration of the plight of slaves to be found on the Restoration and eighteenth-century stage.

Perhaps it is no surprise why Dryden turns to this remarkable examination of the limited options available to those who are defeated and enslaved since, at the time of the production and publication of *Don Sebastian*, he had encountered a tragic reversal of his own, moving from the Laureateship to the desperate position of a persecuted religious minority who had aligned himself with the losing side in the latest political upheaval. The Dryden who brought *Don Sebastian* to the stage was certainly not a heroic resister of the new order—after all, he neither exiled himself and joined the Stuart court in France—nor does he seem to have actively or clandestinely promoted the Jacobite cause in England.[23] The fact that so many scholars have debated at such length about the exact political meaning of *Don Sebastian* demonstrates just how cagey Dryden was on this occasion—the play engages with the political issues of the day and contains some sly critiques of the new Whig order, but it never comes close to issuing a heroic denunciation of the sovereignty of William and Mary.

Rather, Dryden's self-portrait in both the preface and the prologue align him much more with the type of resistance offered by Antonio than with the heroic confrontation of Sebastian and Almeyda. In these texts, he depicts himself as a beleaguered, reduced figure who has lost his position and income, who is subject to the power of his enemies, and who has returned to the stage despite his best intentions. In the preface, he tells his readers that he was brought "*against his will*" to write another play and that: "*While I continue in these bad circumstances, (and truly I see very little probability of coming out:) I must be oblig'd to write*" (65). Surrounded by "*Enemies enow to wish me yet in a worse condition*," Dryden returns to the stage, despite his reservations about the "*worn out*" nature of the genres he helped to popularize and the general denigration of theater culture in England. Later, he figures himself as a type of prisoner or slave who is "*condemn'd to dig in those exhausted Mines*" (65–66). The way that Dryden positions himself, as a person forced to "*please by writing*" (65) in order to better his position as a defeated, oppressed subject, is fascinating for the ways it parallels that of Antonio in the lower plot—both men turn to "diversion" in order to mitigate their reduced circumstances as, respectively, persecuted subject or abject slave.

This impression is further reinforced by the jocular prologue, in which Dryden addresses his degraded social and economic position in a different, more comedic register. In this text, he jokes about his "*loss of Pension*," and he meekly grovels before the audience by having the speaker acknowledge their power and implore their mercy towards Dryden: "*Your looks are cheerful; and in all this place/ I see not one, that wears a damning face./ The* British *Nation, is too brave to show,/ Ignoble vengeance, on a vanquish'd foe./ At least be civil to the Wretch imploring;/ And lay your Paws upon him, without roaring*" (5–10). Here, Dryden figures himself as a defeated subject who is beset by those who will surround and mishandle his body, much like Antonio in the chaotic slave market scene in the play. Later in the prologue, Dryden jokes about the extra restrictions and taxes imposed on Catholics and implores the new regime to "*Fine him to daily Drudging and Inditing;/ And let him pay his Taxes out, in Writing*" (45–46). This image draws a suggestive parallel to Antonio's sexual "drudgery" on behalf of Johayma in Act 4—each man is required to provide entertainments and pleasures to those who have power over him and is forced to beg for mercy and compassion from those same. Showing that they understand their new, subordinate positions, both speak in a comic, self-deprecating register and joke about their constrained circumstances in an attempt to disarm and partly subdue those who can do them harm.

At the end of the play, Antonio's path of non-resistance opens up fantastic possibilities of escape, wealth, and sexual happiness, while the heroic resistance of Sebastian and Almeyda ultimately leads only to incest and shame. The play gestures at the dark fates that await most slaves—rape, torture, abuse, and death—but swerves away from these into a fantasy world in which all the Portuguese slaves are freed in one way or another and in which, at least for Antonio, a triumphant Christian victory is snatched from the jaws of defeat, slavery, and death. In the epilogue to the play, Antonio and Morayma skewer the heroic values and self-sacrificial resolutions of the upper-plot. Discussing the fact that Sebastian and Almeyda forever part from each other after discovering that their marriage was incestuous, Morayma says that "*Without question/ Their Conscience was too queazy of digestion*" (Epilogue 15–16). Dryden suggests that while there is something magnificent about the heroic resistance and stubborn resolution of the tragic upper-plot characters, not all parties have the strength or even desire to follow their rigorous path, which adheres strictly to heroic and moral codes.

Rather, there is something to be said for those who show flexibility in matters of honor or morality when the situation calls for it and who employ their talents to entertain and please to further their own ends. Perhaps this is not the most "honorable" way to deal with political defeat or slavery, but the play suggests that it may be the more effective all the same. After all, a slave whose "honor" does not allow him to comply with his master's desires will be tortured and killed and in no position to take advantage, like Antonio, of a change in circumstances and an unlikely opportunity for freedom and effective resistance. While the open-ended tragicomic form allows no easy or final answers, Dryden seems especially attracted to this idea since it is quite useful for formulating a suggestive defense of his own diverting strategy for dealing with the Glorious Revolution. If this is true, then the preface and prologue to *Don Sebastian* ultimately leave us with an image of Dryden as a type of defeated and enslaved man, a talented and entertaining "drudge" who is willing, for the time being, to divert the Williamite nation with expertly crafted and formally complex drama and to bide his time, waiting for one more miraculous historical reversal to restore him to his past positions and freedoms. At the same time, the play as a whole gives us the impression of Dryden as a person who was deeply engaged with the issue of slavery, its grotesque violations of the human body and spirit, and the possible responses of those held in its grasp. Bringing together these two critical emphases is the best way to engage with the formal and intellectual complexity of the play and with Dryden's central place in a Restoration literary culture that was concerned not only with domestic politics but also with global affairs of empire and slavery.

NOTES

1. For a rare example of a scholar who reads *Don Sebastian* with *Oroonoko*, see Rose A. Zimbardo, "The Late Seventeenth-Century Dilemma in Discourse: Dryden's *Don Sebastian* and Behn's *Oroonoko*," in *Rhetorics of Order/Ordering Rhetorics in English Neoclassical Literature*, ed. J. Douglas Canfield and J. Paul Hunter (Newark: Univ. of Delaware Press, 1989), 46–67. The essay, however, has almost nothing to say about literary representations of slavery, but focuses on questions of literary form.

2. Patterson, *Slavery and Social Death: A Comparative Study* (Cambridge, MA: Harvard Univ. Press, 1982). Patterson's account remains one of the most valuable and comprehensive studies of slavery to date.

3. Kroll, *Restoration Drama and 'The Circle of Commerce': Tragicomedy, Politics, and Trade in the Seventeenth Century* (New York: Cambridge Univ. Press, 2007), 21, 23. For an excellent earlier reading of the thematic relationship between the two plots, including an insightful discussion of slavery, see Derek Hughes, "Dryden's *Don Sebastian* and the Literature of Heroism," *The Yearbook of English Studies* 12 (1982): 72–90.

4. For the most recent readings of *Don Sebastian* that emphasize the political issues of the play as well as its engagement with the events and theories surrounding the Glorious Revolution, see Jeffrey Galbraith, "The Performance of 'Pious Fraud': Reading Passive Obedience in Dryden's *Don Sebastian* (1689)," *Restoration* 36 (2012): 23–40; Stuart Sim and David Walker, *The Discourse of Sovereignty, Hobbes*

to Fielding: The State of Nature and the Nature of the State (Burlington, VT: Ashgate, 2003), 115–31; Duane Coltharp, "Radical Royalism: Strategy and Ambivalence in Dryden's Tragicomedies," *Philological Quarterly* 78 (1999): 417–37; Steven N. Zwicker, *Lines of Authority: Politics and English Literary Culture, 1649–1689* (Ithaca: Cornell Univ. Press, 1993); Hugh MacCallum, "'A track of Glory': Dryden's *Don Sebastian* and the Tragedy of Heroic Leadership," *Restoration* 19 (1995): 43–54; David Bywaters, *Dryden in Revolutionary England* (Berkeley: Univ. of California Press, 1991); and James Anderson Winn, *John Dryden and His World* (New Haven: Yale Univ. Press, 1987), 438–42.

5. Visconsi, *Lines of Equity: Literature and the Origins of Law in Later Stuart England* (Ithaca: Cornell Univ. Press, 2008). In Visconsi's account, plays like *The Indian Emperor* allow Dryden to confront his audience with ambiguous and unsettling questions that have no easy answers in the attempt to help them cultivate their powers of "equity," which is the ability to decide difficult cases or issues with openness and fairness (35–74).

6. Orr, *Empire on the English Stage 1660–1714* (Cambridge: Cambridge Univ. Press, 2001), 3.

7. Kroll extends this type of reading to Aphra Behn's *Oroonoko* as well. In "'Tales of Love and Gallantry': The Politics of *Oroonoko*," *Huntington Library Quarterly* 67 (2004): 573–605, he argues that: "*Oroonoko* is therefore not a novel; nor is it a quasi-sociological account of the conditions of slavery or emerging colonialism. It is in fact Behn's desperate attempt between 10 and 29 June 1688 to warn James II that if he continues on the path he has described since his accession, he risks suffering the same fate as his father" (578). This argument is rather rigid in its insistence that the novel can only be about one subject and also that Behn's interests in colonial slavery and the fate of James II were mutually exclusive.

8. Orr, *Empire on the English Stage 1660–1714*, 167.

9. Orr, *Empire on the English Stage 1660–1714*, 169. For a similar argument that Dryden uses the play to critique Whig claims about supposed political "slavery" in England, see Zwicker, *Lines of Authority*, 191–2.

10. Matar, *Britain and Barbary, 1589–1689* (Gainesville: Univ. Press of Florida, 2005), 167–70, and de Sousa, "Portugal, North Africa, and Dryden's *Don Sebastian*," *CLIO* 37 (2008): 339–63.

11. Dryden, *Don Sebastian, King of Portugal* in *The Works of John Dryden*, Vol. 15, ed. Harold Miner (Los Angeles: Univ. of California Press, 1976), 72. All subsequent citations will be found in the text.

12. Patterson, *Slavery and Social Death*, 173.

13. Matar, *Britain and Barbary*, 169–70.

14. For a discussion of Dryden's engagement with the doctrine of "passive obedience and non-resistance" that informed political debate at the time of the Glorious Revolution, see Galbraith, "The Performance of 'Pious Fraud'." For an important recent discussion of these issues in *Oroonoko*, see Corrinne Harol, "The Passion of Oroonoko: Passive Obedience, The Royal Slave, and Aphra Behn's Baroque Realism," *ELH* 79 (2012): 447–475.

15. The term "postures" recalls both the thirty-six sexual "postures" depicted in

Pietro Aretino's *La puttana errante* as well as Pepys's comments on the "postures of lust and buggery" performed in public by the libertines Charles Sedley and Charles Dorset. For an account of both, see James Grantham Turner, *Libertines and Radicals in Early Modern London: Sexuality, Politics, and Literary Culture, 1630–1685* (Cambridge: Cambridge Univ. Press, 2002), 129 and 209. For another reading of the episode with Sedley and Dorset, see Jeremy W. Webster, *Performing Libertinism in Charles II's Court: Politics, Drama, Sexuality* (New York: Palgrave Macmillan, 2005), 3–8.

16. Orr, *Empire on the English Stage 1660–1714*, 169. For a reading that claims the scene is farcical, see Zimbardo, "The Late Seventeenth-Century Dilemma in Discourse," 59.

17. Matar, *Turks, Moors, and Englishmen in the Age of Discovery* (New York: Columbia Univ. Press, 1999), 109–27.

18. Colley, *Captives* (New York: Pantheon Books, 2002), 129. For an important work that investigates homosexuality in the Arab-Islamic world and that provides a valuable supplement to the work of Colley and Matar, see Khaled El-Rouayheb, *Before Homosexuality in the Arab-Islamic World, 1500–1800* (Chicago: Univ. of Chicago Press, 2005). For my purposes, El-Rouayheb's account of Arab-Islamic attitudes towards the homosexual rape of slaves is invaluable in that he quotes many Arabic sources that condemn this practice but that also assume that it was widespread. See for example 39–41.

19. If so, Dryden is participating in a wider discourse on this subject that equated rape with the political defeat of the Stuarts. On this point, see Toni Bowers, *Force or Fraud: British Seduction Stories and the Problem of Resistance, 1660–1760* (New York: Oxford Univ. Press, 2011), 46.

20. On this point, see the work of Aliyyah I. Abdur-Rahman, "'The Strangest Freaks of Despotism': Queer Sexuality in Antebellum African American Slave Narratives," *African American Review* 40 (2006): 223–37. I have been inspired by Abdur-Rahman's argument that slave institutions create both male and female slaves as "socially and sexually abject" (230), which renders them vulnerable "to nearly every conceivable violation" (231) at the hands of their masters. While developed in relation to plantation slavery in the American south, her insights seem widely applicable to the lives of all slaves.

21. In "Dryden's *Don Sebastian* and the Literature of Heroism," Hughes argues for a strong tonal shift once Antonio is enslaved in the Mufti's garden. He comments that "Antonio seemingly moves into a less menacing world," that "he quickly becomes inured to and oblivious of his slavery," and that he now inhabits a "benign dream world of comedy" (88).

22. See Toni Bowers, *Force or Fraud*, for an argument that similar explorations of resistance were central to Tory thinking from the 1670s on and especially after 1688. She shows how Tory novelists like Behn, Manley, and Haywood turned to seduction stories and their representations of "sexual coercions" in order to "comment on the possibility and meaning(s) of virtue in any relation of unequally distributed power" (51). Dryden is clearly thinking through similar issues in *Don Sebastian*. While few would think of Antonio as trying to maintain "virtue" in the same manner

as the heroines of Tory-inflected seduction fiction, he does work through his own particular version of what Bowers calls "'collusive resistance'—a paradoxical exercise of *resistance through submission*" (4).

23. For an excellent account of Dryden's extremely cautious maneuverings in the immediate aftermath of the Revolution, see Winn, *John Dryden and His World*, 433–47.

"Interloping with my Question-Project": Debating Genre in John Dunton's and Daniel Defoe's Epistolary Periodicals

RACHAEL SCARBOROUGH KING

In the first decades of the eighteenth century, two of London's most notorious and influential print pioneers engaged in a personal and professional dispute that left a lasting impact on what would become the public genre *par excellence*: the periodical. This essay explores the underappreciated connection between John Dunton and Daniel Defoe, and its consequences for developing concepts of authorship, publication, and authority, as it materialized in the epistolary periodical, a crucial turn-of-the-century genre. While the wide-scale use of reader letters in early periodicals has been acknowledged if not fully appreciated in contemporary scholarship, Dunton and Defoe devoted copious space to both printing and commenting on submitted correspondence. In Dunton's question-and-answer paper, *The Athenian Mercury* (1691–7), and Defoe's periodical essay, the *Review* (1704–13), and journalistic work, *The Storm* (1704), the authors debated the role of manuscript letters in the "public prints" in a way that highlighted the periodical as a vehicle for community information, opinion, and expertise. In the early, experimental periodical form, an epistolary metadiscourse emerged that filtered the status of print publication through the discussion of letters. This pervasive self-reflexivity would remain a defining feature of the periodical genre.[1]

Printed periodical news and opinion was still a "new thing," in Defoe's words, when the two men began writing, and they emerged from the same community of dissenting printers and preachers.[2] But while they were at one time collaborators, their relationship quickly soured. In Dunton's memoirs, the prolific bookseller, author, and printer accused Defoe of plagiarism, or of what Dunton termed "Interloping with my *Question-Project*."[3] The "Question-Project," also known as "Athenianism," was Dunton's phrase for his genre-defining periodical, *The Athenian Mercury*, which scholars now agree was Britain's first question-and-answer paper.[4] It consisted of purportedly reader-supplied questions and the answers of the "Athenian Society," which claimed up to a dozen members but in fact included only Dunton and two associates. In a 1706 work, Dunton wrote that Defoe had "done me a sensible Wrong" by adopting the question-and-answer format in Defoe's own news miscellany, the *Review*.[5] While Dunton had no qualms about plagiarism of content, as *The Athenian Mercury* constantly reprinted existing texts as answers to questions, he considered the genre of the question-and-answer his literary "Property," calling the "Design" the "Child of my Brain."[6] The quarrel with Defoe concerned Dunton's self-perceived prominence as a generic inventor.

Dunton's ire notwithstanding, the extent of Defoe's plagiarism is highly debatable.[7] While the *Mercury* consisted entirely of lists of readers' queries, the *Review* followed its news sections with supplemental letters, not all of which drew responses from the author. I will return to the question of Defoe's debt to Dunton. But what I want to emphasize here is how Dunton's unfamiliar notion of intellectual property—which located originality not in the author's writing but in the print worker's novel use of genre—modeled a cyclical and communal version of authorship and readership, one that depended on the cooperation of readers as contributors. By foregrounding reader letters, Dunton and Defoe were able simultaneously to take a number of actions necessary in their unstable literary milieu: to foster and coordinate reader communities; to put forward a notion of collectivity that helped legitimate their anonymous, unfamiliar texts; and to interrogate the shifting relationship between manuscript and print as media of publication. Jody Greene and Mark Rose have each demonstrated the instability in concepts of originality and literary property evident in the period between the lapse of the Licensing Act in 1695 and the first "Copyright Act" of 1710, an instability that I argue Dunton and Defoe both assuaged and took advantage of through their extensive incorporation of reader letters.[8] Early periodicals created literary circuits in which participants could oscillate between the positions of reader and writer; their insistent heterogeneity and multi-vocality offered readers a stake in the texts through the possibility to challenge the editors on matters of fact, politics, and literary style.[9]

At the same time as these periodical authors trumpeted communal knowledge, they began to differentiate between manuscript and printed texts and to elevate the editor for his role in mediating between letter writers and public readers.[10] As Dunton attacked Defoe for "stealing" the question-and-answer format, and as Defoe defended his methods against both Dunton and later competitors, a shift materialized: while the earlier author displayed an omnivorous media appetite that viewed any piece of writing as fodder for circulation, the later began to divide manuscript and print into what we would recognize as a more modern hierarchical schema. As Defoe praised manuscript for its authenticity but print for its preservative and authoritative status, his self-reflexive commentary on printed letters initiated nascent divisions between writing and printing, readers and authors, private and public. These topics would remain at the forefront of periodical writing throughout the eighteenth century.

In this essay, I draw together two fields of inquiry that have recently received prominent scholarly attention—periodical and epistolary studies—to offer a new understanding of the centrality of letters to early periodicals. Scholars of periodicals have established the genre as an "especially important and lively subfield" of print culture, showing how its takeoff signaled print's impact and set the stage for the emergence of the novel.[11] Printed periodicals have been "given a place of privilege in the foundation of the public sphere" because they were seen to enable, for the first time, the wide-scale discussion of politics and culture.[12] Meanwhile, studies of seventeenth- and eighteenth-century letters describe epistolarity as multimodal, not print-centric. The prominence of the letter genre in periodicals, novels, and magazines demonstrates that the "relationship between script and print is emphatically simultaneous not sequential: that is, correspondence and printed letters co-existed in multiple and complex ways."[13] Even as critics recognize this media interconnection, however, recent epistolary studies have tended to shift away from printed letters—in particular, from the epistolary novel, the focus of much earlier scholarship—and toward archival study of manuscript correspondence.[14] Despite the acknowledged scope of printed letters, scant attention has been paid to the complicated nature of epistolary periodicals.[15]

Given the ongoing scholarly divide between printed periodicals and manuscript correspondence, the letters in early periodicals have generally been understood in two ways. First, they served as "truth claims" whose goal was to establish credibility and legitimacy. J. Paul Hunter argues that documents like letters, diaries, and eyewitness notes are important to late seventeenth-century narrative because they "assert factuality" and "claim to represent what the present-day world was like."[16] Such fact-establishing writings were part of a larger trend in which all sorts of texts, including those we now identify as fictional, included elaborate declarations of truth. Second, letters played a role in generating the public sphere by, paradoxically, representing the private. Critics including Kathryn Shevelow, Michael McKeon, and Manushag Powell explain the early periodical as a site for the public discussion of private concerns, such as familial relationships and gender roles, which often appeared in the guise of reader letters.[17] The periodical was crucial to the public sphere, these critics argue, because it drew a contrast between the publicity of print and the privacy of manuscript.

But early modern and eighteenth-century letters complicate binary distinctions between manuscript and print and between the present-day categories of private and public with which each medium is often associated. Readers and writers did not see a direct relationship between the genre of the letter and privacy or the domestic sphere: letters were often written in groups and read aloud, with multiple people advising or adding notes in a process of "social transaction."[18] Letters from this period also raise multilayered questions of authorship, since they were frequently dictated to clerks or compiled from the stock phrases of epistolary manuals and commonplace books.[19] They were metadiscursive texts, almost always including discussion of systemic features such as handwriting, postage, paper quality, length, and the possibility of interception. As studies of social authorship—Margaret Ezell's term for the communal, fluid nature of manuscript publication—have shown, manuscript continued to be a vital medium for the creation and circulation of literary and scientific texts into the mid-eighteenth century, one that emphasized "interactive, dynamic, and ongoing exchange" among groups of readers.[20] By grounding discussions of authorship, authority, and medium in the genre of the letter, the era's epistolary periodicals engaged, complicated, and, perhaps, subverted many of these characteristics of manuscript circulation. For Dunton, attention to epistolary discourse and media of communication brought to the fore questions of authorship, originality, and literary property. For Defoe, it led to concerns with proof, truth, and authenticity. The capacious form of the epistolary periodical enabled each author to propose and scrutinize printing innovations at a moment of almost unprecedented change in the literary marketplace.

Epistolary community in *The Athenian Mercury*

John Dunton's breakout hit, *The Athenian Mercury*, offers a useful starting point for consideration of eighteenth-century periodical publishing trends, but Dunton's claims of absolute novelty notwithstanding, it also emerged from an existing tradition of printed letters.[21] The first printed news sources, including newsbooks in the 1640s and newspapers in the 1660s, gathered their news from diplomatic, mercantile, and personal correspondence, referring constantly to "letters received" as their source of information. Political pamphlets frequently styled themselves as letters from "a gentleman in town to his friend in the country," while collections of "found" letters, such as *Familiar Letters: Written by the Right Honourable John late Earl of Rochester, and several other Persons of Honour and Quality (1697)* and *The Post-boy Rob'd of His Mail: Or, The Pacquet Broke Open* (1692), provided both actual letters and early epistolary fiction.[22] And a scholarly periodical like the *Philosophical Transactions of the Royal Society*, while not presented in the question-and-answer format, printed ongoing reader correspondence and distributed questionnaires for foreign travelers. Whether readers believed they were reading "real" letters or saw the letter genre as a convenient framing device, "[t]he reading public in Britain and the colonies was thoroughly accustomed to encountering letters everywhere in print culture."[23]

From this perspective, Dunton seems a figure of pure print culture, a proto-Benjamin Franklin who viewed his own life as a printer's "case" to be set, impressed, and altered like so many pieces of type. His constant writing and printing displayed a new mode of expressing subjectivity in print, in which "knowing himself became publishing himself, personal identity a matter of finding himself on the page," and the "discursive mobility" of the printing press enabled a series of "experiments at getting print to work in his favor."[24] He was aware of both the material and imaginative possibilities of the press, which he viewed as an extension of himself—a technological "prosthesis"—that was an appropriate medium for almost all of his writings.[25] But he was no less interested in the possibilities and procedures of manuscript composition and, in particular, in the omnipresent genre of the letter, which formed the backbone of his most famous literary novelty. Epistolarity allowed Dunton to engage a number of themes that recurred across his career: a disavowal of the title of author (he preferred "scribbler" or "rambler" when describing himself) combined with a fierce claim to generic originality; a tenuously upheld promise to maintain his own and his correspondents' anonymity; and a sense that any text was open to future improvement and emendation through an ongoing cycle of provocation and response. He operated in a literary environment in which the border between personal letters and print was not clearly demarcated; his *Mercury* made this state of affairs apparent.

Dunton seems to have viewed almost any text, written or printed, as material for his own authorial efforts, a fact his surviving correspondence reveals. Over the course of his career, he rarely published a work that did not include significant epistolary aspects, whether it was his use of letters from his wife and mother-in-law to "prove" that he was justified in seeking a loan of £300 from his wife's jointure, or his frequent reprinting of a "letter to his creditors" to avoid arrest for his debts. He marked incoming letters with brackets and other printing instructions. For example, at the top of a tender, conciliatory, and laboriously inscribed letter from his estranged wife, Sarah, dated July 1699, Dunton scrawled, "For a letter to Incognito," a name he used to sign printed epistles.[26] Two years later, Sarah lashed out at him for using her letters "too banter an laugh att me an my mother by your magoty printen."[27] Another correspondent, who signed his 1710 letter "JW" and warned Dunton against printing more letters from a female acquaintance, ended with a similar accusation: "There's no writing to a man that prints every Thing."[28] The question-and-answer concept obviated this objection; in the periodical, Dunton printed not "found" or "rob'd" letters but those whose authors affirmatively wanted to see their words in print.

Claiming ownership in the genre of the question-and-answer, which he described as his "sole Right and Property," thus allowed Dunton the benefits of both novelty and imitation.[29] He could use reader letters to produce large quantities of text and tap into the existing trend for printed letters while offering greater participation and interaction to the reading community. He could also assert his property in the paper and its "design" even though his two collaborators, Richard Sault and Samuel Wesley, did much of the actual writing. Dunton did have some justification for his grandiose claims as he appears to have been one of the earliest authors explicitly to solicit letters to the editor and to use the conceit of a club of respondents to create the sense of collective investigation. This sense spread rapidly: by the paper's second weekly number, the authors were thanking readers for their "encouragement by a great many Letters to continue our Gazett" and promising to "endeavour as general a satisfaction as we can."[30] While there is no known cache of letters sent to the *Mercury* to prove actual reader response, as exists in the case of *The Tatler* and *The Spectator*, the authors' constant references to incoming letters, and their requests to readers not to re-send letters or ask previously answered questions, indicate a popular reaction. Dunton stimulated reader identification with the periodical as he claimed to recognize repeat writers' "hands," invited female correspondents and set aside special women's issues, and noted that his paper provided an ideal source of coffeehouse "Chatt and Entertainment."[31]

Because the process of writing and receiving letters was so central to the printed periodical's stated mission, epistolary topics soon came to comprise a significant chunk of the paper's content. The *Mercury*, like any letter, featured constant and sudden shifts from topic to topic. The fourth number, of April

4, 1691, began with the question "Whether there is a Vacuum?" followed by "What is the cause of Titillation?" (meaning tickling), "Why doth the Hair and Nails of dead People grow?" and finally "What sort of Government is the best?"[32] There was a steady stream of interest in the publication itself, the letters it received, the people who sent them, and the timeliness with which the authors responded to readers. In the advertisement to the first issue, of March 17, 1691, readers were told to expect the "Resolution" of their questions "by the next Weekly Paper after their sending."[33] By the third number two weeks later, the authors noted that, since "the Questions grow so fast upon us, among which are several Duplicates with Complaints of their not being yet answered," they had decided to increase the publication schedule to twice weekly, on the post days of Tuesday and Saturday.[34] On April 11, correspondents were asked to hold off on sending more questions until the current backlog had been addressed. The authors claimed in the preface to the second volume, just two months after beginning the project, that they had already received more than 4,000 questions; this theme of an overworked Athenian Society continued for years. In September 1691 they appealed, "we must earnestly desire all persons whom it may concern, to hold their *Hands* and *Pens*, and let us take *Breath a while*, and get rid of those *CART-LOADS* of *Questions* which are yet upon the File, and are likely to press us to death under their weight."[35]

Indeed, the paper's author-editors were unequivocal about the debt they owed to their "Querists" in supplying content. The device was ideal not only because it was, in Dunton's words, "surprizing and unthought-of," but also because it provided easy copy.[36] In the preface to the first volume, Sault and Wesley wrote, "those concerned in the Composition … are not very ambitious to the name of Authors."[37] The goal was not to produce new knowledge, but to circulate it in a new form. The writers noted that they should "be glad of better Information; and when it appears will very willingly retract their Errors."[38] The Athenians deferred to readers and cited their sources, naming Aristotle, Descartes, Boyle, and the *Philosophical Transactions of the Royal Society* as authorities. They acknowledged the benefits of the epistolary genre, writing in December 1691, "'tis to Us much easier to write the Volume than the Preface, because half of one is supply'd to our Hands, but all the other must be pure Invention."[39] But they faced reader critique that the periodical read too much like a commonplace book; as one querist asked in July 1691, "Why [do] you pretend to such strange things, and yet in effect tell the World nothing but what we all know already?" Dunton's response: "what one may know, another does not, and diffusing knowledge is a sort of improving it, perhaps the best way."[40] The best defense of his design was to "diffuse" knowledge and authority through a community of readers and writers. The "epistolary pact" of the *Athenian Mercury* meant that any reader was also potentially a correspondent: "To read the periodical was, at least theoretically, to be empowered to write, thus to assume complicity in the production of the text."[41] But while Dunton disclaimed authorship of his text, he jealously guarded the question-and-answer format of the work and attacked those, including but not limited to Defoe, who "interloped" upon his terrain.

This not-quite-modern notion of literary property stands counter to the contemporary distinction between an idea in general and the copyrightable expression of that idea. It allowed Dunton to position his readership as an interactive community and to disperse authority for the text among the group. By figuring periodical publication as epistolary conversation, in which any reader unhappy with an answer could request "a fuller satisfaction in the next Paper," Dunton integrated the continuous, exchange-oriented logic of letter writing into the realm of print.[42] But the new medium also afforded changed possibilities; as Dunton wrote in his memoirs, the genesis of the "question-Project" lay in anonymity: "the first rude *Hint* of it, was no more than *a confus'd Idea of concealing the Querist and answering his Question.*"[43] The authors continued in the preface to the first volume: "The Design is briefly… to remove those Difficulties and Dissatisfactions, that shame or fear of appearing ridiculous by asking Questions, may cause several Persons to labour under, who now have opportunities of being resolv'd in any Question without knowing their Informer."[44] While some correspondents signed their real names to their questions, and while the makeup of the "society" may "have been an open secret at least within bookselling and publishing circles,"[45] the normative stance of the publication was to favor "secrecy." And as Lawrence Klein and Patricia Meyer Spacks have shown, this was the primary eighteenth-century meaning of "privacy," which referred more to a distinction between open and closed intelligence than to one between public and domestic spheres.[46] While we now associate personal letters with privacy, they in fact lacked secrecy, as they were subject to interception by parents, husbands, or government agents, or to requests to be read aloud. The Athenian Society, meanwhile, was "fix'd … both as to Number and Privacy," but was "willing to receive any Gentleman's Thoughts upon what we write."[47] The printed letter, as the Athenians figured it, enabled a level of "privacy" that surpassed that of manuscript.

By focusing on the importance of epistolary secrecy and anonymity, insisting that the *Mercury* was written by a society and never signing his name to the paper even as he claimed the "sole Right and Property" in the question-and-answer genre, Dunton positioned himself simultaneously as printer, bookseller, newsmonger, author, editor, reader, and correspondent.

This profusion of paradoxical impulses may help explain why he was unable to keep up with the print marketplace as tastes apparently shifted toward a more codified, hierarchical relation between readers and producers. In 1710, Dunton's correspondent "JW" advised him, "if you have Essays or Letters that are valuable, call 'em Essays & Letters in short and plain language, & if you have any thing writ by men of sense & on subjects of consequence it may sell," but added, "Such Titles as Athenian Phoenix … are so senseless & impertinent that 'twould spoil the credit of any author that should use them."[48] Indeed, Dunton seems to have been unable to cope with the overall surge in competition occasioned by the lapse of the Licensing Act in 1695 as the *Mercury* rapidly declined before folding in 1697. While he tried to continue capitalizing on the paper's success, signing books "by a member of the Athenian Society," he never recaptured the *Mercury*'s influence and spent his later years ineffectually ranting against former colleagues in hundreds of pages of memoirs.

It is in these texts that Defoe, known at the time as a Whig hack writer, repeatedly appears. One of Defoe's first published poems was titled "To the Athenian Society" and appeared, attributed to "D.F.," among other dedicatory poems at the opening of Charles Gildon's *History of the Athenian Society* (1692). In his memoirs, Dunton praised Defoe as "a Man of good Parts, and very clear sense," but added that Defoe suffered from "not only the ITCH and Inclination, but the *Necessity* of writing."[49] These attacks stemmed from the question of literary property; as Dunton wrote, "To this (sneaking) Injustice of *Interloping*, Foe has added that of *Reprinting a Copy* he gave me," an act that usurped Dunton's rights as a printer.[50] Dunton blamed Defoe for adopting the question-and-answer form in the *Review*, but the innovation had already become a transportable genre divorced from any individual progenitor. In the experimental literary environment of the early eighteenth century, Dunton—who advocated for reinstatement of the Licensing Act—was unable to maintain his "property" in the question-and-answer.

Authenticity and authority in Defoe's print periodicals

The first issue of Defoe's *Review of the Affairs of France* appeared in February 1704, when Dunton was busy trying to recover his Athenian authority. Despite the widespread adoption of reader letters in other periodicals, Dunton seems to have singled out Defoe, whom Dunton critiqued in multiple texts and quoted by name on the title page of his self-justifying memoirs, *The Life and Errors of John Dunton Late Citizen of London* (1705): "He that has all his own Mistakes confest,/ Stands next to him that never has transgrest,/ And will be censur'd for a Fool by none,/ But they who see no ERRORS of their own./ *Foe*'s Satyr upon himself."[51] Regardless of Dunton's continual plagiarism charges, Defoe varied the *Athenian Mercury* model in the *Review*. He used readers' letters not as the main text but as a supplement, or, as he wrote, a "little Diversion … at the end of every Paper."[52] Not all of the letters to the *Review*'s "Scandalous Club" required specific answers; many were commentaries on the *Review* or other periodicals, while others discussed public affairs or readers' remarks in earlier numbers. That is, the letters in the *Review* functioned much more like present-day letters to the editor than like the "Dear Abby" style of the *Athenian Mercury*. As with letters to the editor, Defoe dispensed with them when space demanded.[53] While presenting his work as a newspaper, he had actually shifted to essayistic opinion writing, subordinating reader response to his own polemical articles on politics, finance, and culture: "He was there to argue about the events of the time—to satirize the wrong view and to assure his readers that his interpretation of events was the proper one."[54] By altering Dunton's question-and-answer format, Defoe moved the periodical toward a model in which a central eidolon would monitor and coordinate a more authoritarian reading experience.[55]

Defoe's periodicals included extensive reflection on his own and other news writers' use of the letter genre. From the beginning to the end of his career and in works of poetry, news, and fiction, he dwelled constantly on the material circumstances of writing for "the World" in the early eighteenth century. In doing so, he developed a media-centric interest in fact, proof, and authority that laid the groundwork for later associations of print with fixity and truth and of manuscript with ephemerality and rumor.[56] But even as his writing normatively contrasted the reliability of print with the instability of manuscript, in practice he positioned letters as proof of his printed assertions, delegating authority to the handwritten "original." By reading the *Review* alongside his journalistic work of the same year, *The Storm*, we can better understand how Defoe used reader correspondence not merely to claim a (perhaps spurious) factuality, but also, and more broadly, to work through the oscillating relationship between manuscript and print as media of authority. In the question-and-answer sections, he engaged directly with the print marketplace and the shifting nature of periodical authorship in the early eighteenth century.[57]

While Defoe, unlike Dunton, rarely mentioned his rival by name, he appears to have been self-conscious about potential comparisons; in the preface to the 1705 collected edition of the *Review*'s first volume, he noted that "Receiving or Answering Letters of Doubts, Difficulties, Cases and Questions … was the remotest thing from my first Design of any thing in the

World; and I could be heartily Glad, the Reader of this Paper would excuse me from it yet,—But I see it cannot be, and the World will have it done."[58] He did, however, continually critique the best-known newspapers of the new century, not by claiming ownership in the periodical genre but by claiming competency in its conventions—one of which was the use of letters. Part of almost every *Review of the Affairs of France* was taken up with commentary on what Defoe terms the "Errors and Nonsense of our News-Writers."[59] He gave an example in the first issue, as he mocked "*The London Post* of the 21st of *August* last, where in Advice from the *Hague*, by way of *Lisbon*, we are acquainted with some News from *Paris*." He sarcastically continued: "this is just as Direct an Intelligence, as if they shou'd say, *There are Letters from* Jamaica, *by the last* East India *Ship, which give a more particular Account of a great Fight in* Flanders."[60] A few weeks later, Defoe charged the author of *The Post-Man* with "filling up his Papers with long Harangues of his own, and making News for us, when the Posts were not come in to supply."[61] That is, while other authors only pretended to have letters to authenticate their news, Defoe repeatedly promised to leave the "originals" of his readers' letters with his printer, "for any Person to peruse that doubts the Truth of them."[62] This verification was the more necessary in a "publick print," he noted, as "I cannot satisfie my self to say any thing in Print, without either being very sure of my Authorities, or letting the World know upon what Foot, as to Credit, they are to take it."[63] "Credit" and "Authority" derived from the letter, the backup to Defoe's printed assertions.[64]

As in the *Review*, where Defoe affirmed communal authorship by denying that he was the actual author of his printed letters, in *The Storm* he repeatedly asserted the material existence of the correspondence he used to create the text; the "fact" of the letters' existence served to authenticate the "facts" conveyed in the writing. In this, his first book-length work, he married the innovations of periodical publication to the established position of the codex format. When the Great Storm struck in late 1703—killing more than 8,000 people and destroying innumerable buildings, particularly in Bristol and London[65]—Defoe immediately interpreted it as a national news event. Five days after the storm, he placed advertisements in two London papers, the *Daily Courant* and the *Gazette*, in which he announced his intention to "preserve the Remembrance of the late Dreadful Tempest" with an "exact and faithful Collection" of stories.[66] He asked witnesses to send him letters describing the storm, and the account he produced presented about 70 letters interspersed with his own narration, selections from scientific treatises, and sermons given before and after the hurricane. As had Dunton before him, Defoe deflected his authorial position in *The Storm*, calling himself the "Editor" or "Compiler" of the work and writing that he gave "the World the

Particulars from [his correspondents'] own Mouths, and under their own Hands."[67] His "Method … of Printing Letters from the Country in their own Stile" allowed him to "keep close to the Truth, and hand my Relation with the true Authorities from whence I receiv'd it."[68] He included his correspondents' names, places of residence, and, often, occupations. Once again, communal knowledge was required to produce journalistic authority.

But while Defoe insisted that the epistolary, handwritten source of the work's content vouchsafed its authenticity, the letters' remediation into print created concerns as well. Large portions of the book were taken up with asserting and explaining the truth of his narrative and in particular with exploring the role that print could play in creating a factual record. He established a hierarchy of scale in the first line of the work, writing, "Preaching of Sermons is Speaking to a few of Mankind: Printing of Books is Talking to the whole World." He continued: "[I]f a Book Printed obtrudes a Falshood, if a Man tells a Lye in Print, he abuses Mankind, and imposes upon the whole World, he causes our Children to tell Lyes after us, and their Children after them, to the End of the World."[69] Thus, before he could begin his narrative of what happened, he felt compelled to discuss the question of how he knew what happened and what was the best way to transmit this information. Print publication, he argued, placed more rigorous requirements on the author and historian than did speech or manuscript: "where a Story is vouch'd to him with sufficient authority, he ought to give the World the Special Testimonial of its proper Voucher."[70] In *The Storm*, that voucher is the handwritten letter, amplified and given additional weight, but also complicated and perhaps undercut, by the medium of print.

The letter genre offered Defoe a method to prove through print, a function that was in need of explicit elaboration in the early eighteenth century. In *The Storm*, he contrasted the letters' supposedly reliable authenticity with the sections of his narrative that were "abstracted from the publick Prints" and, therefore, "not particularly vouch'd." As he continued, "several Branches of this Story … were too easily credited, and put in Print," a mistake he rectified by collecting "Letters from the respective Places where such things have happen'd."[71] Whether or not *The Storm* and the *Review* included "actual" letters (although it seems safest to assume that both works comprise a mix of letters that Defoe received in the mail and wrote himself), his recourse was to the media characteristics of the source text. Manuscript represented a personal level of proof that print could not yet attain. The epistolary metadiscourse of the early periodical created an emphasis on secrecy and testimony—on the specific, perceived ability of the letter to bear witness to the truth within a community of readers. By relying on letters to structure and support his news writings, Defoe placed his works in the world of epistolary communication, with which readers were familiar, and he brought this world into the realm of print.

But Defoe's epistolary journalism also always exposed a gap that print could not cover, whether it was between the printed letter and its manuscript original—with irreproducible elements such as handwriting, postmarks, and folding—or between the letter and the speech in whose place it supposedly stood. His early works often expressed a sense of this abyss, which he tried to cover but, in fact, further revealed by stressing his sources' status as eyewitnesses of the events he was reporting. As author of *The Storm*, he described himself as an "Eye-witness and Sharer of the Particulars," and the "Testimony" of the letters came from those who were also "Eye-witnesses."[72] By reading the letters, the reader transforms into a kind of eyewitness as the plain style of the prose enhances its factual status: "The Plainness and Honesty of the Story will plead for the Meanness of the Stile in many of the Letters, and the Reader cannot want Eyes to see what sort of People some of them come from."[73] But he also betrayed doubts about his ability to convey the "literal truth" of his facts and feelings to the reader. "No Pen can describe it, no Tongue can express it, no Thought conceive it, unless [of] some of those who were in the Extremity of it," he wrote of the storm, questioning the reliability of his printed book despite the apparent superfluity of "authentick Vouchers" in the form of letters.[74] Remarkably, he repeated this sentence almost verbatim in *Roxana* twenty years later; when Roxana reunites with her long-lost daughter, she writes, "No Pen can describe, no Words can express, *I say*, the strange Impression which this thing made upon my Spirits."[75] Defoe's early journalism offered a language for describing not only proof and truth but also the failure of print accurately to depict and transmit.

Scholars have tended to look to Defoe's journalistic writings to explain his later novels, and they have offered persuasive analyses of the relationship between the two.[76] I argue, however, that we should view Defoe's journalism not primarily as preparation for the series of fictions he wrote toward the end of his life but as essential to understanding his methods and preoccupations throughout his prolific career, and as central to developing definitions of the periodical genre. These writings offer key evidence of his authorial strategies and self-positioning in the media landscape. The *Review*'s overt concern with its own relationship to other periodicals betrays a fixation on the conditions of the marketplace as almost every issue of its first two years included some critique of the London newspapers' reporting, grammar, or subject matter. Defoe highlighted questions of proof and fact in order to differentiate his own writing in a forum that was already beginning to seem crowded. The letter became important as a genre of proof because it was a personal document that could stand in for a named source of authority, lending that authority to the more anonymous and, thus, undependable print medium.

In this way, the *Review* and *The Storm* point toward a shift in ideas about the printed letter. Readers eventually would cease to expect claims about accuracy or rely on assurance that the "originals" actually existed. In the epistolary periodicals, Defoe insisted that the materiality of the "hand" writing the letter was proof of the text's factual existence and of its moral authority; at the same time, he emphasized the growing dominance of the print medium. Defoe occasionally deferred, like Dunton, to the authority of his readers, requesting, for example, "the Assistance of the more Capable Part of the World" as he protested that he was "not, as was pretended in the *Athenian Mercury*, a Professor in all the Heads."[77] Yet he also lectured and condescended to them in a way that emphasized the growing split between author and consumer. In the preface to the *Review*'s first volume, he complained about readers' assumption of correspondence, writing of these "importunate Cavils," "I am Letter baited by Querists, and think my Trouble to write civil, private Answers to teazing and querulous Epistles, has been equal, if not more troublesome, than all the rest of this Work."[78] As editor he began to arrogate to himself the right to instruct his readers without incorporating their feedback, a stance that became more prominent over the course of the *Review*'s lifetime as reader letters became less so.

Both Defoe and Dunton thus alternated between asserting the primacy of print and demonstrating their continued reliance on manuscript letters and personal reading communities. As I have shown, a clearer understanding of the function of epistolary periodicals can help us to dislodge the teleological narrative that sees print as having an inherent fixity and authority. Dunton's vacillating comment in answer to the question, "Whether has Gunpowder or Printing done the greatest Mischief to the World," that "Printing has done more service and disservice too," indicates the ongoing debate around the expanding uses of the print medium that became a topic of such concern for the early periodical.[79] Dunton was also unable to articulate a clear relationship between his paper, his readers, and "the publick." In response to a query in August 1692, "Can you tell us what good was ever yet done by your *Athenian Mercury*?" he cycled between the practical and the imaginative, the particular and the national:

> Not therefore to insist on the mighty *benefits*, which (if they are not very ungrateful) the Stationers, Printers, Hawkers, Coffee-houses, *&c.* (very profitable Members of the Commonwealth) must own they have receiv'd by our *Mercury*, nor to boast of its merits in helping to carry on the *War against* France, by advancing the Royal Revenue some thousands *per An.* (pence we mean) by

> the *Penny Post* ... And lastly, to say nothing how helpful we have been to the *Pastry-Cooks*, &c. we think we may in earnest, and without *vanity* pretend that our Paper has been of some real *use* both to the *publick*, and in many particular cases of high moment: For the first, none can deny but we have rais'd a kind of *Learned Ferment* in the Nation ... since we have set the World a *talking*, they have fallen a writing too."[80]

This, again, was a trope with legs: Mr. Spectator would go on to joke about the benefits *The Spectator* provided to "the publick" in the form of paper with which to wrap spices, light pipes, and line pie-pans.[81] The *Mercury* and its generic descendants activated a readership of potential authors who experienced a continuous literary sequence that ran from wastepaper through personal letters to periodical and book publication.

The turn of the eighteenth century marked an experimental, self-reflexive moment in which authors across a range of printed publications turned their attention to their own conditions of reading, writing, and circulation. The ongoing analysis of reader letters and the genre of the question-and-answer allowed Dunton and Defoe to articulate a version of the periodical that favored communal authorship arising out of a mixed-media environment. The familiar genre of the letter helped readers understand new genres of print and signaled to them the importance of building reading communities that would engage in ongoing exchange and interaction. Letters bridged manuscript and printed worlds, offering a shortcut to authorship and readership for emerging constituencies. At the same time, the periodicals' commentary upon the appearance of printed letters within their pages allowed authors to begin separating out the categories that would come to define eighteenth-century literature: of public print, private manuscript, and the authorial figures who had a special ability to span the two spheres.

The first general-interest periodicals appeared at a crucial moment of flux in the literary marketplace. Rose argues that the shift from licensing to copyright constituted a shift from a "regime of regulation" to a "regime of property" in which the author was established as the sole creator of a text. But the 1710 Statute of Anne appeared at an early moment for this "specifically modern" view of authorship, and "in the first decade of the eighteenth century the conception of the author as proprietor was still in an early phase of development"—a point emphasized by Dunton's attempt to claim ownership over a genre rather than a text.[82] His failure to maintain his "property" reveals the changing circumstances of print publication in the early eighteenth century. Dunton and Defoe, I contend, were negotiating a transition from a circumscribed literary sphere wherein the authority of a book derived from its writer's reputation to a literary market flooded by anonymous books and requiring new methods of credentialing.[83] Each dealt with this unstable literary environment by highlighting his paper's epistolary makeup. Reader letters were a metonym for interactive literary communities and dispersed authorship. Epistolary periodicals offered a mode of proof that bridged the conventions of manuscript and print publication, and in the early eighteenth century this multimodality could vouch for a work to an extent unattainable by print alone.

NOTES

I would like to thank Collin Jennings and Pamela Smith for their advice on early drafts of this article. This essay developed from a paper on the panel "Interactions between Eighteenth-Century Authors, Readers, and Publishers" at the 2013 ASECS Annual Meeting, and I am grateful to the panelists and audience members, and particularly to the convener, Eve Tavor Bannet, for their feedback. Finally, thanks to the anonymous reviewers at *SECC* for their insightful responses.

1. Manushag Powell notes that from the eighteenth century on, "Periodicals have a tendency toward self-reflexivity that seems to surpass that of other genres." Michael Warner has also highlighted the self-reflexivity of early periodicals, arguing that publications like *The Athenian Mercury* and *The Spectator* included "feedback loops" in order to demonstrate the existence of the public they claimed to be addressing. Christina Lupton, focusing on the novels of the mid-eighteenth century, argues that discussion about literary media was a key feature of the century's popular literature. Manushag Powell, "Afterword: We Other Periodicalists, or, Why Periodical Studies?," *TSWL* 30, no. 2 (Fall 2011): 447; Michael Warner, "Publics and Counterpublics," in *Publics and Counterpublics* (New York: Zone Books, 2005), 11–12, 99–100; Christina Lupton, *Knowing Books: The Consciousness of Mediation in Eighteenth-Century Britain* (Philadelphia: Univ. of Pennsylvania Press, 2012), x, 1.

2. Daniel Defoe, *A Review of the Affairs of France, and of All Europe, as Influenced by That Nation* (London, 1705), n.p. The first British newspaper, the bi-weekly London (Oxford) *Gazette*, appeared in 1665; weekly, bi-weekly, and tri-weekly periodicals only began to multiply after the lapse of the Licensing Act in 1695. Paula Backscheider consistently calls Dunton and Defoe "friends," despite their later quarrel, and highlights Defoe's dissenting education at Newington Green where a key pedagogical influence was Samuel Annesley, later Dunton's father-in-law. But Maximillian Novak, while noting the ongoing literary relationship, questions "whether Defoe ever actually worked with Dunton or was a close friend," since Dunton's business reputation was already declining at the end of the seventeenth century. Paula Backscheider, *Daniel Defoe: His Life* (Baltimore: Johns Hopkins Univ. Press, 1989), 18–20 and passim.; Maximillian E. Novak, *Daniel Defoe, Master of*

Fictions: His Life and Ideas (Oxford: Oxford Univ. Press, 2001), 110.

3. John Dunton, *Dunton's Whipping-Post: Or, A Satyr Upon Every Body* (London, 1706), 88.

4. James Tierney points out that Sir Roger L'Estrange's periodical *The Observator: In Question and Answer* (1681–83) was the first to use the Q&A format. The paper worked as a kind of catechism, using only the form, not the function, of letters; it did not solicit reader letters or present itself as an actual collection. James Tierney, "Periodicals and the Trade, 1695–1780," in *The Cambridge History of the Book in Britain Volume 5: 1695–1830*, ed. Michael F. Suarez SJ and Michael L. Turner (Cambridge: Cambridge Univ. Press, 2003), 481.

5. Dunton, *Dunton's Whipping-Post*, 88.

6. Dunton, *The Life and Errors of John Dunton Late Citizen of London* (London, 1705), 257.

7. Defoe was not the only one to adapt the question-and-answer format or to face Dunton's wrath. Thomas Brown and William Pate started the *London*, later *Lacedemonian*, *Mercury* in February 1692 as both satire of and competitor to *The Athenian Mercury*, criticizing Dunton's claim to have "an uncontrovertible Patent for answering all Queries exclusive of all men else." Other periodicals, including the *Jovial Mercury* (1693) and the *British Apollo* (1708–11), also used the question-and-answer device. Stephen Parks, *John Dunton and the English Book Trade: A Study of His Career with a Checklist of His Publications* (New York: Garland Pub., 1976), 94–7; Tierney, "Periodicals and the Trade, 1695–1780," 481.

8. Greene argues that the 1710 Act of Anne codified a privileged role for the author as the figure with both the commercial benefits and legal liability of ownership while Rose notes that "in the first decade of the eighteenth century the conception of the author as proprietor was still in an early phase of development." Jody Greene, *The Trouble with Ownership: Literary Property and Authorial Liability in England, 1660-1730* (Philadelphia: Univ. of Pennsylvania Press, 2005), 4–8, 127; Mark Rose, *Authors and Owners: The Invention of Copyright* (Cambridge, MA: Harvard Univ. Press, 1993), 37. See also Michel Foucault, "What is an Author?" in *The Book History Reader*, eds. David Finkelstein and Alistair McLeery (New York: Routledge, 2006), 281–91; David Saunders and Ian Hunter, "Lessons from the 'Literatory': How to Historicise Authorship," *Critical Inquiry* 17, no. 3 (Spring 1991): 479–509.

9. Clifford Siskin has argued that this "transformation of reader into writer" was a fundamental aspect of the ways in which writing induced generic differentiation in the eighteenth century as it became a feature of the periodical and influenced later developments in novel writing. Clifford Siskin, *The Work of Writing: Literature and Social Change in Britain, 1700–1810* (Baltimore: Johns Hopkins Univ. Press, 1998), 4, 160–8.

10. Jared Gardner has focused on the key role of the "editorial function," as opposed to the author function, in early American magazines, arguing that the "careful guidance of the editor" created a "collaborative and interactive ... periodical space" that "worked to collapse the distance between author and reader." Gardner, however, focuses on the political valence of this stance, seeing the heterogeneous magazine as an embodiment of federalist values. Jared Gardner, *The Rise and Fall*

of Early American Magazine Culture (Urbana, Chicago, and Springfield, IL: Univ. of Illinois Press, 2012), 103, 74–5.

11. Sean Latham and Robert Scholes, "The Rise of Periodical Studies," *PMLA* 121, no. 2 (March 2006): 520–1. See also Lennard Davis, *Factual Fictions: The Origins of the English Novel* (Philadelphia: Univ. of Pennsylvania Press, 1996); William B. Warner, *Licensing Entertainment: The Elevation of Novel Reading in Britain, 1684–1750* (Berkeley and Los Angeles: Univ. of California Press, 1998); J. Paul Hunter, *Before Novels: The Cultural Contexts of Eighteenth-Century Fiction* (New York and London: W.W. Norton & Company, 1990).

12. Powell, "See No Evil, Hear No Evil, Speak No Evil: Spectation and the Eighteenth-Century Public Sphere," *Eighteenth-Century Studies* 45, no. 2 (Winter 2012): 256. In Jürgen Habermas' influential analysis of the eighteenth-century split between public and private "spheres," print is the foremost "institution" of the public sphere, since "the public" is necessarily a reading public. Jürgen Habermas, *The Structural Transformation of the Public Sphere: An Inquiry into a Category of Bourgeois Society*, trans. Thomas Burger (Cambridge, MA: MIT Press, 1991), 18, 23, 27, 46.

13. Clare Brant, *Eighteenth-Century Letters and British Culture* (Basingstoke, U.K., and New York: Palgrave Macmillan, 2006), 9.

14. Important exceptions include Brant's *Eighteenth Century Letters and British Culture* and Gary Schneider's *The Culture of Epistolarity* (Newark: Univ. of Delaware Press, 2005), both of which emphasize the interrelation of manuscript epistolary practices and printed letters.

15. This is true even of *The Spectator* where the prominence of letters has long been acknowledged but under-theorized. Apart from Richmond P. Bond's introduction to his *New Letters to the* Tatler *and* Spectator (Austin: Univ. of Texas Press, 1959) and Eve Tavor Bannet's essay "Epistolary Commerce in *The Spectator*," I am unaware of any extensive considerations of the periodical's letters. Bannet focuses on the style of the letters to argue that *The Spectator* served as a letter-writing manual, demonstrating polished epistolary style for diverse readers. Powell has analyzed the epistolary *Rambler* essays but argues that they diverge from earlier epistolary periodicals in that Johnson wrote almost all of the letters himself and did not solicit reader correspondence. Eve Tavor Bannet, "Epistolary Commerce in The Spectator," in The Spectator: *Emerging Discourses*, ed. Donald J. Newman (Newark: Univ. of Delaware Press, 2005), 221, 224–5; Powell, "Johnson and His 'Readers' in the Epistolary *Rambler* Essays," *Studies in English Literature, 1500–1900* 44, no. 3 (Summer 2004): 572, 577.

16. Hunter, *Before Novels*, 186.

17. Kathryn Shevelow, *Women and Print Culture: The Construction of Femininity in the Early Periodical* (London and New York: Routledge, 1989), 4; Powell, *Performing Authorship in 18th-Century English Periodicals* (Lewisburg, PA: Bucknell Univ. Press, 2012), 35.

18. James Daybell, *The Material Letter in Early Modern England: Manuscript Letters and the Culture and Practices of Letter-Writing, 1512-1635* (Basingstoke, U.K., and New York: Palgrave Macmillan, 2012), 9; Eve Tavor Bannet, *Empire of*

Letters: Letter Manuals and Transatlantic Correspondence, 1688-1820 (Cambridge: Cambridge Univ. Press, 2005), xvii.

19. Daybell, *The Material Letter in Early Modern England*, 12, 202; Bannet, *Empire of Letters*, 6.

20. Margaret J.M. Ezell, *Social Authorship and the Advent of Print* (Baltimore: Johns Hopkins Univ. Press, 1999), 111. See also Harold Love, *The Culture and Commerce of Texts: Scribal Publication in Seventeenth-Century England* (Amherst, MA: Univ. of Massachusetts Press, 1993) and Arthur Marotti, *Manuscript, Print, and the English Renaissance Lyric* (Ithaca, N.Y., and London: Cornell Univ. Press, 1995).

21. Hunter has highlighted Dunton's obsession with novelty, reflected in his exaggerated claims of originality in the "Question-Project." His "pursuit of novelty for its own sake" is representative, Hunter argues, of "a whole sprawling context of attention to the new, strange, and surprising" that was a necessary precursor to the emergence of the novel. Hunter, "The Insistent I," *Novel: A Forum on Fiction* 13, no. 1 (Autumn 1979): 20; Hunter, *Before Novels: The Cultural Contexts of Eighteenth-Century English Fiction*, 103, 14.

22. Dunton was the bookseller for the latter, written by Charles Gildon, whom Dunton later commissioned to write a *History of the Athenian Society*.

23. Konstantin Dierks, *In My Power: Letter Writing and Communications in Early America* (Philadelphia: Univ. of Pennsylvania Press, 2009), 152.

24. Hunter, "The Insistent I," 33; Jody Greene, "Ego Non Sum Ego: John Dunton and the Consolations of Print," *The Eighteenth Century: Theory and Interpretation* 50, no. 2–3 (Summer/Fall 2009): 131.

25. Greene, "Ego Non Sum Ego," 128.

26. Bod. Lib. MS. Rawl. D. 71, 71.

27. Bod. Lib. MS. Rawl. D. 71, 73.

28. Bod. Lib. MS. Rawl. D. 71, 119.

29. Dunton, *Life and Errors*, 257.

30. *The Athenian Mercury* 1.2 (24 March 1691). Because copies of the *Mercury* survive in different formats and with varying pagination, I provide the volume and issue numbers, along with the date of the issue, for easiest reference; I have silently changed old-style dates to new style. The issues of the *Mercury* cited here were accessed via the *ProQuest British Periodicals* database, which lists the publication as the *Athenian Gazette*, a title Dunton used for the first few numbers before switching to the *Mercury* for the remainder of the run.

31. *AM*, "The Preface to the Third Volume," 3.1 (28 July 1691).

32. *AM* 1.4 (4 April 1691).

33. *AM* 1.1 (17 March 1691).

34. *AM* 1.3 (31 March 1691).

35. *AM*, "The Preface to the Fourth Volume," 4.1 (29 Sept. 1691).

36. Dunton, *Life and Errors*, 256.

37. *AM*, "The Preface to the First Volume," 1.1 (17 March 1691). According to Dunton's agreement with Sault and Wesley, the collaborators were responsible for the prefaces affixed to the collected volumes. Bod. Lib. MS. Rawl. D. 71.

38. *AM* 2.17 (21 July 1691).
39. *AM*, "Preface," 9.1 (13 Dec. 1692).
40. *AM* 2.17 (21 July 1691).
41. Shevelow, *Women and Print Culture*, 79.
42. *AM* 1.1 (17 March 1691).
43. Dunton, *Life and Errors*, 248–9.
44. *AM*, "The Preface to the First Volume," 1.1 (17 March 1691).
45. Helen Berry, *Gender, Society and Print Culture in Late-Stuart England* (Burlington, VT: Ashgate Publishing Company, 2003), 20.
46. Lawrence Klein, "Gender and the Public/Private Distinction in the Eighteenth Century: Some Questions About Evidence and Analytic Procedure," *Eighteenth-Century Studies* 29, no. 1 (Fall 1995): 97–109; Patricia Meyer Spacks, *Privacy: Concealing the Eighteenth-Century Self* (Chicago: Univ. of Chicago Press, 2003).
47. *AM*, "The Preface to the Second Volume," 2.1 (26 May 1691).
48. Bod. Lib. MS. Rawl. D. 71, 119.
49. Dunton, *Life and Errors*, 240.
50. Dunton, *Dunton's Whipping Post*, 89.
51. Dunton, *Life and Errors*, n.p.
52. Defoe, *A Review of the Affairs of France*, 4.
53. J.A. Downie, "Stating Facts Right About Defoe's *Review*," in *Telling People What to Think: Early Eighteenth-Century Periodicals from the* Review *to the* Rambler, ed. J.A. Downie and Thomas N. Corns (London and Portland, OR: Frank Cass, 1993), 13.
54. Novak, "Defoe's Political and Religious Journalism," in *The Cambridge Companion to Daniel Defoe*, ed. John Richetti (Cambridge: Cambridge Univ. Press, 2008), 26.
55. Powell has focused on the importance of the eidolon to the development of the periodical in *Performing Authorship*, arguing that authorship involved self-commodification that was made visible through the eidolon. The eidolon enacts authorship so that "periodicals require rather than avoid interaction with their readers." Powell, *Performing Authorship in 18th-Century English Periodicals*, 3–4, 14.
56. Paula McDowell argues that in his *Journal of the Plague Year* (1722), Defoe asserts a (factually incorrect) lack of printed news in the 1660s in order to contrast the modern reliability of print with a backwards, oral past. In this text, she writes, "media forms that are in reality copresent and interdependent are modeled as in some sense competing with each other." A similar dynamic, I argue, exists in the epistolary periodicals. Paula McDowell, "Defoe and the Contagion of the Oral: Modeling Media Shift in 'A Journal of the Plague Year'," *PMLA* 121, no. 1 (January 2006): 104.
57. Greene argues that Defoe's writings on licensing and copyright—she focuses on another 1704 production, the *Essay in Favor of the Regulation of the Press*—typify his period's attitudes toward the emerging centrality of the author figure. Greene, *The Trouble with Ownership*, 107.
58. Defoe, *A Review of the Affairs of France*, n.p.

59. While Defoe remained interested in the periodical marketplace in *A Review of the State of the British Nation*, he spent less space explicitly critiquing other newspapers in this second iteration of the *Review*. I focus here on the *Review of the Affairs of France*, which ran from 1704–5.

60. Defoe, *A Review of the Affairs of France*, 5.

61. Defoe, *A Review of the Affairs of France*, 35.

62. Defoe, *A Review of the Affairs of France*, 115. The editors Defoe criticized defended themselves in open letters "to the author of the *Review*." In July 1704, the author of the *Daily Courant* denied that he had misquoted from the *Leiden Gazette* a month earlier. "I was wrongfully accus'd of imposing upon the Publick," he wrote, adding that Defoe "ought not to publish such a Letter"—in which the original charge was made—"unless he were satisfied the Fact related in it were true." "To the Author of the Review of the Affairs of France," *The Daily Courant* (London), July 19, 1704.

63. Defoe, *A Review of the Affairs of France*, 85.

64. Mary Poovey has highlighted these as key terms in Defoe's works across the "fact/fiction continuum, arguing that Defoe often returned to the question of how the print medium could inspire belief even in a factually untrue narrative. *Genres of the Credit Economy: Mediating Value in Eighteenth- and Nineteenth-Century Britain* (Chicago: Univ. of Chicago Press, 2008), 105–10.

65. Richard Hamblyn, "Introduction," in *The Storm* (London and New York: Penguin Books, 2005), x.

66. Qtd. in Hamblyn, "Introduction," xxiii.

67. Defoe, *The Storm* (London and New York: Penguin Books, 2005), 157.

68. Defoe, *The Storm*, 8.

69. Defoe, *The Storm*, 3–4.

70. Defoe, *The Storm*, 4.

71. Defoe, *The Storm*, 139, 65.

72. Defoe, *The Storm*, 64.

73. Defoe, *The Storm*, 8.

74. Defoe, *The Storm*, 53.

75. Defoe, *Roxana: The Fortunate Mistress* (Oxford World's Classics: Oxford Univ. Press, 1996), 277.

76. See, for example, Davis, *Factual Fictions*, and Hunter, *Before Novels*. An important counterexample is the series of essays in a recent volume, *Positioning Defoe's Non-Fiction: Form, Function, Genre,* ed. by Aino Mäkikalli and Andreas K.E. Mueller (Newcastle upon Tyne, U.K.: Cambridge Scholars Publishing 2011).

77. Defoe, "A Supplementary Journal to the Advice from the Scandal Club; For the Month of September 1704," in *A Review of the Affairs of France* (London, 1705), 3.

78. Defoe, *A Review of the Affairs of France*, n.p.

79. *AM* 1:14 (9 May 1691).

80. *AM* 8:1 (12 July 1692).

81. Joseph Addison and Richard Steele, *The Spectator*, ed. Donald F. Bond, vol. 3, 5 vols. (Oxford: Oxford Univ. Press, 1965), 380.

82. Rose, *Authors and Owners*, 15, 3, 37.

83. Johns, *The Nature of the Book*, 31–2. Defoe emphasized this transition in the *Essay on the Regulation of the Press*, in which he argued that under the Licensing Act an individual licenser might reject a work "because the Man was not approv'd that wrote it, and a Book was Damn'd for the Author, not the Author for the Book." *An Essay on the Regulation of the Press* (London, 1704), 5.

Anna Barbauld's Authorial Self-Fashioning: From "fair pedagogue" to "fatidical spinster"

KELLY E. BATTLES

Anna Laetitia Barbauld's legacy has been dominated by the shadow of her career's end. According to the conventional narrative, devastating reviews of Barbauld's *Eighteen Hundred and Eleven* cowed the author into retreating from the public eye, despite a successful career that spanned over forty years. *Eighteen Hundred and Eleven,* a fiery political poem denouncing the policies of the British government in the Napoleonic wars and predicting a dystopian future, elicited viciously negative reviews. Consequently, she never published again. Most infamously, John Wilson Croker writing in the *Quarterly Review* lamented that Barbauld ventured away from her role as the "fair pedagogue" in this political poem. For Croker, the poem marked her transformation into a "fatidical spinster," a term that brings to mind the misogynist image of a wizened, solitary old hag given to witchery and false prophecy. Although his sarcastic tone obscured whether he truly held her in high esteem as a "fair pedagogue," the label would resonate with those who did respect her in that role. He attacked Barbauld for her gender and her established reputation as a children's author.[1] "We had hoped, indeed," he writes, "that the empire might have been saved without the intervention of a lady-author."[2] Many others agreed with Croker's negative assessment, both publicly and privately. William Keach has surveyed the critical response to

Eighteen Hundred and Eleven and has shown that even Barbauld's friends did not fully support her in the wake of this negative reception, with Henry Crabb Robinson lamenting the "very bad" tone of the poem and Maria Edgeworth balking at the possibility of defending her friend in public.[3]

Ultimately, it is vital to note the impact Barbauld's career trajectory had on the poem's reception. *Eighteen Hundred and Eleven* appeared after Barbauld had rebranded herself as a purveyor of domestic literature for children following her marriage. Croker and other reviewers seemed to have selectively forgotten that Barbauld was heralded by early commentators as worthy to stand with the best male poets before the emergence of the "fair pedagogue" when she was still Miss Aikin. Her biographer William McCarthy cites an early reviewer, William Woodfall, who in 1773 compared her to "Milton and even Shakespeare."[4] Such comparisons were not anomalous. Barbauld's engagement in the masculinized space of public political discourse was acceptable to the reading public for most of her life. McCarthy ventures to say that Barbauld's "influence on the culture met with no resistance" in her earlier days.[5] Similarly, Penny Mahon writes that Benjamin Flowers of the *Cambridge Intelligencer* printed extracts of Barbauld's 1793 pamphlet *Sins of Government, Sins of the Nation,* and she offers the opinion that "he must have perceived its radical Dissenting tone and he had no qualms about ascribing it to Barbauld."[6] This is not to say that Barbauld completely escaped critique for her departure from gendered norms in her early writings. For example, Horace Walpole notably labeled her an "*Unsex'd Female*" due to the strident tone in which she forwarded her progressive political opinions.[7] Her political essays addressed the most contentious issues of her day, ranging from the abolition of slavery to advocating for full civic rights for Dissenters. In such a context, Croker's objection that Barbauld should not have "dash[ed] down her shagreen spectacles and her knitting needles … to sally forth" into the realm of grand public, political discourse strikes a discordant note, evincing an amnesia about her earlier career.[8] This amnesia, I argue, is still apparent in contemporary narratives of Barbauld's career. These narratives do not consider that the negative reaction to her final poem related both to Barbauld's turn towards children's literature and to the periodical press's efforts to condition subsequent reader-reception of Barbauld. It is my intention here to correct this critical forgetting by asserting a new explanation of the public's reaction to *Eighteen Hundred and Eleven*. I also explain its role in the end of her career by considering both the way her persona was fashioned by the periodical press and the impact of her own self-fashioning as an author.

Contemporary scholars have overlooked one important aspect of the way that the periodical shaped Barbauld's persona. Too often, literary scholars, when they consider the material conditions of how poetry was presented in the contemporary periodical press, look exclusively at reviews of the poems, overlooking the frequent appearance of extracts tucked away in the midst of articles not ostensibly related to the reception or interpretation of the poetry. These framed interpolations provide important information for how periodicals framed and how the public perceived Barbauld. I will offer some examples of such references to Barbauld appearing in *The Universal Magazine of Knowledge and Pleasure* as a case study to illustrate this act of framing.

Even though for most of her career she carefully managed her public image, in *Eighteen Hundred and Eleven* the power to do so escaped her. There was a shift in her reputation, an erasure of her political power. The dominance of the "safe" maternal role in her children's literature for the majority of the last part of her career derailed her attempt to resume her strong, direct political voice in *Eighteen Hundred and Eleven.* As McCarthy writes, "the fact that Barbauld performed as a pedagogue came eventually to count against her in literary history; the very books for which she was long remembered came to be regarded as grounds for dismissing and even reviling her."[9]

The impact of Barbauld's children's literature must be taken into consideration in a revised narrative of her career that explains her withdrawal from the literary marketplace as a function of how her authorial persona changed over the course of her lifetime. Despite the fact that Barbauld sometimes exerted careful control over her persona, the periodical press took a greater role in how the reading public received her writing. When Barbauld's *Lessons for Children* and *Hymns in Prose for Children* are considered in dialogue with the rest of her work, a continuous trajectory becomes clear that belies the discontinuity that her contemporaries perceived and critiqued when she published *Eighteen Hundred and Eleven.* From her support of the freedom fighters in her early poem *Corsica* to her public advocacy for abolition as well as political and social recognition to Dissenters, Barbauld expressed a conviction for universal and global rights.

Reframing Barbauld in the Periodical Press

The extreme swing in Barbauld's reputation over her lifetime has not gone unnoticed by scholars. Harriet Guest writes that "[w]hat this range of responses to Barbauld's work has in common is that for all of them it is the gendered character of her writing that is at issue: it is her willingness or failure to appear properly feminine that is the central focus of their criticism."[10] I want to provide a possible explanation for this range of responses that offers a diachronous reading of Barbauld's appearances in the periodical press over time. Because most readers encountered Barbauld's poetry in excerpts carefully curated and framed by the editors of the periodicals, a narrative of Barbauld's shifting authorial persona must also include a discussion of the material conditions in which readers encountered her writing in the press. A fuller explanation of the poem's harsh reception and Barbauld's subsequent withdrawal from the literary marketplace can be achieved by recognizing the dissonance between the Barbauld persona created by periodicals that represents a patriotic and laudatory vision of the British landscape and the dark, politically critical vision she presents in *Eighteen Hundred and Eleven*.[11]

An important turning point for the British nation and for Barbauld's career occurred in 1790–1791, coinciding with a flurry of public reactions to the ongoing French Revolution and Barbauld's return to public writing with her essay about Dissenters following Parliament's failure to repeal the Test and Corporation Act. As a periodical with Whiggish leanings, *The Universal Magazine* was generally supportive of the progressive politics of its time. Its progressive politics were always, however, in the service of a deep sense of British nationalism and a positive view of the British future, an outlook that has come to be known in later times as a "Whiggish" view of history. During the two years in question, *The Universal Magazine of Knowledge and Pleasure* included numerous references to Barbauld in anonymous essays on natural history and topographical essays, among others, alongside excerpts from Helen Maria Williams and Edmund Burke on the French Revolution. The references to Barbauld in this one magazine during this condensed time frame show the mediation or recontextualization of eighteenth-century poetry in essays, which conditioned readers to interpret Barbauld's poems as a celebration of the English landscape and traditional political power structures. Set in contrast to this manner in which her audience had been disciplined to receive her poems in these alternative contexts, the negative reaction to her poem *Eighteen Hundred and Eleven* can be more fully understood as emerging from the conditions of how Barbauld's poetry had been appropriated and framed in the periodical press earlier in her career.

An article appearing in February 1791 in the *Universal Magazine* exhibits a telling pattern.[12] The article, "An Account of the New College, at Hackney: With a fine View of the principal Front of that Edifice," is an anonymous topographical essay with an accompanying engraving. It lauds the English landscape in "these enlightened times" and concludes with a rather long excerpt from Barbauld's early poem "The Invitation to Miss B-."[13] In fact, the excerpt from Barbauld's poem runs much longer than the original text of the essay's author. The author reappropriates Barbauld's poem describing Warrington Academy to apply to the new context of the New College at Hackney. The author praises the New College (which like Warrington was founded by Protestant Dissenters) for the service it would provide to the nation-building project through educating the youth, or as Barbauld refers to them in "The Invitation," the "embryo statesmen." Whereas the author himself maintains a positive and approving tone consistent with the general tone of the long excerpt he quotes from Barbauld, other lines from Barbauld's poem included in the excerpt references the exclusion of Dissenters from earning college degrees and contain language that foreshadows the angrier, harsher tone of *Eighteen Hundred and Eleven.* In that poem, she protests the "bigot Rage" that "Crush'd [Science's] strong pinions, and her flight withheld."[14] As a result of decontextualization, Barbauld's specific social critique, buried within a long excerpt and framing essay that was generally positive and future-oriented, becomes a generic and rather toothless objection to any barrier to knowledge rather than a sharp criticism of how Dissenters were legally shut out of the major universities. Barbauld's poem builds up to a nationalistic fervor, proclaiming a "patriot passion," "ardent, and glowing with undaunted zeal" that "with lips of fire shall plead his country's cause."[15] As if to emphasize that the female poet's place was not to speak out with such fiery passion, the excerpt selected by the essayist continues all the way to the end of the poem, at which point the female poet meekly and humbly protests her inability to do justice to the lofty purpose of celebrating the British nation, which she calls "arduous themes," and retreats back into a more passive and appropriately feminine stance: "My drooping Muse folds up her fluttering wing, / And hides her head in the green lap of spring."[16] This excerpt amounts to 99 lines of poetry and over one half of the length of the printed space of the essay. Even though the last stanza turns toward a focus on the poet rather than the school as nursery to "embryo statesmen," I suggest that the excerpt continues through to the end of the poem in order to reassert Barbauld's passive femininity to counterbalance the fact that the male essayist has briefly allowed her voice to speak for him.

The framing of Barbauld's poetry in the *Universal Magazine of Knowledge of Pleasure* in the early 1790s was symptomatic of how the periodical press as a whole neutered Barbauld's depiction of the English landscape of its bite, thus conditioning readers to receive her work in kind. Moreover, other uses of Barbauld's poetry in the magazine reveal an even sharper delineation of Barbauld as a poet who celebrated the English landscape. For instance, one unsigned article in the June 1790 issue, "A View of the Insect Tribes," was part of a series on natural history in the magazine called "The Contemplative

Philosopher." The author begins with an epigraph from Barbauld's poem "To Mrs. Priestley, With Some Drawings of Birds and Insects":

> What atom-forms of insect life appear!
> And who can follow nature's pencil here?
> Their wings with azure, green, and purple gloss'd,
> Studded with colour'd eyes, with gems emboss'd,
> Inlaid with pearl, and mark'd with various stains
> Of lively crimson thro' their dusky veins.[17]

The Contemplative Philosopher does not make any remarks on these lines, but they precede an article that maintains a highly scientific, analytical tone, with the opening announcing that the "fourth order of insects is distinguished by the name of *neuroptera.*"[18] Barbauld's lofty lines to her friend Mrs. Priestley, wife of Joseph Priestley, ask "who can follow nature's pencil here?" The Contemplative Philosopher suggests that he is the one for this task. These poetic interpolations indicate that Barbauld's poetry was elevated to the important position of becoming a filter for how people could come to understand the phenomena of the natural world around them.

In an earlier issue in February of that same year, The Contemplative Philosopher makes more extensive use of the same poem Barbauld addressed to Mrs. Priestley. The essay "On the Feathered Creation" extracts 24 lines of "To Mrs. Priestley, With Some Drawings of Birds and Insects," and then concludes with the following statement: "I shall only add, at present, that from the consideration of the providential care so evidently manifested in the preservation of the aerial tribes, the Divine Teacher of our holy Religion has drawn an argument, to prevent our sinking into anxiety and despondence, and to induce us to rely with filial confidence and piety in the goodness of our Heavenly Parent."[19] In terms of how the Contemplative Philosopher frames this poem, Barbauld's tone twenty years later in *Eighteen Hundred and Eleven* can be seen not just as a reversal of the mandate to avoid "sinking into anxiety and despondence," as the Contemplative Philosopher terms it, but also as a rebellion against both God and Country. In fact, Barbauld's reversal of tone in *Eighteen Hundred and Eleven* from that she employed in this early naturalist poem becomes even more evident in light of William McCarthy and Elizabeth Kraft's assertion that Barbauld wrote the poem on native British insects and birds in response to "a patriotic challenge issued by British naturalist (and her brother's friend) Thomas Pennant."[20] That Barbauld succeeded in tapping into a sense of British patriotism through her exploration of the natural world was evidenced by the frequent quotations from her poetry that the author of the "Contemplative Philosopher" drew upon. Besides the aforementioned essays "On the Feathered Creation" and "A View of the Insect Tribes," he also quoted her in the same year "On the Migration of Birds" alongside Milton, Pope, and the Bible.[21]

Despite these examples of the high regard in which Barbauld was held by her contemporaries twenty years prior to the publication of *Eighteen Hundred and Eleven,* Barbauld's social critiques were acceptable only within sharply defined contexts. They had to remain positive about the British future even when she harshly targeted the policies of the present government. This unspoken mandate that political critique must maintain a rosy view of Britain's future prospects was one that she broke in *Eighteen Hundred and Eleven,* which Penny Bradshaw has called a "damning and sweeping [vision] of the failure of the European Enlightenment."[22] Evan Gottlieb, building on the work of Emily Rohrbach, identifies Barbauld's deviation from the optimistic Whiggish view of history, or the stadialist notion of history associated with the Scottish Enlightenment, as her "greatest 'crime'" in *Eighteen Hundred and Eleven.*[23]

Her previous poetry lacked such harsh criticism of the British nation's essential character and its potential for goodness in the future. Even the harshest lines of her abolitionist poem, *Epistle to Mr. Wilberforce*, imply that the contamination came from without. "By foreign wealth are British morals chang'd" (line 104), the poem states, and this moral contamination could by implication be resisted. In contrast, Croker's infamously scathing review of *Eighteen Hundred and Eleven* in the *Quarterly Review* leveled some of its harshest condemnations against the poem's vision of the Americas as the frontier of liberty and hope for the future, sarcastically blasting Barbauld's "blissful visions of American glory" and ending his review with the reassurance that "we should not by any means impute it to want of taste or patriotism on her part, if, for her own country, her fears were less confident, and for America her hopes less ardent."[24] From Croker's review, we can gather that it was acceptable to launch revolutionary social critique as long as one remained optimistic about the future of the British nation.

The terms in which *The Universal Magazine* responded to the appearance of *Eighteen Hundred and Eleven* are especially interesting to set alongside the same magazine's earlier words of praise for Barbauld's feminine restraint. Despite the frequent appearance of her poetry in the pages of the magazine in the rather mild, nonthreatening contexts of topographical and natural history essays, the *Universal Magazine* then appeared to turn against her for these very nonthreatening, modest qualities. In its review of *Eighteen Hundred and Eleven, The Universal Magazine* states that she "is one of those writers who acquire a sort of celebrity for negative merits; that is, for the absence of all glaring faults, with an equal absence of all striking excellencies. She has produced books for children, criticisms for young gentlemen and ladies, and poetry for both, together with psalms, hymns, and tales; and in all these various and opposite productions there prevails the same cold regularity, the same frigid observance of what is right without any thing that is very good."[25] However, the modest feminine beauty and restraint of her poetry had always been a construct in which the magazine participated. After all, one of her earliest poems, "Corsica," engages in a fiery discussion of the righteousness of armed rebellion. The *Universal Magazine*'s response after *Eighteen Hundred and Eleven* did not recognize the magazine's own complicity in conditioning readers to receive Barbauld in such terms of predictable and "cold regularity."

Authorial Agency and Barbauld's Self-Fashioning in her Children's Literature

Ultimately, not all of the blame for the cognitive dissonance that the reading public experienced upon the appearance of the revolutionary Barbauld in *Eighteen Hundred and Eleven* can be placed at the feet of periodical essayists reappropriating and recontextualizing her poetry. Barbauld herself employed careful framing techniques and filters that sometimes render it difficult to pin down her politics. And, of course, she did plenty of her own framing of other authors in the multi-volume *British Novelists*.

One example of the enduring effects of Barbauld's obscuring of her politics is the disagreement among contemporary scholars on the question of Barbauld's progressiveness, especially when it came to her seemingly anti-feminist response to Mary Wollstonecraft in "The Rights of Woman," a poem that McCarthy and Kraft speculate may have either been ironic or written in a "fit of anger at Wollstonecraft's having criticized her earlier poem, 'To a Lady, with some Painted Flowers,'" or possibly may have been a "[bad] misread[ing]" of Wollstonecraft.[26] Harriet Guest points to one potential explanation for why Wollstonecraft would single out Barbauld for criticism. Wollstonecraft so admired Barbauld's other writing that she felt betrayed by the way "To a Lady, with some Painted Flowers" allows women only a purely decorative social role. Guest writes, "Wollstonecraft accuses Barbauld of adopting a masquerade of femininity, a disguise that conforms to the 'supposed sexual character' that the language of men creates."[27] This language of "masquerade" is what Wollstonecraft's criticism of Barbauld had in common with her conservative detractors. The sense that Barbauld somehow "masqueraded" as either more masculine or more feminine than her innate character or that she manipulated others' perception is a more grievous sin than the nonconformity itself. Barbauld's authorial self-fashioning suggests an awareness of gender as performance, but one that is in keeping with the fluid nature of gender itself rather than as a disingenuous masquerade. The "Mother" in Barbauld's children's literature, thus, forms part of the dialogical interplay that Barbauld engages in with her readers and society at large about whether a woman could simultaneously be feminine and claim a public voice.

Barbauld's construction of the "Mother" of her children's literature, which became closely aligned in public perception with Barbauld herself, resembles what Linda Kerber terms the "Republican Mother."[28] In fact, Guest explicitly aligns Barbauld with the Republican Mother.[29] However, I argue that Barbauld's mother is not the ultimately conservative ideological figure of the Republican Mother that sustains the civic virtue of the nation primarily through the inculcation of civic virtue in male children. Rather, Barbauld's mother is the refraction of that figure, which provides for a much more radicalized role: one that calls more closely to mind the female allegorical figures of Reason and Liberty of the French Revolution. This radicalism exists despite common critical interpretations that set her at odds with the feminism of Wollstonecraft.

Previous to *Eighteen Hundred and Eleven,* the conditions of Barbauld's writings were carefully crafted to both allow for social critique and to insulate her personally from any accusations of impropriety. McCarthy and Kraft argue that after her *Hymns* and *Lessons* for children, "Barbauld needed an identity which would be socially allowed to a woman and therefore realizable in action, but which would also make the most of what was socially allowed to woman: an identity which could be not merely realized, but made a stage from which to intervene in her culture," and that the role she chose to cultivate in her writing was that of "Mother."[30] Again, it is important to caution against the way in which modern scholars as well as Barbauld's contemporaries fall into the habit of using language that implies deceit and subterfuge to characterize the fluidity of Barbauld's gender performativity, the fact that it changed over time, and that it existed in a dialogical relationship with her reading public.

Admittedly, there is quite a bit of change in Barbauld's gendered expression in her writing over time. Excluding "Corsica," most of her early poetry features humble domestic scenes. Early poems are addressed to specific friends and read more like personal letters, with titles that point towards their personal context like "The Invitation: To Miss B--" or "On the Death of Mrs. Jennings." Other political poems have the appearance of occasional domestic poems such as "The Mouse's Petition" or "Washing-Day." Susan Rosenbaum describes the majority of Barbauld's poetry as "miniaturist" literature, often addressed directly to friends or containing the names of domestic objects in the titles. Such literature "advertises itself as the product of feminine, domestic handicraft [and] in doing so, it appears to accept its 'minor' status, its role as adornment, the themes of domestic life and moral virtues," although it succeeds in engaging the public sphere by subtly blurring the lines between the domestic and the public.[31] However, Barbauld herself does not delineate between the language of the political and the domestic spheres as much as her readers did; thus, it would be inaccurate to characterize domestic poems such as "Washing-Day" as masking political messages. Daniel White and Harriet Guest, among others, have argued that Barbauld integrated advocacy for public political change with the femininized domestic role, for White, via a collaborative model with her brother that melded the feminine qualities of sensibility, warmth and intimacy with the "masculinist features of nonconformity."[32] For Guest, Barbauld adapted the trope of the patriotic matrons of the Roman republic such that "the proper province or bounded sphere of femininity in familial domesticity" became "the source of civic virtue."[33]

While reviewers praised her children's literature as an appropriate and useful outlet for the literary talent of the now-married and properly domesticated "Mrs. Barbauld" in contrast to her maiden identity as "Miss Aikin," this praise represents an ultimate misreading of the maternal subject position in her children's literature. Generally, her literature for children is read by scholars today as a subversion of traditional gender roles and common notions of motherhood.[34] For example, Whitney Helms, speaking specifically about Barbauld's *Lessons for Children* and *Evenings at Home* (coauthored with her brother), notes that her children's stories "gave Barbauld the means to manipulate established gender roles and subvert the very ideologies that rendered women private and quiet."[35] Barbauld's self-fashioning of the maternal identity in her writing forced an unsettling notion on the readers of her time: how the gender positioning of an author can differ from the author's biological identity as a woman and a mother. Barbauld pointed toward the radical idea of gender performativity when the full spectrum of her writing is taken into account with its ever shifting authorial subject positions. This radical notion of motherhood predated and exceeded her writing that specifically addressed children as an audience. As discussed previously, we can see it functioning as early as her "Invitation to Miss. B--," in which she refers to the nonconformist Warrington Academy as a nursery to "embryo statesmen." Here, as elsewhere, the maternal function of the educator is unhinged from the biological maternal body and resides, rather, in the pedagogical function of the educational institution as a whole, where the educators were primarily male.

Barbauld fashions the "mother" of the *Lessons* and *Hymns* as a figure that performs an integral public function residing in the domestic realm of properly educating young sons into citizens. The "mamma" in *Lessons for Children* is a fully embodied maternal character speaking to her child. The "Advertisement" begins, "This little publication was made for a particular child, but the public is welcome to the use of it."[36] From a biographical standpoint, this particular child was presumed to be her adopted son Charles. However, while the advertisement emphasizes the private nature of the pedagogical work, Barbauld quite consciously maneuvers the text to have a public pedagogical function. The opening sentence is a hedge—a conscious framing, a construction that plays on the insistence that the ideal mother remains in the private domestic sphere; an author, such as Barbauld, who publishes her voice intrudes dangerously into the masculine public sphere. This initial sentence is an inoculation, the constructed voice of Barbauld's idealized "Mother." Not all of Barbauld's contemporaries accepted her blending of the domestic and maternal with the public pedagogical function in her writing for children. Michelle Levy has shown how Sarah Trimmer warned readers against exposing their children to the radical agenda she perceived to be evident in Barbauld and John Aikin's *Evenings at Home,* and that, to safeguard Barbauld's reputation, Lucy Aikin later claimed that her aunt had only a limited role in the composition of the work.[37]

In my reading of Barbauld's children's literature, I move away from overly biographical interpretations that map onto the texts a psychological reading about Barbauld's personal status as an adoptive mother to her nephew Charles or contemplate that Barbauld's children's literature is marked by her feelings of never having given birth to a child. It has been argued that "Barbauld may have been writing partially out of an anxiety over her state of unnatural motherhood," a state that was an "awkward and undoubtedly painful situation" and that her children's literature "compensates for her real-life maternal shortcomings."[38] Rather, Barbauld's subject position outside of the realm of literal, biological motherhood perhaps allowed her to more fully inhabit the role of collective national mother. As the collective national mother, nobody could lay claim to her body as a specific maternal body.

I intervene in the critical conversation about Barbauld's figuration of motherhood in her children's literature by arguing that it was part of a continuous trajectory, a thread that extended throughout her career. Barbauld's poetry is consistently full of powerful and influential female figures that she represents as having an active role on the public stage, appearing in a continuum ranging from the subtle influence of the mamma in *Lessons for Children* to the heroic female allegories such as Liberty, Reason, and Virtue. The disconnect that her critics perceived between her literature for children in contrast to her poetry and political pamphlets is owing to a shift in the way she presented the mother figure's mode of intervention in the public sphere. The women in her poetry actively instigate revolutions and stand in judgment of the actions of men. Significantly, as McCarthy notes, her early poem "Corsica," (1769) written in support of the Corsican freedom fighters resisting Italian rule, casts the female figure of Virtue as a mother: "the Corsicans and, by implication, all who struggle for liberty are her sons."[39]

Taking a close look at the pronouns Barbauld uses in her work reveals telling hints at how she constructs voice and, particularly, the way that a female authorial persona could inhabit and deploy different subject positions. In her *Hymns in Prose for Children*, she opens Hymn 1 with a call to worship, "Come, let us praise God," then continues with repeating statements in the first person, presumably the voice of the child. "I will praise God with my voice; for I may praise Him, though I am but a little child."[40] As this statement illustrates, Barbauld's *Hymns* give a voice to children and women who are typically rendered voiceless. The presumably female voice prompts the child in a call and answer to say, "A few years ago, I was a little infant, and my tongue was dumb within my mouth: And I did not know the great name of God, for my reason was not come unto me. But now I can speak, and my tongue shall praise Him."[41] The mother as teacher is giving the child his voice by giving him reason, and so the role of pedagogue is elevated as the giver of voice, identified as the source of reason and power in this hymn. Similarly, in the *Lessons,* Mitzi Myers has argued that the mother figure "controls access to literacy and culture, naming the world and defining reality."[42] However, this naming function has special theological resonance within the religious context of the *Hymns*.

The hymns continues to centralize specifically maternal functions; for instance, Hymn 2 praises the return of spring and glorifies the natural process of giving birth. Each part of nature is framed as maternal. "The hen sits on her nest of straw, she watches patiently the full time, then she carefully breaks the shell, and the young chickens come out. The lambs just dropt are in the field, they totter by the side of their dams."[43] The narrator calls on the young devotees to praise God as the enabler of their birth. "The young animals of every kind are sporting about, they feel themselves happy, they are glad to be alive—they thank Him that hath made them alive."[44] However, lacking a voice, the animals can only thank him in their hearts, and so the Mother instructs the child that it is his duty to speak for the lamb who lacks a voice, just as she gave him a voice when he lacked one: "[L]ittle lambs that skip about, if you could you would say how good he is; but you are dumb, we will say it for you."[45] God's live-giving force directly follows an enumeration of mothers' birthing function among various species and elevates the mother to a position next to God, bypassing the role of the earthly father in reproduction.

In Hymn 2, the dominant pronoun shifts to "us." It should be asked, who is included here in this "us" pronoun? Visual illustrations that typically accompany the hymns and textual analysis suggest that adult men are not included. The word of God comes from the mother to the child, not from the paternal voice preaching a sermon from the pulpit. In a time when most Christian denominations did not allow women to be ordained as church leaders, the maternal voice in the *Hymns* conveys the religious message to the child.[46] Only the mother and child are accorded voices in these hymns, with sparing references to fathers (other than God the Father).

In addition to these subtle signals encoded in pronouns, the *Hymns* tackles a more explicitly political controversy. For example, in Hymn 8, Barbauld instructs children to count Africans and other colonized peoples in the family of God. "Many kingdoms and countries full of people, and islands, and large continents, and different climates, make up this whole world—God governeth it. The people swarm upon the face of it like ants upon a hillock; some are black with the hot sun; some cover with furs against the sharp cold; some drink of the fruit of the vine; some the pleasant milk of the cocoa-nut, and others quench their thirst with the running stream. All are God's family."[47] Just as Barbauld's *Hymns* accord women and children voices, she also accords a voice to women subjugated by slavery and colonialist policies. The female voice of the *Hymns* calls to these women in their shared identity as mothers. "Negro woman, who sittest pining in captivity, and weepest over thy sick child: though no one seeth thee, God seeth thee; though no one pitieth thee, God pitieth thee; raise thy voice, forlorn and abandoned one; call upon Him from amidst thy bonds, for assuredly He will hear thee."[48] Again, the power of voice for the voiceless and marginalized appears as an ongoing theme in the *Hymns*. In Barbauld's supposedly meek and mild *Hymns in Prose for Children*, Croker's "fair pedagogue" in fact taught those children to give a voice to the mothers enslaved across the empire.

However, these powerful invocations of voice went unnoticed by reviewers. Prior to her marriage, reactions to the poetry of Miss Aikin, while consistently positive about her talent, often exhibited an anxiety that McCarthy notes was centered on the sense that she wrote "like a man." McCarthy cites a 1776 article in the *Westminster Review* that noted her "masculine force."[49] After her marriage, though, the language used to describe Barbauld shifted to a more traditional gendered vocabulary. Her poetry was, above all, "beautiful," as the Contemplative Philosopher wrote.[50] In 1786, the *European Magazine* describes Barbauld's "useful and unambitious performances" in her publications for children, and ends with praise cast in telling language: "every part of her works exhibit marks of a refined and vigorous imagination, of cultivated genius, elegant manners, unbigoted religion, and unenthusiastical devotion."[51] Barbauld was praised for her emotional restraint and modesty that was, above all, suited to her gender. However, tellingly, this profile occurred after Barbauld's marriage, and the article notes with favor that Barbauld's writing career had become suitably domestic after her marriage, focusing primarily on her works for children.

Perhaps Barbauld at the end of her career turned away from her role as the "fair pedagogue" of the nation because, while the mamma in her children's literature may model for women some limited participation and power in the political sphere through the act of educating future male legislators, this role ultimately took too long to effect real change. One example often cited of Barbauld's political influence as an educator is her student Thomas Denman, who was deeply involved in the 1832 Reform Act over 50 years after he first enrolled as a young boy at the Barbaulds' Palgrave School.[52] However, Barbauld was concerned about political problems that were imminent. Barbauld's description of the mamma function on the advertisement page of *Lessons for Children* points toward the long trajectory of change even as she praises it, writing that "[t]he task is humble but not mean; for to lay the first stone of a noble building, and to plant the first idea in a human mind, can be no dishonor to any hand."[53] Those stones of the noble building accumulated slowly. Barbauld includes a similar metaphor in Hymn 10 that can be read simultaneously as praise for the fruits of youthful education and lamentation for the long timeline. Comparing the child to an acorn, the hymn states that "It was long before this oak showed its greatness; year after year passed away, and it had only shot a little way above the ground, a child might have plucked it up with his little hands; it was long before any one called it a tree; it is long before the child becomes a man."[54] While the education of young sons was a noble task, Barbauld's interest in contemporary political issues and the suffering they caused meant that she could not be satisfied with influence in such a long temporal trajectory. To effect immediate change, a more urgent voice became necessary, and Barbauld boldly took up that voice again in *Eighteen Hundred and Eleven.*

Besides the long trajectory of maternal influence, Barbauld's Mother persona carried with it a more serious problem. While the maternal position allowed her a certain kind of freedom, she couldn't take off that disguise without paying an enormous price. No matter how much agency children's literature afforded women authors, it ultimately became a trap for Barbauld, framing her public authorial persona in such a way that the shift she made back to an authoritative masculinized voice in *Eighteen Hundred and Eleven* created a sharp dissonance for readers. Barbauld utilized her children's literature in just the way that Mitzi Myers argues that it operates for women authors, as a space of female agency and a bridge between the domestic and the public. I argue, however, that the shock of this sudden shift from her persona as the "mamma" of *Lessons* and the gentle devotional guide in *Hymns* back to the fiery voice of *Eighteen Hundred and Eleven* created a backlash much more severe than if her readers had read the poem as continuous with the trajectory of Barbauld's entire body of work.

Turning from how the *Hymns* constructed a particular subject position to the poem that ended her career, it is evident that voice continued to be Barbauld's primary tool for opening a space for women to intervene in public discourse. The voice in the first half of *Eighteen Hundred and Eleven* is very authoritative and omniscient, proclaiming truth to "thou," the nation of Britain, foretelling the future fall of the great nation with cold certainty. The voice Barbauld appropriates in this poem brutally passes judgment on the future of the nation. In line 67, the voice shifted from distant observer to one that speaks with a more personal plea to the nation with the line "Yet, O my Country! Name beloved and revered," and continues this more personal voice, proclaiming that the image of her country "to my infant senses came/ Mixt with Religion's light and Freedom's holy flame" (lines 69–70).[55] Further along in the poem, the poetic voice shifts to a hypothetical future Briton with a "musing mind" who takes American tourists through the ruins of the future British Isles (line 187). In the final stanzas of the poem, the narrator again takes on an omniscient, distant voice with the introduction of the "Spirit" (line 215) or "Genius" (line 241) described with male pronouns. This Genius is "capricious," alternately desolating the land as he turns his sights away from Britain, inspiring rebellion among the subjugated peoples of the British colonies, and turning towards the Americas to bestow goodness, benevolence, and wealth. The last line is a prediction for the future: "Thy world, Columbus, shall be free" (line 334). Barbauld gave herself the power to proclaim, and for this the reviewers punished her.

Although contemporary reviewers cited these shifts in voice in *Eighteen Hundred and Eleven* as an aesthetic flaw, they can be likened to a condensed version of the shifting voices that Barbauld used throughout her career. Her poetry has often been characterized as a throwback to the poetry of the Enlightenment with its omniscient voice rather than the more subjective personal voice characteristic of her Romantic contemporaries later in her life. The authorial voice in the children's literature is identifiably female, whereas her essays were often anonymous and gender-neutral, with the default assumption being male. When Barbauld wrote "we" and "us" in her pamphlets, she referred to a masculinized public body of fellow Dissenters or to the collective British nation, not to a feminized collective. Her pamphlets had an aggressive voice, according to Emma Major, although they were often published anonymously.[56]

She claimed her own voice in *Eighteen Hundred and Eleven* by using her own name. She did not choose to write it as an "anonymous" political pamphlet, to write it under a general pseudonym such as "Dissenter," nor filter it through the "mamma" of the children's literature or even link it to her brother's name as co-author. She stood alone, unguarded and defiant in *Eighteen Hundred and Eleven,* claiming her own voice and identity. It was a return to the political poetry of her youth, of Miss Aikin. Unfortunately, her public was not ready for their beloved schoolmistress to turn politically radical. The failure of her contemporaries to recognize the subtly subversive figure of motherhood in her children's literature and how this prefigured the more explicitly authoritative voice she claimed in her other writing presents a potential explanation for the dissonance experienced by readers and critics upon the publication of *Eighteen Hundred and Eleven.* Croker's "fair pedagogue of our former life," was in reality always there, rooted in her literature for children and continuing through in her political pamphlets, her politically critical poetry, and her domestic poetry. Recognizing this continuous thread requires placing Barbauld's children's literature in dialogue with her poetry rather than positioning it as an anomaly in her oeuvre, a temporary hiatus from the rest of work.

NOTES

1. This is a gendered attack that Croker incidentally also used to the same effect in his review of two reform pamphlets by William Roscoe, Barbauld's "compatriot" and author of the "Butterfly's Ball," appearing in the same issue. He mockingly praised Roscoe's children's poems *The Butterfly's Ball* and *The Butterfly's Funeral* as "a *pair of brilliants*. They are very pleasing specimens of that description of poetry, the excellence of which consists not in strength of wing, but in beauty of plume and lightness of movement, and, by their prettiness and *volancy*, seem altogether suited to their subject." Further linking the two reviews, Croker also noted that Roscoe, like Barbauld, also wore presumptuous "spectacles." See John Wilson Croker, "Art. II. *A Letter to Henry Brougham, Esq. M.P on the Subject of Reform in the Representation of the People in Parliament …*," *Quarterly Review* (June 1812): 266.

2. John Wilson Croker, "Art. VI. Eighteen Hundred and Eleven. A Poem," *Quarterly Review* (June 1812): 309. It would be inaccurate to characterize Croker as harboring a particular grudge against opinionated "lady-authors," of course, since he came to be known as a notoriously vicious reviewer, numbering Keats and Tennyson among his victims, but rather that he deployed gendered language against his foes regardless of biological sex.

3. William Keach, "A Regency Prophecy and the End of Anna Barbauld's Career," *Studies in Romanticism* 33.4 (Winter 1994), 570–1.

4. William McCarthy, *Anna Letitia Barbauld: Voice of the Enlightenment* (Baltimore: Johns Hopkins Univ. Press, 2008), 117.

5. William McCarthy, *Anna Letitia Barbauld*, x.

6. Penny Mahon, "In Sermon and Story: Contrasting Anti-war Rhetoric in the Work of Anna Barbauld and Amelia Opie," *Women's Writing* 7.1 (2000): 26.

7. See Harriet Guest, *Small Change: Women, Learning, Patriotism, 1750–1810*, (Chicago and London: Univ. of Chicago Press, 2000), 224.

8. Croker, "Art. VI. Eighteen Hundred and Eleven. A Poem," 309.

9. William McCarthy, "Mother of All Discourses: Anna Barbauld's *Lessons for Children*," in *Culturing the Child 1690–1914: Essays in Memory of Mitzi Myers*, ed. Donelle Rae Ruwe (Lanham, MD: Scarecrow Press, 2005), 86–7. See also, for example, Whitney Helms: "[I]t has been argued that the children's literature she authored not only diminished the overall quality of her work, but also lowered her respectability in literary circles" in "Appropriating Maternal Authority and Politicizing the Domestic: Anna Barbauld and Children's Literature," *Eighteenth-century Women: Studies in Their Lives, Work, and Culture,* ed. Linda V. Troost (Brooklyn, NY: AMS Press, 2011), 6:210.

10. Guest, *Small Change,* 226.

11. Mahon has connected the language Barbauld employs in her children's literature to that used in her anti-war sermons. However, Mahon does not extend her discussion of Barbauld's anti-war rhetoric to include *Eighteen Hundred and Eleven* or explain why it received such a drastically different reception than her sermons published almost twenty years earlier.

12. "An Account of the New College, at Hackney: With a fine View of the principal Front of that Edifice," *Universal Magazine of Knowledge and Pleasure* 88.611 (Feb. 1791): 81–3.

13. Penny Bradshaw argues that this poem can be read as exhibiting a mixed enthusiasm about the Enlightenment project, with the building of the canal representing a darker side of progress, masculinized by Barbauld, that is intent on controlling nature. Bradshaw, "Gendering the Enlightenment: Conflicting Images of Progress in the Poetry of Anna Laetitia Barbauld," *Women's Writing* 5.3 (1998): 358.

14. *The Invitation,* lines 98–99, quoted in "An Account of the New College, at Hackney," 82.

15. "An Account of the New College, at Hackney," 82.

16. "An Account of the New College, at Hackney," 83.

17. "The Contemplative Philosopher, Number LIX. A View of the Insect Tribes,"

Universal Magazine of Knowledge and Pleasure 86.602 (June 1790): 307.

18. "The Contemplative Philosopher, Number LIX," 307.

19. "The Contemplative Philosopher, Number LV. On the Feathered Creation," *Universal Magazine of Knowledge and Pleasure* 86.598 (Feb. 1790): 92.

20. William McCarthy and Elizabeth Kraft, eds, *Anna Letitia Barbauld: Selected Poetry and Prose* (Peterborough, ON: Broadview, 2002), 44.

21. "The Contemplative Philosopher, Number LVI. On the Migration of Birds," *Universal Magazine of Knowledge and Pleasure* 86.599 (March 1790):146.

22. Bradshaw, "Gendering the Enlightenment," 365.

23. Evan Gottlieb, "Fighting Words: Representing the Napoleonic Wars in the Poetry of Hemans and Barbauld," *European Romantic Review* 20.3 (July 2009): 339; Emily Rohrbach, "Anna Barbauld's History of the Future: A Deviant Way to Poetic Agency," *European Romantic Review* 17.2 (April 2006): 180.

24. Croker, "Art. VI. Eighteen Hundred and Eleven. A Poem," 313.

25. "Original Criticism," *The Universal Magazine, New Series* 17: (March 1812): 217, quoted in William McCarthy, *Anna Letitia Barbauld*, 476. Perhaps by no coincidence, this same issue of the revamped *Universal Magazine* contains a short anecdote that lauds the young Edmund Burke for disproving rumors of his Jacobitism, and praising both his "manliness of sentiment" and his conservative "reflections on the French Revolution." "Anecdotes of Edmund Burke," 190.

26. McCarthy and Kraft, eds., *Anna Letitia Barbauld,* 55 and 130.

27. Guest, *Small Change*, 223–4.

28. Linda Kerber, "The Republican Mother: Women and the Enlightenment, American Perspective," *American Quarterly* 28.2 (1976): 187–205. For a recent application of Kerber's term, see, for example, Jane Donawerth, *Conversational Rhetoric: The Rise and Fall of a Women's Tradition, 1600–1900* (Carbondale and Edwardsville, IL: Southern Illinois Univ. Press, 2012). Kerber linked her term to a uniquely American expression of the political ideology of the Enlightenment. Although I depend on the tenets of the term "Republican Mother" for my formulation of Barbauld's authorial persona, I modify it to accommodate the fact that Kerber's term is heavily associated with an American context and with the affirmation of an existing political status quo.

29. According to Guest, "Her sermons of the 1790s suggest that Barbauld might best be understood within the context of an ideal of 'republican motherhood' which represents the 'household virtues' as continuous with and necessary to more obviously patriotic virtues because their privacy is the basis for an inclusive conception of the civic" (251).

30. Guest, *Small Change*, 19.

31. Susan Rosenbaum, "'A Thing Unknown, Without a Name': Anna Laetitia Barbauld and the Illegible Signature," *Studies in Romanticism* 40.3 (Fall 2001): 372.

32. Daniel White, "The 'Joineriana': Anna Barbauld, the Aikin Family Circle, and the Dissenting Public Sphere," *Eighteenth-Century Studies* 32.4 (Summer 1999): 515.

33. Guest, *Small Change,* 236.

34. I rely on the definition of the function of children's literature set forth by Mitzi

Myers, "The Erotics of Pedagogy: Historical Intervention, Literary Representation, 'the Gift of Education,' and the Agency of Children," *Children's Literature* 23 (1995): "[P]edagogy unites domestic education and public event, [and] it legitimates the female writer's agency as well as that of the child protagonist" (3–4). Further, Myers's work establishes that children's literature by eighteenth- and nineteenth-century authors like Barbauld and Edgeworth "might constitute a radical gesture, an intervention in public history" (3) that provides a way for women to bridge the gap between the domestic sphere and the public masculinized realm of what Myers refers to as "big" history.

35. Helms, "Appropriating Maternal Authority," 210.

36. Barbauld, Mrs. [Anna], advertisement to *Mrs. Barbauld's Lessons for Children* (London: J. Johnson, 1791).

37. Michelle Levy, "The Radical Education of *Evenings at Home," Eighteenth-Century Fiction* 19.1–2 (2006–7): 1, 9.

38. Helms, "Appropriating Maternal Authority," 217.

39. McCarthy, *Voice of the Enlightenment*, 103.

40. Mrs. [Anna] Barbauld, *Hymns in Prose for Children. By the Author of Lessons for Children*, 6th ed. (London: J. Johnson, 1794), 7, 9.

41. Barbauld, *Hymns*, 9–10.

42. Mitzi Myers, "Of Mice and Mothers: Mrs. Barbauld's 'New Walk' and Gendered Codes in Children's Literature," in *Feminine Principles and Women's Experience in American Composition and Rhetoric,* ed. Louise Wetherbee Phillips and Janet Emig (Pittsburgh: Univ. of Pittsburgh Press, 1995), 269.

43. Barbauld, *Hymns*, 13.

44. Barbauld, *Hymns*, 15.

45. Barbauld, *Hymns*, 17.

46. Early Wesleyan denominations in the eighteenth century allowed women to preach publicly. However, this changed following Wesley's death in 1791. See Methodist Archives and Research Center, "The Role of Women within Methodism," The University of Manchester Library, http://www.library.manchester.ac.uk/searchresources/ guidetospecialcollections/methodist/using/womeninmethodism/roleofwomen/

47. Barbauld, *Hymns,* 64–5.

48. Barbauld, *Hymns*, 66–7.

49. McCarthy, *Voice of the Enlightenment,* 117–8.

50. "The Contemplative Philosopher, Numb. LIX. A View of the Insect Tribes": "I shall conclude this with some beautiful verses by Mrs. Barbauld" (312).

51. "An Account of Mrs. Anna-Laetitia Barbauld, formerly Miss Aikin. [With an Elegant Engraving of Her]," *European Magazine, and London Review* 9 (March 1786): 140.

52. See McCarthy, Introduction to *Voice of the Enlightenment*: "Thomas Denman, the man who drafted the 1832 Reform Act that began to modernize the British electoral system, had been a pupil at her school and remained devoted to her memory all his life" (x).

53. Barbauld, Mrs. [Anna], advertisement to *Mrs. Barbauld's Lessons for Children* (London: J. Johnson, 1791).

54. Quoted in McCarthy and Kraft, eds., *Anna Letitia Barbauld,* 253. According to McCarthy and Kraft, this hymn was added in 1814. See Barbauld, *Hymns in Prose for Children by the Author of Lessons for Children* (London: J. Johnson, 1814): 91–92.

55. This line calls to mind the Preface to Barbauld's *Hymns* in which she cited the importance of inculcating a reverence for God through sensory stimulus for the pre-linguistic child: "to impress them by connecting religion with a variety of sensible objects; with all that he sees, all he hears, all that affects his young mind with wonder or delight" (v).

56. Emma Major, "Nature, Nation, and Denomination: Barbauld's Taste for the Public," *ELH* 74.4 (Winter 2007): 910.

Novel "Modes" and "Indian Goods": Textilic Nationalism in *A Patch-Work Screen for the Ladies* and *The Lining of the Patch Work Screen*

SAMARA ANNE CAHILL

Nancy Armstrong's recent provocation to see the "network as the model of a nation increasingly dependent on international trade" was a salutary development in studies of the novel.[1] Armstrong focused on Jane Austen's novels, but envisioning the nation as a "network" can also be a useful method for studying earlier writers such as Jacobite novelist Jane Barker (1652–1732). Barker wrote three novels centering on her semi-autobiographical Jacobite heroine Galesia. Scholars call this set of novels the "Galesia Trilogy" and the final two novels are associated by the textile references in their titles: *A Patch-Work Screen for the Ladies* (1723) and *The Lining of the Patch Work Screen* (1726). Situating the two final "patchwork" novels of Barker's trilogy against the backdrop of the Anglo-Portuguese-Dutch trade network between Europe and South Asia explains the heroine's perplexing suggestion that "Indian" textiles signify true English identity. Theorizing the nation as a trade network reveals two of Barker's central images—the tea table and the patchwork screen (and its lining)—to be interlocking synecdoches of Anglo-Portuguese-Indian cultural hybridity that Barker used to articulate a complex model of national belonging that excluded the Dutch.[2] Barker's network model placed Jacobite exiles at the center of English identity while decentering arriviste "BUGGS" that represented, as I will argue, the political and financial innovations of William III and the Dutch.[3]

Barker aligned her fiction not only with the feminocentric activities of patchworking and presiding over the tea table, but also with the women of London who participated in these activities. She did so by representing all of them as mutually vulnerable to a fire that could only be warded off by investing in the virtues she allegorized as "Indian" textiles (calicoes). With this gesture, Barker would condemn the realist fiction—or "HISTORIES at Large"—of the pro-Dutch, anti-calico Daniel Defoe to an apocalyptic conflagration.[4] Barker used references to the Anglo-Dutch-Portuguese trade network to valorize an alternative English subjectivity to that cultivated by the increasingly realist fiction of the early eighteenth century.

Barker wrote in a variety of modes, including translation, Jacobite coterie poetry, and novels. She also wrote for a variety of audiences and, as Tonya Moutray has demonstrated, sometimes adjusted her work to conform to audience expectations.[5] While Barker never explicitly called for an overturning of Hanoverian rule, at least in her mainstream fiction, she clearly presented Hanoverian England as a place where virtues were not recognized, to the endangerment of anyone who did not want to "patch" the virtuous Jacobites into the national fabric. Barker dared to present the Jacobite exile as the bearer of English identity. In this article, I tease out Barker's complex network of meaning through the five sections below, including an explanation of the term "textilic nationalism"; the association of predatory BUGGS with the Dutch and the South Sea Bubble; the ladies' tea table as a synecdoche of Anglo-Portuguese hybridity; the patchwork as a synecdoche of Anglo-Indian hybridity; and, finally, Barker's use of apocalyptic fire to valorize her own Jacobite fiction over that of her contemporary Daniel Defoe.[6]

Textilic Nationalism

In a famous passage from *A Patch-Work Screen*'s prefatory "TO THE READER," Barker described the tea table as a site of female sociability that enabled women to combine conversation and tea-drinking with the domestic work of patching, an activity roughly equivalent to ornamental quilting. As she said, when

> *a Set of Ladies* [are] *together, their Sentiments are as differently mix'd as the* Patches *in their Work: To wit,* Whigs *and* Tories, High-Church *and* Low-Church, Jacobites *and* Williamites, *and many more Distinctions, which they* divide *and* sub-divide, *'till at last they make this* Dis-union *meet in an harmonious* Tea Table *Entertainment.*[7]

From the outset, Barker mapped the act of patchwork—the uniting of diverse materials—onto a model of national unity envisioned as harmonious ideological hybridity. This unity was important to Barker as a Jacobite who spent several years in exile at the court of the ousted James II in St. Germain, France.

Continued support for the exiled Stuart monarchs in the wake of the "Glorious Revolution" of 1688 made the political threat of Jacobitism linger in England as a national security threat until at least the Jacobite rebellion of 1745. Indeed, as Toni Bowers has noted, the "elimination of the Jacobite threat was by no means as sudden as historians sometimes imply; it was years after the decisive Battle of Culloden [in 1746] before Britons could be certain that the Jacobites would not rise again, and degrees of security varied regionally."[8] The Jacobites were a diverse group; some remained in England as objects of suspicion while others, like Barker, went into exile with James II. And among those Jacobites who remained in England, there existed a range of attitudes toward the exiled Stuarts, including those who "withheld full ideological commitment, or whose commitment mutated over time."[9] Nevertheless, Jacobites were viewed as a potential national security threat whether they went into exile or remained in England. Barker's project was to reintegrate English national identity by recasting the threatening figures of the Jacobite diaspora as allies of the English body politic against the depredations of the financial and political elites who she felt had concocted the disastrous stock market fiasco of the South Sea Bubble. In a practice that I am coining "textilic nationalism" Barker interlinked sociability and delimited diversity in a patchwork fashion that enabled her to portray Jacobite exiles as integral patches of the national fabric while urging BUGGS to accept Stuart rule or risk being cut out.

Barker enshrined her marginalized religio-political perspective in her Jacobite poetry but also in the mainstream "Galesia Trilogy," which includes *Love Intrigues* (1713, revised 1719) and the two "patchwork" novels: *A Patch-Work Screen for the Ladies* and *The Lining of the Patch Work Screen*.[10] Galesia's sociable interactions with strangers provide the pretext for storytelling in the "Trilogy." *Love Intrigues* is only significant to this argument because, by setting it at St. Germain, Barker immediately identified Galesia as a member of the Jacobite diaspora. As *A Patch-Work Screen for the Ladies*—the middle novel of the trilogy and the first of the "patchwork" novels—begins, a middle-aged Galesia is a respectable but poor single woman. Having suffered a mishap while traveling in the countryside, she is taken in by a benevolent unnamed Lady. The Lady invites Galesia to join her in creating an ornamental "patchwork" screen for display in a richly furnished room. The process of creating this domestic textile product structures the narrative and that of the sequel, *The Lining of the Patch Work Screen*. The women sew together diverse patches, some of them manuscript pages of Galesia's writing, including "Pieces of *Romances*, *Poems*, *Love-Letters* and the like" which they "mixed in due Order, and thereof compose[d] a SCREEN."[11] The conflation of text and textile enables Galesia to narrate episodes according to the ostensibly random selection of patches.

But Barker's textile narratives created meaning according to a gradual, associative accretion; the patches were not randomly selected at all. This becomes clear when we see that interlocking synecdoches of cultural hybridity anchor the final two novels of the trilogy. The first of the two synecdoches, the ladies' tea table, represented the Anglo-Portuguese alliance of Charles II and Catherine of Braganza. The second, invoked by the novels' titles—the "screen" and its "lining"—represented the Stuart-associated global textile trade. Understanding the tea table and patchwork as synecdoches, however, first requires some background on Barker's antipathy to the Dutch.

Going Dutch

Barker had to be circumspect in her criticism of the Revolution of 1688, so in *The Lining to the Patch Work Screen*'s introductory "TO THE LADIES" she suggested that England had become a "Jargon of *Babel*" in which "old *English*" had been displaced and incoherence and pride had become the "Mark of good Breeding."[12] In Barker's view, a "Colony of BUGGS" had installed itself in England and this colony was partly to blame for the frivolous, consumerist "Court" that rejected "Poetry" and used "Greek and Latin" simply to "garnish their Dedications." Fashionable society had turned away, not only from poetry and real engagement with classical literature, but also from an original, unifying, conversational "old *English*."

England was not itself and Barker considered several possible culprits: the BUGGS; the proliferation of gin ("JINN"); or the lingering influence of radical Protestants—the "Saints" of "Oliver's time"—who "spoke a Dialect so different" from "the Ungodly" that "one might almost take it for two Languages."[13] Barker never specified the identity of the invasive colony of BUGGS; yet I contend that she meant them to represent the Dutch in general and, specifically, the Dutch-influenced institutions that took over London's political and financial centers after William III came to the English throne.[14]

Barker associated Oliver Cromwell, William III, and their respective supporters as violent usurpers of Stuart rule. But the defeated Roundheads were not the real problem. Rather, the most troubling BUGGS were those who had come to power due to the Revolution of 1688: the Dutch and, subsequently, the Hanoverians. The engine behind Barker's sustained critique of William III and the Dutch was her tacit contention that the near destruction of national welfare by Dutch financial innovations contrasted with the flourishing of England under just Stuart rule.

Charles II's reign was racked by the Anglo-Dutch Wars and by the trade rivalry between England and Holland. This rivalry was only resolved by what Niall Ferguson called the "Anglo-Dutch business merger" of the Dutch and English East India Companies brought about by the Revolution of 1688. As Ferguson has said, a "powerful oligarchy of English aristocrats" joined with the "merchants of the City of London" to invite "the Dutch Stadholder William of Orange to invade England" in order to replace James II.[15] This coup resulted in Dutch businessmen becoming "major shareholders in the English East India Company" and introducing the English to the institutions of "modern finance" that the Dutch had "pioneered." These institutions included the Bank of England (founded in 1694 on a model similar to Amsterdam's Wisselbank, according to Ferguson) and "the Dutch system of a national public debt, funded through a Stock Exchange" that "allowed the government to borrow at significantly reduced interest rates."[16] Barker also seems to have believed that the Dutch-influenced financial systems and the cheap credit they made possible also laid the groundwork for the national financial disaster known as the South Sea Bubble, a stock market scheme that failed not only because of rampant over-speculation and because the wildly exorbitant profits expected of a trade monopoly in the Spanish Americas never materialized, but because the South Sea Company's stocks had been tied to the national debt.[17]

So it is significant that while Galesia and the Lady are at their patchwork and Galesia is narrating her life story, they are informed that "*South-Sea* Directors" from London plan to visit the Lady's husband to entice him to "lay a Debt upon his Estate" to involve himself in the "profitable Fund."[18] Yet the patch that Galesia selects from her collection at that moment is a poem prophesying that when "a Noise in the South" arises, England ought to "beware of Undoing." Writing from a post-crash vantage point, Barker manipulated her narrative to present Galesia as prophetic while also leveraging the knowledge her readers in 1723 would have had of this recent financial disaster. Further, Galesia's warning to her host occurs directly before she resumes narrating her autobiography. She resumes her life story by recollecting that King Charles's death was soon followed by that of Galesia's beloved, pro-Stuart mother. This narrative contiguity equated a Dutch-associated financial disaster with the loss of a Stuart king and a mother.

Barker associated William III and his Dutch influences—gin (a Dutch import) and the modern financial systems represented by the South Sea directors and other merchants of the "City"—with the invasive colony of BUGGS. This context clarifies what is at stake when the wives of the "City" gentlemen reject Galesia's "Indian" textiles in *The Lining*. Recognizing the tea table and the patchwork as two interlocking synecdoches of Anglo-Portuguese-Indian cultural hybridity identifies Galesia's "Indian" textiles as the true English virtues that would save Barker's readers from divine punishment.

Tea Table Hybridity

The tea table was not an innocent site of feminine sociability and political harmony. Rather, it represented a foreign import that had been successfully domesticated. Although tea has become the quintessentially British beverage, it was actually Charles II's bride, Catherine of Braganza, who popularized tea. As a Portuguese princess, Catherine had greater access than the English to the exotic commodities of Asia. Indeed, the Portuguese trade network occupied a place on the world stage that the Stuart kings strove to emulate.

At various points in her textile narratives Barker alluded to each item of Catherine of Braganza's dowry. Roy Moxham has observed,

> Catherine of Braganza with her dowry tea … made tea a fad at court. … There were other presents in the queen's dowry, too. There was the gift of the African trading enclave of Tangier; there was the right to trade freely to Brazil and to the East Indies—rights previously regarded by the Portuguese as exclusively theirs; and there was the gift of Bombay (Mumbai).[19]

Thus, Catherine's dowry connected the Stuarts to the much more established and powerful trade network of Portugal. As Eric Gilbert and Jonathan Reynolds have observed, Portugal was "instrumental in creating … the 'First Globalization.'"[20] But this was not to last. Over time "the Dutch became the masters of the Indian Ocean's sea lanes," marginalizing the Portuguese "because of their superior access to capital, their more efficient bureaucracies, and because, to a greater extent than the Portuguese, they were able to internalize their costs." While the Anglo-Dutch wars were an ongoing source of worry during Charles II's reign, the arrival of William III on the English throne resulted in the Dutch East India Company (VOC) and the English East India Company's (EIC) negotiating trade routes.[21] So Barker's "old" (pre-1688) England was aligned with the Portuguese, the Indian textile trade, tea, and the Stuarts together against the Dutch, gin, financial chicanery, successful trade expansionism, and William III. Using this backdrop, Barker wove a subtle, tapestried argument in favor of Stuart rule.

In Barker's view, English unity could be achieved under the Stuarts because they were a cosmopolitan and hybrid monarchical family, able to harmonize diverse elements in a profitable global trade to benefit the nation. Barker paired a successfully domesticated foreign import with hybrid imports associated with a Stuart textile network to model the kind of relationship that English citizens ought to cultivate with the Jacobite exiles, their seemingly threatening alien compatriots. The domestication of tea indicated that what was initially foreign and strange could eventually be a valued asset, indeed, a cherished symbol of national identity.

Further, Barker associated each item of Catherine's dowry with sympathetic exiles. In one story, "Tangerine," the gentleman gypsy of the story's title had been stationed at Tangier; in another, Galesia's friend Captain Manly set out to trade in the Caribbean only to be captured by pirates off the coast of Africa (near the Portuguese-held Madeira Islands); and, in Barker's final novel, Galesia purchased and tried to market "Indian" textiles. These three individuals—associated with the dowry items brought to Charles II by Catherine of Braganza—suffered rejection, criminalization, and misrecognition by loved ones or potential companions in England. It was the tea popularized by Catherine of Braganza that brought together "Whigs" and "Tories" in a "harmonious Tea Table Entertainment."[22]

Though Barker did not mention her by name, Catherine of Braganza made an appearance in the "Galesia Trilogy" as the "Queen" in the "Tale of the Unaccountable Wife," a narrative of domestic usurpation that coincided with Barker's later critique of the usurpers in the corrupt City and Court.[23] In the tale, Queen Catherine significantly promises the "Unaccountable Wife" a pension and gives her "Five Guineas" to abandon her non-traditional, cross-class relationship.[24] This gift-giving associates Catherine of Braganza with Galesia's Fairy Queen who, in a fantastical dream sequence leading up to the conclusion of the trilogy, gives Galesia the "Fairie Treasure" with which Galesia purchases her Indian wares. The connection would have been significant for Barker's eighteenth-century readers because fairies were associated with the "old profession" of Roman Catholicism.[25] Stuart patronage and the female gift-giving it enabled were thus contradistinguished from the financial predations of the "*South-Sea* Directors." Barker's textilic hybridity would similarly indict "City" wives.

Textilic Hybridity

The *Lining* draws to a close with a fantastic allegorical vision: Galesia dreams that she attends a ceremony, presided over by the Queen of the Fairies, crowning Orinda (Katherine Philips) as "Queen of Female Writers."[26] Yet the Queen of the Fairies inexplicably insists that Galesia leave the ceremony, dismissing her with a gift of gold. Galesia subsequently awakens to receive a sum of gold from an anonymous gentleman. She chooses to invest this "*Fairie*-Treasure" in "*Indian* Goods" (allegorized as "*Female Vertues*") imported by a friend who had been trading in the Indies. Galesia seems blithely unaware of her own social satire when she agrees with her friend that such foreign virtues were sure to "sell well in this Country, where there was so great a Scarcity." But her economic model—the assumption that where there is scarcity there must also be demand—does not serve her well.

Galesia believes it to be "her Duty and Interest to send to the Court in the first place" the virtue of "Sincerity," yet the ladies of fashion, while admitting that the goods are "curiously wrought, and safely brought over," decline the virtue of sincerity since "that kind of Merchandize, was quite out of fashion." More significantly, the "rich and haughty Dames," the wives of merchants in the financial and trading center of the City, do not discern the value of "*Humility*" and remind Galesia's representative that because Indian textiles are prohibited, she could be arrested. They tell her they have plenty of "Home-made" humility and so need none of her "right *Indian*" kind. Yet their explanation reveals that their wrongheaded understanding of humility consists in aping the "Fashions" of "Ladies" at Court.

Moreover, after this benighted rejection of humility, the ladies rail, "to come into the City with your prohibited Ware, is Insolence in a high degree; Therefore be gone, before my Lord Mayor's Officers catch, and punish you according to your Deserts." Virtue, in Barker's view, was entirely too exotic for the fashionable London elite. No wonder that after her entrepreneurial disappointments in the City Galesia elects to return to the Country with her patroness "in hopes the Women of all Ranks and Stations would be better Customers" of her female virtues.

However, one Londoner, the prostitute Mrs. Rottenbones, recognizes the names on the packages containing Galesia's Indian textiles as belonging to her former colleagues in the business of petty crime: Betty Bilk, Sarah Shuffle, and Polly Picklock. These women had been displaced, yet their professional industry suggests that they had been integrated as productive members into an English society abroad and were now sending seemingly foreign virtues back to England. Among the lowliest of social outcasts displaced across the globe, English virtue had found a home.

This scenario raises two questions: (1) In light of new research on the early modern global textile network, to what extent could these "Indian wares" really be considered "foreign"? (2) India was not an English colony at this time, so why would the female criminals have been transported there? These questions are important to consider because only slight critical attention has been paid to the implications of the textile form of Barker's last two Galesia novels in relation to the "Calico Craze" that was roughly coterminous with the publication of these novels. One exception, Rivka Swenson's excellent article on the surprising modernity of Barker's patchwork aesthetics, offers the following tantalizing footnote:

> Galesia's goods are "prohibited" because they are "Indian"... During the speculative activities that led to the disastrous South Sea Bubble, Spitalfield weavers rioted to protest the East India Company's importation of calicoes. ... [Thus] the significance of the cloth "Vertues" may reside less in their East Indian origin than in the fact of their prohibition and the necessity, perceived by Galesia, of importing them in from outside England in the first place.[27]

I would like to complicate this persuasive argument by qualifying the description of the "Indian wares" as having an exclusively "East Indian origin." The assumed origin of the textiles must be considered further since the importation of calicoes was a Stuart project in which royal support of native wool manufacturers was enmeshed with support of the East India Company. Additionally, by the time Barker was writing, the calicoes were essentially hybridized Anglo-Indian designs.

Importantly, the "Calico Craze" highlighted an internal conflict within the English body politic. On the one hand, royalty, aristocrats, and anyone who could afford them desired the breathtakingly ornate Indian cotton textiles that far surpassed in vibrancy of color and artistic intricacy what domestic textile workers were capable of producing. On the other hand, England was a nation that prided itself on its woolen manufacture. According to Prasannan Parthasarathi and Giorgio Riello,

> The late seventeenth-century passion for imported India cottons was seen as a 'calico craze,' but not all in Europe were pleased with these developments. While Indian cottons enriched the East India companies as well as the merchants, traders, and shopkeepers connected to the trade in these new clothes, they aroused the opposition of manufacturers of woolen and silk cloth who argued that the import of calicoes, the generic term for Indian cottons, decreased the wealth of the nation.[28]

Thus, it seems impossible that Barker could defend the importation of Indian textiles while simultaneously defending the domestic woolen industry. This conflict is, however, precisely why Galesia's Indian textiles function as a synecdoche of cultural hybridity, for under the Stuarts the potential conflict could have been seen, by a pro-Stuart writer, to be harmoniously balanced: Charles II had protected the woolen industry while importing these luxurious Indian calicoes. Under the Stuarts, Barker could reasonably have believed, domestic and foreign textile production were not engaged in a zero-sum competition.

The Great Fire of London came on the heels of a devastating plague that caused such havoc in the domestic woolen trade that Charles II, out of his "Clemency and tender Compassion," issued a proclamation that as the King he gave

> free Liberty and License to all and every person whatsoever, as well Natives and Denizens, as Strangers and Foreigners, from the day of the Date hereof [15th day of April, 1666], until the five and twentieth day of December next, to Transport and Carry out of this Kingdom, all Woollen Manufactures whatsoever, to any Port or place beyond the Seas, lying within the Limits and Bounds of the said Merchant-Adventurers Patent.[29]

The plague and "the present War" were two disasters that united King, nation, a global merchant company, and even "Strangers and Foreigners" in the shared endeavor of recovering national welfare through trade. It was this united England of shared interests under a Stuart monarch to which Galesia wished to return.

Further, under the Stuarts the East India Company (EIC) established an economic, if not a political, presence in India. Though the Stuarts had established colonial holdings in North America and had granted a charter to the EIC before the marriage of Charles II and Catherine of Braganza, it was Charles II who granted the EIC

> new and extraordinary powers. It was given the right to send out its own ships of war, men and ammunition, and to authorize their commanders to "continue or make peace or war with any Prince or People (that are not Christians) in any place of their trade"...With these privileges the East India Company was set to become the most powerful multi-national corporation the world has yet seen.[30]

In other words, the empire that expanded over the course of Hanoverian rule was enabled by the conjunction of a Stuart monarch's support of the corporate power of the EIC and that same monarch's marriage to a Roman Catholic Portuguese princess.

So the "Indian" wares were not so foreign to Barker's "Old" London after all. The point could be pushed further. Though Indian textiles would have come to England through English merchants, the designs of the wares, too, were hybrid English productions. As John Styles has recently argued,

> From the 1660s it became normal English East India Company practice to send patterns from London to determine the design of the quilts that had been the main form of Indian decorated textiles sold in England in the first half of the seventeenth century and the chintzes that enjoyed success in the second half of the century. *This was a system of manufacture in which London remained the principle arbiter and source of design.*[31]

In his response to Styles, Parthasarathi agreed that "the designs that appealed to English consumers were complex hybrid products," but he also proposed "that we no longer speak of English or Indian textile design. Instead, let us speak of textile design in England and in India (actually, not India either, but regions of the subcontinent)."[32] And as Beverly Lemire and Giorgio Riello have observed, "routine consultation between the East India companies and their factors in India attempted to ensure that the imported textiles met local European standards and tastes." [33] Indeed, this hybridity has recently received significant attention in various catalogues based on the holdings of the Victoria and Albert Museum (London) and the Metropolitan Museum of Art (New York).[34] The Metropolitan Museum's most recent textile exhibition, *Interwoven Globe: The Worldwide Textile Trade, 1500–1800* (September 16, 2013–January 5, 2014) focused on the dynamism and hybridity of the early modern global textile trade, a trade network within which the Stuart monarchs desired to be key players.

In other words, the directive from the EIC to the Indian factors to produce English designs largely coincided with the Restoration of Charles II (also the "threescore and six years ago" so celebrated by Barker in her final, 1726 novel) and his subsequent marriage to Catherine of Braganza.[35] Galesia's "Indian" textiles were actually the hybrid products of an England uncorrupted by BUGGS. No wonder, then, that the ladies of the Court and City were not interested in purchasing these virtues: English virtues were not only foreign to them, the virtues also represented the return to the "Old" London of the Stuart monarchs. Indian textiles were hybrid products that the

Stuarts not only encouraged but also used in their official self-fashioning as global trade leaders.[36]

But were there Englishwomen in EIC factories in the years 1690–1720, as Galesia implied—transported criminals whose repentance and piety would signal their allegiance to England? As Peter Carleton Craft has pointed out, English trading posts were established in India in the seventeenth century under the EIC, but these were allowed only at the sufferance of powerful Mughal emperors like Aurangzeb. After several years of squabbles with the already established Portuguese traders, the English were able to acquire Mughal permission to establish their first factory at Surat in 1615. As Craft has observed, in "the late seventeenth and early eighteenth centuries, the total number of Englishmen in South Asia never exceeded a few hundred and their overseas territories were primarily 'factories,' or trading posts, rather than large-scale colonial occupations as in the Americas."[37]

More research is needed on the presence of women in the English factories in India, starting with Bombay in the 1660s (Craft has noted that European women were barred from factories like Surat and Madras, which had been established early in the seventeenth century).[38] Nonetheless, sources do point to women's presence in these settings and suggest that, while they do not seem to have been technically transported as Barker suggested, they did have reputations as heavy drinkers and petty criminals. Writing in the nineteenth century, Philip Anderson explained the reasoning behind the importation of English women to Bombay when he reported that Gerald Aungier, Governor of Bombay between 1672 and 1675, had suggested that male factory employees

> ought to be encouraged and assisted in contracting marriages with their countrywomen. Consistently [sic] with his character he took a religious view of the question, and pointed out that the men being Protestants were in the habit of marrying native Portuguese women, the consequence of which was that their offspring were, "through their father's neglect, brought up in the Roman Catholic principles to the great dishonor and weakening of the Protestant religion and interest." He therefore recommended that a supply of women should be sent out from England. This proposal was acceded to by the court of Directors. . . . Unhappily . . . a judicious observer, who visited the island soon after, was shocked to see how sickly their children were in consequence of the free and easy way in which the mothers lived, and their inveterate habit of taking strong liquors.[39]

Thus, the Englishwomen who went to Bombay did resemble the petty criminals described by Barker (though perhaps they were not, ultimately, so very reformed). Also, the anxiety about Englishmen's hybrid children being trained up by Roman Catholic Portuguese mothers underscored not only that the Portuguese presence in India was much stronger than that of the English, but also that Bombay had come to the English as part of the dowry of a Portuguese princess.

Barker, in other words, constructed a fantasy in which the exile who seemed to lack virtue was capable of "piety" and "reform" in a new, international location where she could contribute to something valuable to be sent home. But would the English—overrun with "BUGGS" and "Jinn" and living in a Babel of their own creation—recognize their own community? Barker was not sure, for she presented even Galesia's agent as being misrecognized by the city guards and "Centinels" as a "Spectre."[40]

If the English could not recognize their friends, it was no wonder that they did not recognize or properly value exiled virtue. Moreover, the rejection of Galesia's "*Indian* Goods" by the City wives was particularly damning because Barker could lean on her English readers' identification of the patchwork as an example of a distinctively English material culture that combined both foreign and domestic products in an adornment for the domestic space. Barker's "patch work" functioned synecdochically. Heather Audin has noted that the "earliest known dated British patchwork in existence [the 1718 patchwork coverlet in the Quilter's Guild Collection]… is completely made of silk apart from six pieces of wool and velvet."[41] The various fabrics selected for patchworks also included cotton and particularly sought after were "Indian cottons with their exotic multi-colored chintz designs" which were "unparalleled in Europe, making them a desirable commodity for fashionable garments and bed covers." This very desirability, of course, led to the protests by domestic textile producers that resulted in Parliament passing protectionist legislation that applied to "both Indian and British-made cotton."

The diversity of fabrics used in patchwork was certainly important for Barker's recuperation of the Jacobites, but also significant was the status of patchwork as a collection of family artifacts. As Audin observed of the 1718 coverlet, the "range of silk fabrics represents nearly a century's worth of collecting, showing how valuable and treasured these fabrics were." The fabrics of another rare surviving example (1726, McCord Museum of Canadian History) also represented "nearly a century of fabric collecting." Thus, patchwork served as a visible reminder that history could be recycled and made new, useful, and pleasurable. Barker gambled that, if her patchwork were an effective display of national belonging, there would be no reason not to "patch" in the Jacobites, too.

So the discussion of the fashion dynamic between the country and the City when Galesia's representative tries to sell her Stuart-associated Indian wares to the wives of the City men is significant. These women scoff at the Indian merchandise of "Humility," declaring that too much of that merchandise circulates in the City already. They insist that their own "Humility," the fashionable rivalry between City wives and "Ladies" of the court and country,

> appears daily…by giving your Ladies place every where, by following their Fashions at all times; Whereas our Riches give us a right to be fantastical, and setters-up of new Modes; But 'tis our *Humility* that pervails [sic] with us, and makes us their Apes, at the same time; many of them being but meanly descended, they often run in our Debt, for their gaudy Trappings; and their Husbands borrow of ours, to support their Equipage, on the credit of their Acres.[42]

Yet while the City wives may be erstwhile conformers to English aristocratic taste, what really gives these "setters-up of new Modes" pleasure is knowing that the credit their husbands offer is destroying the financial stability of the landed gentry. Clearly, Barker positioned the wives of the City's financial elites, which would include the Directors of the South Sea scheme, as not only opposed to the sartorial culture of the Stuarts but also as proponents of a fashion cycle that vampirically destroyed the country estates of "old" England. Barker saw the "new" mode of fiction as equally destructive, particularly the mode promoted by Daniel Defoe.

Fiction Aflame

In her essay on European responses to "Eastern" textiles, Melinda Watt identified Defoe as "one of the most eloquent advocates for the European domestic textile industries," one who "produced a number of pamphlets against the importation of Indian goods."[43] Defoe's antipathy perhaps explains Barker's use of Indian textiles to defend her hybrid fiction against the modern fiction of Defoe. For Barker, novels like *Robinson Crusoe* and *Moll Flanders* were "HISTORIES *at* Large" and she explicitly contrasted them with her own "HISTORY *reduc'd into* Patches."[44] Barker, in other words, was competing with Defoe for dominance in the literary market.

Barker always appealed to her female readers as commercial judges. At the end of her letter "TO THE LADIES" in the *Lining*, she acknowledged that they had been "kind to my Booksellers in favour of the SCREEN" and hoped that "this LINING will not meet with a less Favourable Reception from Your Fair Hands."[45] However, Barker played on the fact that a book is not only an experience, but also a material artifact. She assured her readers that if the ladies did not approve of her work, they could use it to fuel the fire to boil water: "if it have but the honour to light your Lamps for your Tea-kettles," she tells them, "its Fate will be propitious enough." Either way she would have contributed to their communal enjoyment.

But there was an edge to Barker's submission to her judges that hinged on her complex association of the textile trade with her defense of exiles, the welfare of London, her fiction, and her readers. As she told the Ladies in the same letter, the larger patches, or "pane" work, of the *Lining* resembled the "Composure in your Petticoats" which in turn "bears some resemblance to Old *London*, when the Buildings were of Wood and Plaister." She hoped that the ladies would enjoy her panels rather than consigning them to the same fate as Old London, which had been ravaged by the Great Fire of 1666. Fire, then, was an important motif in Barker's fiction, a motif that associated a threat to London's security with a threat to the intimate apparel of her reader, to her own work, and, as we shall see, to domestic textile production.

Fire was both politically and religiously significant for Barker. As Galesia describes her youthful self in *A Patch-work Screen*, she was isolated upon first moving to London because her country upbringing had made her knowledge of rural life (with its truly productive agrarian economy) laughable in the sophisticated city. Galesia explicitly criticizes herself as a country bumpkin, but her censure tacitly reflects on the members of the sophisticated urban elite who neither understand nor care about maximizing domestic productivity. This binary opposition between rural production and urban apathy was key, because in one of Galesia's most explicit criticisms of Parliament Barker presented a failure to protect domestic textile production as directly leading to fire, the very fate to which she hoped her female readers would not subject her writing.

The young Galesia had censured Parliament for the "Decay of the Wooll-Trade" and for "taking no better Care of the Country-Trade, by prohibiting Cane-Chairs and Wainscot; by which means, the Turkey-work, Tapistry, and Kidderminster Trades were quite lost; and in them the great Manufacture of the Nation; and not only so, but perpetual Fires intail'd on the City of London."[46] Yet Barker was not simply contrasting a youthful Galesia and the urban elite; she was also intervening in a historical debate. The perceived decline of the wool trade was certainly an element in the protectionist reaction to the Calico Craze but it was also a point of contention in the approach of an assembly of Cane-Chair makers to Parliament in 1689. According to the "Case" made by the cane-makers:

> We find (by a true and exact Account) that there is not Six thousand Dozens of Cane-Chairs, Stools, Couches, and Squobs, made in *England* in any one Year, whereof above Two thousand Dozens are yearly Transported into almost all the Hot Parts of the World, where the Heat renders the Turky-work, Serge, *Kidderminster*, and other Stuffed Chairs and Couches useless. ...Whereby it appears, that the Making and Using is not one eighth part of that Detriment to the Woollen Manufacture, as it is Asserted to be.[47]

In other words, by asserting a causal link between the proliferation of cane chairs and that of fires, Barker intervened in a decades-old trade competition between the wool manufacturers and cane-chair makers.[48] Not surprisingly, given her association with the country and with textiles, the young Galesia sided with the woolen manufacturers against the cane-makers, even though the latter had insisted that their products were not a significant threat to the domestic wool market. In Galesia's view, Parliament's support of the cane-chair makers did indeed harm the domestic textile market. The "Case" also roughly coincided with the Revolution of 1688, and it was, therefore, no wonder that Galesia characterized the Stuart-associated Indian wares as less of a threat to domestic textile trade, despite the Calico Craze, than cane-chairs, even if these could be exported.[49]

Galesia does not explain why a decrease in the wool trade would increase fires in London. She may have been suggesting that cloth-covered furniture in the damp English climate was less flammable than cane-chairs composed only of wood. In any case, she argues that not only did the Parliament fail to support its own domestic wool manufacturers, but the proliferation of wood in the capitol had made it more vulnerable to fire. Fire was a constant threat to Barker's fiction, to her reader's petticoats, and to London, and it was because the current political establishment neither understood nor cared about national welfare. Barker's position was, to be sure, biased and self-interested. But her representation of national belonging as textilic sociability—true Englishness meant adapting to the messy patchwork of reconciling an English body politic under the aegis of a Stuart monarch—should be recognized as an ambitious and complex public relations campaign for Jacobite exiles.

Yet while Barker was in the business of persuasion, she was not above suggesting that a rejection of her "vertues" would have dire consequences. She walked a fine line between offering pleasure and threatening punishment. As she lamented,

> Those honourable Romances of old Arcadia, Cleopatra, Cassandra, &c. discover a Genius of Vertue and Honour, which reign'd in the time of those Heroes, and Heroines, as well as in the Authors that report them; but the Stories of our Times are so black, that the Authors, can hardly escape being smutted, or defil'd in touching such Pitch.[50]

After this narratorial interjection vilifying modern fiction, Galesia hears a noise and sees "every body gazing up at a strange Light in the Sky" that appears to be "the general Conflagation [*sic*]...when the Almighty will purge the World from its Dross, by Fire as heretofore he did from its Filth by Water." The vocabulary of "smutted" and "defil'd" linked the modern fiction Barker primarily identified with Defoe to the sins of London that deserved a just and divine retribution, a final destruction by fire. Barker's fiction and Galesia's Indian textiles—the female virtues that, in Barker's view, London's political and financial elite had to choose to integrate into their homes—were the answer to saving the nation.

Survival, however, might not be possible for Londoners who reject her "Indian" virtues. Galesia and her friend Miranda, on the other hand, pointedly go to sleep while the fire continues to rage. The narrator accounts for this astonishing behavior by asserting that "Vertue and Innocence are always safeguards; and screen'd our two Friends from fear that dreadful Night." With this phrasing Barker called to mind the dual use of Galesia's original textilic production: the decorative patchwork fire screen served both to ornament and to protect the household. Thus Barker's fiction modeled female sociability while representing it as protection from divine punishment — at least for the kind of women who preferred "Romances of old" to the "Stories of our Times." Clearly, it was in the readers' own interests to be receptive to Barker's salvific fiction. Yet Barker presented her contemporary Londoners as perhaps too corrupt to escape punishment by fire, and it was no accident that Barker organized the episode of the fire to precede the episode of Galesia's Indian goods. At the end of the *Lining*, after the disappointing sales of the Indian textiles, Galesia leaves London for the country and the significance of this apparently anti-climactic conclusion is clear: the fire next time may not be avoidable for those who failed to value the prohibited virtues offered by Barker's Jacobite fiction.

This argument dovetails with Rachel Carnell's contention that "when we move beyond traditional Whig histories of the novel and uncover the early British novel's multifaceted partisan history, we discover that male and female writers were equally significant in shaping the features of novelistic realism and in determining which partisan version of reality would be allowed to be counted as 'real.'"[51] Indeed, one revelation in this analysis of Barker's fiction is her sustained engagement of Daniel Defoe's textile politics.[52] Their opposition on the matter of textile imports informed her construction of their respective modes of fiction as explicitly, ideologically, opposed. Juxtaposing Barker and Defoe instantiates Carnell's claim that "from the 1680s into the 1750s, this Whig version of reality had not yet emerged as normative, and the novels written during those decades reveal the spectrum of different partisan versions of realism that were still competing for cultural dominance."[53] We can read Barker's reference to the London conflagration as a warning to English readers that fiction like Defoe's ought not to dominate. The older, heroic romances of the Stuart era—the kind that had been patched into her own hybrid Jacobite fiction—would save the nation. The Jacobite exile, if patched into the body politic, would screen England from destruction, if only English readers would recognize the true worth of the dispossessed.

To date, Defoe's fiction outranks Barker's in terms of canonization, general recognition, and presence in university curricula. But scholars of early eighteenth-century fiction by women and other marginalized groups are now correcting this distortion by attending to how these perspectives are informed by a distrust of what Margaret Doody calls "Prescriptive Realism"—the "all-or-nothing Realism" that "cuts out fantasy and experiments, and severely limits certain forms of psychic and social questioning."[54] Accepting Barker into the canon of the English novel requires a healthy decentering of such "Prescriptive Realism."

Swenson was right to observe that Barker's aesthetics seem surprisingly "modern": the interpretive contingency of the "real" and the interconnectedness of the global community are now widely recognized.[55] Governments, banks, national borders, even the Anglo-Scottish partnership of "Great Britain," are increasingly provisional.[56] Barker saw this provisionality all along. Having spent several demoralizing years at the impoverished Stuart court in exile, Barker came back, haunted, to an England in which she could only live the life of the dispossessed: doubly conscious, always masked, imagining another reality. Perhaps it would have gladdened her to know that in a strange and distant century—that of the internet and worldwide web, of virtual realities and online social networks—her exilic patchwork fictions could finally find a home.

NOTES

I am grateful to the editors and anonymous *SECC* readers for their incisive comments throughout the editing process. Thanks are also due to Mark Brantner, Leung Wing Sze Evelyn, and Anne Thell for their helpful feedback at an early stage of the project and to Kevin Riordan for a useful perspective on Defoe's travel narratives. Thanks to Eileen and Victor Botting for their generous mentorship. For conversations that enriched the development of this article, grateful thanks to the global tea-table: Martine Brownley, Mary Cahill, Chandrava Chakravarty, Rachel Carnell, Shirley and Jennifer Chew, Akankasha Dewan, Margaret Doody, Kathryn Duncan, Anne Gardiner, Emily Kugler, Bhuvaneswary Narayanan, Manushag Powell, Krishna Sen, Priya Sharma, Rivka Swenson, Nanci Takeyama, Cassandra Teo, Hsu-Ming Teo, Phyllis Thompson, Jean Tsai, Rajee Vissa, Bethany Williamson, Chienhui Yang, and Joyce Zonana.

1. As Armstrong wrote, "I'm contending that each Austen novel tears open the traditional household and disperses its members (especially daughters) by putting them into circulation. … It is thus because Austen's novels propose a network as the model of a nation increasingly dependent on international trade that I now see them as the very examples of what a novel is and does." See Nancy Armstrong, "Austen's Domestic Fiction and The Network Form," *The 18th-Century Common*, 26 August, 2013. http://www.18thcenturycommon.org/austens-domestic-fiction-and-the-network-form/.

2. For an alternate reading, see Courtney Wigston Smith, *Women, Work and Clothes in the Eighteenth-Century Novel* (Cambridge: Cambridge Univ. Press, 2013), 5.

3. All references to Jane Barker's fiction are taken from the following edition: *The Galesia Trilogy and Selected Manuscript Poems of Jane Barker*, Carol Shriner Wilson, ed., (Oxford: Oxford Univ. Press, 1993). I refer to the two last novels in notes as follows: *A Patch-work Screen for the Ladies* (*PWS*) and *The Lining of the Patch Work Screen* (*LPWS*). See Carol Shiner Wilson's note, *LPWS*, 178n3.

4. Barker, *PWS*, 51. For Daniel Defoe's pro-Dutch stance, see Ton J. Broos, "Did Daniel Defoe do Dutch?" *Canadian Journal of Netherlandic Studies/Revue canadienne d'études néerlandaises* 33.1 (2012), 1–13. For Defoe's hostility to the importation of Indian calicoes, see Paula Backscheider, *Daniel Defoe: His Life* (Baltimore: Johns Hopkins Press, 1989), particularly 461 and 513.

5. See Tonya Moutray McArthur, "Jane Barker and the Politics of Catholic Celibacy," *Studies in English Literature, 1500–1900* 47.3 (Summer 2007), 595–618.

6. "BUGGS" was an ambiguous umbrella term that could mean Quakers, general troubles, typhus, or the Dutch.

7. Barker, *PWS*, 52.

8. Toni Bowers, "Representing Resistance: British Seduction Stories, 1660–1800" in Paula R. Backscheider and Catherine Ingrassia, eds., *A Companion to The Eighteenth-Century English Novel and Culture* (Chichester: Wiley-Blackwell, 2009), 140–163. 150–151.

9. Toni Bowers, "Jacobite Difference and the Poetry of Jane Barker," *ELH* 64.4 (1997), 857–869. 858.

10. For Barker's references to "Old London" and the "Buggs" see *LPWS*, 178.

11. Barker, *PWS*, 74.

12. Barker, *LPWS*, 178.

13. Barker, *LPWS*, 178 n.3, 179.

14. Barker's argument could also be read as a belated response to Daniel Defoe's satirical poem "The True-Born Englishman" (1701) in which he defended William III by ridiculing the notion of England's cultural purity. In other words, Barker and Defoe propounded competing models of English cultural hybridity.

15. Niall Ferguson, *Empire: How Britain Made the Modern World* (London: Penguin Books, 2004), 22.

16. Ferguson, *Empire*, 23.

17. Defoe is quoted in Ferguson, 23. For references to the South Sea Company and Bubble, see Ferguson, 20 and Wilson, 53n7. For an overview of the South Sea scheme and Defoe's complex and conflicted attitude toward it, see Backscheider, *Daniel Defoe*, 447–457.

18. Barker, *PWS*, quotations from this section can be found on 151–2.

19. Roy Moxham, *Tea: Addiction, Exploitation, and Empire* (New York: Carroll & Graf Publishers, 2003), 19.

20. Erik Gilbert and Jonathan T. Reynolds, *Trading Tastes: Commodity and Cultural Exchange to 1750* (New Jersey: Pearson Education, Inc., 2006), 42–43. Gilbert and Reynolds take the phrase "First Globalization" from the title of Geoffrey C. Gunn's *First Globalization: The Eurasian Exchange, 1500–1800* (Lanham: Rowman and Littlefield Publishers, Inc., 2003).

21. Ferguson, *Empire,* 23–24. Significantly, the Dutch never banned calicoes as the English did. See Beverly Lemire and Giorgio Riello, "East & West: Textiles and Fashion in Early Modern Europe," *Journal of Social History* 41.4 (2008), 887–916. 898.

22. Barker, *PWS*, 52.

23. The unnamed "Queen" is certainly Catherine of Braganza because the episode occurs just before Charles II's death in Galesia's retrospective account. See *PWS*, 148–153. For an alternate reading of the tale, see Kathryn King, *Jane Barker, Exile: A Literary Career 1675–1725* (Oxford: Clarendon Press, 2000), 226.

24. Barker, *PWS*, 148.

25. Many thanks to Professor James Lake for drawing my attention to the early-modern association of fairies, Roman Catholics, the Virgin Mary, and the gift of prophecy, and for furnishing me with a copy of Richard Corbett's "The Fairies' Farewell." As both M.E. Bradford and Patricia Springborg have pointed out, Corbett was drawing on a conventionally accepted early-modern association of fairies and Roman Catholics. Stanza six begins, "By which we note the Fairies / Were of the old profession; / Their songs were Ave Marys, / Their dances were procession" Quoted in M.E. Bradford, "The Prescience of Richard Corbett: Observations on 'The Fairies' Farewell,'" *The Sewanee Review* 81.2 (1973), 313 and Patricia Springborg, "Hobbes, Heresy, and the Historia Ecclesiastica," *Journal of the History of Ideas* 55.4 (1994), 566.

26. Barker, *LPWS*, quotations for this section can be found on 279–289.

27. Rivka Swenson, "Representing Modernity in Jane Barker's *Galesia Trilogy*: Jacobite Allegory and the Patch-Work Aesthetic," in Catherine Ingrassia and Jeffrey S. Ravel, eds., *Studies in Eighteenth-Century Culture* 34 (Baltimore and London: Johns Hopkins University Press, 2005), 55–80. 79n107.

28. Prasannan Parthasarathi and Giorgio Riello, "India to the World: Cotton and Fashionability," in Frank Trentmann, ed., *The Oxford Handbook of the History of Consumption* (Oxford: Oxford Univ. Press, 2012), 145–170. 158–9.

29. By the King. *A PROCLAMATION For the Free Exportation of Woollen Manufactures until the 25th Day of December next* (London, 1666).

30. Moxham, 20–21. Moxham quotes Charles II's 1661 charter to the EIC. See England and Wales, Sovereign [Charles II], "The *East-India* Companies CHARTER, Granted by the KINGS Most Excellent MAJESTY *CHARLES the Second*, under the Great Seal of *England*, Dated the third day of *April*, in the 13th. Year of His Majesties Reign, 1661" (London, 1661), 13. There are no parentheses around the phrase "that are not Christians" in the *Early English Books Online* copy of the Charter.

31. John Styles, "Indian Cottons and European Fashion, 1400–1800," in Glenn Adamson, Giorgio Riello and Sarah Teasley, eds., *Global Design History* (London and New York: Routledge, 2011), 37–46. 43. My emphasis.

32. Prasannan Parthasarathi, "Response," in Adamson, Riello and Teasley, eds., *Global Design*, 47–49. 49.

33. Lemire and Riello, "East & West: Textiles and Fashion in Early Modern Europe," 895.

34. Melinda Watt, "'Whims and Fancies': Europeans Respond to Textiles from the East," in Amelia Peck, ed., *Interwoven Globe: The Worldwide Textile Trade, 1500–1800* (New York: Metropolitan Museum of Art; distributed by Yale Univ. Press, New Haven, 2013), 87; Rosemary Crill "Indian Floral Patterns," in *V&A Patterns: Indian Florals* (London: V&A Publishing, 2009), n.p. For a useful review of the *Interwoven Globe* exhibit, see Brijraj Singh, "The Interwoven Globe: The World-wide Textile Trade, 1500–1800," *The Eighteenth-Century Intelligencer* 28.1 (2014), 23–28.

35. Barker, *LPWS*, 179.

36. See, for example, the table carpet panel that shows figures resembling Charles II and Catherine of Braganza presiding over the world in *Interwoven Globe Catalogue* (247, cat. 86B). See also Rosemary Crill, *Chintz: Indian Textiles for the West* (London: V&A Publishing, 2008), 29, note to plate 31; images on 70–71.

37. Peter Carleton Craft, "Warfare, Trade, and 'Indians' in British Literature, 1652–1711" (PhD diss., Univ. of Illinois at Urbana–Champaign, 2010), 2.

38. Craft, 10–11.

39. Philip Anderson, *The English in Western India; Being the Early History of the Factory at Surat, Of Bombay, and the Subordinate Factories on the Western Coast. From the Earliest Period Until the Commencement of the Eighteenth Century. Drawn from Authentic Works and Original Documents* (Bombay: Smith, Taylor and Co.; London: Smith, Elder and Co., 65, Cornhill, 1854), 101. Anderson draws on two sources in this passage. The first, regarding the weakening of Protestant principles, is

from a letter addressed to the EIC by Aungier and the "Councell at Surrat" ("Proposals Touching Bombay Island," February 5, 1671) available in *Selections from the Letters, Despatches, and Other State Papers Preserved in the Bombay Secretariat.* Home Series, Volume 1. Ed. George W. Forrest (Bombay: Government Central Press, 1887), 55. The second, describing the inveterate drinking of the English women, is from John Fryer, *New Account of East-India and Persia, in Eight Letters. Being Nine Years Travels, Begun 1672. And Finished 1681* (London, 1698). See Letter 2, Chapter 1, 69.

40. Barker, *LPWS*, 280.

41. Heather Audin, *Patchwork and Quilting in Britain* (Oxford: Shire Publications, 2013), 14. All subsequent references to Audin are from this section, 14–18.

42. Barker, *LPWS*, 281.

43. Watt,"'Whims and Fancies,'" 88.

44. Barker, *PWS*, 51.

45. Barker, *LPWS*, quotations for this section can be found on 178–9.

46. Barker *PWS*, 108.

47. Anon., "*The CASE of the Cane-Chair Makers humbly Presented to the Consideration of the Honourable the Commons in Parliament Assembled*" (London, 1689).

48. For the woolen manufacturers' perspective, see J. F. Houston, *Featherbedds and Flock Bedds: The Early History of the Worshipful Company of Upholders of the City of London* (Sandy, Bedfordshire: Three Tents Press, 2006), 61–63. Houston notes that the "efforts to suppress the cane chair failed," 63.

49. See, however, the account of contemporary economic theorist and Member of Parliament Nicholas Barbon, *A Discourse of Trade* (1690), reprinted by Jacob H. Hollander, ed., (Baltimore: The Johns Hopkins Press, 1905), 6.

50. Barker, *LPWS*, quotations for this section can be found on 252–3.

51. Rachel Carnell, *Partisan Politics, Narrative Realism, and the Rise of the British Novel* (New York: Palgrave Macmillan, 2006), 4.

52. See Defoe's anti-Portuguese, pro-Dutch observations in the overview of global trade that he co-authored, *Atlas maritimus & commercialis* (London, 1728), particularly 101, 103, and 155–6.

53. Carnell, 8.

54. Margaret Anne Doody, *The True Story of the Novel* (New Brunswick, NJ: Rutgers Univ. Press, 1996), 294.

55. Swenson, 56.

56. As I write this, the Scottish independence referendum is scheduled for 18 September 2014. Scotland could become an independent nation for the first time since 1707.

Mercier's Revolutionary Theater: Reimagining Pantomime, the Aesthetic of the Unfinished, and the Politics of the Stage

YANN ROBERT

Few eighteenth-century men were as well versed in the scenic arts as Louis-Sébastien Mercier, a frequent theatergoer, a leading critic of classical drama, and the author of some sixty plays. Yet this familiarity with the stage did little to prepare him for the most powerful dramatic experience of his life, while in Mannheim in 1787: A performance of Schiller's *The Robbers* in German, a language he did not know. After reflecting on his experience, Mercier concluded that the emotions he had felt that day were the result of his transmutation from a receptive stance to a creative one: "Il y a du plaisir à deviner une action, à interpréter le geste, le regard, tous les mouvements et les accessoires de la scène; on compose alors la pièce avec l'auteur, et, je l'ai remarqué, la sensation que l'on se crée est plus vive que celle que l'on reçoit."[1] Forced to rely on his imagination to compose the dialogue that he could not understand, Mercier had experienced at once the pleasure of the creator and that of the spectator. Scholars of the eighteenth century will undoubtedly recognize the influence of two crucial aesthetic movements on Mercier's explanation—the popularity of pantomime and the fascination with unfinished works of art. Yet Mercier's account, while clearly drawing from these artistic movements, actually differs from them in significant ways. In fact, his experience in Mannheim would inspire him to publish articles a decade later promoting a unique form of theater, strikingly different from the didactic *drames bourgeois* he remains best known for. In what follows, I will highlight the originality of this new conception of the dramatic arts, paying particular attention to the ways in which it challenged the revolutions in artistic and political thought of the late eighteenth and early nineteenth centuries.

Reimagining Pantomime

As Mercier notes in the quotation above, his inability to understand the meaning of the actors' speech inspired him to focus his attention on their gestures, movements and props. Thus, the performance became for him a pantomime—a polysemic term that, in the eighteenth century, could be applied not only to silent plays, but also to any fragment of a performance in which gestures are foregrounded and speech is interrupted or unintelligible. Sophia Rosenfeld is not the first scholar to note the eighteenth century's "widespread fascination with gestures and pantomime as means of communication and expression," but in *A Revolution in Language*, she provides perhaps the most thorough examination of this fixation's philosophical foundations.[2] Her work draws particular attention to the belief among defenders of pantomime that gestures constituted a primeval means of communication, which preceded the development of spoken language and, as a result, retained a closer link to nature and truth. In fact, it was precisely because gestures were not mediated through language that they were deemed to be so much more poignant than words. More instinctive and instantaneous than speech, gestures could affect the spectators without requiring any intellectual involvement from them. The eighteenth-century critic Jean-François Marmontel opposed silent plays for that very reason: when watching a pantomime, he lamented, "on peut s'épargner presque la peine de penser."[3] But for proponents of pantomimes, the greater poignancy of silent gestures revealed the failure of language to convey accurately the sensations of the characters on stage. Accordingly, many theorists in the second half of the eighteenth century argued that scenes of heightened emotional intensity should depict a collapse of language, with gestures and unarticulated cries taking the place of speech.

For most eighteenth-century thinkers, however, pantomime was not just a way of indicating an emotional breaking down of spoken language; it was a language in its own right. In other words, gestures and screams did not simply allude to the existence of ideas and emotions beyond communication; they were themselves a mode of communication. Diderot, for instance, praises the scene in which Lady Macbeth compulsively washes the hands she had used to murder her father, noting that this gesture conveys her remorse better than any speech.[4] As this example suggests, in Diderot's theater, silent gestures do not seek, as they often do in modern drama, to open up a space of ambiguity; their aim is, in fact, the very opposite: to express a specific idea in the most effective way possible. Thus, Arnaud Rykner regrets that Diderot "ne conçoit pas pour cette dernière [la pantomime] un autre mode de fonctionnement que celui du discours, auquel, précisément, elle s'oppose. Il veut en privilégier l'usage, certes, mais il veut surtout privilégier en elle un substitut de la parole, c'est-à-dire, en un sens, un ersatz silencieux de la parole."[5] Indeed, in the eighteenth century, pantomime and verbal language were not held to be incompatible. On the contrary, they were regarded as alternate forms of communication, with different strengths, but the same aim: the unequivocal expression of a specific emotion or idea.

Mercier's conception of pantomime differs in significant ways from his contemporaries', partly as a result of his experience in Mannheim.[6] Indeed, it can hardly be a coincidence that in an article published in 1798, he praises pantomimes in almost exactly the same terms that he had used to describe his experience in Germany: "Pourquoi la perfection de l'art dramatique réside-t-elle dans la pantomime?... C'est que le spectateur, sans cesse ému, sans cesse interrogé, compose les paroles pour ces êtres muets dont il interprète les moindres mouvements, et la sensation que l'on se crée est plus agréable et plus profonde que celle que l'on reçoit."[7] According to Mercier, only silent plays can recreate the intense emotions that he had felt ten years earlier. His contemporaries attributed the unique poignancy of gestures to the notion that they required neither mediation through language nor intellectual involvement on the part of the audience. However, Mercier takes the very opposite view, arguing that the spectators of a pantomime find themselves "sans cesse interrogé[s]" and, as a result, compelled to study every gesture and invent a dialogue to match what they see. In such a scenario, silent gestures do not signal a failure of language, indicative of its shortcomings in the face of a true emotion, nor are they superior means of communication that offer a solution to such a failure. In fact, they are as distant as can be from an indictment of speech since they actually function as an invitation to *more* language. Mercier makes a similar claim about music, which, like pantomime, was often portrayed in the eighteenth century as a primeval means of communication, anterior and superior to verbal language. In an unpublished note, Mercier contends that the power of music lies not in its capacity to communicate, but rather in its ability to give birth to language in the mind of the listener: "Non, la musique n'est point une langue ... Mais la musique développe en nous et très puissamment le langage intérieur."[8] Likewise, what makes pantomimes so powerful for Mercier is that silent gestures are indeterminate signs in need of interpretation. They inspire the spectators to create their own dialogue—a creative impulse that blurs the distinction between author and audience and transforms the theater into a space of improvisation.

Reimagining the Aesthetic of the Unfinished

Mercier's belief that a work of art's pathos lies in its indeterminacy not its clarity places him firmly among the supporters of an aesthetic of the unfinished. While this artistic movement has a rich history, it attained its greatest influence in the second half of the eighteenth century.[9] Diderot, in particular, lavished frequent praise on the emotional impact of sketches, noting that their blank spaces and partial strokes encourage a greater involvement on the part of the viewer: "L'esquisse ne nous attache peut-être si fort, que parce qu'étant indéterminée, elle laisse plus de liberté à notre imagination, qui y voit tout ce qu'il lui plait."[10] Yet in the eighteenth century, the aesthetic of the unfinished, so prevalent in the visual arts, was only rarely applied to the stage.[11] The theater was widely believed to be the most complete art form, at once verbal and visual and able to appeal to multiple senses simultaneously. According to Saint-Albine, the theater was the least likely of all art forms to stimulate the spectator's imagination: "Notre imagination est presque toujours obligée de suppléer à l'impuissance des autres arts imitateurs de la nature. Celui du comédien n'exige de nous par lui-même aucun supplément."[12] In spite of Saint-Albine's assertion, however, Diderot attempted to amend the theater so it would inspire greater imaginative involvement. In a letter to Madame Riccoboni, who had warned that the more realistic acting style advocated by Diderot would confuse the spectator (who would be unable to hear or see the actors fully), Diderot explains that brief moments of visual or textual indeterminacy produce a deeper emotional impact by stirring the spectator's imagination: "Mettez mon imagination en train, et je verrai au plus loin, et je devinerai ce que je ne verrai pas, et peut-être y gagnerez-vous."[13] To Madame Riccoboni's understanding of the theater as a totality, as an art subjugated to an ideal of complete visibility and audibility, Diderot opposes a conception of the stage as a space of (temporary) indeterminacy.

Diderot's promotion of tableaux perhaps best exemplifies his advocacy of the unfinished on stage. He describes tableaux as fleeting moments of stillness, usually occurring when scenes of pathos reach such poignancy that language and action break down. Like pantomimes, tableaux seek to communicate intense emotions that cannot be translated into words. They compel the spectators to focus their attention on the performers' frozen bodies that express physically the sincerity and intensity of their emotions. More than just tears, it is the suspension of the actors' speech and movements, rendering visible their inability to articulate their emotions, which triggers an emotional experience in the audience both simultaneous and identical to the one felt by the characters on stage. For Diderot, tableaux affect the viewers in much the same way as sketches do by producing an unmediated emotional communion between creator and beholder. Indeed, as he proposes in his *Salon* of 1765, the power of sketches derives from their ability to transmit the artist's emotional state without alterations produced by reflection and artistic technique: "C'est le moment de chaleur de l'artiste, la verve pure, sans aucun mélange de l'apprêt que la réflexion met à tout."[14] A sketch, like a tableau, remains necessarily incomplete because it originates from an overwhelming emotion only expressible in the manner the artist experiences it—suddenly, fragmentarily and fleetingly. One may question, however, how much imaginative freedom the unfinished work truly gives the beholder. Unlike Mercier in Germany, the spectators of a Diderotian tableau do not create their own sensations, but rather experience the same emotions as the playwright and actor. The incompleteness of Diderot's tableaux is simply not intended to be a source of ambiguity, serving to unshackle the spectators' imagination from the artwork. On the contrary, it seeks to manipulate the audience into losing itself in an emotional communion with the performers on stage.

By contrast, Mercier aims above all else to stimulate the audience's creativity, leading him to espouse a far more radical conception of dramatic indeterminacy than his contemporaries. Whereas Diderot calls for discrete moments of silence in otherwise word-filled plays, Mercier advocates entirely speechless performances. In Mercier's eyes, the brevity and fixity of Diderot's tableaux betray an understanding of the aesthetic of the unfinished too wedded to the sketch and, therefore, to the affective power of the visual (the name "tableau" itself lends weight to this critique). To seek to transform parts of a performance into a sketch is to overlook the fact that the visibility of the theater differs from that of a painting. Mercier notes that, unlike a dramatic production, a painting does not unfold in time: "La peinture n'a qu'un instant.—Qu'elle avoue donc son éternelle impuissance!"[15] This immediacy initially heightens the painting's emotional impact, but it also restricts the spectator's imagination, since everything is communicated at once. Moreover, the visual arts only appeal to one sense (sight). Even in cases where the beholders of a sketch experience the desire to complete the unfinished work of art in their minds, they inevitably imitate the original act of creation by adding shapes and colors to the indeterminate spaces of the sketch. In so doing, they become painters, but painters restricted to building upon existing forms, compelled to follow and complete the vision of another. Like the tableau, the sketch thus favors communion, not individual creativity. By contrast, because the theater appeals to multiple senses, it becomes possible to stage a performance that deliberately refrains from engaging one of these senses—like hearing in the case of pantomime.[16] Such a performance, by its genuine ambiguity, encourages the spectators to compose their own artistic creations from the limited information they have, a far more imaginative act than the completion of a preexisting, fixed and framed work of art. Moreover, unlike painting, theater has a temporal dimension, as well as a spatial one. Because of this diachronicity, a pantomime triggers the human impulse to organize discrete moments into a coherent narrative. By inventing a plot, along with dialogue to sustain it, the spectator does not mimic the artist (the mute performer) but rather engages in a completely different, verbal mode of creation, that of a playwright. For these reasons, indeterminacy onstage jolts the beholder from a receptive stance to a creative one far more effectively than indeterminacy on a canvas. A true pantomime, bereft of words from start to finish, inspires in its spectators an act of literary invention, not just of completion.

Mercier's praise for the indeterminacy of total silence set him apart from nearly all eighteenth-century thinkers. Even those in favor of pantomime viewed it as a *complement* to verbal language, unable to function effectively in the absence of speech.[17] For instance, the story of Diderot covering his ears at the theater in order to concentrate on the actors' gestures is well known; less frequently noted, however, is the fact that he admits only doing so at plays where he knows the text nearly by heart.[18] Likewise, boulevard theaters of the eighteenth century fought back against the restrictions on the use of language imposed by the crown, resorting to printed programs, placards, and puppets (with voice actors hidden behind the curtains) to ensure that their pantomimes were not devoid of a verbal element. Such anecdotes reflect the widespread belief among Mercier's contemporaries that pantomime, for all its emotional potency, was powerless to communicate abstract notions and plot details.[19] In *Idées sur le geste et l'action théâtrale*, Johann Engel goes so far as to contend, against the conventional wisdom of his day, that the Ancient Greeks were no exception: even the most celebrated virtuosos of the art of pantomime, he argues, confined their repertoire to famous myths and historical events, to ensure that the plot would be well known to the audience.[20] Engel cannot fathom any other explanation for the popularity of pantomimes in antiquity because he agrees with Louis Gachet that when confronted with a truly silent, unfamiliar play, "l'esprit du spectateur erre au gré de son imagination, qui de moment à autre a la mortification de reconnaître son erreur, en voyant qu'elle est entrée dans des pensées souvent différentes de celles qu'elle croyait deviner."[21] Such a statement confirms that, for most eighteenth-century thinkers, ambiguity was not the aim of pantomime, but its enemy. To prevent any confusion, verbal language had to be present in a supporting role, helping to protect the spectators from their drifting imaginations and guide them towards the correct interpretation. By eliminating all language from his vision of pantomime, Mercier sought to achieve the opposite goal—namely, to encourage the spectators' imaginations to wander freely and arrive at their own linguistic creations.

More than any other aspects of Mercier's new conception of the theater, this fixation on giving the spectators unlimited imaginative freedom amazed and amused his contemporaries. Just eight days after the publication of Mercier's article promoting nonverbal plays, A. L. Villeterque responded in a letter, also printed in the *Journal de Paris*, ridiculing Mercier's belief that art derives its value from its ability to awaken its beholders' creativity: "Si l'imagination seule pouvait… achever ce que l'artiste a ébauché, pourquoi s'arrêter en si beau chemin et ne pas dire que l 'admirateur doit tout créer?"[22] Why not build, Villeterque continues sarcastically, galleries of blank paintings, gardens full of unsculpted blocks of marble and theaters in which completely silent plays are performed every night? Wouldn't such art forms leave even more to the beholder's imagination? While Villeterque clearly considers such examples to be ludicrous, they perfectly illustrate what made Mercier so troubling to his contemporaries—no one in the eighteenth century had dared push the taste for the unfinished to such extremes. Villeterque criticizes this topsy-turvy conception of art, which places such faith in the creativity of its spectators that it almost dispenses with writers altogether: "On peut conclure de tout cela que, pour atteindre la perfection de la pantomime, il faudra que les acteurs et les spectateurs soient tous des hommes de génie, on n'en dispense que les auteurs."[23] Therein lies the reason, according to Villeterque, for the inevitable failure of Mercier's indeterminate theater; thc average spectator simply does not possess the talent of a Corneille, Molière, or Voltaire, and can thus never hope to imagine anything close to their masterpieces. Although Mercier never claims otherwise (he only asserts that individual spectators will be more affected by their own creations than by those of others), Villeterque can hardly be faulted for concluding that Mercier's new vision of the theater seeks to undermine the exalted status of the author. In that regard, it is perhaps telling that Mercier's wording changes slightly between 1787 and 1798. Following his experience in Germany, he initially writes that "on compose alors la pièce avec l'auteur." However, when he reprises the passage in his article on pantomime, "l'auteur" disappears, leaving the spectator to compose alone. Nevertheless, it should be noted that for Mercier, the decline in prominence of the professional author does not constitute an end in itself, but is a byproduct of the birth of many more authors, as each spectator sets out to fill in the blank page that is a pantomime.

This transformation into an author constitutes for Mercier the ideal response not only to the theater but to all art forms. Indeed, Mercier's endorsement of pantomime belongs to a larger artistic vision outlined in a series of articles and books published between 1797 and 1801. When these relatively obscure texts are cited today, it is usually to highlight two recurrent themes: Mercier's fierce condemnation of the visual arts and his equally passionate embrace of the art of writing. Angelica Goodden has struggled to reconcile Mercier's praise for pantomime with these two features of his artistic vision, noting that his endorsement of a nonverbal art is inconsistent with his preference for the textual over the visual.[24] Yet one should be careful not to repeat Diderot's mistake (in Mercier's eyes) of treating pantomimes as identical to paintings simply because of the absence of speech. As we saw earlier, the creative impact of a pantomime upon its viewers differs from a painting's—and this, for Mercier, is what matters most when evaluating the merit of art forms. Hence, in his article on Schiller's play, he equates the experience of watching a performance devoid of intelligible speech, not to viewing a painting, or even a sketch, as one might expect, but to reading a novel: "l'imagination voyage comme quand on lit un Roman, un Poème épique."[25] This parallel might seem peculiar (shouldn't purely verbal artworks have a different impact on the imagination than nonverbal gestures?) until one realizes that for Mercier a reader's creative involvement is not limited to the visualization of images. Like many of his contemporaries, Mercier praises the immateriality of language for allowing readers to imagine different objects while enjoying the same text, but he goes even further by arguing that the vagueness of language inspires readers to start substituting their own words for the author's. To quote Enrico Rufi, for Mercier, "l'effort du lecteur est de même nature que l'effort du poète, un effort éminemment linguistique."[26] As a result, whereas a sketch turns its beholder into a painter, a novel transforms its reader into an author—the most laudable form of creativity, in Mercier's estimation.[27] His admiration for pantomime is, therefore, entirely consistent with his praise for writing and with his condemnation of the visual arts, since a silent play, like a novel but unlike a painting, inspires its spectators to engage in an act of linguistic creation. In fact, at the end of an article on the *Musée central des arts*, in which he spends more time describing the museumgoers than the paintings on display, Mercier advises his readers to likewise turn away from "materially imitative" works of art and observe instead the people moving silently around them. It is by focusing on this unintended pantomime, not the static paintings, that they can hope to fulfill the exhortation with which Mercier ends the article: "Soyez poètes!"[28]

Mercier's broad artistic program in the final years of the eighteenth century, including his endorsement of pantomime, derives its originality as well as its coherence from its allegiance to this very injunction addressed to the audience: "Soyez poètes!" Such a creed entails a redefinition of imagination, which traditionally and etymologically refers to the formation of mental images often in response to a verbal stimulus. Without abandoning this vision of imagination, Mercier makes it subordinate to an alternate—and inverted—model, in which imagination denotes instead the mental composition of texts often in response to a visual stimulus. The value of an art form lies, therefore, in its ability to transform its spectator into an author, not in any objective measure of its beauty.[29] Mercier's fixation on the creative rather than purely emotional impact of an artwork leads him to develop a strikingly modern conception of art, built on the systematic rejection of all elements liable to impede on the spectator's imaginative freedom. As we saw earlier, the professional author is among the first victims, his or her exalted status as the origin of the true meaning of a work of art sacrificed in favor of the infinite rewritings of individual spectators. The plot, another traditional source of meaning, suffers the same fate. In an article published in 1799, Mercier describes his habit of breaking the spines of books and mixing the pages together before reading them.[30] Such an unusual practice calls to mind his elimination of all language, including expository speeches, from his conception of pantomime insofar as both grow out of the same desire to undermine the clarity, sequentiality and causality that a plot imparts to a work of art. Detached pages, like silent gestures, encourage the readers to create connections between discrete events and, in this manner, construct their own narrative structure instead of inertly following a fixed storyline to its conclusion.

Even art itself appears at times to be imperiled by Mercier's crusade against all imaginative boundaries. The belief that artistic creations lack any intrinsic beauty leads him to challenge the value that societies place on certain works to the detriment of others: "Tous les livres sont parfaitement égaux."[31] From this contention follows the inevitable, but still shocking, conclusion that there need not exist more than one book: "Anéantissez toutes les bibliothèques de l'univers, ne conservez qu'un volume, prenez-le au hasard."[32] With these words, Mercier comes very close to endorsing what Villeterque feared when he asserted that Mercier would next call for uncarved blocks of marble and utterly blank canvases—the death of art itself. It is telling that in his article on the *Musée central des arts*, Mercier advises becoming a poet not by looking at a theatrical pantomime but at a scene from ordinary life—a museum visit. Indeed, as Mercier's writings (notably the *Tableau de Paris*) illustrate, nearly anything, not just art, can serve to stimulate one's creativity. Nor is the resulting act of imagination expected to yield a new work of art, since for Mercier, this amounts to giving a finite, material form to an idea or a vision that, in the mind, exists entirely free of limitations and imperfections. Moreover, were the spectators of a pantomime to commit to paper the dialogue and storyline that they invented, they would inevitably impede on the imaginative freedom of other spectators. Thus, Mercier devises an artistic program that paradoxically has no essential need of artworks, neither as catalysts nor as end results, because it locates art, in its purest form at least, solely within the mind.

Reimagining the Politics of the Stage

Mercier's fixation on the freedom of individual spectators offers a unique contribution to the age-old debate on the political function of the theater. More than any other art form, the dramatic arts allow for a communal experience. This ability to move a crowd, not just a single individual, is what made the theater the most political art form in the eyes of eighteenth-century thinkers, for it meant that plays could be used to transform a heterogeneous audience into a united society. Starting in the 1750s, pantomime became widely regarded as the theatrical genre most effective at forming "un peuple" out of a divided "public." This faith in pantomime rested on the new vision of gestures I described earlier, which held that they were natural and instinctual, and, therefore, intelligible to all. As Rosenfeld has noted, many late eighteenth-century thinkers condemned spoken language for segregating spectators on the basis of education and rank,[33] in stark contrast to silent gestures, which they believed lacked the social markers found in speech and made up, in the words of Charles-Nicolas Cochin, "[une] langue muette et commune à tous les hommes."[34] Partisans of pantomime maintained, in fact, that the egalitarianism of a silent gesture could be seen not only in its intelligibility to men and women from all walks of life, but also in its dramatic impact since the ability of silent gestures to bypass reason and appeal directly to the senses meant that they produced emotions of the same nature and intensity in every spectator. This shared experience of powerful emotions revealed to men and women from different social backgrounds their common humanity and revived the sense of civic belonging that had been denied to them by the stratified society of prerevolutionary France.

In the 1760s and 1770s, Mercier stood out as one of the most enthusiastic proponents of this political vision of the theater, most notably in *Du Théâtre*. The simple act of watching a play could, Mercier believed, fuse men and women of all classes into a cohesive people.[35] However, this belief in an act of fusion hinged on an implicit rejection of the value of a unique subjective experience. As a result, it differed from Mercier's subsequent obsession with inspiring each spectator to engage in a distinctive act of imaginary creation. In fact, during the final years of the eighteenth century, Mercier asserted again and again that no two individuals ever respond to a work of art in the same fashion: "On ne trouve dans un ouvrage que ce qu'on a en soi-même. Tel lit dans un livre cent choses que tel autre n'y a pas lues."[36] Pantomimes appealed to Mercier for that very reason: their indeterminacy rendered it inevitable that they would elicit a multiplicity of interpretations. Indeed, by the century's end, Mercier no longer believed that pantomimes should seek to produce an emotional fusion in the auditorium, viewing them instead as ideal catalysts for individual acts of creativity.[37]

Therefore, one may wonder what inspired such a reversal in Mercier's understanding of the political function of theater. Mercier appears to have developed his new vision gradually, starting even before the Revolution. In his *Tableau de Paris*, he imagines an unusual spectacle, allegedly imitated from the Chinese, in which an entire city is reconstructed, with live actors in the role of the inhabitants. The audience is invited to enter the space of representation and interact with it so that each spectator creates his or her own theatrical experience, much as Mercier had done in Mannheim. As Joanna Stalnaker has shown, this uniquely interactive performance epitomizes the "innovative descriptive poetics" employed by Mercier in his *Tableau de Paris*.[38] According to Stalnaker, Mercier embraces a descriptive technique that allows for the inclusion of multiple points of view and encourages the readers to compose and recompose the object—and indeed the text itself—in their imaginations. The *Tableau de Paris* thus displays, in its form as in its content, the first signs of Mercier's shift from an aesthetic centered on communion to one promoting individual creativity. It was not until the final years of the eighteenth century, after the Reign of Terror had opened Mercier's eyes to the potential for political misuse lurking within the dream of artistic fusion, that he explicitly set out to explore the political implications of this new aesthetic vision and to develop it into a concrete, wide-ranging artistic program.

Indeed, Mercier's experience of the Terror played a vital role in his evolution away from his former vision of the theater as a site of communion. The grisly crimes of vast unified crowds rattled his faith that the emotional fusion of disparate individuals would necessarily reveal a virtuous core to humanity. In *Le Nouveau Paris*, written soon after the Terror and partly as a response to it, Mercier describes a moment of emotional communion in a theater of the Revolution, seemingly reverting to his earlier political vision of the dramatic arts: "Tous les cœurs tressaillent alors de plaisir, tous les yeux se remplissent de larmes, tous les auditeurs éprouvent les mêmes sensations."[39] But he immediately follows this idyllic description with the question: "Sont-ce bien réellement ces mêmes Parisiens qui par milliers ont agi en tigres féroces?"[40] By juxtaposing a group of spectators crying in unison with the transformation of thousands of Parisians into bloodthirsty animals, Mercier suggests that for every example of emotional communion leading to virtuous sensations, there exists another in which the fusion originates from anger and results in acts of violence. In fact, the image of the audience as a people, so prevalent in *Du Théâtre*, disappears in *Le Nouveau Paris*, replaced by such terms as "tourbe" (rabble), "populace d'échafaud" (riffraff of the scaffold), and "horde infernale" (infernal horde). The act of gathering individuals into a crowd no longer enlightens them about their duty as compassionate beings to a larger whole; on the contrary, it renders each individual more pliable to manipulation by substituting a collective opinion, often based on the lowest common denominator, to one's unique perspective.[41] Such examples from *Le Nouveau Paris* reveal that the Terror had shattered Mercier's dream of achieving a virtuous and cohesive society through artistic communion.

Given his own affiliation with the Girondins, Mercier not surprisingly blamed the Jacobins for the destruction of this dream. As a man obsessed with politics, drama, and the nature of the links between them, he could not have failed to notice that the Jacobins' vision of the theater bore certain similarities to the theories espoused by prerevolutionary supporters of pantomime. Indeed, the vast majority of Jacobins believed the theater to be a unique site of communion, essential to national unity. As Judith Schlanger has noted, the theater became increasingly programmatic under Jacobin rule, replete with simplistic stories of Republican heroism and virtue intended to inspire the spectators to cheer and repeat the political mantra on stage. The principal objective of such a theater was to join all voices together in support of the Revolution, fusing the stage and the auditorium in a moment of genuine harmony.[42] Yet the theater of the Jacobin era departed in crucial ways from the ideals of the early supporters of pantomime. In the eyes of the latter, silent plays represented an opportunity for socially diverse spectators to rediscover a shared humanity, a primeval, instinctual core obscured by the cultural differences and social hierarchies introduced by language. Thus, the resulting community came from within (since it was built on a preexisting, albeit latent, uniformity) and lacked a specific political agenda (since it transcended the divisions and categories which underlie political thought). To be sure, it promoted an ideal of solidarity, but offered no concrete proposals on how to attain this ideal outside of the auditorium. By contrast, the theater of the Jacobins sought to produce a deeply ideological uniformity, by encouraging its spectators to internalize the political beliefs and values extolled on stage. Unity was no longer defined as a hidden origin, but as a cultural construction, the result of a process that would impart upon all individuals a particular set of ideological principles. Such divergent views explain why the Jacobins set out to achieve fusion not through pantomime but through its very opposite: full, constant speech. The endless repetition onstage of the same inspirational phrases and stories made it possible to trigger an emotional communion and to define the nature of the resulting community.

The Jacobins' embrace of political declarations and oaths as a means of fusion led them to develop a profound distrust of dramatic silence, all the more remarkable given the popularity of pantomime among the previous generation of thinkers. Nowhere is this more evident than in the following rant from the *Feuille du salut public*, a Jacobin newspaper: "Quand un acteur parle de la paix, si celui qui est en scène avec lui, ne lui répond: Point de paix tant que les ennemies souilleront notre territoire: point de paix tant que les tyrans n'auront point rendu hommage à notre république: point de paix jusqu'au moment où la république sera vengée, alors l'acteur a tort, et on peut l'accuser de modérantisme."[43] This passage essentially advises actors to ignore the script and use the stage to express their own political beliefs (so long as they are in line with the Jacobins'), rather than those of their characters. This fascinating collapse of the boundary between actor and character and between debating and roleplaying suggests that the theater of the Terror had grown so ideological that it no longer operated as a space of fiction distinct from reality but functioned instead as a political tribune wherein speech was both mandatory and closely supervised. Such a theater constituted the opposite of a pantomime in that no performer was allowed to stay silent even for a brief moment, for to do so might suggest that he or she did not fully partake in the act of communion onstage. Silence was no longer perceived as an alternative means of communication, more effective than verbal language in conveying heartfelt emotions. Rather, it was perceived as a deliberate refusal of language, indicating a lack of enthusiasm for the Republican régime. Once regarded as an essential catalyst to the communion of the audience, it was now deemed a threat to it. All needed to speak, constantly and loudly, in order to show their devotion to the Revolution and prove, thereby, their civic belonging.

In the eyes of the Jacobins, playwrights were, like actors, citizens first and artists second. As citizens, staying silent when they had the power to reach a wide audience amounted to nothing less than a dereliction of duty. In 1793, Michel-Jean Sedaine, enjoying a well-deserved retirement at the age of 74, was attacked in the *Journal des Spectacles* for his lack of recent contributions to the Parisian stage: "Où est [Sedaine]? Que fait-il? Si son ardent civisme ne m'était connu, j'accuserais son *silence* de modérantisme et je le rendrais responsable de ne pas mettre actuellement au théâtre [de] pièce patriotique."[44] This was not simply an isolated incident, instigated by a relatively powerless journalist. Perhaps for the first time in French history, one finds during the Terror examples of political officials publicly chastising playwrights for a few years of silence. In particular, the Comité de salut public and the Comité d'instruction publique did not deem it beyond their powers to order a writer back to work. In April of 1794, Barère, Saint-Just and Collot d'Herbois, among others, signed the following directive: "Le Comité de Salut Public… requiert le citoyen Pigault-Lebrun, auteur dramatique, pour être employé à faire des pièces patriotiques."[45] Six months later, the Comité de salut public approved a similar statute, this time ordering Népomucène Lemercier to start writing patriotic plays at once, despite his suffering from what the decree itself described as convulsive asthma and partial paralysis.[46] This official war on silence highlights just how much the Jacobins' political vision of the theater differed from that of the absolutist monarchy. Under the ancien régime, a deep anxiety about speech hostile to the crown, or at least, uncontrolled by it, inspired the government to attempt to suppress the use of language in all but a few state-supervised theaters— an approach which played a key role in the development of pantomime in France. In a near perfect inversion, the Jacobins' fear of the ambiguity and secrecy of silence prompted efforts to impose speech to everyone, even those wishing to remain quiet. While these two approaches may seem to represent two sides of the same coin, since both seek to restrict freedom of speech, the Jacobins' war on silence is in many regards more oppressive and insidious in that it strives to control what is said *and* what is left unsaid. As the Jacobins understood, a far greater power lies in compelling others to say what one wants them to say than in prohibiting them from saying what one does not want them to say.

In *Le Nouveau Paris*, Mercier repeatedly condemns the Jacobins' ideological vision of the arts with a particular focus on the linguistic excesses it cultivated. He argues in several chapters that new writers and orators arose in droves in the years immediately before and during the Terror, all of them using the same hyperbolic, republican language drawn from classical tragedies in an attempt to please the Jacobins and the uneducated masses. This seemingly ubiquitous melodramatic tone made every decision a matter of life and death, casting out all moderation and justifying the crimes of the Terror: "ce sont toutes ces phrases insignifiantes, et même celles qui étaient les plus inintelligibles qui ont été le ciment des prisons et des échafauds."[47] Irrespective of tone and content, the new writers and orators simply spoke too much according to Mercier: "On a trop abusé de la parole. Jadis créatrice, elle n'est plus qu'un vain son…le style verbeux a anéanti la pensée."[48] The Terror's torrent of words left little creative freedom to the reader or listener—a flaw that Mercier stresses at the end of his article by praising Pythagoras who instructed his pupils to retreat into silence and reflect individually on his brief lessons. Perhaps the most worrisome aspect of the new regime of speech under the Terror derived from the tendency of the droves of novice writers to adopt the same style, tone and vocabulary. In *Le Nouveau Paris*, Mercier frequently expresses the fear that the repetitive, overblown speeches of the Revolutionaries might obliterate once and for all the originality of individuals. As Pierre Frantz has noted, few if any of the Jacobins' crimes were as ghastly, in Mercier's eyes, as their attempt to transform the stimulating mosaic that was eighteenth-century Paris into an undifferentiated mass.[49] Under the Jacobins' influence, the dream of many prerevolutionary thinkers, that of unity through art, was perverted into the nightmare of a tedious—and harmful—conformity.

Le Nouveau Paris was published within a year of Mercier's article calling for a new kind of theater, and there is much to indicate that Mercier's hostility towards the Jacobins' ideological vision of the arts directly affected his own artistic program. His contempt for the repetitive, hyperbolic speeches favored by the Jacobins likely influenced his decision to embrace dramatic silence. His opposition to the Jacobins' pursuit of ideological conformity, meanwhile, inspired him to promote a practice of silence unlike that of previous partisans of pantomime, one less interested in creating a homogeneous community than in freeing the spectators from any such uniformity. Indeed, if Mercier came to place the highest value on art forms that recognize and affirm the uniqueness of individuals, it was partly due to his conviction that the crimes of the Terror had grown out of the Jacobins' distortion of the ideal of equality. In a telling passage, he condemns the hordes of public orators during the Terror for behaving "comme des hommes qui, ayant rejeté l'inégalité des conditions, avaient admis l'égalité des talents."[50] For Mercier, the Terror illustrated the perils of confusing true equality—that of rights and conditions—with a uniformity founded on the suppression of individual differences.

This interpretation of the Terror as an attempt to force naturally gifted men and women to adopt the beliefs and behaviors of the mindless majority was not unique to Mercier and led many of his contemporaries to respond by embracing an esoteric conception of the arts. Rufi and Yolande Coste-Rooryk have suggested that Mercier was influenced by this current of esotericism, as evidenced by the post-Thermidorian works in which he expresses both his admiration for artists who disregard the whims of their spectators and his contempt for the unthinking masses who failed to grasp the beauty of Enlightenment ideals.[51] Yet other texts by Mercier reveal that he never surrendered to the temptation of esotericism. In 1797 and 1798, he published several articles attacking the notion that the arts should be the exclusive domain of a cultural elite on the grounds that artistic progress came not from singular men of genius (who have never existed, according to Mercier) but from the circulation of new ideas and the gradual accretion of a vast number of individual operations.[52] Mercier's novel critique of the concept of "genius" hints at the two reasons behind his dislike of esotericism. First, esotericism is evocative of the ancien régime in that it treats art as a privilege that risks being sullied if practiced by the majority. Second, it violates Mercier's core belief in the social and political value of art, by positing the existence of an unbridgeable chasm between men of genius and the uncultured multitude. It would be wrong therefore to see Mercier's new conception of the theater as a contrarian reaction to the Jacobins' ideological vision of art on a par with the turn towards esotericism. While the propagandistic art of the Terror undeniably had an impact on Mercier, it did not inspire him, as it did many esoteric thinkers, to lose faith in the notion that art can serve a social purpose; rather, it motivated him to devise a new political role for the arts, wholly unlike that of the Jacobins.

Indeed, Mercier's vision of art as a creative catalyst can hardly be described as esoteric. As we saw earlier, it challenges the exalted status accorded to authors by situating the value of the work of art in its reception. The true artist is not the superior man or woman whose work of genius dazzles the initiated and confuses the unsophisticated, but the one who encourages all spectators, regardless of talent, to replace his or her creation with their own. In fact, elitism of any sort has no place in Mercier's artistic vision, which seeks to cultivate a unique form of egalitarianism described by an acquaintance of Mercier, Jean Charles Levacher de Charnois, as follows:

> L'action muette convient également à tous les états, à tous les caractères. L'homme sensible, le philosophe, l'ignorant, le noble, l'artisan, dans ce silence que la musique seule remplit, fait parler les acteurs en lui-même, comme il parlerait. Chacun y attribue son style, ses passions. Tout le monde est content. L'imagination ajoute encore quelquefois: on ne fait dire aux personnages que ce

> qu'il faut qu'ils disent pour nous intéresser. Eh! Quel est l'auteur assez heureux pour oser espérer de deviner ainsi ce qui pourrait convenir absolument à chacun![53]

A lowly worker can enjoy a pantomime as much as the most erudite philosopher because each individual spectator is free to give the characters his or her own speaking style, passions and interests. What could be more egalitarian than an art form that adapts to the different desires and beliefs of its spectators, satisfying all and excluding none? Of course, other forms of theater—notably that of the prerevolutionary partisans of pantomime, and the Jacobins'—had also laid claim to a degree of egalitarianism, but they understood equality as largely synonymous with homogeneity, which they tried to realize through an emotional or ideological fusion. After the Terror, Mercier could no longer accept such a conception of equality due to the restrictions that it imposed on individual originality. This led him to build his new vision of the theater around a different definition of equality, that of opportunity. In Mercier's vision, all spectators, regardless of social class, education or talent, are offered the same opportunity to create their own work of art, and no individual spectator can boast of being a superior artist since each is most pleased with his or her own creation. Thus, Mercier attempts to redefine art from a pursuit restricted to sociocultural elites or ideological factions to a universally-practiced and yet deeply personal habit, embedded in the daily life of each individual. His ideal society resembles the audience at one of his silent plays; it consists of a gathering of authors who are equal precisely because they are free to be different from one another: "une nation lettrée dans presque tous ses individus dont chacun aurait sa physionomie propre, et absolument libre dans son expression."[54] This resemblance is no coincidence. Far from losing faith in the political value of the dramatic arts, Mercier turned to silent plays in the final years of the eighteenth century as a way to accomplish the two tasks that had bedeviled the Revolutionaries: Reconcile equality and liberty in such a way that neither is sacrificed to the other and create that seeming contradiction, a cohesive community of unique individuals.

NOTES

1. “There is pleasure in deciphering an action, in interpreting the gesture, the gaze, all of the movements and accessories of the stage; one then composes the play with its author, and—I have observed this—the sensation that one creates for oneself is more intense than the sensation that one receives.” *Journal de Paris*, November 7, 1787.

2. Sophia Rosenfeld, *A Revolution in Language: The Problem of Signs in Late Eighteenth-Century France* (Stanford, CA: Stanford University Press, 2001), 9.

3. “One can nearly spare oneself the trouble of thinking.” Jean-François Marmontel, *Éléments de littérature*, in *Œuvres complètes*, vol. 4 (Geneva: Slatkine reprints, 1968), 823.

4. Denis Diderot, *Letter on the Deaf and Dumb*, in *Diderot’s Early Philosophical Works*, trans. Margaret Jourdain (London: Open Court Publishing, 1916), 167–8.

5. “[Diderot] does not grasp that pantomime could have a different way of operating than speech, which is, after all, its opposite. It is true that he wishes to give priority to the use of pantomime, but what he particularly wants to prioritize through pantomime is a substitute to speech – that is, in a sense, a mute ersatz of speech.” Arnaud Rykner, *L’envers du théâtre: Dramaturgie du silence de l’âge classique à Maeterlinck* (Paris: José Corti, 1996), 214.

6. I disagree with Rykner who depicts Mercier as a paltry imitation of Diderot and not a true innovator. Rykner, *L’envers du théâtre*, 14–5.

7. “Why does the perfection of the dramatic arts reside in pantomime? …It is because the spectator, ceaselessly moved, ceaselessly interrogated, composes the dialogue of these mute beings, whose slightest gesture he interprets, and the sensation that one creates for oneself is more pleasing and profound than the sensation that one receives.” *Journal de Paris,* August 6, 1798.

8. “No, music is not a language… But music develops in us, and with great power, an internal language.” Cited in Philippe Barr, “Le ‘je’ et son ombre: La Mort imaginaire de Louis Sébastien Mercier à la lumière de Saint Martin,” *Orbis Litterarum* 64, no. 3 (2009): 182.

9. On the role of the unfinished in eighteenth-century aesthetic thought, see Angelica Goodden, “Painting for the Eye and Painting for the Mind: Correspondences of the Arts in Eighteenth-Century France,” *Oxford Art Journal* 7, no. 1 (1984): 3–14. On the rich history of the sketch, see George P. Mras, “Literary Sources of Delacroix’s Conception of the Sketch and of the Imagination,” *The Art Bulletin* 44, no. 2 (1962): 103–111.

10. “Sketches perhaps only engage us so forcefully because, being indeterminate, they leave more freedom to our imagination, who sees in them anything it pleases.” Denis Diderot, *Salon de 1767*, in *Diderot, Œuvres,* vol. 4, ed. Laurent Versini (Paris: R. Laffont, 1996), 715.

11. Not surprisingly, Mercier also had a fondness for sketches, which he credited with inspiring a greater creative involvement on the part of the spectator than

finished paintings. In fact, in an article dating from 1797, he describes the experience of seeing a sketch in the same terms he had used to communicate the emotions that he had felt in Mannheim: "On aime mieux la sensation que l'on se crée à soi-même, que celle que l'on reçoit" ["One prefers the sensation that one creates for oneself to the sensation that one receives"]. As we will see, however, the way in which the beholder creates his or her own sensation varies depending on whether the impetus comes from a sketch or a pantomime, leading Mercier to maintain that reading and pantomime- watching are more intellectually-liberating and artistically-stimulating activities than viewing a sketch. *Journal de Paris*, February 13, 1797.

12. "Our imagination is almost always forced to compensate for the impotence of other art forms imitative of nature. The art of the actor does not by itself require from us any supplement." Pierre Rémond de Sainte-Albine, *Le Comédien*, in *Mémoires de Molé et Le Comédien* (Paris: E. Leroux, 1825), 106.

13. "Put my imagination in motion, and I will see as far as possible, and I will guess what I cannot see, and perhaps this will benefit you." Denis Diderot, *Les Entretiens sur le Fils naturel*, ed. Jean Goldzink (Paris: GF Flammarion, 2005), 350.

14. "It's the artist's heated moment, pure eloquence, without there being mixed in the affectation that reflection adds to everything." Denis Diderot, *Salon de 1765*, in *Diderot, Œuvres,* vol. 4, ed. Laurent Versini (Paris: R. Laffont, 1996), 388.

15. "Painting has only one instant.—Let her therefore confess her eternal impotence!" *Journal de Paris*, June 8, 1797.

16. Mercier also explored, as another possibility, a theater that would refrain from engaging the sense of sight. In a couple of unpublished notes, he describes a theater in which only one person speaks in total darkness to the assembled spectators. It is unknown why he chose not to publish such a unique vision of the theater when he had shown no such hesitations about his conception of a silent theater. See Martine de Rougemont, "Le Dramaturge," in *Louis Sébastien Mercier, un hérétique en littérature*, ed. Jean-Claude Bonnet (Paris: Mercure de France, 1995), 150–1.

17. This was the case, notably, of Diderot. Angelica Goodden, *Actio and Persuasion: Dramatic Performance in Eighteenth Century France* (New York: Clarendon Press, 1986), 108.

18. "I used to frequent the theatre, and I knew by heart most of our best plays. On the days when I meant to examine actions and gestures I would climb to the gallery, for the further I was from the actors the better. As soon as the curtain was raised, and the rest of the audience disposed themselves to listen, I put my fingers in my ears, much to the astonishment of my neighbours; not knowing my motives, they looked on me as a madman who only came to the play to miss it. I paid no attention to their remarks, and kept my fingers obstinately in my ears as long as the gestures and actions of the actor corresponded with the dialogue which I remembered. When I was puzzled by the gestures I took my fingers from my ears and listened." Diderot, *Letter on the Deaf and Dumb*, 173–4.

19. Johann Jakob Engel, *Idées sur le geste et l'action théâtrale*, vol. 2 (Paris: Chez H. J. Jansen et Comp., 1794), 24. Several other authors make the same claim, including Ange Goudar, Jean-Baptiste Dubos and Louis Gachet.

20. Johann Jakob Engel, *Idées sur le geste et l'action théâtrale*, vol. 1 (Paris: Chez H. J. Jansen et Comp., 1794), 22.

21. "The mind of the spectator wanders at the whim of his imagination, which from time to time has the mortification of realizing its mistake, upon seeing that it has entered into thoughts often different from those it had wrongly believed to have deduced." Louis Gachet, *Observations sur les spectacles en général, et en particulier sur le Colisée* (Paris: Chez P. Alex. Le Prieur, 1772), 21.

22. If the imagination by itself could ... complete that which the artist has begun, why stop there, when success is assured? Why not say that the admirer should create everything?" *Journal de Paris,* August 14, 1798.

23. "One can conclude from all this that, to attain the perfection of pantomime, it will be necessary that the actors and spectators all be men of genius; only the authors are exempt from this." *Journal de Paris,* August 14, 1798.

24. Goodden expresses surprise that "Villeterque does not point out the most glaring inconsistency in Mercier's argument for pantomime, that he had shortly before declared his preference for verbal art over visual." Goodden, *Actio and persuasion*, 44.

25. "The imagination travels, as when one reads a Novel, an epic Poem." *Journal de Paris*, November 7, 1787.

26. "The reader's effort is of the same nature as that of the poet, an eminently linguistic effort." Enrico Rufi, *Le Rêve laïque de Louis-Sébastien Mercier entre littérature et politique* (Oxford: Voltaire Foundation, 1995), 186. Mercier's own works bear witness to this philosophy of active reading. See Shelly Charles, "L'écrivain journaliste," in *Louis Sébastien Mercier, un hérétique en littérature*, ed. Jean-Claude Bonnet (Paris: Mercure de France, 1995).

27. "Tant que l'art d'écrire ne sera pas réputé le premier de tous, je combattrai les autres arts imitatifs qui ne lui rendront pas cet hommage." ["So long as the art of writing will not be renowned above all others, I will fight against the other imitative arts that do not pay it this homage."] Louis Sébastien Mercier, *Néologie ou Vocabulaire de mots nouveaux,* vol. 1 (Paris: Chez Moussard et Maradan, 1801), lxxv.

28. "Be poets!" *Journal de Paris*, May 18, 1799.

29. "La beauté d'un poème n'est pas dans le livre, mais dans l'âme de celui qui le lit." ["The beauty of a poem is not in the book, but in the soul of its reader."] *Journal de Paris*, December 29, 1797.

30. *Journal de Paris*, January 9, 1799.

31. "All books are perfectly equal." Cited in Rufi, *Le Rêve laïque de Louis-Sébastien Mercier*, 127.

32. "Annihilate all the libraries of the universe; preserve only one volume; pick it randomly." Cited in Rufi, *Le Rêve laïque de Louis-Sébastien Mercier*, 127.

33. Rosenfeld, *A Revolution in Language*, 75.

34. "[A] mute language, common to all men." Cited in Pierre Frantz, *L'Esthétique du tableau dans le théâtre du XVIIIe siècle* (Paris: Presses Universitaires de France, 1998), 124.

35. Rufi notes that Mercier reiterates "almost obsessively" in *Du Théâtre* that the magic of theater lies in its ability to link socially disparate men together and found thereby a nation. Rufi, *Le Rêve laïque de Louis-Sébastien Mercier*, 59. See also Pierre Frantz, "L'usage du peuple," in *Louis Sébastien Mercier, un hérétique en littérature*, ed. Jean-Claude Bonnet (Paris: Mercure de France, 1995).

36. "One only finds in a work that which one has in oneself. One reads in a book a hundred things that another did not read in it." *Censeur des journaux*, July 15, 1796.

37. On the political implications of audience participation in the eighteenth century, see Paul Friedland, *Political Actors: Representative Bodies and Theatricality in the Age of the French Revolution* (Ithaca: Cornell UP, 2002) and Susan Maslan, *Revolutionary Acts: Theater, Democracy and the French Revolution* (Baltimore: Johns Hopkins UP, 2005). Mercier's new vision of the theater does not coincide perfectly with either Friedland's or Maslan's portrayal of eighteenth-century drama. To some extent, the silent theater endorsed by Mercier brings to mind Maslan's arguments in that it operates as a site of individual emancipation and not of collective indoctrination. Yet the participation of the spectator does not take the form of a vocal, political contestation but of a silent, aesthetic creation. In that regard, one could argue that Mercier's theories reflect the evolution traced by Friedland towards a more passive and primarily imaginary involvement among theatrical audiences.

38. Joanna Stalnaker, *The Unfinished Enlightenment: Description in the Age of the Encyclopedia* (Ithaca: Cornell UP, 2010), 152.

39. "All hearts quiver with pleasure; all eyes fill with tears; all listeners feel the same sensations." Mercier, *Le Nouveau Paris*, 609.

40. "Are these really the same Parisians who by the thousands acted like ferocious tigers?" Mercier, *Le Nouveau Paris*, 609.

41. Yolande Coste-Rooryck thus notes that the manipulation of revolutionary crowds is one of the principal themes of the *Nouveau Paris*. Yolande Coste-Rooryck, *Le Pari fou de Louis-Sébastien Mercier dans* Le Tableau de Paris *(1781–1789) et* Le Nouveau Paris *(1799): Un Réalisme militant* (Paris: Champion, 2009), 356.

42. Judith Schlanger, *L'Enjeu et le débat* (Paris: Denoël, 1979).

43. "When an actor speaks of peace, if the one who is on stage next to him does not respond: No peace so long as enemies sully our land; no peace so long as the tyrants have not paid homage to our republic; no peace until our republic is avenged— then the actor is wrong, and one can accuse him of 'modérantisme'." *Feuille du Salut Public*, October 30, 1793.

44. "Where is Sedaine? What is he doing? If his fervent civic-mindedness was not known to me, I would accuse his silence of 'modérantisme', and I would hold him responsible for not currently putting a patriotic play on the stage." *Journal des Spectacles*, August 11, 1793.

45. "The Comité de Salut Public…calls upon the citizen Pigault-Lebrun, playwright, to be employed in the creation of patriotic plays." Cited in Paul d'Estrée, *Le Théâtre sous la Terreur (Théâtre de la peur), 1793–1794* (Paris: Emile-Paul Frères, 1913), 147.

46. D'Estrée, *Le Théâtre sous la Terreur*, 146.

47. "It is all of these insignificant phrases, and even those that were the most unintelligible, that were the cement of the prisons and the scaffolds." Mercier, *Le Nouveau Paris*, 18–20.

48. "We have overused speech. Once creative, she is now only pointless sound … the verbose style has annihilated thought." *Censeur des Journaux*, August 14, 1797.

49. Pierre Frantz, "Heurs et malheurs de l'écriture: le *Nouveau Paris* de Mercier," *Littérature* 69 (1988): 100–110.

50. "Like men who, having rejected the inequality of conditions, had accepted the equality of talents." Mercier, *Le Nouveau Paris*, 257.

51. Rufi, *Le Rêve laïque de Louis-Sébastien Mercier*, 188. Coste-Rooryck, *Le Pari fou de Louis-Sébastien Mercier*, 373–6.

52. "A-t-il jamais existé un homme de génie? …Tout se fait à tâtons, et par une infinité de mains: chaque art est donc le résultat d'une foule d'opérations particulières." ["Has there ever existed a man of genius? …Everything is done blindly, and by an infinity of hands: each art is thus the result of a multitude of individual operations."] *Journal de Paris*, December 12, 1797. See also, *Journal de Paris*, December 29, 1797 and February 15, 1798.

53. "Pantomime is equally well suited to all conditions, to all temperaments. The sensitive man, the philosopher, the simpleton, the aristocrat, the craftsman, in this silence that only music fills, makes the actors speak inside him, as he would speak. Each attributes to the pantomime his style, his passions. Everyone is happy. Imagination adds even more sometimes: one makes the characters say only that which they need to say to interest us. Who is the author fortunate enough to dare hope of finding that which can suit everyone absolutely!" *Journal des Théâtres*, August 1, 1777.

54. "A nation with nearly all of its citizens literate, each with his own physiognomy, and with absolute freedom of expression." Louis Sébastien Mercier, *Satyres contre Racine et Boileau* (Paris: Hénée, 1808), xi.

View From the Luxembourg: David and the French Landscape Tradition

HEIDI E. KRAUS

> Je suis dans un abandon total, je sens combien votre amitié m'était chère, je vous cherche en vain les soirées, et je ne vous retrouve plus. Je gémis seul; une consolation me reste, c'est que vous êtes plus heureux que moi; vous jouissez au moins de votre liberté.[1]

In 1794, while imprisoned in the Luxembourg Palace for his Revolutionary activities, Jacques-Louis David painted a landscape scene from his upper floor prison window (Fig. 1).[2] Known in the literature as the *Vue presumée du jardin du Luxembourg*, the painting's subject matter and attribution are fraught with controversy. At the forefront of the discussion lies scholars' hesitation to view David within the French landscape tradition. David is known as the father of Neoclassicism and, Eugène Delacroix would argue, the father of Modernism because he painted moralizing depictions of men and women from the classical past as well as grand events from contemporary French history. First and foremost, David was a history painter, yet what could be learned about David and his prolific career if we looked beyond the prescribed academic hierarchy of painting in the eighteenth century? What could be gained concerning David and his oeuvre by investigating the artist's engagement with landscape?

It is the purpose of this article to examine David's landscapes anew, demonstrating that he was conversant with the genre throughout his career.

Figure 1. Jacques-Louis David, *Vue présumée du jardin du Luxembourg* (*View from the Luxembourg*), 1794. Oil on canvas. 55 x 65 cm. Musée du Louvre, Paris, France. Photo: Erich Lessing. Photo credit: Réunion des Musées Nationaux/Art Resource, NY.

I will focus on the attribution of David's *View from the Luxembourg* from a new perspective by reexamining the painting within the context of the artist's little-studied Roman drawings of landscape views. In these Roman drawings, sketched *en plein aire*, David often emphasized perspective, atmospheric conditions, and the transient effects of light and shadow on the Italian landscape and surrounding architectural structures. While it is reasonable to assume that these landscape drawings were the result of the Academy's prescribed curriculum, I will demonstrate that their subtle beauty, enigmatic qualities, and interest in the transience of nature distinguish them from mere works of artistic pedagogy. I will also pay close attention to the landscape sketches of Pierre-Henri de Valenciennes (1750–1819), the renowned late eighteenth-century French landscape painter, who shared David's interest in nature's effects on landscape and the built environment. The influence of Valenciennes's aesthetic, coupled with a deep knowledge of and appreciation for the French landscape tradition, had a significant effect on the way David came to view and utilize landscape in his work.

The *View from the Luxembourg* is organized in a geometric fashion. This is important to emphasize because David's preference for the rational, the ordered, and the visually restrained characterize the artist's mature style. By the late 1790s, David's compositions appear almost formulaic in their rigid arrangement of space. The painting, marked by its high viewpoint, is divided in half horizontally by a row of mature trees that extend across the center of the canvas and intersect with another row of trees at left. In the foreground, this horizontality is echoed by the dilapidated fence that outlines the stark confines of the prison yard. Within this vast empty space, antique philosophers actively engage with one another while a solitary young figure dressed in white walks along the inside of the fence. Another figure is identifiable on the left of the painting, also walking, although she is not enclosed within the prison yard. Rather, the woman, shown with a pot on her head, strolls freely down a path in between the fence and an adjacent row of trees. The only architecture represented in the painting is a group of white Italianate buildings on the right and a campanile-like structure in the center of the canvas, barely visible within the dense foliage. In the distance at right, in a scene that prefigures similar nineteenth-century Italian landscapes by Jean-Baptiste Camille Corot, David explored the effects of color, light, and atmospheric effects on the landscape. The warm, autumnal palette and deep cast shadows leave little doubt that David was interested in capturing a specific time of day and season. A single tree in the center of the painting has lost its branches, foreshadowing the arrival of winter and the dormancy it inevitably brings. It is this unique and highly sophisticated juxtaposition of the philosophical and the psychological, the moral and the political, the metaphorical and the actual, that makes the *View from the Luxembourg* unmistakably modern and unquestionably a painting that, in 1794, few artists were capable of producing.

The literature references extant primary documentation that convincingly supports David's attribution of the *View from the Luxembourg*, including a letter by Madame David, an entry by the artist citing the painting in question, and a correspondence by P. M. Delafontaine dated August 1794.[3] Delafontaine, himself a student of David's, made note of "deux paysages" by his master painted from his window in the Luxembourg Palace. Until recently art historians had largely accepted that the painting was indeed by David, but a second landscape by the artist—as purported by Delafontaine—has never surfaced. The existence of a second landscape is further drawn into question by Étienne Delécluze who wrote in his 1855 biography of David, "Des croisées de sa prison il peignit les arbres du jardin et fit le seul paysage qu'il ait jamais exécuté."[4] It is important to reiterate that Delécluze was writing thirty years after David's death, and it is possible that he was mistaken in his assertion. It would seem that the letter by Delafontaine, written at the time of the painting's execution, is a more reliable source.

All of the sources mentioned above confirm that David painted at least one landscape scene. Despite the existence of such compelling and rare primary sources (including the painting's well-documented provenance), a 1992 article by Anna Ottani Cavina and Emilia Calbi argue that the *View from the Luxembourg* is not by David, and they boldly claim that the artist showed "no inclination towards landscape-painting during his long career."[5] The article credits Antoine Schnapper for first questioning the painting's authorship in the catalog for the 1989 David retrospective at the Louvre.[6] Chief among Schnapper's concerns was the depiction of the buildings in the background of the painting, which although he asserts are French in style, never existed in the Luxembourg quarter. Doubt was cast over the location depicted in the painting and thus its attribution too was questioned.

Alphonse de Gisors's *Le Palais du Luxembourg* (published in 1845) provided Ottani Cavina and Calbi with the evidence they felt proved the Louvre landscape is not by David. The authors suggest that the immediacy of a specific quote indicates that Gisors composed it directly in front of the canvas, although it is not clear where he physically saw the painting. Because of its relevancy to my argument, I have included the quote from Gisors in its entirety:

> Il reste de lui [David] une esquisse assez curieuse d'une partie du jardin du Luxembourg, prise de la chambre où il était renfermé, à l'étage supérieur de l'ancien pavillon d'angle situé à l'ouest du palais. On aperçoit sur le premier plan un vaste enclos en planches qui devait exister sur l'emplacement qu'occupent actuellement les jardins particuliers du palais et de la Chancellerie; au-delàs sont les allées mises en culture pendant la Révolution. Plus loin à travers les arbres plantés sans symétrie, on voit les bâtiments du café tels qu'ils sont encore aujourd'hui; ils avaient été construits depuis peu pour y établir les bureaux d'administration des ateliers d'armes qui furent, à cette époque, organisés dans l'ancien clos des Chartreux. Dans le lointain se dessinent les collines de Meudon et Bellevue …[7]

While the view from the west of the palace and the "vaste enclos en planches" in the foreground are similarities between Gisors's passage and the painting, this is where the comparison ends, specifically with regards to the buildings in the background. In addition, Gisors omits the figures in the painting from his description. Based on the aforementioned quote, Ottani Cavina and Calbi conclude that the landscape is not the one Gisors saw and wrote about; it does not show the Luxembourg gardens and, therefore, cannot be by David.[8] While the description does seem at odds with the *View from the Luxembourg*, nowhere do Ottani Cavina and Calbi suggest that Gisors might have viewed and described the second now missing landscape by David mentioned in Delafontaine's letter. Instead they discredit attribution of the painting to David and attribute the work to Louis Gauffier, a contemporary of David.

According to Ottani Cavina and Calbi, the painting's high viewpoint, rigid geometric organization, and the quick graphic nature of the figures in the foreground reoccur in landscapes painted by Gauffier—most notably in his Vallombrosa series and in his *bozzetti* or exploratory sketches located today in the Musée Fabre in Montpellier.[9] The authors take the position that the Luxembourg painting is in fact a *bozzetti* by Gauffier, as is evidenced by its small format and irregular course-weave canvas. Moreover, the free and spontaneous technique exhibited by the artist (in addition to areas where the painting seems unfinished) suggests its purpose as a sketch rather than a finished painting. While the authors acknowledge the rapid, sketch-like application of paint found in similar works by Gauffier, they fail to mention that David also exhibited a more relaxed style of brushstroke throughout his career. For instance, in 1794, while imprisoned in the Hôtel des Fermes, David painted a portrait of himself as an artist with palette and brush held tightly in hand. His expression is one of honesty, bewilderment, anxiety, and frustration with what he viewed to be an unjust imprisonment (Fig. 2).[10] To convey these feelings in the *Self-Portrait* (painted the same year as the *View from the Luxembourg*), David abandoned his characteristically tight, controlled brushstroke for a looser, more rapid one. In his self-portrait, as is the case with the *View from the Luxembourg*, we are aware of the artist's hand and his role in the painting's creation.

Figure 2. Jacques-Louis David, *Self-Portrait*, 1794. Oil on canvas. 81 x 64 cm. Musée du Louvre, Paris, France. Photo: Erich Lessing. Photo credit: Réunion des Musées Nationaux/Art Resource, NY.

Self-Portrait is not the only example of David's divergence from the refined brushstroke and smooth surfaces that characterize his finished paintings. David was experimenting with the application of paint prior to the Revolution—specifically with regard to portraiture—in works like *Psyche Abandoned* (1787), where both the modeling of the figure and background is conceived with a more precipitous touch than we have come to expect in his completed canvases. Many of his paintings carried out during the Revolution, including the *Portrait of Louise Trudaine* (1791–92) and the *Death of Bara* (1794), share aspects of this more relaxed, sketchlike style of brushwork, often accompanied by a stippling technique and monochrome background.[11] *The Fortune Teller* (1825), a finished work painted at the very end of David's career in Brussels, likewise shows David's experimentation with this use of sketchlike style.[12] Yet at issue is not whether or not the aforementioned paintings by David were considered "finished works" or sketches—an argument central to Ottani Cavini and Calbi in linking the *Luxembourg* painting to Gauffier. What is essential in regards to the *View from the Luxembourg* is the acknowledgment that David was constantly experimenting with and diverging from stylistic conventions over the course of his career. His breaking with artistic norms and questioning the traditional hierarchy of genres demonstrated his artistic virtuosity and provided him with an alternative mode of expression. Thus, it should not surprise us that David could paint in the more sketchlike style that characterizes the *Luxembourg* painting and, moreover, that he would diverge from grand history painting to depicting landscape.

Further evidence of David as a landscape painter can be found in his Roman albums. The nature and scope of David's corpus of drawings completed while a *pensionnaire* at the French Academy in Rome from 1775–1780 has only recently been given scholarly attention, thanks in large part to the publication of a voluminous two-tome *catalogue raisonnée* of the artist's drawings by Pierre Rosenberg and Louis-Antoine Prat.[13] The catalogue, published in 2002, includes the dozen extant Roman albums posthumously assembled by David's two sons, Jules and Eugène, and has afforded scholars—for the first time—access to the vast compendium in one location. Many of the drawings in David's Roman albums contain landscape scenes, and some even depict what can be considered pure landscapes—that is, landscapes free from narrative content.[14] Landscapes found in the Roman albums exhibit the artist's skill at rendering nature, specifically trees and rocky formations. In the albums, David frequently places architectural structures within landscape settings in the manner of some of the most famous landscape painters in the history of Western art, namely, Annibale Carracci, Domenichino, Nicolas Poussin, and Claude

Lorrain.[15] The landscapes contained in David's Roman albums demonstrate that the artist was engaged with the French landscape tradition and did so with a sensitivity and proclivity towards landscape that has been largely dismissed in the literature.

We can also turn to the Roman albums for an explanation of the buildings in the back right of the painting, which, as mentioned earlier, bear no resemblance to any such structures in the Luxembourg quarter. Ottani Cavina and Calbi discuss the presumed location of the landscape at length in their article, suggesting that both the landscape and architecture depicted in the painting are French—perhaps even identifiable in the Faubourg Saint-Antoine where Gauffier might have stayed during his brief visit to Paris in 1789.[16] I think it much more likely that the landscape and architecture depicted by David in the *View from the Luxembourg* was based largely on memory and his imagination rather than any specific, identifiable location. As was the case throughout the Roman albums, David would often combine different architectural structures and elements—both real and imagined—to create his own unique views in the manner of Giovanni Battista Piranesi, Hubert Robert, and Giovanni Paolo Panini.[17] Of particular note is the bell-tower-like structure, barely visible within the line of lime-trees on the garden's perimeter. The structure bears a striking resemblance to an Italian campanile, examples of which can be found throughout David's Roman albums.[18] The deep brown roofs on the buildings on the right of the composition, the rolling hills and hazy atmosphere visible in the distance, and the Claudian yellow-brown glow that evokes the distinctive light of the Roman *Campagna* all suggest that David has brought Italian elements to an otherwise French scene. It must also be remembered that the design of Luxembourg Palace—the location of David's imprisonment—was based on the Palazzo Pitti in Florence, the childhood home of Marie de'Medici.[19] Thus, the Luxembourg Palace, much like the architecture represented in David's painting, is a hybrid of French and Italian inspiration. Seeing these Italian influences in the *View from the Luxembourg* is entirely in keeping with David's aesthetic, imagination, and memory of his period of study in Rome.

Another significant piece of evidence to support the painting's attribution to David is his representation of the sketched figure group in the foreground. The classical nature of the figures might at first glance seem strange when juxtaposed with the "modern" surroundings of late eighteenth-century Paris. Several scholars—including Toussaint, Schnapper, and Schmoll—have all commented on the classical group, although efforts to definitively prove the specific antique source for the figures have been largely inconclusive.[20] Most convincing is the argument put forth by J.-A. Schmoll who claims the figures in question represent a scene preceding the death of Archimedes.[21]

According to Schmoll, David's choice to depict such an episode would be appropriate, and it can be read as an autobiographical allusion by the artist to his presumed fate.[22] The inclusion of an episode from a classical source elevates the painting's status to that of *paysage historique*—a far more acceptable genre for an artist of David's status than a non-narrative landscape (I will address the importance of the *paysage historique* to eighteenth-century landscape theory in the pages that follow).[23]

If we look to the Roman albums, we see that David frequently included quickly sketched figure groupings in his drawings to establish scale and depth. Often these figures were placed in front of or even within monumental works of architecture in an effort to reiterate the timelessness of such ancient structures and the relative impermanence of man. The figures represented in *La Place du Panthéon à Rome (avec une calèche traversant la place sur la gauche, des personnages autour d'une table)* are characteristic of this type (Fig. 3). In the drawing, David sketched the figures in the foreground with a rapid touch—a technique that is at odds with the clarity and dexterity associated with the artist's depiction of the human body in his finished paintings. Instead of his strong sculptural aesthetic and trademark corporeal expressivity, David uses quick abstract lines and splotches of dark wash to give a sense of three-dimensionality to his figures. When compared to the group in the *View from the Luxembourg*, similarities with the figures in David's Roman albums become immediately apparent. In the painting, David renders the figures in a similar sketchlike fashion, using deep shadows, line, and spatial voids to establish form. As in the Roman albums, the figures grouped in the *View from the Luxembourg* appear emotionless and generic in their anonymity. The smallness of the figures in relation to the landscape they inhabit conveys feelings of isolation and insignificance, as it does throughout the Roman albums. These feelings are enhanced by the presence of a small, child-like figure in the painting (perhaps a young boy), dressed in white and shown walking alone along the high garden fence.

Perhaps the child dressed in white is an allusion by David to the innocence of childhood, a metaphorical reference to his own virtue amid the confines of an unjust imprisonment. Moreover, this association of white with innocence, purity, and virtue is echoed in the central figure in the sketched figure group in the foreground. This classically inspired figure, shown in the act of drawing in the earth before his followers, also wears white. One well-acquainted with David's oeuvre cannot help but recall his *Death of Socrates* (1787) in which the artist portrays the stoic philosopher partially clothed in a white garment surrounded by his disciples. David represents Socrates in this significant moment as the embodiment of the *exemplum virtutis*. It seems plausible that during his imprisonment David aligned himself with Socrates—the

Figure 3. Jacques-Louis David, *La Place du Panthéon à Rome avec une calèche traversant la place sur la gauche, des personnages autour d'une table*, c. 1775-80. Black ink and grey wash over graphite on laid paper, .153 x .210 cm (6 x 8 ¼ in). 1998.105.1.jj Patrons' Permanent Fund, Image courtesy of the Board of Trustees, National Gallery of Art, Washington.

ultimate virtuous teacher who, not unlike himself, was jailed and ultimately laid down his life for what he ardently believed. David would again use a solitary figure dressed in white to convey notions of purity and virtue in his *Sabine Women* (1799), a work likewise planned by the artist in prison and executed shortly thereafter. In the *Sabine Women*, David portrays Hersilia, dressed in white with arms outstretched, as a heroine—literally placing herself physically and emotionally between her warring Sabine father and the Roman husband she has grown to love. The inclusion of the child-like figure dressed in white in the *View from the Luxembourg* and the references it affords suggest that—at least in 1794—David still harbored intense feelings of persecution as a result of his incarceration and was left to wonder if he, like Socrates, would be left to drink the proverbial hemlock.

A central question persists: Why an artist made famous for his grand history paintings and elegant portraits of the French elite would turn to what was considered to be the "lesser" genre of landscape?[24] In order to understand this choice, let us examine the French landscape tradition at the end of the eighteenth century, specifically, the impact of an artist who, I believe, had a significant effect on the new way David viewed landscape: Pierre-Henri de Valenciennes. Valenciennes and David had much in common. Both artists worked during a period of immense social, political, and artistic change in France and each would become known as the chief exponents of their respective genres—David in history painting and Valenciennes in landscape. Valenciennes, like David, was markedly influenced by the classical tradition and archaeological discoveries of Italy, first visiting Rome in 1769 and again in 1777.[25] He would remain in Italy, firmly committed to landscape until 1784, with the exception of a brief visit to Paris in 1781–82.[26] While in Italy, Valenciennes was surrounded by some of the most brilliant artistic minds of the period including Giovanni Battista Piranesi, Thomas Jones, Phillip Hackert, J.-R. Cozens, Henry Fuseli, Jean-Baptiste Regnault, and Jacques-Louis David.

While the extent of the relationship between David and Valenciennes remains uncertain, during his second trip to Rome Valenciennes received an unspecified drawing from David that he would treasure for the rest of his life.[27] Clearly this indicates the high esteem Valenciennes had for David's work and, conversely, the respect David must have had for Valenciennes. What is apparent from their respective drawings is that both artists shared a strikingly similar view of the Italian landscape and how to approach it in their art. Like David, Valenciennes made countless drawings (Valenciennes was particularly fond of the oil sketch) during his two trips to Italy that document the Eternal City as well as his visits to Tivoli, Naples, Paestum, and Sicily.[28] In these drawings, we can picture Valenciennes—like David—wandering the streets of Rome, climbing the sides of ancient hills, meandering through ruins, and venturing throughout the countryside. Throughout his expeditions, Valenciennes paid close attention to both ancient and modern architectural structures and, above all, the changing effects of light and atmosphere on such buildings and the Italian landscape.

It is this last point that makes the Italian drawings of Valenciennes so relevant to David's conception of landscape and foreshadows nineteenth-century advances in the genre by Achille Etna Michallon, Jacques Bertin, and Jean-Baptiste Camille Corot.[29] Prior to Valenciennes, eighteenth-century artists like Jean-Honoré Fragonard and Hubert Robert used landscape primarily as a context for displaying ruins and monuments. Their focus was often not on the landscape itself or a historical moment, but rather on the archaeological-romantic sentiment such monuments conveyed.[30] Certainly David's Roman albums pay tribute to this monument-centered ideology, one that focused on the splendors of ancient civilizations, death, decay, and the legacy of the artist. As mentioned earlier, evidence of an appreciation for landscape in its purest form is also evident in David's Roman albums. In some drawings, specifically those illustrating expansive views of Rome, David uses architecture simply as an element in a landscape composition.

For example, in his drawing *Vue de Rome avec l'église San Sebastiano fuori le Mura sur la gauche*, no one building or monument is given visual precedence over the other; the architecture was not David's primary concern (Fig. 4). Rather the drawing emphasizes perspective, atmospheric conditions, and the transient effects of light and shadow on the landscape. The movement of the clouds and the deep shadows cast by the warm Italian sun reflecting against the buildings all indicate that David was interested in capturing a specific time of day and even time of year—as he did in the *View from the Luxembourg*. Rather than using ruins to provide commentary on the fleeting aspect of life, here he uses the changing effects of nature on the landscape to convey the passage of time. The simplicity and functionality of the architecture in the drawing, coupled with the absence of a figural narrative component, suggest that David's interest in the drawing was solely in depicting the Roman landscape. For David and his School, as Pierre Rosenberg has discussed, representations of Rome held the same moralizing, philosophical, and ideological content as history paintings.[31] The severity of style identifiable in Roman buildings and the spirit of antiquity that permeates the Italian countryside are translatable to David's conception of history painting rather than being at odds with it.

David captured the transient aspects of landscape in his Roman drawings in a way that Fragonard, Robert, and many of his contemporaries like François-André Vincent and Joseph-Benoît Suvée did not through his choice of medium. Both David and Valenciennes abandoned the traditional red and black chalk in their Italian landscape sketches in favor of pen and wash—a medium frequently used by seventeenth-century artists like Claude and Poussin to explore the effects of light and shade on the landscape. By using pen and wash, both David and Valenciennes constructed their landscapes and the architecture included therein in terms of broad masses of light and dark. The artists' distinctive use of pen and wash to establish form is clear in their drawings of the Roman church of Sant'Onofrio (Figs. 5–6). An examination of the two drawings side-by-side reveals uncanny similarities in the artists' shared technique, subject matter, perspective, and use of light and shade. The dramatic, expansive shadows created by the wash in both works conveys a sense of movement and repetition as the eye moves from planes of empty space to those characterized by darkness. In their two drawings, David and Valenciennes were principally interested in capturing the changing effects of light on the landscape, specifically with regards to the architecture. Given the striking similarities between their drawings

Figure 4. Jacques-Louis David, *Vue de Rome avec l'église San Sebastiano fuori le Mura sur la gauche*, c. 1775-80. Album factice, No. 8. 1998.1 The Pierpont Morgan Library, New York. Purchased as the gift of S. Parker Gilbert and Eugene Victor Thaw.

Figure 5. Jacques-Louis David, *Vue de l'église Sant'Onofrio à Rome*, c. 1775-80. Grey wash over black chalk on pale blue laid paper, 16.7 x 21.5 cm (6 9/16 x 8 7/16 in). 1998.105.1.vv Patrons' Permanent Fund, Image courtesy of the Board of Trustees, National Gallery of Art, Washington.

Figure 6. Pierre-Henri de Valenciennes, *Rome: l'église Sant'Onofrio* (*View of a Building*), c. 1782. Brown wash, graphite, 20 x 31.2 cm. Inv. F13035R. Musée du Louvre, Paris, France. Photo: Thierry LeMage. Photo credit: Réunion des Musées Nationaux/Art Resource, NY.

of Sant'Onofrio, it is plausible that the two artists created their respective renderings at the same time and worked *en plein-air*. The possibility that Valenciennes might have informally instructed David on landscape during his period at the French Academy in Rome seems logical and merits further investigation.

The stylistic similarities between the landscape sketches of Valenciennes and David suggest that the artists shared a common interest in nature's effects on landscape and the built environment and, we can feel certain, prominent theories concerning the genre and its depiction. Prior to the sixteenth-century, landscape played a minimal compositional let alone narrative role. Artists like Brueghel and Titian were among the first to push the boundaries of landscape by no longer strictly relegating it to the background of their narrative compositions. Of unquestionable influence on the French conception of landscape was the Bolognese artist Annibale Carracci (1561–1609). While Annibale both painted and sketched pure landscapes, it was his creation of an "ideal landscape" that warrants our attention.[32] Annibale's ideal landscapes combined the pastoral landscapes found in the Venetian tradition as well as his own views of the Roman *Campagna*. Paintings from his mature period placed classical and religious subjects in ordered outdoor settings often enhanced by Roman ruins—a reminder of our own decay and the passage of time. One of six lunettes by Annibale commissioned for a chapel in the Palazzo Aldobrandini (today in the Galleria Doria-Pamphili) entitled *The Flight into Egypt* (1603–04) exemplifies this type of landscape in which nature, architecture, and humanity are in perfect accord.[33] A series of intersecting diagonals emphasize the importance of the Holy Family in the foreground while the architecture in the background is seemingly absorbed into the surrounding landscape. The line between where the architecture ends and the landscape begins is barely distinguishable in Annibale's harmonious painting.

The rise of the ideal, historicized landscape promulgated by Annibale is critical to understanding how Valenciennes, David, and other French artists would come to view the genre. While Annibale's pupil, Domenichino, would preserve the ideal landscape tradition in Italy, it was seventeenth-century French painters (namely Poussin and Claude) that advanced landscape painting within the established aesthetic hierarchy.[34] Claude best carried on Annibale's remarkable ability to create this seemingly indistinguishable boundary between architecture and landscape evident in the Roman landscapes of David and Valenciennes. Claude achieves this harmonious effect by bathing both his landscapes and buildings in the same radiant light so characteristic of the central Italian countryside. In a late painting, *Landscape with Ascanius Shooting the Stag of Silvia* (1682), Claude uses the columns and entablature of a dilapidated classical structure on the left of the composition as a *repoussoir*, directing the viewer's attention to the figures below and the stag at right. Rather than relying on the more typical usage of trees to draw the viewer into the painting, Claude uses architecture and nature interchangeably—the four long column shafts mimicking the thin, elegant tree trunks to the right of the ruinous structure. What remains of a weighty classical entablature finds its counterpart in the full leaves and branches that comprise the adjacent tree canopy. While Claude maintains Poussin's desire for order and rationality amidst a classical setting, he does so in a decidedly less rigid, more naturalistic fashion.

The question of how an artist should envision nature and, consequently, how he should portray it became exceedingly important in the eighteenth century. At issue was the significance of the artist's imagination. Should the artist depict "true" nature or should he attempt to render nature as "beautiful" even beyond his own observations?[35] A vast number of texts from the period discuss this duality of nature, yet Roger de Piles' chapter on landscape from his *Cours de peinture par principles* (1708) was arguably the most famous and it had a substantive effect on Valenciennes and, I believe, David as well. In the *Cours de peinture*, De Piles limits his discussion of landscape to two types: *le paysage heroïque* and *le paysage pastoral* or *champêtre*. Concerning the heroic style (a composition that finds inspiration from both art and nature) De Piles makes note of two visions of nature all the while notably attempting to raise the status of the landscape painter within the academic hierarchy:

> Et si la Nature n'y est pas exprimée comme le hazard nous la fait voir tous les jours, elle y est du moins représentée comme on s'imagine qu'elle devroit être. Ce style est une agréable illusion, et une espèce d'enchantement quand il part d'un beau génie et d'un bon esprit, comme étoit celui du Poussin: lui qui s'y est si bien exprimé.[36]

De Piles also includes a discussion of buildings in his chapter on landscape. He claims buildings were more appropriate for heroic landscapes rather than rural scenes. He writes:

> Les Fabriques en général font d'un grand ornement dans le paysage, quand même elles seroient gothiques, ou qu'elles paroîtroient inhabitées et à moité ruinées: elles élèvent la pensée par l'usage auquel on s'imagine qu'elles ont été destinées ... Le Poussin a peint dans ses ouvrages des fabriques romaines d'une grande élégance, et Bourdon des fabriques gothiques qu'elles font, ne laissent pas de jetter un air sublime dans ses paysages.[37]

For De Piles, the purpose of buildings within a landscape was to evoke history—as epitomized in the paintings of Poussin and Bourdon. Yet it is significant to note his comment concerning the poetics of ruins and their ability to "raise the imagination." This sentiment is in keeping with the ideas of Diderot, who encouraged meditation on ruins as a means of reflecting upon the human condition.[38] Thus, De Piles emphasized both the historical and emotional sensibilities that buildings are capable of conveying—an idea that is central to understanding David's conception of architecture both in his Roman albums and later paintings like the *View from the Luxembourg*.

Encouraged by his students to publish his theoretical system on perspective, Valenciennes wrote his own treatise on landscape with the young artist in mind. *Elémens de perspective pratique à l'usage des artistes* was the most detailed and complete study on landscape painting published in the eighteenth century.[39] Yet the title of the book is misleading because only the first half of the nearly three-hundred-page treatise is devoted to perspective.[40] The second half was concerned with raising the status of landscape by equating it to *le beau idéal*. To do this, Valenciennes applied many concepts to landscape previously used to glorify history painting. For Valenciennes, the landscape painter created only one type of painting: the *paysage historique*.[41] The *paysage historique* was an expression of the ideal in nature—how nature should be. This perfection in nature was not limited to aesthetics. Rather it extended to a careful scholarly study of ancient texts and mythology as a moral foundation for the composition, as was mandated in history painting and promoted by Diderot. In order to create these ideal representations, it was necessary for the artist to master the vocabulary of nature as Valenciennes and David had achieved during their respective periods in Italy.[42] The best way to master nature and its elements, according to Valenciennes, was to copy it directly. A close observation of nature would afford the student a first-hand knowledge of the contrasts and harmonies of nature, as well as an understanding of its imperfections. In keeping with the ideas of Poussin, nature was not always beautiful and—according to Valenciennes—required the artist to improve upon it.[43] To do this, the artist must rely on his imagination. Although the *Elémens* was not published until 1800, I suggest that David knew Valenciennes' ideas concerning landscape during their time in Italy in the 1770s and 1780s. An examination of David's landscape drawings from his Roman albums reveals the extent to which Valenciennes' and De Piles' views of nature influenced his own conception of the genre. Rather than depict Rome and its environs as they actually existed, David frequently made a conscious decision (as Piranesi did) to depict the landscape, its architecture, and inhabitants as he imagined it to be.

David's interest in depicting landscapes did not end with the Roman albums or his *View from the Luxembourg*. On 7 July 1815, David, accompanied by a servant, left Paris for Switzerland to embark upon a "voyage pittoresque."[44] Numerous landscape drawings by David document the journey through the Franche-Comté and depict the environs surrounding Besançon, Chamonix, and Geneva. The drawings provide keen insight into the artist's state of mind only months prior to his exile from Paris in January 1816, revealing an interest in the serenity of the landscape—its expansive valleys, mountains, and trees. With rare exception, the pen and brown ink drawings are void of narrative content and serve as reflections on nature itself. Landscape also continued to serve a vital narrative role in David's paintings including, *The Sabine Women*, *Napoleon Crossing the Alps* (1800), *Leonidas at Thermopylae* (1814), *Amor and Psyche* (1817), and *The Anger of Achilles* (1819). This interest in and the importance of landscape in David's work can and must be linked back to his period of study in Rome where, surrounded by some of the most brilliant artistic minds of the late eighteenth century, David was exposed to the metaphorical possibilities landscape could provide.

In the *View from the Luxembourg*, the imprisoned artist was free to exercise his stylistic range, retrospective sentimentality, active imagination, and intellectual prowess while simultaneously contemplating nature and his place within it. The *View from the Luxembourg* is a kind of melancholy reverie—a meditation on physical nature as well as human nature.[45] Yet the painting also provides a glimpse into France's artistic future, foreshadowing Romanticism and the major role landscape painting would play in the nineteenth century. Anne-Louis Girodet, one of David's most gifted pupils, perhaps best carried on this legacy, one that ascribed a metaphorical and symbolic importance to landscape in history painting as well as portraiture.[46] In the *View from the Luxembourg*, David did not abandon his classical ideals. Rather he turned to landscape as yet another vehicle for expression and self-identity.

NOTES

I would like to thank Wallace Tomasini, John Beldon Scott, Robert Rorex, Wendelin Guentner and Christopher Johns for their invaluable insights and support of this project. I would also like to extend my appreciation to the readers of *SECC*. It is with deep gratitude that I dedicate this essay to Dorothy Johnson, mentor and friend, for her years of generous advice and unceasing encouragement.

1. Letter from David to his friend M. de Mainbourg, 8 November 1794. Reproduced in Daniel and Guy Wildenstein, *Documents complémentaires au catalogue de l'oeuvre de Louis David* (Paris: Fondation Wildenstein, 1973), no. 1143. "I feel utterly abandoned; I understand how dear your friendship was to me. I look for you, in vain, in the evenings but I no longer find you. I am moaning, alone. Only one consolation remains and it is to know that you are happier than I; at least you are enjoying your freedom." English translation from the original French by Athina Alvarez with Dorothy Johnson.

2. Following the fall of Robespierre on 27 July 1784, David was twice imprisoned for his Revolutionary activities—from 2 August to 29 December 1794 in the Hôtel des Fermes and the Luxembourg Palace, respectively, and 29 May to 3 August 1795 in the Collège des Quatre Nations. David was transferred to the Luxembourg Palace on 15 September 1794 where he was held on the upper floor of the pavilion at the southwest of the palace. See Dorothy Johnson, "David and Napoleonic Painting," in *Jacques-Louis David: New Perspectives*, ed. by Dorothy Johnson (Newark: University of Delaware Press, 2006), 13; Anna Ottani Cavina, "Rome 1780: le thème du paysage dans le cercle de David," Regis Michel, ed., *David contre David: actes du Colloque David, Musée du Louve, 1989* (Paris: La Documentation française, 1993), I, 81–92; and Anita Brookner, *Jacques-Louis David* (London: Thames and Hudson, 1980), 124.

3. The letter by Delafontaine is reproduced in Wildenstein, *Documents complémentaires*, no. 1131. For the content of Mme. David's letter, see Wildenstein, *Documents complémentaires*, no. 1212; the painting in question is mentioned by David in a checklist of his works completed in 1817. See Wildenstein, *Documents complémentaires*, no. 1810.

4. Étienne Delécluze, *David, son* école *et son temps* (Paris: Editions Macula, 1983), 178.

5. Anna Ottani Cavina and Emilia Calbi, "Louis Gauffier and the Question of J.-L. David's 'Vue présumée du jardin du Luxembourg'," *The Burlington Magazine* 134 (Jan., 1992): 27. For an account of the painting's provenance beginning in the Collection Sosthène Moreau, see *Jacques-Louis David 1748–1825*, ed. by Antoine Schnapper (Paris: Réunion des Musées Nationaux, 1989), no. 136.

6. Schnapper, *Jacques-Louis David 1748–1825*, no. 136.

7. A. de Gisors, *Le Palais du Luxembourg* (Paris, 1845), 67–68. Quote reproduced in Ottani Cavini and Calbi, "Louis Gauffier and the Question of J.-L. David's 'Vue présumée du jardin du Luxembourg'," 30. "He (David) left behind a rather curious sketch of part of the Jardin du Luxembourg, seen from the room in which he was imprisoned, on the upper floor of the former pavilion at an angle located to the west of the Palace. In the foreground, we notice a vast wooden enclosure that must have existed in the location that the private gardens of the Palace and the Chancellerie currently occupy. Beyond this are the pathways planted during the Revolution. Father away, through the randomly planted trees, one sees the buildings of the café such as they still are today. They had been constructed a little earlier to establish in that location the administrative offices of the armories that were, at the time, situated in the former grounds of the Carthusians. In the distance the hills of Meudon and Bellevue are outlined." English translation from the original French by Athina Alvarez with Dorothy Johnson.

8. Gisors, *Le Palais du Luxembourg*, 67–68 qtd by Ottani Cavini and Calbi, "Louis Gauffier and the Question of J.-L. David's 'Vue présumée du jardin du Luxembourg'," 30.

9. Gisors, *Le Palais du Luxembourg*, 67–68 qtd by Ottani Cavini and Calbi, "Louis Gauffier and the Question of J.-L. David's 'Vue présumée du jardin du Luxembourg'," 30. Louis Gauffier, identified primarily as a history painter and portraitist, painted the well-known landscape series during his Italian sojourn in the late 1790s. Gauffier won the Prix de Rome in 1784 (sharing his win with Jean-Germain Drouais in painting and Antoine-Denis Chaudet for sculpture) and remained in Italy with rare exception until his death in 1801. See P. Marmottan, "Le peintre Louis Gauffier," *Gazette des Beaux-Arts* 13 (1926): 281–300; M. Sandoz, "Oeuvres de Louis Gauffier nouvellement apparues," *Revue des Arts* 4 (1958): 195–8; and Celia Alegret, "Gauffier, Louis," in *Grove Art Online, Oxford Art Online*, http://www.oxfordartonline.com.proxy.lib.uiowa.edu/subscriber/article/grove/art/T031007 (accessed March 11, 2009).

10. See the letter from David to the representatives of the Committee of General Security, 15 September 1794. Reproduced in Wildenstein, *Documents complémentaires*, no. 1138.

11. Dorothy Johnson has suggested that the *Bara* is unfinished, which was likely the artist's intent. The painting—like the child martyr himself—remains fragile, undeveloped, and incomplete. Dorothy Johnson, *Jacques-Louis David: Art in Metamorphosis* (Princeton, NJ: Princeton Univ. Press, 1993), 112.

12. Johnson, *Art in Metamorphosis*, 229.

13. See Pierre Rosenberg and Louis-Antoine Prat, *Jacques-Louis David, 1748–1825: Catalogue raisonné des dessins*, 2 vols. (Milan: Leonardo Arte, 2002), 391–407; and Heidi E. Kraus, "David's Roman *Vedute*," in *Studies in Eighteenth-Century Culture* 38 (Baltimore: The Johns Hopkins Univ. Press, 2009): 173–198.

14. Rosenberg and Prat, *Catalogue raisonné des dessins*, nos. 703, 880, 893, 896–899, 1028, 1079, 1080, 1168–1170, and 1254.

15. Ottani Cavina and Calbi make note of the high viewpoints and rigid geometric organization as being characteristic of Gauffier's landscapes, but these so-called identifying characteristics also occur in sketched views by David and countless other French artists working in Rome in the later part of the eighteenth century. Ottani Cavini and Calbi, "Louis Gauffier and the Question of J.-L. David's 'Vue présumée du jardin du Luxembourg'," 30–31. At least two extant drawings in David's Roman albums bear a striking resemblance to Italian drawings by Gauffier. See Rosenberg and Prat, *Catalogue raisonné des dessins*, nos. 877, 877s, 897, and 897a.

16. "The landscape, despite the *all'antica* figures, is an actual one, painted on the spot on a particular day in late summer: the rye is already being cut, the lime-trees have an autumnal brown tint, and the shadows are long and marked. It is not, however, an Italian landscape, however tempting it may be to think so, bearing in mind Gauffier's long stay in Italy. Too many elements point further north. In the first place, the stockade: the scarcity of timber means that in Italy fences have always been made of more readily available materials such as stone. The vegetation of the park is also not very Italian, with spotted lime-trees and others, of the species *tilia cordata*, pruned into a line. The architecture is not Italian: the white-washed houses with exposed beams, the crossed wooden members at the base of the façade, the wooden girders that support the construction and the high chimneys of the workshops are foreign to any kind of Italian building technique. The location seems rather to be French, and the bell-tower visible between the dry branches of the tree seems to have an aperture with louvres or *abat-sons* for deflecting the sound downwards like those found in the French architectural tradition stretching from the gothic onwards." Ottani Cavini and Calbi, "Louis Gauffier and the Question of J.-L. David's 'Vue présumée du jardin du Luxembourg'," 33.

17. See Heidi E. Kraus, "David, Architecture, and the Dichotomy of Art," Ph.D. diss. (Ann Arbor: UMI Publishing, 2012), 36–38; fig. A14.; and Kraus, "David's Roman *Vedute*," 173–197.

18. Rosenberg and Prat, *Documents complémentaires*, no. 628–633.

19. The Luxembourg Palace was under construction from 1615 to 1622. For the seminal sources on the palace, its history, architecture, and decoration, see Arthur Hustin, *Le Luxembourg, ses transformations, son agrandissement, ses architectes, sa décoration, ses décorateurs* (Paris: P. Mouillot, 1904); Pasteur Pannier, *Un Architecte*

Français au commencement du XVIIe siècle, Salomon de Brosse (Paris: Université, diss., 1911); Reginald Blomfield, *History of French Architecture 1494–1661* (London: G. Bell and Sons, 1911); and G. Hirschfeld, *Le Palais du Luxembourg* (Paris, 1931).

20. See Serguisz Michalski, "Stepping Out from Popilius' Circle: David's Symbolic View of His Revolutionary Experience," *Gazette des Beaux-Arts* (July 1993): 51–56.

21. J.-A. Schmoll gen. Eisenwerth, "J-.L. David's 'Vue du jardin du Luxembourg' von 1794 als Parabel der Gefangenschaft des Malers," in *Florilegium Artis. Festschrift für Wolfgang Götz anlässlich seines 60 Geburtstag, Searbrüch* (1983), 125–32.

22. Ottani Cavina and Calbi, however, reject Schmoll's assertion because the scene is missing the figure of the Roman soldier who kills Archimedes for drawing circles on the ground. Ottani Cavini and Calbi, "Louis Gauffier and the Question of J.-L. David's 'Vue présumée du jardin du Luxembourg'," 31–32.

23. Ottani Cavina and Calbi assert the "generic" nature of the figures, included by Gauffier at the last minute, they presume, to give a sense of scale and depth to the painting. Ottani Cavini and Calbi, "Louis Gauffier and the Question of J.-L. David's 'Vue présumée du jardin du Luxembourg'," 31.

24. Kraus, "David, Architecture, and the Dichotomy of Art," 26–27.

25. Wendy M. Watson, "Tradition and Innovation: Pierre-Henri de Valenciennes and the Neoclassical Landscape," in *Valenciennes, Daubigny, and the Origins of French Landscape Painting* (South Hadley, MA: Mount Holyoke College Art Museum, 2004), 25. The seminal text on Valenciennes is Robert Mesuret, *Pierre-Henri de Valenciennes*, exh. cat. (Toulouse: Musée Paul-Dupuy, 1956). Other important studies include: Paula Rea Radisich, *Eighteenth-Century Landscape Theory and the Work of Pierre-Henri de Valenciennes* (Los Angeles: Univ. of California at Los Angeles, 1977); Whitney Wheelock, "Pierre-Henri de Valenciennes (1750–1819)" (M.A. thesis, Courtauld Institute of Art, London, 1975); and Geneviève Lacambre, "Pierre-Henri de Valenciennes en Italie: Un Journal de voyage inédit," *Bulletin de la Société de l'Histoire de l'Art français, année 1978* (1980): 139–72.

26. Peter Galassi, "The Nineteenth Century: Valenciennes to Corot," in *Claude to Corot: The Development of Landscape Painting in France*, ed. by Alan Wintermute (New York: Colnaghi, 1990), 233. Due to his status as a landscape painter, Valenciennes was not a recipient of the Prix de Rome which, at this point, was reserved exclusively for history painters. During his trip to Paris in 1781–82, Valenciennes met Claude-Joseph Vernet who proved instrumental in teaching him perspective as it applied to painting.

27. Radisich, *Eighteenth-Century Landscape Theory and the Work of Pierre-Henri de Valenciennes*, 216. David was a student at the French Academy in Rome from 1775–1780 and returned to the Eternal City in 1784–85 to paint the *Oath of the Horatii*.

28. Watson, "Tradition and Innovation," 27. The majority of Valenciennes's Italian sketchbooks and oil sketches are located today in the collections of the Louvre and Bibliothèque Nationale, Paris. In 1930, the Louvre acquired one hundred and

twenty-five sketches by Valenciennes from the collection of the Princesse de Croÿ, who inherited them from her grandfather, M. de l'Espine. De l'Espine purchased the sketches in 1819 and 1825 at the posthumous sales of Valenciennes and his pupil Anne-Louis Girodet. See Geneviève Lacambre, "Les paysages de Pierre-Henri de Valenciennes 1750–1819," *Dossier du département des Peintures, Louvre II* (1976), n.p.; and Philip Conisbee, "Pierre-Henri de Valenciennes at the Louvre," *The Burlington Magazine* 118, no. 878 (May, 1976): 336–334.

29. See Galassi, "The Nineteenth Century: Valenciennes to Corot," 233–249.

30. *French Landscape Drawings and Sketches of the Eighteenth* Century, ed. by Roseline Bacou (London: British Museum Publications Ltd., 1977), 99.

31. Pierre Rosenberg, *From Drawing to Painting: Poussin, Watteau, Fragonard and Ingres* (Princeton: Princeton Univ. Press, 2000), 117–118.

32. *River Landscape*, c. 1590 (National Gallery of Art, Washington, D.C.), serves as an example of a pure landscape by Annibale. The painting is reproduced in John Varriano, *Italian Baroque and Rococo Architecture* (New York: Oxford University Press, 1986), 10, fig. 4. For the seminal text on the Carracci, see Giovanni Pietro Bellori, *The Lives of Annibale and Agostino Carracci*, trans. by Catherine Enggass (University Park: Pennsylvania State Univ. Press, 1968).

33. Varriano, *Italian Baroque and Rococo Architecture*, 10–11.

34. Varriano, *Italian Baroque and Rococo Architecture*, 11. This is not to dismiss the influence of Domenichino on David's oeuvre. Several drawings from David's Roman albums are studies completed after Domenichino, one of which is a landscape. See Rosenberg and Prat, *Documents complémentaires*, nos. 634, 736, 1021, and 1134.

35. Marianne Roland Michel, "Landscape Painting in the Eighteenth Century: Theory, Training, and its Place in Academic Doctrine," in *Claude to Corot*, 99.

36. Roger de Piles, *Cours de peinture par principes* (Paris: Jacques-Estienne, 1708), 158–9. "And if Nature appear not there, as we every day casually see her, she is at least represented as we think she ought to be. This style is an agreeable illusion, and a sort of enchantment, when handled by a man of fine genius, and good understanding, as Poussin was, who has so happily expressed it." Roger de Piles, *The Principles of Painting*, trans. by John Osborn (London, 1743), 124.

37. De Piles, *Cours de peinture par principes*, 174. "Buildings in general are a great ornament in landscape, even when they are *Gothick*, or appear partly inhabited, and partly ruinous: they raise the imagination by the use they are thought to be designed for… Poussin has very elegantly handled the *Roman* manner of architecture in his works as *Bourdon* has done with the *Gothick*." Roger de Piles, *The Principles of Painting*, trans. by John Osborn, 173.

38. M. Michel, "Landscape Painting in the Eighteenth Century: Theory, Training, and its Place in Academic Doctrine," 101.

39. Radisich, *Eighteenth-Century Landscape Theory and the Work of Pierre-Henri de Valenciennes*, 177.

40. See Pierre-Henri Valenciennes, *Elémens de perspective pratique à l'usage des artistes* (Paris: Libraire Duprat, 1800).

41. Radisich, *Eighteenth-Century Landscape Theory and the Work of Pierre-*

Henri de Valenciennes, 179–180.

42. Watson, "Tradition and Innovation," 26.

43. Valenciennes, *Elémens de perspective*, preface.

44. Rosenberg and Prat, *Documents complémentaires*, nos. 1883–1887; See also Sandoz, "Dessins peu connus du peintre Louis David dans la vallée de Chamonix en 1815," in *La Revue Savoisienne* (1981): 56–59; and Thomas Crow, "The Imagination of Exile in David's *Anger of Achilles*," in *David after David. Essays on the Later Work*, ed. Mark Ledbury (New Haven: Yale Univ. Press, 2007), pp. 123–137.

45. See Dorothy Johnson, "Rousseau and landscape painting in France," *The Nature of Rousseau's Rêveries: physical, human, aesthetic*, ed. by John C. O'Neal (Oxford: Voltaire Foundation, 2008), 37–57.

46. Johnson, "Rousseau and landscape painting in France," 51–53.

The New Heathens: A Pandemic of Heresy in Late Eighteenth-Century Prussia

JONATHAN BLAKE FINE

On September 15, 1785, the conservative civil servant Johann Christoph Woellner delivered a treatise concerning the proper governmental regulation of religion to the Prussian crown prince, who would soon ascend the throne as Friedrich Wilhelm II. In response to Friedrich II's declining health, Woellner had spent the previous year grooming the presumptive monarch for his imminent assumption of power with a series of lectures concerning practical matters such as rural serfdom and the kingdom's fiscal affairs. This "Abhandlung über die Religion" delivered by Woellner on that September day, however, was far more ambitious.[1] Indeed, it should be read as the Counter-Enlightenment pendant to the seminal debate on the meaning of the Enlightenment that had played out publicly only a year beforehand in the pages of the *Berlinische Monatsschrift*.[2]

However, Woellner's definition of the Enlightenment was purposefully bereft of the nuances seen in the contributions to that prior debate by such paragons of the moderate Enlightenment as Immanuel Kant and Moses Mendelssohn. According to Woellner, the Enlightenment was neither an escape from self-incurred immaturity nor less politically suspect through division into civic and humanistic components.[3] Instead, it became clear in the treatise that, for Woellner, the Enlightenment fundamentally entailed the seditious propagation of blasphemy to a populace incapable of properly evaluating complex thought let alone wading through the vagaries of biblical hermeneutics. When Woellner looked back at the preceding decade, he saw scant evidence of an *Aufklärung* divided into an enlightened public sphere for intellectual discourse via print on the one hand and, on the other hand, the private use of reason that could be practiced by civil officials so as to ensure societal order.[4] In other words—and to avail myself of the helpful, albeit slightly reductive triangular heuristic developed by Jonathan Israel in his trilogy on the European Enlightenment—the leading figure of the Prussian Counter-Enlightenment did not see the preceding decade as the maturation of the moderate Enlightenment with its support for a measured and highly circumspect pedagogical approach to dealing with the common people.[5] Instead, he saw in the last decade of Friedrich II's reign the eruption of the Radical Enlightenment out of the sequestered domain of academics and clerics and into the nascent, bourgeois public sphere. Radical ideas had been unscrupulously injected into this public sphere in order to bring about public Enlightenment with undue haste. The absence of strong, centralized leadership in the kingdom's religious affairs, which should have been provided by Karl Abraham von Zedlitz, the chief of the kingdom's department of spiritual affairs, had allowed numerous radical, self-ordained *Aufklärer* to peddle sacrilegious, printed wares, the consumption of which had contributed to the successful transformation of Prussia into the most irreligious land in Europe. A chief aim of the revanchist project that Woellner would lead was ensuring that the faith of the common people was no longer undermined by contact with blasphemy delivered under the guise of educating people via involvement in the momentous religious debates that used to occur behind closed doors.

Woellner had good reason to be wary of religious debates. Since there was, in comparison to England, little space for true political dissent in the Prussian public sphere, theological polemic often served as an ersatz method to debate the prerogatives of the state. Indeed, such hybrid religious-political debates had long been a key feature of the German offshoot of the *république des lettres*.[6] This had not necessarily been dangerous at a time when the majority of scholarly discourse was conducted in Latin; however, over the course of the eighteenth century, the linguistic barrier that had kept these occasionally heretical debates from infecting the masses broke down. The earliest phases of the Enlightenment in the seventeenth century had featured the circulation of clandestine manuscripts written in Latin or occasionally French amongst members of the philosophical underground, as Martin Mulsow has shown.[7] But as the eighteenth century drew to a close, religious debates increasingly took place both in print and in the vernacular, a development that ensured that theological polemic became increasingly comprehensible to those without a formal education, as Ursula Goldenbaum has demonstrated in her recent magisterial study *Appell an das Publikum: Die öffentliche Debatte in der deutschen Aufklärung 1687–1796*.[8] Given the steady rise in the literate percentage of the population and the ongoing reading-revolution, by Woellner's time, heresy had become, at least in theory, easily accessible to the common people.

Woellner was certainly reacting to the dangers that he perceived in this century-long trend toward accessibility when he composed the treatise on religion, which, upon Friedrich Wilhelm II's accession, would form the basis of the two religious edicts that subsequently governed intellectual discourse in the public sphere. Recent research on Woellner that has taken advantage of newly available manuscripts to examine the development of the edicts has provided a thorough contextualization of this altogether not-unprecedented attempt to regulate the way intellectuals communicated.[9] Although revisionist accounts such as Michael Sauter's have occasionally swung the pendulum too far in the direction of pro-Woellner apologetics, they have undoubtedly delivered a more nuanced view of Woellner's efforts to prevent enlightened thought from infecting the common people. Thus, it is quite curious that no critical attention has been devoted to the offshoot of the tradition of Enlightenment-era public debate directly responsible for the viral spread of heretical ideas that Woellner wanted to curtail, especially since he explicitly named two of the men involved in the treatise.[10] Woellner's contemporaries had a quite provocative sobriquet to refer to these men; they were called the new heathens.

The phenomenon of the new heathens is too diffuse to be captured in a micro-history (such as those written by Mulsow) that would explain the effects of individual texts. Moreover, the speed with which their heresies were expunged from the public consciousness ensured that the heretical pandemic they unleashed would be difficult to incorporate in a diachronic study that aimed to discern a thread of continuity in the fits and starts that characterized the *Aufklärung*. Perhaps for these reasons—along with the fact that many of the heathens' texts were both highly derivative and not particularly cogent—there has never been a sustained scholarly reflection on the new heathens. Thus, there has been no account of the role that this collection of individuals (I hesitate to say group given the fact that the heathens were neither personally acquainted nor were they always intellectually simpatico) played in provoking the Counter-Enlightenment backlash that would both silence the new heathens and claim the moderate *Aufklärung* as collateral damage. This is not to say that the controversialist paradigm in intellectual history with its focus on reviving and contextualizing forgotten theological debates has completely ignored the individuals seen by their compatriots to be members of the new heathens.[11] To date, however, the most salient link connecting this concatenation of individuals has been ignored. Although they did not act collectively in an organized manner, they were nonetheless viewed by their contemporaries as co-conspirators in a dangerous movement. Scholarship addressing this conception of a conspiracy of apostates remains a desideratum.

This essay can but offer a brief overview of this forgotten attempt to incorporate the non-elite in theological debates. As such, I shall only focus on the three men of letters that were held by some of their contemporaries to be the leaders of the new heathens: The playwright Gotthold Ephraim Lessing, whose theological agitation has been the topic of innumerable studies even though his personal theological views remain enigmatic;[12] Karl Friedrich Bahrdt, a malcontent theologian and firebrand who has received an increasing amount of critical attention in recent years;[13] and Christian Ernst Wünsch, whose theological writings, to my knowledge, have over the course of the last century only been addressed in one article.[14]

Lessing was the first to realize that the ongoing reading revolution of the late eighteenth century offered the possibility of widely disseminating anti-Christian texts, which had long been popular but had been both too expensive and oftentimes too encumbered by debates on philology to achieve widespread publicity. When Baruch Spinoza unleashed his system on seventeenth-century Holland, the intellectual impact on the elite may have been profound and immediate, but the popular reaction was much more limited, even though it was still greatly feared. A century later, when Hamburg's senior pastor Johann Melchior Goeze preached that Lessing's publication of the *Fragmente eines Ungenannten* had inaugurated the "Stunde des Satans," the congregants could hasten to a local bookstore the very next day and buy their own copies of one of the dozens of readily available texts written by participants in the public dispute.[15] As the circulation and popularity of these blasphemous texts increased, Lessing, Bahrdt, and Wünsch sensed that there had been a previously unmet need in the intellectual marketplace for works that used a popular tone to challenge the state religion, and they ruthlessly took advantage of the opportunity presented to them to cast off the yoke of superstition while they still had the chance.

Lessing and the Response to the *Fragmente eines Ungenannten*

It was Lessing who first succeeded in creating a new genre of controversial theological texts that would also appeal to a lay public.[16] As Burckhard Dücker has shown, he intended the consumption of these texts to lead to a new type of knowledge that would challenge the ossified agglomeration of superstitions that passed as religion in the Germanic states.[17] A full understanding of the response that Lessing's publication received requires a short introduction to the various religious doctrines vying for dominance in the late eighteenth-century German cultural arena. Although the *Fragmentenstreit* that we will be considering in this section is oftentimes viewed through the narrow prism of Lessing's dispute with Goeze (the epitome of Lutheran orthodoxy who was nonetheless actually Lessing's old drinking buddy), Lessing's primary aim was not to challenge the orthodox. Nor did Lessing intend to enter into a dialogue with rural preachers such as the atheistic Johann Heinrich Schulz, whose eventual downfall has drawn critical attention in recent years.[18] The true targets were enlightened neologians such as Johann Salomo Semler and Johann Friedrich Wilhelm Jerusalem. It was their attempt to unite Wolffianism, deism, and pietism that Lessing found to be especially inconsistent. Particularly galling to Lessing were the neologians' attempts to maintain belief in revelation even though their own doctrines would seem to demand that they abandon belief in revelation and miracles such as the resurrection.[19] Given the various religious forces battling for domination, Leonard Wessell has averred that the intellectual landscape in which Lessing operated resembles Thomas Kuhn's depiction of the period of time before one scientific paradigm emerges triumphant after contention among various paradigms.[20] It was in this ideological ferment that Lessing decided to launch his intervention into the public sphere.

When Lessing departed Hamburg in 1770 to take up his new position as the librarian at the Herzog August Bibliothek in Wolfenbüttel, a post held previously by Gottfried Wilhelm Leibniz, he brought with him a curious manuscript.[21] Likely begun some time in the late 1730s in the immediate aftermath of the suppression of Johann Lorenz Schmidt's so-called *Wertheimer Bibel*, the manuscript was the work of a celebrated professor at the Gymnasium in Hamburg, an outwardly pious churchgoer by the name of Hermann Samuel Reimarus. Reimarus was well known in the Republic of Letters for his works on physico-theology and ethology. A small circle of his friends, however, knew that those texts on natural religion and animal behavior began as parts of a lengthy manuscript, the final version of which bore the title *Apologie, oder Schutzschrift für die vernünftigen Verehrer Gottes*. It was an early draft of this manuscript that Lessing smuggled across the border into the duchy of Braunschweig-Lüneburg. When published in fragmentary form as the *Fragmente eines Ungenannten*, it unleashed the most destructive public theological controversy of the late eighteenth century.

Reimarus was fully aware of the danger posed by his text to a public unaccustomed to unfiltered expressions of heterodoxy. In the introduction to the final manuscript, which was first published in its entirety only in 1972, Reimarus wrote,

> Die Schrift mag im Verborgenen, zum Gebrauch verständiger Freunde liegen bleiben; mit meinem Willen soll sie nicht durch den Druck gemein gemacht werden, bevor sich die Zeiten mehr aufklären. Lieber mag der gemeine Hauffe noch eine Weile irren, als daß ich ihn, (obwohl es ohne meine Schuld geschehen würde) mit Wahrheiten ärgern, und in einen wütenden Religions-Eiffer setzen sollte. Lieber mag der Weise sich, des Friedens halber, unter den herrschenden Meynungen und Gebräuchen schmiegen, dulden und schweigen, als daß er sich und andere, durch gar zu frühzeitige Äusserung, unglücklich machen sollte.[22]

How exactly the times were to become more enlightened without receiving some external impetus did not receive Reimarus's attention. Lessing, however, had long believed that it was the duty of intellectuals to provide the whole truth, and he thought confrontation with unwelcome ideas to be one of the surest ways to combat erroneous traditions.[23] Lessing came to see Reimarus's text as the perfect instrument to accomplish two of his overriding goals. First, the manuscript could potentially serve as the catalyst that impelled the German people to undertake its own process of enlightenment. Second, as noted above, Lessing had a very negative opinion of what passed as enlightened theology. He hoped that the publication of Reimarus's manuscript would ensure that the theological edifice would be so thoroughly destroyed that no one would ever attempt to reconstruct it.[24]

In 1774, Lessing published an initial fragment in the third volume of *Zur Geschichte und Litteratur: Aus den Schätzen der herzoglichen Bibliothek zu Wolfenbüttel*, his vehicle to make important, unpublished works from the ducal library available to the public. Although portions of the fragment, entitled "Von Duldung der Deisten," touch upon the distinction between the historically contingent facts of history and the necessarily true doctrine of reason that would become so crucial for Lessing in his dispute with the theologians, the majority of the first publication was an earnest and rather platitudinous plea for the toleration of the views of free-thinkers, deists, and adherents of natural religion. Although this argument might have been controversial when Reimarus first formulated it in the 1740s, it had lost much of its bite by the time of the text's publication. Lessing's erstwhile collaborators, Mendelssohn and Friedrich Nicolai, correctly surmised that this text was not sufficiently threatening to the theological status quo to attract significant opposition. A slightly disappointed Lessing had to continue on in his quest to ignite a large controversy.

Under the pretext that he had been asked to publish the "Dreisteste und Stärkste" passages from the papers of the "Ungenannte," Lessing published five additional fragments in the fourth issue of *Zur Geschichte und Litteratur*, which appeared in 1777.[25] They are of uneven quality, but Lessing managed to start the dispute that he desired, nonetheless. The first fragment, bearing the title "Von Verschreiung der Vernunft auf den Kanzeln," continued the line of thought from the initial publication in 1774. The second fragment was a bricolage of assorted deistic statements loosely grouped around the assertion that provided the fragment with its title, namely the "Unmöglichkeit einer Offenbarung, die alle Menschen auf eine gegründete Art glauben könnten." Neither Reimarus nor Lessing was concerned that claiming the impossibility of a properly proven revelation begged questions of how such standards would be applied to religious belief. The third fragment was notable for its meticulous dismantling of the story of the Red Sea crossing from *Exodus*. Reimarus concluded that the story quite simply could not have happened; moreover, he had the math to prove it. This fragment would eventually be published as a separate pamphlet and proved to be quite popular throughout the 1780s. The fourth, much less memorable fragment, entitled "Daß die Bücher A. T. nicht geschrieben worden, eine Religion zu offenbaren," construed the absence of the doctrine of the immortality of the soul in the Pentateuch as a sign that it was not written to reveal a religion. Ever the dramatist, Lessing saved the most dangerous fragment for the end. In the denouement to this five-act drama, entitled innocently enough "Über die Auferstehungsgeschichte," the assault on Christian theology merely adumbrated in the first pieces became clearer: Reimarus identified ten specific contradictions in the story of the resurrection, and he proceeded to use these inconsistencies to poke holes in the apostles' accounts. He argued that the story of the resurrection seemed, at best, arbitrarily fabricated. The unarticulated suggestion gleaned by Lessing's opponents was that these errors would call into question the entire edifice of Christianity.

Even more scandalous, however, were the "Gegensätze des Herausgebers" that Lessing appended to the fragments. In this text, Lessing developed the key points that he would return to in each of his interactions with his detractors: Lessing argued that a true, and in fact more authentic Christian religion existed before the writing of the Bible and that revealed religion ultimately contained a reasonable core, which was crucial for Lessing's attempt to reconcile the most acute of Enlightenment problems, namely the relationship between faith and reason. Given that this essay will not examine the individual texts that Lessing published in response to his opponents in order to expound his own thoughts on religion and theology, I will not here enter into the longstanding intellectual debate on what, if any, of the ideas that Lessing developed could be said to represent his genuine beliefs.[26]

Such blasphemous ideas as those expressed in the *Fragmente* and the "Gegensätze" called out for a response, but Lessing was disappointed in the quality of the first refutations. Although texts such as those by Johann Daniel Schumann and Johann Heinrich Reß prompted Lessing to produce some of his most succinct reflections on the true religion of Christ—in contrast to the Christian religion preached from the pulpit—Lessing recognized that more was needed to implant Reimarus's ideas deeply into the public sphere. It was Goeze whose very public agitation against him provided Lessing with the perfect pretext to unleash the most salacious attack on Christianity yet, the second part of the fifth fragment on the resurrection, to which Lessing gave the title *Vom Zweck Jesu und seiner Jünger*, which contained Reimarus's true thoughts about Christianity.

Lessing prefaced *Vom Zweck Jesu* with a lament: The dispute that had just begun was so important, but the proceedings thus far had been decidedly lacking.[27] Lessing admitted that some of the responses demonstrated great learning, but they collectively suffered from the same problem: They purported to thoroughly refute what they took to be Reimarus's *coup de grâce* against Christianity, namely that doubts about the veracity of the resurrection cast doubt upon Christianity as a whole. Given how Lessing arranged the publication of individual parts of the manuscript, these opponents could not know that the argument they believed to have demolished was little more than a straw man. This was because the "Ungenannte" did not question the totality of Christianity on account of the ten contradictions he identified in the story of the resurrection. Rather, Reimarus doubted the story of the resurrection because he contended that the entirety of Christianity was based upon deception. The falsity of the story of the resurrection followed naturally from the falsity of Christianity as a whole, and not the other way around.

In *Vom Zweck Jesu*, Reimarus asserted that Jesus was a committed Jew who had deluded himself into believing that he might be the man to achieve the liberation that was the Jews' most fervently pursued political goal. His disciples, upon whose flawed testimony so much depends, followed Jesus because they hoped that they might aggrandize themselves and acquire material goods when Jesus became the political redeemer of his people. It was only after the crucifixion that the frustrated political hopes of Jesus's followers were sublimated into the belief that Jesus was a divinely ordained messiah who might offer the possibility of spiritual redemption. What really happened, Reimarus argued, was that after the crucifixion, the disciples had quickly realized that their leader's death did not preclude them from advancing their ambitions; in fact, by preaching the gospel of a divine savior, their future could be just as remunerative. After Reimarus adduced this true story of the founding of the Christian religion, he proceeded to look for traces of the real story in the official, established legend. With the narrative set up in this manner, it was not at all surprising that Reimarus was able to identify quite a few submerged traces that revealed the nefarious misdeeds of Jesus's followers. Unlike the first six fragments, which were printed entirely in quotation marks in order to emphasize that they were cited text, Lessing dispensed with this formality for the publication of *Vom Zweck Jesu*. Moreover, since Lessing did not append any refutation to this work as he had done for the *Fragmente* published only a few months beforehand, it was widely assumed to represent his real views.[28] With this last publication, Lessing finally achieved his goal, a full theological war conducted entirely within the public sphere.

Nearly all of the polemical replies from the first full year of the controversy concern the effects of the *Fragmente* upon a lay public and seek to speak to that public.[29] Moreover, what ultimately made the *Fragmentenstreit* so important for the still developing German public sphere was the fact that it became the first multi-media scandal. In addition to the numerous refutations by the many minor and several major theologians, the *Fragmentenstreit* was also portrayed in poetry.[30] Lessing's battle with Goeze was also depicted in popular literature: In one of the most popular works of the 1780s, a "travestied" version of Virgil's *Aeneid*, Goeze was memorably depicted blessing the Trojan horse.[31]

As might be expected, the faculties of theology at German universities were soon in an uproar. On Wednesdays at 2 P.M. during winter semester 1779–1780, the theologian Johann Georg Rosenmüller delivered a course completely dedicated to a defense of the story of the resurrection against the *Fragmente*.[32] As the neologian Semler's refutation of the *Fragmente* attested, impressionable students in the faculty of theology in Halle started to question their choice of a vocation after reading the blasphemy spewed by Lessing.[33] Parish priests were particularly interested in the progression of the dispute.[34] Franz Anton Knittel, the superintendent of priests in the duchy of Braunschweig, advised in a speech to his synod that the people must remain in the dark lest the pulpit be turned into a battlefield.[35] Notwithstanding this official admonition, commoners soon heard of Reimarus's heresies, as is shown by the feverish efforts on the part of numerous country preachers to fortify the ramparts of orthodoxy.[36] Reimarus, who had hoped that his writings would remain unpublished until the Enlightenment had fully penetrated the German public sphere—a time that he felt was not at all imminent—was denounced at numerous pulpits barely a decade after his death.[37] Although Goeze had explicitly argued in another context against turning the pulpits into "Streitplätze" since doing so would expose the common man to "ein Same des Unkrauts," the dispute was often a topic or crucial subtext in his own sermons.[38]

Lessing's opponents despaired that uneducated readers could not see what was so blatantly obvious to their learned compatriots, namely that the *Fragmente* were little more than nets of contradictions and falsities.[39] Within the *Gelehrtenrepublik*, scholars had refuted such anti-Christian texts for decades. However, since few members of the broader public had come into contact with undiluted examples of heterodoxy, they were eager consumers. It is unknown how many individuals actually became infected with Lessing's poison. A priest by the name of Treumann from the vicinity of Berlin, writing as "Agm" in the *Allgemeine deutsche Bibliothek*, hyperbolically inflated the number of people contaminated by the *Fragmente* into the millions.[40] Johann Bernhard Basedow, on the other hand, estimated that the *Fragmente* had, at most, 3,000 readers.[41] What is known for sure is that the fourth volume, which contained the five main fragments, sold as many as the first three combined.[42] Moreover, one journal described the readership of the *Fragmente* as comprising a class of people for whom the reading of religious writings would not be expected.[43]

Although it is unclear ultimately how many individuals read the *Fragmente* given the lack of reliable information on circulation as well as the widespread trafficking in unauthorized reprintings, there is considerably less dissension regarding the enthusiasm with which they were read. In Zürich, the preacher Johann Caspar Lavater devoted his "Synodalrede" on May 4, 1779 to the struggle against deism and rationalism as exemplified by the righteous battle against "jener neue fürchterliche Ausbruch des giftigsten Unglaubens in der allbekannten und von unserer männlichen Jünglingschaft heißhungrig verschlungenen Lessingschen Schrift 'Vom Zweck Jesu und seiner Jünger.'" In Lavater's personal opinion, as articulated to the congregated theologians, Lessing's last publication from Reimarus's manuscript was unique among all anti-Christian texts with respect to both its "Bösheit und Zweklosigkeit" as well as its "List und taschenspielerscher Raisonnirkunst." What was worse, however, to the deacon Lavater, who had become increasingly inimical to enlightened theology over the course of the prior decade, was the popularity of *Vom Zweck Jesu*. Lavater wrote,

> Diese Schrift ist in Aller Händen, sie liegt oder lag in unsern Buchläden; unsere Dienstboten holen und tragen sie hin und her; während daß sie gebunden werden, lieset sie der Buchbinder und sein Gesell, erhascht der Hausgenoß und der Nachbar

> tiefvergiftende Gedanken daraus; unsere Jünglinge tragen sie in ihrer Tasche und triumphieren damit in ihren Kreisen.

As Lavater went on to remark, the poison in the *Fragmente* and *Vom Zweck Jesu* had even infected learned women.[44]

With each new fulmination against the *Fragmente*, Reimarus's texts penetrated deeper into the public sphere. Lessing's opponents did not realize until it was too late that that was part of the plan from the beginning; the work of exposing the public to heterodoxy required them to react and turn the publication of the *Fragmente* into a public scandal. When considered strictly as a theological battle, however, Lessing actually lost the *Fragmentenstreit* according to the standards of his time. It was Lessing, after all, to whom the Duke of Braunschweig-Lüneburg's order of censorship applied. Moreover it was Lessing, half-heartedly applauded by some but fully supported in his mission by not one of his contemporaries—in fact, furtively repudiated by some, such as Nicolai, that he counted amongst his friends—who died under threat of imperial indictment.[45] Nevertheless, this sad fate did not, as we shall see, prove to be a particularly strong deterrent.

A Spreading Epidemic: Bahrdt and Wünsch

By the time that Lessing died on February 15, 1781, the immense public outcry over the *Fragmente eines Ungenannten* had mostly subsided. Lessing's death was mourned by the majority of Germany's men of letters, but welcomed by those who thought it to be just recompense for his steadfast determination to conduct the *Fragmentenstreit* publicly and for the harm to society it caused. In the opinion of these scrupulous intellectuals, the "Erzseelenlosen Sophisten Leßing," as Lavater besmirched him in a letter to Friedrich Heinrich Jacobi, had gotten what he deserved.[46]

The danger, however, was not past. Only a few months after Lessing's death, the former Jesuit Joseph Anton Weissenbach sounded the alarm in *Die Vorbothen des neuen Heidenthums* about a new movement of latter-day heathens who did not see the exact nature of Lessing's defeat in the *Fragmentenstreit* as an admonition against such acts of public defiance.[47] After all, Lessing had manifestly succeeded in his attempt to set off a chain reaction that would both threaten the core of the theological edifice and penetrate the public sphere. Weissenbach painted a foreboding picture of what might happen should these polemicists succeed. Such a course of events would lead to the complete "Zerfall des Glaubens."[48]

The prospect of a complete inversion of societal structure was also imminent: According to Weissenbach, after they came into contact with any of the numerous heretical texts, laymen began "in das Lehramt ein[zu] greifen" and numerous women "ohne was gelernet zu haben, sich an die Schwierigkeiten der Metaphysik, und der Gottesgelehrtheit waget."[49] In such an era when the wise had enthroned their own reason and understanding above God himself, good Christians had to guard against even seemingly minor deviations from orthodoxy because "Irrglaube gerade zu dem Unglaube führ[t]."[50] Thus, even the seemingly benign calls for tolerance such as those contained in the initial fragment "Von Duldung der Deisten" concealed an assault on the peace of Jesus Christ.[51] Behind such appeals for freedom of conscience lay the true goal of these new heathens; the downfall of all legitimate authorities and the anarchy that would surely ensue.[52] According to Adam Sigismund Fleischer, at the core of this rapidly expanding group of new heathens was a triumvirate composed of Lessing and two others who had learned from him how to market "Mäusekoth für Pfeffer, und Gift für Canari Zucker."[53] They were Karl Friedrich Bahrdt, and the man who was widely known as the author of the *Horus*, Christian Ernst Wünsch.

Bahrdt, commonly described as the *enfant terrible* of the German Enlightenment, actually began his career as a theological agitator well before the start of the *Fragmentenstreit*. By 1774, he had already lost the first of many jobs as a preacher on account of his translation of the New Testament, which managed the rare feat of attracting criticism from both Goeze and Johann Wolfgang Goethe.[54] Although Bahrdt was one of the first to use the term *Volksaufklärung*, he initially had little interest in actually enlightening the masses. Indeed, in one of his earliest defenses of his actions, he proclaimed that he would never abuse his position as a preacher by exposing the common people to illicit ideas.[55] Nevertheless, the controversy over Reimarus's *Fragmente* played a crucial role in getting Bahrdt, who cycled through nearly every theological position available to him over the course of his lengthy career, to change his mind about the propriety of using his theological writings to directly communicate with the common people.[56]

In his autobiography, Bahrdt claimed that he was angered by Reimarus's description of Jesus's political program and especially did not like the idea of Jesus as a Jewish king. He wrote,

> Mit empörendem Verdruß hatte ich gelesen, wie ihn der Verfasser der Fragmente zum elenden Politiker herabgewürdigt und ihm den armseligen Zwek angedichtet hatte, sich eine jüdische Krone zu erringen. Mit wahrem Mitleid und wirklichem Kummer hatte ich die Eindrücke bemerkt, die diese Lessingsche Produkte unter dem Haufen der freidenkenden Menschen hervorgebracht hatte.[57]

It should be noted that this reaction was not primarily motivated by anti-semitism. Instead, it was the explicitly political understanding of Jesus to which Bahrdt objected.

The problem for an aspiring disseminator of heterodox thought was how to differentiate one's wares in an intellectual marketplace that was increasingly saturated with blasphemous texts. As the politically-inclined theologian Johann August von Stark, a critic of these writers, noted, "Es geht mit diesen Schriften gerade so, wie mit den Alchimistenbüchern: wer eines gelesen hat, hat alle gelesen. Alles kommt darauf hinaus, daß die Bibel unzuverläßig, die positive Religion nichts, und daß der Naturalismus der eigentliche Kern ist." Stark went on to note that the only major difference between these texts was in how "frey" and "unverschämt" they proceeded in their assaults.[58]

Bahrdt personally chose to differentiate his products by constructing a new vision of Jesus as a proto-*Aufklärer*. In his *Briefe über die Bibel im Volkston*, published weekly beginning in January 1782, Bahrdt began offering this new, enlightened vision of Jesus as an antidote to anyone whose faith was disturbed by the overly Semitic presentation in the *Fragmente*.[59] In his *Ausführung des Plans und Zwecks Jesu*, Bahrdt furthermore asserted that Jesus wanted to destroy superstition, to suppress positive religion, and to restore to reason the rights that priestly deception had denied it.[60] In subsequent years, Bahrdt became ever more convinced that "die Zeit der Kindheit des Menschengeschlechts ist vorbey, wir sind iezt Männer und brauchen strarke Speise, reine Wahrheit," which he began to serve to the people.[61] Eventually, this desire to serve the people pure truth would lead to Bahrdt's downfall and imprisonment.

The third member of the triumvirate under consideration was Christian Ernst Wünsch. A doctor of philosophy and medicine, Wünsch is remembered today, if he is remembered at all, as one of Heinrich von Kleist's favorite teachers as well as for his relatively minor contribution to the study of color theory, which earned him Goethe's condemnation in the *Xenien*.[62] During his lifetime, however, Wünsch was widely known as the anonymous author of a scandalous anti-Christian tract filled with what the physicist/aphorist Georg Christoph Lichtenberg denounced as the "entsetzlichsten Gotteslästerungen."[63] The text bore the thoroughly descriptive and pompously verbose title: *Horus oder Astrognostisches Endurtheil über die Offenbarung Johannis und über die Weissagungen auf den Messias wie auch über Jesum und seine Jünger. Mit einem Anhange von Europens neuern Aufklärung und von der Bestimmung des Menschen durch Gott. Ein Lesebuch zur Erholung für die Gelehrten und ein Denkzeddel für Freimaurer* (1783). In contrast to both the vision of Jesus as a Jewish king advanced by Lessing and Reimarus and the conception of Jesus as a forerunner of the *Aufklärer*, Wünsch provocatively avowed that the Messiah developed by the Jews actually originated in the ancient Egyptian cult surrounding the falcon-headed god Horus, son of the Egyptian God of the Dead Osiris and his consort, the mother goddess Isis. It should be noted that such an association of Christianity with paganism and, in particular, the religion of the Ancient Egyptians, was not entirely *sui generis*. Indeed, as the recent boom in interest in the seventeenth-century, Jesuit polymath Athanasius Kircher has demonstrated, the idea of such a link had been part of intellectual discourse for decades by the time that Wünsch decided to popularize it.[64] For many of Wünsch's contemporaries, however, this was one step too far.

To German-speaking men of letters, *Horus* was doubly appalling. First, it was universally acknowledged that the book's reasoning was not at all cogent. Johann Georg Hamann claimed that he could not continue reading the book beyond the preface.[65] In the 1787 edition of the *Kirchen-und-Kezer-Almanach*, Bahrdt wrote that Wünsch "soll der Verfasser des Horus seyn. Ich weiß es nicht. Er sey es aber, oder sey es nicht, so ist der Horus ein Meisterstück einer lebhaften Phantasie, aber kein Produkt eines philosophischen Geistes."[66] Second, Wünsch embedded his heresies in popular genres, such as mythology and pseudo-science, so as to attract more readers. However, this combination of bad writing and popular genres was not seen to be a disqualifying defect. On the contrary, these factors made the book incredibly dangerous.

In a polemical short story published in 1785, Weissenbach analogized Wünsch to a doctor who dabbled privately in poisons before deciding to sell his wares to the masses.[67] According to Weissenbach, *Horus* was "das giftigste Buch, welches Deutschland in seiner Sprache erblicket hat." Weissenbach noted that the entire book was "dunkel, schwämerisch, übertrieben, abgeschmackt" and designed to compel readers who might have considered themselves Christians to renounce their faith and pledge allegiance to the cult of reason. With regard to Wünsch's theology, Weissenbach explained that the author of *Horus* denigrates Jesus, viewed the books of the prophets as "verworrene Uebergaben der alten ägyptischen, chaldäischen, und persischen Sterndeuter," and considered the gospels to be "ein Mischmasch von Wahnwitz, und Widersinn."[68] According to Weissenbach, the foremost problem with Wünsch's book was that it showed "nicht nur den Gelehrten, nicht nur den Freymäurern, sondern auch dem Pöbel, daß die Bücher, welche sie bisher für Gottes Wort hielten, nichts denn Aberglauben, Menschentand, Träumerey, Widersprüche, Fabeln, und aus der alten Sternkunde hergeholte Bilder sind."[69] The new heathens had succeeded in their quest to provoke "den niedersten Pöbel" to read "alles Böse."[70] *Horus* had become a "Handbuch aller Stände,"and a "Lehrbuch der Heiden."[71]

With the rapid spread of the *Fragmente* barely behind them, the authorities did not wait to see what would happen next. The Leipzig magistrate confiscated the book immediately after its publication and severely fined Wünsch's publisher, who refused to name the text's author, nonetheless.[72] Although all copies of the book that could be found were publicly burned in Frankfurt, one copy did manage to make its way to Zedlitz, who to Woellner's horror promptly invited Wünsch to teach in Prussia.

Lessing, Bahrdt, and Wünsch were soon joined in their assault on all that the traditionalists held to be inviolable. In a book that he styled as a defense of Christianity, Christian Ludwig Paalzow announced that every revealed religion was based on falsity and could only be maintained by violence and deception.[73] In a book entitled *Auch Fragmente* as an homage to Lessing, the aristocrat-general Woldemar Hermann von Schmettow said the way forward was to overthrow all the priests, since they used the educational system to inculcate their worldview in every generation.[74] The playwright Heinrich Keller provocatively suggested that the members of the new heathens should take the place formerly occupied by the priests, since they would be able to instruct the people in the true path of reason.[75]

The new heathens' opponents were divided when it came to the proper way to respond to these texts. Relatively disinterested observation was one possibility. In the book *Rasereyen des achtzehnden Jahrhunderts*, the anonymous author broadly labeled these aspiring propagators of heterodoxy as charlatans and fanatics who have brought upon themselves much deserved retribution on account of their unending desire for reform.[76] As the anonymous author noted, these reformers, who considered themselves to be pedagogues, sought to make the eighteenth century into the dawn of a new era, and they certainly succeeded in getting everyone to talk about them.[77] However, by attempting to make the world clever against its will, they had forced their opponents to rise up to give them bitter medicine.[78]

For both traditionalists and adherents of enlightened theology, however, the way forward was much more uncertain. The publication of texts refuting the new heathens only seemed to make matters worse. Furthermore, there was no guarantee that impressionable members of the public would deliberately choose to spend their money on texts that restated the catechism when something scandalous and more enjoyable was available at a similar price. Goeze, for example, regretted how much more eagerly the public consumed texts written by the heterodox than they read the texts meant to combat these heresies. He wrote,

> Nun ist zu beklagen, daß die Vertheidigungen der Religion gemeiniglich nicht so begierig als die Schriften des angreifenden

> Theils gelesen werden. Denn die Feinde der Religion erlauben sich wilde Spöttereyen, an welchen sich der Pöbel unter den Lesern, zumal in diesen witzsüchtigen Zeitcn, belustiget, dergleichen sich der ernsthafte Bekenner der Religion niemahls erlauben kann.[79]

A previously unthinkable suggestion soon took hold. Perhaps the new heathens had truly proven that religion was little more than a "Zaum für den Pöbel," as the rural clergyman Johann Ernst Schmidt put it.[80] Even worse was the intimation that this might not be that terrible. Semler, who in the midst of the *Fragmentenstreit* had published a pamphlet that attacked Lessing as an arsonist, responded to the rapid advance of blasphemy with a book that asked whether the Antichrist had finally arrived.[81] In spite of all the invective that, Goeze and others had directed at the new heathens, Semler's somewhat surprising answer was no, it was not the age of the Antichrist. In fact, after the onslaught of these sacrilegious texts, Semler had reconsidered his beliefs regarding the flammability of Christianity. The true religion, it turned out, could not be torn down by any manmade force.[82] A few arsonists every once in a while might even be desirable, since it would help true believers fortify their private religion.

Woellner, however, could not disagree more with the traditionalists and neologians who had begun to flirt with abject resignation. The state needed religion; moreover, Woellner foresaw that, as soon as Friedrich II passed on to the eternal damnation that surely awaited him, he would have the opportunity to smother whatever remained of the *Aufklärung* by ensuring that these heathens never again had the opportunity to contaminate the public sphere. Woellner succeeded in his quest. During the reign of Friedrich Wilhelm II, he initiated the marginalization and erasure of these figures and the texts that they had produced. Safely ensconced in Frankfurt an der Oder, Wünsch apparently realized that it was best that he not try to court disaster. Bahrdt could not help himself; he was imprisoned after he decided to lampoon the religious edicts in a satirical play and ended his life as the disgraced owner of an inn/brothel. A similar fate was bestowed upon other heterodox thinkers such as the aforementioned preacher Johann Heinrich Schulz, who was sent to work in a porcelain factory after he continued to act like it was his right to instruct the public in the manner he desired.

With the rapid change in policies, the despair felt by Goeze and Semler for a generation lost to the venom of the new heathens was soon transformed into ridicule of their intellectual pretensions. In the anonymously published *Zween Volkslehrer* (1789), Lavater mockingly portrayed the absurdity of intellectuals proclaiming themselves "Volkslehrer des achtzehnten

Jahrhunderts" when all they could really do was publish their books and send them out into the hopefully receptive public sphere.[83] Lavater's fears from a decade beforehand that the public was all too amenable to such an approach had apparently vanished. Johannes Tobler, Lavater's colleague in Zürich, joined in the mockery. To him it was ridiculous that so many intellectuals had convinced the common people that they were the ones who could lead them out of the "Labyrinthe von Zweifeln." Tobler pointed out that, quite on the contrary, many of the philosophers who had entered this labyrinth had, in fact, never left it. In summation, Tobler offered a fitting lamentation for a formerly widespread phenomenon that had generated an impressive number of texts but, with the resurgence of conservatism, had mostly come to naught. "O ihr Aufklärer!" he wrote, "Was macht ihr bisweilen für entsetzlichen Rauch!"[84]

A fuller investigation of how the controversies discussed in this article were perceived by the public entails reading what John Christian Laursen and Johan van der Zande have termed forms of "lowbrow sociability."[85] All too often, however, works of intellectual history have hesitated to step out of the more comfortable confines of high culture philosophy and theology, which might explain the continued absence of this branch of Enlightenment-era public debate in the already considerable literature on the era. In closing, there is one feature of Tobler's lamentation that warrants further consideration. When he bemoaned the evanescence of the new heathens' influence, it was not the new heathens that he addressed. Instead, it was the *Aufklärer* in general. When Kant was singled out for censorship on account of the "Entstellung und Herabwürdigung mancher Haupt- und Grundlehren der heiligen Schrift und des Christenthums" that Woellner found in *Die Religion innerhalb der Grenzen der bloßen Vernunft*,[86] Kant's reply, which was related in the preface to *Der Streit der Fakultäten*, was that he was not a "Volkslehrer," and the common people should have taken no notice of his book on religion.[87] It was the legacy of the new heathens and the Radical Enlightenment that they attempted to spread to the common people that when the Counter-Enlightenment response finally came, it did not differentiate between the Radical Enlightenment and its mainstream, moderate doppelgänger. It was no longer a safe assumption that radical ideas could be contained; hence, radicals and moderates alike had to be silenced.

NOTES

1. The manuscript copy of Woellner's "Abhandlung über die Religion" remains in the Geheimes Staatsarchiv Preußischer Kulturbesitz in Berlin (Manuscript GStA PK, I. HA, Rep. 92 Woellner I, Nr 7). To date, it has only been transcribed once, albeit in slightly abridged form. See Paul Schwartz, *Der erste Kulturkampf in Preußen um Kirche und Schule (1788–1798)* (Berlin: Weidmann, 1925), 72–92.

2. For a documentation of the full debate, see *What is Enlightenment?: Eighteenth- Century Answers and Twentieth-Century Questions*, ed. James Schmidt (Berkeley, CA: Univ. of California Press, 1996).

3. I am alluding here, of course, to Immanuel Kant's famous opening line in his essay "Beantwortung der Frage: Was ist Aufklärung?" in *Gesammelte Schriften*, ed. Preußische Akademie der Wissenschaften (Berlin: 1923), 8:35, and to the distinction drawn by Moses Mendelssohn in his "Ueber die Frage: was heißt aufklären?" in *Gesammelte Schriften*, eds. Alexander Altmann, et al. (Stuttgart-Bad Canstatt: Frommann-Holzboog, 1981), 6.1:113–9, here 117.

4. Kant's crucial distinction can be found in the essay "Beantwortung der Frage: Was ist Aufklärung?" in *Schriften*, 8:36–37.

5. The three works by Jonathan Israel that comprise the trilogy are *Radical Enlightenment: Philosophy and the Making of Modernity 1650–1750* (Oxford: Oxford Univ. Press, 2001), *Enlightenment Contested: Philosophy, Modernity, and the Emancipation of Man 1670–1752* (Oxford: Oxford Univ. Press, 2006), and *Democratic Enlightenment: Philosophy, Revolution, and Human Rights 1750–1790* (Oxford: Oxford Univ. Press, 2011).

6. So endemic were these debates to this imaginary community that Marcelo Dascal and Cristina Marras have rightfully argued that the peaceable scholars' utopia was in fact a republic of quarrels. See "The République des Lettres: A republic of quarrels?" in *Controversies in the République des Lettres. Technical Report 3: Scientific Controversies and Theories of Controversy*, eds. Marcelo Dascal, Gerd Fritz, Thomas Gloning, and Yaron Senderowicz (Giessen, 2002), 42–79.

7. See Martin Mulsow, *Moderne aus dem Untergrund: Radikale Frühaufklärung in Deutschland 1680–1720* (Hamburg: Meiner, 2002).

8. Ursula Goldenbaum, "Vorwort," in *Appell an das Publikum: Die öffentliche Debatte in der deutschen Aufklärung 1687–1796*, ed. Ursula Goldenbaum (Berlin: Akademie, 2004), viii.

9. See Uta Wiggermann, *Woellner und das Religionsedikt: Kirchenpolitik und kirchliche Wirklichkeit im Preußen des späten 18. Jahrhunderts* (Tübingen: Mohr Siebeck, 2010); and Michael J. Sauter, *Visions of the Enlightenment: The Edict on Religion of 1788 and the Politics of the Public Sphere in Eighteenth-Century Prussia* (Leiden: Brill, 2009).

10. Wiggermann does at least identify the two men. See Wiggermann, *Woellner*, 38.

11. Woldemar Hermann von Schmettow, for example, is somewhat inexplicably mentioned by Israel in connection with Jean-Jacques Rousseau. See Israel, *Democratic*, 108.

12. The literature on Lessing's theology is too vast to name more than a few

of the many excellent works. See, for example, Gerhard Freund, *Theologie im Widerspruch: Die Lessing-Goeze-Kontroverse* (Stuttgart: Kohlhammer, 1989); Leonard P. Wessell, *G. E. Lessing's Theology: A Reinterpretation* (The Hague: Mouton, 1977); and Toshimasa Yasukata, *Lessing's Philosophy of Religion and the German Enlightenment* (Oxford: Oxford Univ. Press, 2002). For a more recent discussion of Lessing's theology, see the essays collected in *Gotthold Ephraim Lessings Religionsphilosophie im Kontext: Hamburger Fragmente und Wolfenbütteler Axiomata*, eds. Christoph Bultmann and Friedrich Vollhardt (Berlin/New York: de Gruyter, 2011).

13. Bahrdt is discussed by Israel in the recent book *Democratic Enlightenment*. See Israel, *Democratic*, 310–315. Bahrdt's role in the theological discourse of his time has received critical attention in several case studies. See Martin Kessler, "Die Götterbote und die Götter. Theologische Diskurse im Teutschen Merkur zur Zeit der Fragmentenstreit," in *"Der Teutsche Merkur"—die erste deutsche Kulturzeitschrift?*, ed. Andrea Heinz (Heidelberg: Winter, 2003), 215–53. See also Andrew McKenzie-McHarg, "Überlegungen zur Radikalaufklärung am Beispiel Carl Friedrich Bahrdt," in *Aufklärung: Radikale Spätaufklärung in Deutschland Einzelschicksale–Konstellationen–Netzwerke*, eds. Martin Mulsow and Guido Nascher, vol. 24 (2012): 207–40, as well as Günter Mühlpfordt, "Außenseitertum. Typologie und Sonderfall. Karl Friedrich Bahrdt—Stimme der schweigenden Mehrheit," in *Außenseiter der Aufklärung*, ed. Günter Hartung (Frankfurt am Main: Lang, 1995), 75–133, and Thomas Hoeren, "Präjakobiner in Deutschland. Carl Friedrich Bahrdt (1740–1792)," in *Zeitschrift für Religions- und Geistesgeschichte* 47, no. 1 (1995): 55–72.

14. The essay concentrates on Wünsch's theory regarding the revelation and does not address the conflict that is considered here. See Jürgen von Kempski, "Apokalypse, 'Horus' und Wünsch," in *Zeitschrift für Religions- und Geistesgeschichte* 47, no. 4 (1995): 304–319.

15. "Hour of Satan," In 1778, Goeze's sermons for the Sunday after New Year's Day; the third, fourth, and fifth Sundays of Lent; the sixth Sunday after Easter; and the fourth Sunday after the Feast of the Trinity all dealt with Lessing and the *Fragmente*. For Goeze's comment regarding the hour of Satan, see Johann Melchior Goeze, *Auszüge aus seinen Sontags- Fest- und verschiedenen Wochen-Predigten des 1778 Jahres* (Hamburg: Harmsen, 1778), 104. All translations are my own.

16. Lessing was certainly not the first German-language writer who attempted to write theological texts that would cause a scandal. For a thorough discussion of these writers, such as Friedrich Wilhelm Stosch and Thomas Ludwig Lau, see Winfried Schröder, *Ursprünge des Atheismus: Untersuchungen zur Metaphysik- und Religionskritik des 17. und 18. Jahrhunderts* (Stuttgart-Bad Canstatt: Frommann-Holzboog, 1998).

17. Burckhard Dücker, "Der Fragmentenstreit als Produktionsform neuen Wissens: Zur kulturellen Funktion und rituellen Struktur von Skandalen," in *Lessings Skandale*, eds. Jürgen Stenzel and Roman Lach (Tübingen: Niemeyer, 2005), 21.

18. See Michael J. Sauter, "Preaching, a Ponytail, and an Enthusiast: Rethinking the Public Sphere's Subversiveness in Eighteenth-Century Prussia," in *Central*

European History 37, no. 4 (2004): 544–67; and Thomas P. Saine, *The Problem of Being Modern, or, the German Pursuit of Enlightenment from Leibniz to the French Revolution* (Detroit, MI: Wayne State Univ. Press, 1997), 285.

19. The most thorough introduction to this strand of eighteenth-century theology remains to this date Karl Aner's *Die Theologie der Lessingzeit.* (Halle: Niemeyer, 1929); (Hildesheim: Olms, 1964). See also Wolfgang Gericke, *Theologie und Kirche im Zeitalter der Aufklärung* (Berlin: Evangelische Verlagsanstalt, 1989), 95–114.

20. Wessell, *Theology*, 41–2.

21. For a discussion of the history of the manuscript, see Gerhard Alexander, "Wie kam Lessing zur Handschrift der Wolfenbütteler Fragmente?" in *Philobiblon* 16, no. 3 (September 1972): 160–172.

22. "The text should remain hidden and only for the use of discreet friends; it should not of my volition become public via print before the times enlighten themselves more. Rather the mass of commoners err for a while than that I (even though it would happen without my guilt) should anger it with truths and set it in an angry religious fervor. Rather the wise man stand back, endure, and remain silent among the ruling opinions and customs for the sake of peace than that he should make himself and others unhappy through a premature pronouncement." Hermann Samuel Reimarus, *Apologie, oder Schutzschrift für die vernünftigen Verehrer Gottes*, ed. Gerhard Alexander (Frankfurt am Main: Insel, 1972), 1:41.

23. For a description of Lessing's pedagogical philosophy, see Willi Oelmüller, *Die unbefriedigte Aufklärung: Beiträge zu einer Theorie der Moderne von Lessing, Kant und Hegel* (Frankfurt am Main: Suhrkamp, 1969), 38–9, and Thomas Höhle, "Einige Wirkungen der Publizistik Lessings," in *Bausteine zu einer Wirkungsgeschichte Gotthold Ephraim Lessings*, ed. Hans-Georg Werner (Berlin/Weimar: Aufbau, 1989), 265.

24. Elise Reimarus shared this summary of Lessing's thoughts in her September 18, 1776 letter to her brother in law, the diplomat August von Hennings. Cited in Alexander Altmann, *Moses Mendelssohn: A Biographical Study* (Tuscaloosa, AL: Univ. of Alabama Press, 1973), 559.

25. "Boldest and strongest." No epistolary evidence for any such request can be found in Lessing's extant letters. It is more likely that he just needed further pretext to justify the continued publication of the fragments. See Hugh Barr Nisbet, *Lessing: Eine Biographie*, trans. Karl Guthke (Munich: Beck, 2008), 706.

26. Wolfgang Kröger has remarked that Lessing's theology developed in a zigzag line that confounded most attempts to explicate it. See *Das Publikum als Richter: Lessing und die "kleineren Respondenten" im Fragmentenstreit* (Nendeln, Liechtenstein: KTO, 1979), 48.

27. See Hermann Samuel Reimarus, *Vom Zweck Jesu und seiner Jünger*, in *Werke und Briefe*, eds. Wilfried Barner, et al. (Frankfurt am Main: Deutscher Klassiker, 1985–2003), 9:219.

28. Kröger, *Publikum*, 125n46.

29. One theologian noted in his response that he would try to be terse so that his text would be widely read. See Johann Christian Blasche, *Kurze auch dem Laien verständliche Verantwortung wider die Beschuldigungen des Wolfenbüttelschen*

Ungenannten in dem Fragmente von dem Zwecke Jesu und seiner Jünger herausgegeben von Gotthold Ephraim Lessing (Jena: Gollner und Rudolph, 1778), 10. Friedrich Wilhelm Mascho remarked in his text that he had decided to avoid foreign phrases that might confuse the uneducated. See Kröger, *Publikum*, 24–5. Johann Balthasar Lüderwald arranged his numerous responses to the *Fragmente* in short sentences as if they formed a catechism. See, for example, his refutation of the third fragment, *Der Durchgang der Israeliten durch das rothe Meer: Gegen die Einwürfe der Ungläubigen völlig berichtiget und vertheidiget* (Helmstedt: Kühnlein, 1779), as well as his *Die letzte Unterredung Jesu mit seinen Jüngern auf dem Gange nach Gethsemane, aus dem Evangelio Johannis Kap. 14–17. Als ein Anhang zur Auferstehungs-Geschichte Jesu, gegen die Ungläubigen vertheidigt* (Helmstedt: Kühnlein, 1779).

30. See, for example, Gottlieb Conrad Pfeffel, "Das Goldstück" in *Neueste Mannigfaltigkeiten* 3 (1780): 191.

31. Goeze was soundly ridiculed in Aloys Blumauer's *Virgils Aeneis travestirt* (Vienna: Grässer, 1784). In the first volume, Goeze was called upon to bless the Trojan horse (60). The second volume featured a description of Goeze's battle with Lessing transposed onto the battle Aeneas hosts before his father's grave (44). In contrast to what actually occurred, Lessing was described as handily winning the battle with the pastor.

32. See Kröger, *Publikum*, 21.

33. Johann Salomo Semler, *Beantwortung der Fragmente eines Ungenannten insbesondere vom Zweck Jesu und seiner Jünger* (Halle: Verlag des Erziehungsinstituts, 1779), ii.

34. For instance, Abraham Philipp Gottfried Schickedanz's contribution to the dispute, *Beurtheilung des Fragments aus der Wolfenbüttelschen Bibliothek die Auferstehungsgeschichte Jesu betreffend* (Frankfurt an der Oder: Strauß, 1779), was republished in the *Handbuch für angehende Prediger, bestehend in Kasualreden und einigen andern Predigten etc. Nebst kurzen Nachtrichten von den neuen theologischen und Erziehungsschriften im Jahr 1778, 3. und 4. Theil* (Frankfurt an der Oder, 1779). See also Kröger, *Publikum*, 21.

35. Knittel advised priests to make themselves aware of the arguments brought forth by this enemy of Christianity so that they would be ready. See Franz Anton Knittel, *Neue Kritiken über das weltberühmte Zeugniß des alten Juden Flavius Josephus von unserm Herrn und Heiland Jesu Christo: Eine synodalische Vorlesung* (Braunschweig/Hildesheim: Schröder, 1779). See also Kröger, *Publikum*, 21–2.

36. Christian Gottlieb Reinhold, the chief pastor in Mulhouse in Alsace, assigned each pastor under his supervision background reading on the controversy so that they might counter the threat represented by the *Fragmente*. See *Epistola pastoralis encyclica qua recentissimas objectiones contra veritatem de resurrectione J.C. in fragmento quinto Guelferbytano, a celeberrimo Lessingio edito, propositas, ductu XX. questionum, in anniversaria r. ministerii synodo ad iuidicium et censuram vocatum iri significant* (Mulhouse: Müller, 1780).

37. Although the exact number of sermons delivered against the *Fragmente* was difficult to ascertain, there was evidence that they were addressed at the

pulpit. Goeze's sermons on the subject dealt oftentimes only peripherally with Reimarus's texts since they were chiefly directed against Lessing. One sermon delivered on the second Sunday in Lent in the Universitätskirche in Leipzig by Christian Gottlieb Wirth clearly addressed Reimarus's works. See *Vernunft- und schriftmäßige Abhandlung von der Absicht des Lehramts Jesu und seiner Apostel, am Sonntag Reminiscere 1779 in der Universitätskirche zu Leipzig vorgetragen; des Wolfenbüttelisch-Ungenannten Zweck Jesu und seiner Jünger vorzüglich entgegengesetzt*. Cited in Kröger, *Publikum*, 174.

38. "Battlefields," "a seed of weeds," See the 40th issue (October 10, 1777) of the *Freywillige Beyträge zu den hamburgischen Nachrichten aus dem Reiche der Gelehrsamkeit*, ed. Ch. Ziegra (Hamburg: C. S. Schröders Wittwe, 1772–9); (Hildesheim: Olms, 2010), 5:314.

39. See the review of Johann Daniel Müller's *Augenscheinlicher Beweis: dass die Abhandlung von dem Zwekke Jesu und seiner Jünger, voll ganz offenbarer Widersprüche und Unwahrheiten sei. Von einem Freunde der Wahrheit* in the combined 14th and 15th issues (February 12, 1779) of the *Freywillige Beyträge*, 6:114.

40. See Kröger, *Publikum*, 21.

41. Johann Bernhard Basedow, *Vorschlag an die Selbstdenker des 19ten Jahrhunderts zum Frieden zwischen dem wohlverstandnen Urchristenthume und der wohlgesinnten Vernunft* (1780), 37.

42. The 1778 edition of the *Buchhändlerzeitung* calculated the text's circulation. See Kröger, *Publikum*, 18.

43. The assertion is from the March 22, 1779 issue of the *Neue Hallische Gelehrte Zeitung*. See Kröger, *Publikum*, 22.

44. "That new dreadful outbreak of the most poisonous disbelief in the text 'On the Goal of Jesus and his Disciples' that is known to all and ravenously devoured by our male youth"; "evilness and purposelessness"; "deceit and cunning art of reasoning"; "This text is in all hands. It lies or used to lie in our bookstores; our servants retrieve it and transport it here and there: during the binding process, the book binder and his apprentice read it, the housemate and neighbor sneak a peek at the deeply poisonous thoughts; our youth carry it in their bags and triumph thereby in their social circles." Johann Kaspar Lavater, "Synodalrede gegen Deismus und kirchlichen Rationalismus, 4. Mai 1779," in *Ausgewählte Werke. 3. Band: Sehet: welch ein Mensch! 1779–1790*, ed. Ernst Staehelin (Zürich: Zwingli, 1943), 9.

45. According to August Friedrich Cranz, who, by virtue of his governmental position appears to have been reasonably well-informed, Nicolai, who had fallen out with Lessing, was the author of an unsigned letter entitled "Ueber die von Herrn Lessing herausgegebenen Fragmente eines Ungenannten, gegen die Wahrheit und Göttlichkeit der christlichen Religion" that urged pastors not to discuss the *Fragmente* from the pulpit. It was published in a popular clerical journal, *Journal für Prediger* 19, no. 1 (Halle: Kümmel, 1778): 24–38. The attribution can be traced via Cranz's *Supplement zum Ersten Stück der Chronika von Berlin, in einem Sendschreiben an den Weltmann in Berlin, wohlmeritirten Tantenbekehrer und Verfasser der Briefe an einen Landgeistlichem[!], das neue Gesangbuch betreffend von dem Verfasser*

der Bokiade (Berlin, 1781). In several library catalogs, Friedrich Germanus Lüdke is noted as a possible collaborator or sole author of the piece. For this attribution, see Kröger, *Publikum*, 126n57.

46. "Arch-soulless sophist Lessing," See Letter 489 (July 1, 1778) from Lavater to Jacobi, in Friedrich Heinrich Jacobi, *Briefwechsel. Gesamtausgabe der Bayerischen Akademie der Wissenschaften*, ed. Walter Jaeschke (Stuttgart-Bad Canstatt: Frommann-Holzboog, 1981), 1.2:75–6, here 76.

47. [Joseph Anton Weissenbach], *Die Vorbothen des neuen Heidenthums, und die Anstalten, die dazu vorgekehret worden sind.* 2 vols. (Basel, 1781).

48. "Destruction of belief." [Weissenbach], *Vorbothen*, 1:2–3.

49. "To meddle in the education authority"; "To venture the difficulties of metaphysics and theology without having learned anything." [Weissenbach], *Vorbothen*, 1:20.

50. "Erroneous belief leads directly to unbelief." [Weissenbach], *Vorbothen*, 1:2.

51. [Weissenbach], *Vorbothen*, 1:49.

52. [Weissenbach], *Vorbothen*, 1:88–9.

53. "Mouse excrement for pepper and poison for sugar from the Canaries." Fleischer dedicated two lengthy volumes to this trio of heretics. The first volume, entitled *Betrachtungen über Leßings Bruchstücken, den Horus und die Briefe über die Bibel in Volcks Ton: allen gelehrten Schriftstellern und Bücher Rezensenten zu einem Probierstein, die Stärcke ihres Geistes daran zu prüffen*, was printed in Vienna in 1786, and the second volume, entitled *Betrachtungen über des Horus Europens neuern Aufklärung und die Bestimmung des Menschen durch Gott, denen Religionslehrern, gelehrten Schriftstellern, Astronomen, Freymäurern, wie auch andern verständigen, Wahrheit liebenden und suchenden Menschen zum Unterricht und weitern Nachdencken gewidmet*, appeared the following year in Vienna. For the comment about pepper and sugar, see pages 16–17 in the first volume.

54. Goethe criticized Bahrdt for putting his own words into Christ's mouth and thus debasing the value of the Bible. See Thomas J. Tillmann, *Hermeneutik und Bibelexegese beim jungen Goethe* (Berlin/New York: de Gruyter, 2006), 71. Goethe satirized Bahrdt's dismissal from his post in "Prolog zu den neusten Offenbarungen Gottes" (1774). One of the most strident critics of Bahrdt's translation was the senior pastor Goeze, who summed up his opinion in the colorful title of his refutation, *Beweis, daß die Bahrdtische Verdeutschung des Neuen Testaments keine Uebersetzung, sondern eine vorsetzliche Verfälschung und frevelhafte Schändung der Worte des lebendigen Gottes sey* (1773).

55. "Popular enlightenment." The justification, entitled *Glaubensbekenntnis, veranlaßt durch ein Kaiserl. Reichhofrathsconclusum* (1779), was a response to the declaration of censorship that Goeze obtained in retaliation for Bahrdt's publication of his translation of the Bible.

56. Israel, *Democratic*, 314–315.

57. "With shocked disappointment I had read how the author of the Fragments had debased him as a mere politician and had credited him with the goal of achieving a Jewish crown. With true pity and real grief I noticed the effects that Lessing's product had brought forth among the mass of free-thinking men." Karl Friedrich

Bahrdt, *Geschichte seines Lebens seiner Meinungen und Schicksale von ihm selbst geschrieben* (Berlin: Vieweg, 1791), 4:124.

58. "With these texts it always goes like it does with books by alchemists: Whoever has read one has read them all. All comes down to the fact that the Bible is untrustworthy, positive religion is nothing, and that naturalism is the true crux"; "free"; "unashamed." Johann August Stark, *Der Triumph der Philosophie im achtzehnten Jahrhundert* (Germantown: Rosenblatt, 1803), 2:64.

59. See, for example, the fourteenth letter in the *Briefe über die Bibel im Volkston* (Halle: Dost, 1782), 215.

60. Karl Friedrich Bahrdt, *Ausführung des Plans und Zwecks Jesu* (Berlin: Mylius, 1784), 480.

61. "The period of humanity's childhood is past; we are now men and we need stronger fare, pure truth." Christoph Friedrich Rinck visited Bahrdt in Halle on December 4, 1783 and noted Bahrdt's comment in his diary. See Hans-Joachim Kertscher, "Carl Friedrich Bahrdt im Urteil der Zeitgenossen," in *Außenseiter der Aufklärung*, ed. Günter Hartung (Frankfurt am Main: Lang, 1995), 71–2.

62. In his *Versuche und Beobachtungen über die Farben des Lichts* (1792), Wünsch argued that all possible colors could be attained via an admixture of primary colors. Goethe criticized Wünsch for this backward theory in *Zur Farbenlehre*. Goethe wrote, "Hier haben wir unsern guten Wünsch wieder und seinen Essig der aus Gurkensalat erzeugt wird" ("Here again we have our good Wünsch who extracts his vinegar from cucumber salad") See *Goethes' Werke. Herausgegeben im Auftrage der Großherzogin Sophie von Sachsen* (Weimar: Böhlau, 1887–1919), 2/5:357. Furthermore, Goethe satirized Wünsch's color theory in one of his contributions to the *Xenien*: In the 125th poem, "Neueste Farbentheorie von Wünsch" ("Newest Color Theory by Wünsch"), he wrote "Gelbrot und Grün macht das Gelbe, Grün und Violblau das Blaue! // So wird aus Gurkensalat wirklich der Essig erzeugt!" ("Yellow-red and green make yellow, green and violet-blue make blue! // So is vinegar truly extracted from cucumber salad!"). See *Werke*, 1/5.1:230.

63. "The most terrible sacrilege." See Albrecht Beutel, *Lichtenberg und die Religion: Aspekte einer vielschichtigen Konstellation* (Tübingen: Mohr Siebeck, 1996), 220n114.

64. See, for example, Daniel Stolzenberg, *Egyptian Oedipus: Athanasius Kircher and the Secrets of Antiquity* (Chicago: Univ. of Chicago Press, 2013), 250.

65. See Karl H. Gildemeister, *Johann Georg Hamann's: Des Magus im Norden, Leben und Schriften* (Gotha: F.A. Perthes, 1857), 2:457.

66. "Is supposedly the author of the Horus. I don't know. But whether he is or he isn't, the Horus is a masterpiece of lively fantasy but not the product of a philosophical mind." Karl Friedrich Bahrdt, *Kirchen-und-Kezer-Almanach* (1787), 206.

67. Joseph Anton Weissenbach, "Horus," in *Erbauliche und angenehme Erzehlungen, zum Zeitvertreib einer christlichen Haushaltung* (Basel: Emanuel Thurneysen, 1785), 204. Weissenbach also explicitly named Wünsch as the author (210).

68. "The most poisonous book to appear in the German language"; "dark, enthusiastic, hyperbolic, vulgar"; "convoluted remainder of the old Egyptian, Chaldean, and Persian astrologers"; "a mish-mash of insane wit and nonsense." Weissenbach, "Horus," 208–9.

69. "Not only the learned, not only the masons, but also the rabble that the books that they used to consider to be God's words were nothing more than superstition, human bric-a-brac, dreams, contradictions, and imagery taken from old astrology," Weissenbach, "Horus," 208.

70. "The lowest rabble"; "everything evil." Weissenbach, "Horus," 209–10.

71. "Handbook of all classes," "textbook of the heathens," Weissenbach, "Horus," 212.

72. Günter Mühlpfordt, "Halle und Leipzig als Zentren des Aufklärerbundes Deutsche Union: eine Reformgesellschaft zur 'Vervollkommnung der Wissenschaften' 1786–1789," in *Gelehrte Gesellschaften im mitteldeutschen Raum 1650–1820* (Leipzig: Hirzel, 2002), 3:207.

73. Christian Ludwig Paalzow, *Hierokles, oder Prüfung und Vertheidigung der christlichen Religion* (Halle: Gebauer, 1785), 362.

74. [Woldemar Hermann von Schmettow], *Auch Fragmente*, 3 vols. (Philadelphia [Altona]: [Sommering], 1783–4).

75. [Heinrich Keller], *Ueber Pfafferey und Religion, Duldung und Religionsvereinigung, hauptsächlich die Protestanten betreffend: Eine Beylage zu den Reformationsvorschlägen des achtzehnten Jahrhunderts* (Berlin/Leipzig/Vienna, 1783), 1:28.

76. *Rasereyen des achtzehnden Jahrhunderts: Ein philantropisch-kosmopolitisches Drama, in welchem die neuern Pädagogen und die Erfinder eines sogenannten Urchristenthums die vornehmsten Rollen spielen; Den Meistern in der Erziehungskunst, und den Erzpriestern der Universalreligion, den Hochgelehrten Herren Basedow, Bahrdt und Trapp ganz ergebenst zugeeignet* (Kosmopolis [Rothenburg]/Göttingen, 1782), 8, 13.

77. *Rasereyen*, 18–19.

78. *Rasereyen*, 35, 17.

79. "Now it should be bewailed that defenses of religion are commonly not read as avidly as the texts by the attacking party. Because the enemies of religion allow themselves wild mockery that amuses the rabble among the readers in these wit-addicted times, which true confessors of religion can never allow themselves." See the 71st issue (March 17, 1778) of the *Freywillige Beyträge*, 5:561.

80. "Bridle for the rabble." Johann Ernst Schmidt, *Solte die Religion wohl weiter nichts als ein Zaum für den Pöbel seyn? Oder Versuche näherer Anwendung der vornehmsten Wahrheiten der Religion auf das wirkliche Leben in einigen Religionsvorträgen. Eine Nachlese zu der Schrift: der unbekannte Gott, aus bekannten Dingen in der sichtbaren Welt* (Berlin/Leipzig: Decker, 1785).

81. Johann Salomo Semler, *Ob der Geist des Widerchrists unser Zeitalter auszeichne?: In freimütigen Briefen zur Erleichterung der Privatreligion der Christen beantwortet* (Halle: Hemmerde, 1784).

82. Semler, *Geist*, 38–39.

83. "Public pedagogues of the eighteenth century." Jonathan Asahel [Johann Kaspar Lavater], *Zween Volkslehrer, ein Gespräch* (Winterthur: Steiner, 1789), 10.

84. "Labyrinths of doubt"; "Oh you enlighteners!"; "What dreadful fumes you make!" Johannes Tobler, *Gedanken und Antworten zur Ehre Jesu Christi und seines Reichs in Bezug auf den Nachlaß der Wolfenbüttelschen Fragmente* (Zürich: Orell, Geßner, Füßli & Comp., 1788), 401–404.

85. John Christian Laursen and Johan van der Zande, "Introduction," in *The Edict of Religion: A Comedy; And, the Story and Diary of my Imprisonment* (Lanham, MD: Lexington, 2000), 5.

86. "Distortion and debasing of some main and fundamental tenets of the holy text and Christianity." Immanuel Kant, "Der Streit der Fakultäten," in *Gesammelte Schriften*, ed. Preußische Akademie der Wissenschaften (Berlin: 1917), 7:6.

87. "Public teacher." Kant, *Schriften*, 7:7–8.

Contributors to Volume 44

Kelly E. Battles is Assistant Professor of English at Maryville College in Maryville, Tennessee. Her publications include articles on James Hogg and George Eliot. Her research interests include historiography, aesthetics, reception and periodicals focusing on British literature of the eighteenth and nineteenth centuries.

Adam R. Beach is Associate Professor of English at Ball State University, and his essays on slavery and colonialism in the British world have appeared in *SEL*, *Eighteenth-Century Life*, and other journals and collections. This essay is part of his larger project on representations of global slave systems in British literature, and he has published previous work from this research in *Philological Quarterly*, *Studies in Eighteenth-Century Culture*, *The Eighteenth Century: Theory and Interpretation*, and *Eighteenth-Century Studies*. He also recently co-edited (with Srividhya Swaminathan) *Invoking Slavery in the Eighteenth-Century British Imagination* (Ashgate, 2013), and the collection contains his essay on the seventeenth-century slave narrative by the Englishman identified as T.S.

Samara Anne Cahill is an Assistant Professor of Restoration and eighteenth-century literature in the Division of English at Nanyang Technological University, Singapore. Her articles have appeared or are forthcoming in the journals *The AnaChronisT, Assuming Gender, Green Humanities, and Religion in the Age of Enlightenment*. She is Vice President of the Southeast Asian Society for Eighteenth-Century Studies (SASECS), Secretary of the Samuel Richardson Society, Asian Liaison to the South Central Society for Eighteenth-Century Studies (SCSECS), and incoming Book Review Editor of Religion in the *Age of Enlightenment*. She recently received a Tier 1 grant from the Ministry of Education, Singapore.

Jonathan Blake Fine obtained his Ph.D. in German from the University of California, Irvine and earned an M.A. in Comparative Literature from New York University. During 2011-2012, he conducted archival research in Germany for the present SECC article with support from the Deutscher Akademischer Austausch Dienst. He is currently revising his dissertation, "*Streitkultur*: Polemic and the Problem of Public Enlightenment in Eighteenth-Century Germany," for publication as a monograph.

Lucas Hardy is Assistant Professor of English at Youngstown State University. An early Americanist, his current research examines the intersections between colonial American theology and early-modern medical history. At present, he is completing a book manuscript entitled *Theologies of Pain: The Human Body and Spiritual Conversion in American Puritanism*, an investigation of the ways in which pain and suffering influenced practices of spiritual regeneration and religious testimony in seventeenth- and eighteenth-century Massachusetts. His 2014 essay "'No Cure': Anne Bradstreet's

Frenzied Brain" appears in a special edition of *Women's Studies* devoted to new critical readings of Anne Bradstreet.

Julie Candler Hayes is Professor of French and Dean of the College of Humanities and Fine Arts at the University of Massachusetts Amherst. Her research focuses primarily on literary and philosophical texts of the French Enlightenment; she has also written extensively on contemporary literary theory and the history and theory of translation. Her most recent book is *Translation, Subjectivity, and Culture in France and England, 1600–1800* (Stanford, 2009). Her current scholarly work looks at seventeenth- and eighteenth-century women moral philosophers.

Paul Kelleher is Assistant Professor of English at Emory University. He has published several articles in the fields of eighteenth-century studies and queer theory, and recently has completed his first book, *Making Love: Sentimentalism and the Literary History of Sexuality*. His current book project explores the intersections of sympathy and disability across several genres, including eighteenth-century moral philosophy and contemporary film.

Rachael Scarborough King is Assistant Professor of English at the University of California, Santa Barbara. She is at work on a book project, developed from her dissertation, on the role of letters and letter writing in the formation of new print genres in the long eighteenth century. Her work has appeared in *Book History*, and she is a member of the Andrew W. Mellon Fellowship in Critical Bibliography at Rare Book School.

Heidi E. Kraus is Assistant Professor of Art History at Hope College, where she is also the Director of The De Pree Gallery. In addition to her current research project on women, art, and social identity in Napoleonic France, she has published "David's Roman Vedute" in *Studies in Eighteenth-Century Culture*, Volume 38, edited by Linda Zionkowski and Downing A. Thomas (2008).

Teresa Michals is the author of *Books for Children, Books for Adults: Age and the Novel from Defoe to James* (Cambridge, 2014). Her new project focuses on representations of disability and masculinity.

Andrew M. Pisano recently earned his Ph.D. in English from The University of North Carolina at Greensboro. His primary area of research is the intersection of Anglophonic ethnic literatures and evangelicalism in American literature before 1800. This article is derived from the first chapter of his dissertation. He was awarded the prestigious UNCG Mildred Kates Dissertation Fellowship in 2013 for innovative scholarship in the field of English studies.

Yann Robert is an Assistant Professor in the Department of French and Francophone Studies at the University of Illinois at Chicago. He received his PhD from Princeton University in 2010, before spending two years as a postdoctoral fellow at Stanford University. His critical edition (with Mark Darlow) of Laya's revolutionary play *L'Ami des lois* was published in 2011 by the Modern Humanities Research Association. He is currently an Andrew W. Mellon fellow at the Newberry Library, where he is working on a book examining the interplay of theater and justice in eighteenth-century France.

ASECS Executive Board 2014–2015

For information about the
American Society for Eighteenth-Century Studies, please contact:

ASECS
P.O. Box 7867
Wake Forest University
Winston-Salem, NC 27109-7867
Telephone: (336) 727-4694
Fax: (336) 727-4697
E-mail: asecs@wfu.edu
Web Site: http://asecs.press.jhu.edu

American Society for Eighteenth-Century Studies

Patron Members 2014–2015

Hans Adler
Richard Shane Agin
Stephen Ahern
Stanford Anderson
Mark S. Auburn
Paula Backscheider
Eve T. Bannet
Joseph F. Bartolomeo
James G. Basker
Denise Baxter
Barbara Benedict
Oliver Berghof
Kevin Binfield
Martha F. Bowden
Theodore E.D. Braun
Fritz Breithaupt
Peter M. Briggs
Jane K. Brown
Marshall Brown
Michael Burden
Joseph A. Byrnes
Ann Campbell
Susan Carlile
Vincent Carretta
Jeng-Guo Chen
Julie Choi
Brian A. Connery
E. Heckendorn Cook
Kevin L. Cope
Brian Cowan
Margaret Mary Daley
Marlies K. Danziger
Jenny Davidson
Joan DeJean
Robert DeMaria, Jr.
Julia Douthwaite
William F. Edmiston
Roger J. Fechner
Frances Ferguson
Riikka Forsstrom
Bernadette Fort
Patsy Fowler
Christopher Fox
Jennifer E. Frangos
Gorden Fulton
Robert Glen
Charles E. Gobin
Scott Gordon
Sayre Greenfield
Monika Greenleaf
Loyd Grossman
Anita Guerrini
Phyllis Guskin
Susan Gustafson
Basil Guy
Knud Haakonssen
Wolfgang Haase
Martha Hamilton-Phillips
Corrine Harol
Phillip Harth
Donald M. Hassler
Julie C. Hayes
Charles Hinnant
Robert D. Hume
Lynn A. Hunt
J. Paul Hunter
Sheila M. Hwang
Catherine Ingrassia
Malcolm Jack
Margaret C. Jacob
Regina Mary Janes
Alessa Johns
Sandro Jung
George Justice
Sarah Kareem
Gary Kates
Michael Keevak
Shirley Strum Kenny
Thomas Keymer
Heather King
Charles A. Knight
Jocelyne Kolb
Scott Krawczyk
Thomas W. Krise
Susan Lanser
Meredith Lee
Elizabeth Liebman
Devoney K. Looser
Aino Makikalli
Elizabeth Mansfield
Robert Markley
Jean I. Marsden
Marie E. McAllister
Christie McDonald
Paula McDowell
Dennis McEnnerney
George C. McElroy
Alan T. McKenzie
James C. McKusick
Heather McPherson
Donald C. Mell Jr.
Eun Kyung Min
Dennis Moore
Anja Mueller-Muth
Yvonne Noble
Felicity Nussbaum
Mary Ann O'Donnell
Frank Palmeri
Virginia J. Peacock
Ruth Perry
Jane Perry-Camp
Stuart Peterfreund
R.G. Peterson
George W. Poe
John Valdimir Price
Ruben D. Quintero
John Radner
Bryant T. Ragan
Tilottama Rajan
Paul Rich

Patron Members 2014–2015 (Con't)

Joseph Roach
James Rosenheim
Laura Rosenthal
Roseann Runte
Elizabeth Samet
Carole Fungaroli Sargent
Steven D. Scherwatzky
Harold Schiffman
Volker Schroder
Norbert Schurer
Richard Sher
Eleanor F. Shevlin
John C. Shields
Craig A. Simmons
Robert Louis Smith
G.A. Starr
Kristina Straub
Susan Staves
Masashi Suzuki
Mika Suzuki
Astrida Tantillo
Ruud N.W.M. Teeuwen
Linda V. Troost
Randolph Trumbach
Bertil Van Boer
David F. Venturo
Joachim Von der Thusen
Cynthia S. Wall
Howard D. Weinbrot
Byron R. Wells
Betty E. White
J. Edmund White
Lance Wilcox
Annie Williams
Karin E. Wolfe
Larry Wolff
Servanne Woodward
James Woolley
Karin Wurst
Myron D. Yeager
Janet E. Aikins Yount
William J. Zachs
Lisa M. Zeitz

Sponsoring Members 2014–2015

Paul Alkon
Misty G. Anderson
Robert Bernasconi
Thomas F. Bonnell
Leo Braudy
Daniel Brewer
Charles Burroughs
Samara Cahill
Michael J. Conlon
Brian Corman
Joyce East
Clarissa C. Erwin
Daniel Timothy Erwin
David Fairer
Jan Fergus
Lisa Freeman
Jack Fruchtman
Michael Genovese
George Haggerty
Daniel Heartz
Deborah Kennedy
Issac Kramnick
Joan Landes
R.W. McHenry
Maureen E. Mulvihill
Melvyn New
John C. O'Neal
David Oakleaf
Douglas Lane Patey
Adam Potkay
Suzanne R. Pucci
Larry L. Reynolds
John Richetti
Albert J. Rivero
Wendy W. Roworth
Treadwell Ruml II
Peter Sabor
Laura Schattschneider
Barbara B. Schnorrenberg
William C. Schrader
Julia Simon
John Sitter
Jeffrey Smitten
Ann T. Straulman
Astrida Tantillo
Dennis Todd
Raymond D. Tumbleson
Ann Van Allen-Russell
Kenneth Winkler

Institutional Members 2014-15

American Antiquarian Society
Colonial Williamsburg Foundation, *John D. Rockefeller, Jr. Library*
Folger Institute
Fordham University
Newberry Library
Ohio State University Libraries, *Thompson Library*
Omohundro Institute for Early American History, *Kellock Library*
Princeton University
Smithsonian Institute, AAPG Library
Stanford University, *Green Library*
UCLA, *William Andrews Clark Memorial Library*
University of California, Santa Barbara, *Division of Humanities and Fine Arts*
University of Kentucky, *Young Library*
University of North Carolina, *Davis Library*
University of Pennsylvania Library
University of Rochester Library
University of Victoria, *McPherson Library*
Yale University Library

Index

Every effort has been made to include references to all identifiable persons living before or during the long eighteenth century, as well as to often cited contemporary critics and commentators, and to provide a selective listing of relevant concepts and keywords. Readers may also wish to consult the endnotes of each essay for more comprehensive information.

F

G

H

I

J

K

L

M

N